Converts, Heretics, and Lepers

Converts, Heretics, *and* Lepers

Maimonides and The Outsider

JAMES A. DIAMOND

University of Notre Dame Press

Notre Dame, Indiana

Copyright © 2007 by University of Notre Dame
Notre Dame, Indiana 46556
www.undpress.nd.edu
All Rights Reserved

Designed by Wendy McMillen
Set in 11.2/13.5 Pavane by Four Star Books

Library of Congress Cataloging-in-Publication Data

Diamond, James Arthur.
Converts, heretics, and lepers: Maimonides and the outsider /
by James A. Diamond.
    p.   cm.
Includes bibliographical references and index.
ISBN-13: 978-0-268-02592-2 (pbk. : alk. paper)
ISBN-10: 0-268-02592-4 (pbk. : alk. paper)
1. Maimonides, Moses, 1135–1204.   2. Other (Philosophy) 3. God (Judaism)
I. Title.
B759. M34D48   2007
296.1'81—dc22

                                                      2007033426

∞ *The paper in this book meets the guidelines for permanence and durability of the Committee on Production Guidelines for Book Longevity of the Council on Library Resources.*

For Moshe Diamond z"l

Contents

	Acknowledgments	ix
	Abbreviations and Citations	xiii
	Introduction	1
1	The Convert (*Ger*): Metaphor of Jewishness	11
2	The Leper: Illness as Contemplative Metaphor	33
3	Elisha ben Abuyah and the Hubris of the Heretic	55
4	The King: The Ethics of Imperial Humility	79
5	The Sage/Philosopher: A Solitude of Universalism	107
6	God, the Supreme Outsider: Indwelling (*Shekhinah*) as Metaphor for Outdwelling	141
7	Deconstructing God's Indwelling: The Challenge to Halevi	159
8	Sabbath: The Temporal Outsider	191
	Notes	227
	Works Cited	301
	Citations Index	317
	Names Index	331
	Subject Index	337

Acknowledgments

I have dedicated this book to the memory of my father, Moshe, who devoted himself to providing his children with the opportunities he was denied. Though he endured unimaginable suffering and loss as a result of being a member of a group branded as "outsider" and singly targeted for death simply for having been born, he managed to maintain a genuine smile, an embracing *shmeichel* throughout his life. In our house there were no outsiders. All were welcome and none were judged. He was often fond of saying in Yiddish, his mother tongue, a language that had been virtually extinguished along with the vast majority of its native speakers, that there is no such thing as a "bad child"—one needs only to smile, welcome, and engage. If the Talmudic approach to pedagogy is correct—that an outsider needs to be "pushed away with the left hand and, at the same time, drawn near with the right"—then my father had two right hands. His smile is etched in my mind forever.

I must mention one other memory of my father who always insisted on extending a warm *shalom,* a hello to whomever he would encounter, familiar or unfamiliar, throughout his life. He would often lament the contemporary loss of this common civility. Though, at the time, I did not fully appreciate its significance, I now understand a rabbinic legend regarding an encounter between Moses and God prior to Moses' receiving of the Torah. God was aghast that Moses did not initially greet him with the customary *shalom*. My father's example has taught me that this *midrash* anchors the entire Law in the greeting, the welcoming of another into one's own space. Without the *shalom*, that which establishes relationship between individuals, there in fact can be no Torah. Rabbinic tradition has it that *shalom* is a name of God for whose common use as an ordinary salutation special dispensation was granted. My father's hello reminds me that the divine resides in the welcome, in the expansion of insider space and conversely in the minimization of outsider space.

The friendship of my brothers Irwin and David and the love of my mother Rose have been of inestimable value in ensuring the success of my late entry into the world of the academy. As always, my wife Florence is living testimony to the truth of the Proverbial maxim, *He who finds a wife finds the Good*. Maimonides addressed his students as his own children for, as he said, to teach is also to engender. The reverse can also be said. The loving listening and responses of my children during the years I worked on this book have enriched my fatherhood and so, in some sense, my sons Shimon and Yonah and my daughter Nina have engendered me in turn.

I would like to extend my gratitude to David Burrell for his sensitive reading of my manuscript and his keen insights as well as his encouragement to publish my work. My deepest appreciation is here also expressed for the profoundly critical input of the readers of my manuscript, Elliot Wolfson and Kenneth Seeskin, which contributed to a final product of much enhanced quality. One could not ask for a better combination of scholarly imprimatur on one's own scholarship. Thanks also to Diane Kriger for her fine editing and indexing. Lastly, thanks to Menachem Kellner, David Novak, and Albert Friedberg for their invaluable feedback, comments, and, most of all, comradeship and willingness to hear me out and set me straight if need be.

■ Earlier versions of parts of this book have appeared in various publications and I would like to express my gratitude for permission to reprint revised chapters of the following:

Chapter 1 from "Maimonides and the Convert: A Juridical and Philosophical Embrace of the Outsider," *Journal of Medieval Philosophy and Theology* 11:2 (2003): 125–46, with the permission of Cambridge University Press.

Chapter 2 from "Maimonides on Leprosy: Illness as Contemplative Metaphor," *Jewish Quarterly Review* 96:1 (2006): 95–122, with the permission of University of Pennsylvania Press.

Chapter 3 from "The Failed Theodicy of a Rabbinic Pariah: A Maimonidean Recasting of Elisha ben Abuyah," *Jewish Studies Quarterly* 9:4 (2002): 353–80, with the permission of Mohr Siebeck.

Chapter 4 from "Maimonides On Kingship: The Ethics of Imperial Humility," *Journal of Religious Ethics* 34:1 (2006): 89–114, with the permission of Blackwell Publishing.

Abbreviations and Citations

GP	*Guide of the Perplexed,* Pines edition (cited by book, chapter, page)
Iggerot	*Iggerot HaRambam,* Shailat edition (cited by page)
MN	*Moreh Nevukhim,* ibn Tibbon edition (cited by page)
MN-S	*Moreh Nevukhim,* Schwartz edition (cited by page)
MT	*Mishneh Torah,* Frankel edition
PM	*Mishnah im Perush Rabbenu Moshe ben Maimon,* Kafih edition
SM	*Sefer Ha-Mitzvot,* Kafih edition
Teshuvot	*Teshuvot HaRambam,* Blau edition (cited by page)

Rabbinic works are cited to standard printed editions, unless otherwise indicated.

Transliteration follows the nonscientific style, with the exception of commonly used words and names.

Converts, Heretics, and Lepers

Introduction

Over the course of my lengthy, and often interrupted, intellectual journeys I have repeatedly returned to Moses Maimonides and his rich corpus of writings, seeking an anchor for my Judaism. Beginning in the *yeshivah,* or traditional rabbinical academy, and through numerous detours eventually landing me within the academy, every genre of his thought—be it law, Talmud, exegesis, or philosophy—spoke to me as no other Jewish thinker could. Maimonides had assorted audiences in mind when crafting such works as his groundbreaking code of Jewish law, the *Mishneh Torah,* or when articulating his lifelong struggle to reconcile the faith into which he was born, and to which he would remain unflinchingly loyal, with equally cherished reason in the *Guide of the Perplexed.* In many ways these audiences are reflected in the various stages through which my own journey has passed from the *yeshivah* to the academy. The constituents of a public readership mirror the various stages reached by an evolving reader, whose repeated turns to a worthy text draw him into greater depths of meaning. The text increasingly discloses itself as the reader liberates himself from his social and literalist constraints.

When Maimonides took his prized student Joseph aside for private instruction, he took all his prospective readers aside for the very same purpose. When he abandoned his earlier project to "explain all the difficult passages in the *Midrashim*" (GP Intro., 9), he gave up any attempt to write for the public at large. His experiment with different literary forms ended in frustration, amounting to the simple exchange of one parable for another and defeating the goals he had set for himself of clarifying, explaining, and ultimately resolving doubt and confusion. Straightforward explication would have offended the very principles that underlie the rabbinic literary form of *midrash,* since the general public would not find its message palatable. Jewish law, or *halakhah,* had also imposed severe restrictions on the public teaching of the esoteric material that is the subject matter of the *Guide* (m. *Hagigah* 2:1), limiting Maimonides' options even further. He was left with no choice but to both disclose and conceal at the same time.[1] Those who do "not find impossibilities hard to accept" (GP Intro., 10) could be comfortably ignored since they already understood *midrash* and contentedly operated in a world of the absurd. Rabbinic authority sculpted their world, and so there was never a clash between *midrash* and science that required any reconciliation. For them, if the prophet heard God then God has a larynx and vocal chords. God is what the prophet describes or sees. There is no standard outside of the text by which to judge prophetic language, and so the prophet shapes the world and God and bequeaths them to an undiscriminating posterity.

Maimonides had an entirely different posterity in mind when he chose the format of the *Guide* to preserve his esoteric teachings. Aside from the obvious philosophical and rabbinic proficiency he expected of his intended readers, the most essential qualifications he anticipated as an entitlement to read his work were angst and confusion caused by "the externals of the Law" (ibid., 5). He was not interested in generating that angst; nor, I believe, was he interested in altogether quelling it. Without the *Guide* the Jew who pledged his allegiance to Torah and sophia could only hold on to both by leading an anxiety-ridden life that "would not cease to suffer from heartache and great perplexity" (ibid., 6).[2] The tension between the two would have to be so overpowering as to demand the surrender of one of them; the choice would be determined by the greater of the pull of either intellectual honesty or religious conformity.

Maimonides offered to transform these opposing pulls from repellent forces into convergent ones by attuning those "distressed" seekers to the literary genre of metaphor. Once prophetic language was understood to be equivocal and its narratives parabolic, a new dimension would open up in which the religious and philosophical flourish. Metaphor was the remedy to restore a bifurcated existence into a holistic one in which religion, law, and science meld into one seamless truth. Maimonides cautioned his readers, however, that the process of attunement to the figurative nuances of prophetic and rabbinic language would itself entail its own angst. He warned them to be realistic in their expectations, for "I do not say that this Treatise will remove all difficulties for those who understand it" (ibid., 6). Maimonides' textual legacy inspired a new productive reading angst to replace the former destructive existential angst by its strategies of scantiness ("chapter headings"), organizational chaos ("Not set down in order or arranged in coherent fashion . . . but rather are scattered and entangled"), and elusiveness ("my purpose is that the truths be glimpsed and then again concealed") (ibid.).[3] The searcher who wishes to enter the Maimonidean academy must be willing to accept an angst-ridden future in which every point of clarity that is achieved paves the way for further perplexity. The end goal of the quest for knowledge is paradoxically the furthest reaches of no knowledge.

Maimonides contended that his writing style follows a long-standing tradition commenced by God Himself and picked up by the sages "following the trail of these [prophetic] books" of communicating in "riddles and parables" (ibid., 7). God is as important an exemplar of writing as he is of pure contemplative thought. The compositions in which Maimonides exploited this strategy of dissemblance were never intended to garner substantial audiences and become insider texts. In the case of the *Mishneh Torah,* he informed his beloved student Joseph ben R. Judah that "I did not compose this *hibbur* to gain prominence in Israel or to garner for myself a reputation but I composed it—and God himself knows—*primarily for myself*" (Iggerot, 300–301, emphasis mine). As far as the *Guide* is concerned, it was written as a private correspondence to the very same student with the stated intention to "address that single man [virtuous man] by himself" (ibid., 16). His two major works are private affairs, conversations with only *myself* or, at their most expansive, with *himself,* emerging out of private spaces. They are self-heuristic exercises, or, at the most, private dialogues into which the reader can eavesdrop. The reader has been duly forewarned: trade in your existential distress for a lifetime of struggle solving the riddles of the very text, which holds the key to solving riddles.

The prerequisites for students who wish to be taught the two most esoteric disciplines within the medieval Jewish studies curriculum—the first chapters of Genesis known as the "Account of Creation" *(ma'aseh bereshit)* and the first chapter of Ezekiel or the "Account of the Chariot" *(ma'aseh merkavah)*—were compared by the medieval commentator Efodi to the seven items of clothing priests were required to wear for the temple service (MN 4a–b). The analogy captures a new theology wherein service of God has moved from the space of the temple to the abstract arena of the mind. The priests have been replaced by the sages/philosophers as its new attendants.[4] They can be identified by their "clothing" (intellectual and ethical constitutions), and the rule "when their clothes are on their priesthood is on, when their clothes are not on their priesthood is not on" (MT *Laws of the Temple Vessels* 10:4) still metaphorically applies. According to Maimonides, certain priestly vestments can not be worn on any occasion other than temple service (MT *Laws of the Temple Vessels* 8:12), and so, analogously, the troubled scholar cannot publicize all of his qualifications. One of those better kept a private affair is the anxiety that would be disturbing to a public unaware that there is anything in their tradition they need be anxious about. A sage who struggles with tradition would pose an unsettling picture for those who look up to him for leadership and guidance.

Another aspect of priestly clothing deepens the significance of the analogy. Just as many of the laws regarding temple sanctity are intended to promote awe and reverence for the temple, so the priests must wear "the most splendid, finest and most beautiful garments"; as Polonius says to Laertes in *Hamlet*, "the apparel oft proclaims the man," and the public judges worth and value based on appearance. Clothing conceals as much as it reveals, "for to the multitude an individual is not rendered great by his true form, but by the perfection of his limbs and the beauty of his clothes" (GP III:45, 579). What goes on within the "true form" of man, that is the intellect, must be covered up to make a positive impression. Maimonides replaced the geographical space, which God and man were once understood to share and where there was divine/human interaction,[5] with intellectual apprehension, in the exercise of which "the divine intellect conjoined with man" (GP I:1, 23).

Maimonides created a textual space restricted to those who complete their preliminary studies of logic, mathematics, and natural science, allowing them to proceed to the final stage of divine science—a group so statistically insignificant as to be limited to "one of a city or two of a family" (Jer 3:14; GP I:34, 75). Finally, after a lifetime of work in the arenas of community activism, politics, public health, and business,[6] he carved out a space on the margins to which he could retreat and invite other "solitary individuals" to share those margins with him. Already in his legal code, the *Mishneh Torah,* he set the stage for camaraderie of the singular and solitary. Historical precedent had shown, however, that the prospects of qualifying as one of those "solitary individuals" Maimonides had in mind were minimal. The attempt by four of "the great men of Israel and great sages" to master the divine and natural sciences ended in a 25 percent success rate and disastrous consequences for the failures; "they did not all possess the capacity to know and grasp these subjects clearly" (MT *Laws of the Foundations of the Torah* 4:13).[7] Those with inadequate preparation and qualifications faced the direst prospects of heresy, insanity, or even death.

Maimonides adopted the rabbinic metaphor of the "garden" *(pardes)* to describe and explain these esoteric disciplines, and the endeavor to comprehend them is correspondingly "a walk in the garden" (ibid.). The first occurrence of this term in the Hebrew Bible is set in a context of impenetrability. The lover of the Song of Songs addresses his "sister," his "bride," as a "locked garden *[gan naʿul]* . . . a locked pool *[gal naʿul]*,[8] a sealed fountain *[maʾayan ḥatum],*" and continues, "Your shoots are a garden *[pardes]* of pomegranates" (Song 4:12–13). Twice locked and once sealed, the original context of *pardes* is shrouded in mystery and exclusivity. In many ways, Maimonides' philosophical project is an attempt to gain access to the primal Garden of Eden where thought reigned free of imaginative constraints (GP I:2). Could it be that Adam's utopian state was shattered once he made the transition from loneliness (Gen 2:18) to companionship? It is no coincidence, from a Maimonidean perspective, that the moment the social circle widened the decline began, from looking only upward to looking at oneself as standing before others: "And the eyes of both of them were opened and they knew that they were naked" (Gen 3:7). It was only then that clothes were needed and concealment became endemic to society. Human beings became *elohim,* defined by Maimonides as "rulers," whose primary concerns are governance and social harmony. The process of concealment shifted from clothes ("and He clothed them" [Gen 3:21]) to language ("And God said to Cain 'where is your brother Abel?' and he responded 'I don't know; am I my brother's keeper?'" [Gen 4:9]).

The language of the prophets is all-embracing, as reflected in the axiom *The Torah speaks in the language of the sons of man* (common human parlance). However, the Torah's popularity is sustained at the expense of unequivocal truth, for "everything that the multitude consider a perfection is predicated of Him, even if it is only a perfection in relation to ourselves—*for in relation to Him, may He be exalted, all things that we consider perfections are the very extreme of deficiency*" (GP I:26, 56; emphasis mine). The Torah describes God in terms of how man views himself and so, curiously, openly espouses a narcissistic theology. Maimonides set out to redirect man's gaze upward.[9]

The chapters that follow discuss one means of redirecting that gaze. Each focuses on a type or character that in some way is an outsider, one who does not quite fit any broad societal norm. They become, in Maimonides' hands, metaphors for something much larger than their own existential predicaments. The external existences of such outsiders are transformed into philosophical archetypes of notions that are marginal and that, in turn, marginalize. Whether it is the convert who enters from the outside in or the heretic who travels from the inside out, they are philosophically suggestive in Maimonides' deft hands. Each one radically reorients theological perceptions and challenges long-standing "beliefs" (as opposed to demonstratively gained knowledge) through a type that itself poses existential and social challenges. There is a heightened urgency to ostracize the leper and the heretic because they pose far greater *philosophical* dangers than previously thought. The convert is far more an insider than acknowledged and, in fact, may be the only authentic insider, leaving his new hosts themselves as outsiders. The sage/philosopher can only pretend to be an insider while he transports himself internally, in the realm where authentic existence abides, to the regions most remote from his religious cohorts. The king starts at the point most distant from the inside and travels in the other direction, pushed inside by the extreme humility his throne embodies. To hold on to any true sense of God, the philosophical traditionalist must be pushed beyond anything familiar, distanced and estranged from man—beyond cognition. Maimonides constructed these metaphors out of his own outsider space, where he may have developed an affinity for outsiders as apt conveyors of philosophical truths.

Maimonides took his literary cue from his perception of nature. The natural analogue of the literary maxim *The Torah speaks in the language of the sons of man* is the rabbinic maxim that governs all of reality, *The world goes its customary way*,[10] which excludes any permanent change in the natural order of the world. Just as language conforms to human nature, so nature persistently conforms to its own design. Miracles, however, are the natural equivalent of the existential outsider and must be accounted for as possible violations of that rule. The solution is to naturalize them, consistent with rabbinic sources stating that "when God created that which exists and stamped upon it the existing natures, He put it into these natures that all the miracles that occurred would be produced in them at the time when they occurred."[11] In a sense, then, every miracle, normally perceived as a suspension of the physical laws of nature, can be viewed as in fact substantiating the natural order by directing our attention back to its origins at creation. The miracle, or the "outsider" phenomenon, is merely another facet of nature, or the "insider" order. Every interruption or extraordinary event indicates the universal order, and its eventual relapse back into a natural state of affairs vindicates the durability of natural causation. From its inception, nature is conditioned to interrupt itself at certain historical junctures. Ruptures in nature are therefore an integral part of the historical chain set in motion at the point of creation.

The rule *The world goes its customary way* will continue to be operative in the messianic era as well: "It should not enter one's mind that during the messianic period any law of nature will cease or that there will be any novelty in the creation. The world will go its customary way" (MT *Laws of Kings* 12:1).[12] It maintains the seamless continuum between the origins of man and the world on one end and the crowning achievement of human potential on the other. Beginnings anticipate ends. The messianic period culminates a historical series of peaks and valleys in the realization of the human "form," the "image of God" *(tzelem elohim)*, commencing with a single human *(adam)* and climaxing with humankind. Every miraculous "outside" event then looks back at creation and forward to messianic utopia by jolting one into an awareness of the principle *The world goes its customary way*. Rather than offending the rule, miracles are shocking reminders of its operational currency. Just as each of the outsiders examined in this book stands as a metaphor for broader philosophical ideals, so the miracle is an empirical metaphor for the workings of nature, which in turn apprises human beings of creation and its originating divine impetus. Increasing awareness of origins (creation) also heightens one's consciousness of destination (the messianic era). The very structure of the *Mishneh Torah* reflects this journey, beginning with "the fundamental of all fundamentals and the pillar of all sciences to know that there is a First Existence and that He has brought everything that exists into existence," and ending with another fundamental principle, anticipation of the messianic period. The latter feeds right back into the beginning, since then "there will be no other preoccupation of the entire world than to know God alone."[13] The *Mishneh Torah* charts a historical current initiated by an individual commandment to know a First Existence ("I am the Lord your God" [Exod 20:2])[14] and evolves into a universal state of affairs in which that knowledge is endemic to all of humanity—the normative becomes the norm.

More importantly, metaphor drives the historical continuum from its inception to its culmination. The Torah's anthropomorphic language cannot be a true description of any being that can be known as a singular First Existence. All such language, therefore, is geared "to the capacity of the public who only appreciate physicality and the Torah speaks in the language of men and they are all figures of speech as it is written *When I whet my flashing sword* [Deut 32:41]. Has God a sword and does He kill with a sword? It is a metaphor and all such phrases are metaphors" (MT *Laws of the Foundations of the Torah* 1:9). Likewise, all prophetic depictions of the messianic period in terms of the fantastic, emblematic of which is "The wolf shall dwell with the lamb and the leopard shall lie down with the kid" (Isa 11:6), "is metaphor and riddle *(mashal, hidah)* . . . and all similar passages regarding the messiah are metaphorical, and in the days of the messianic king the meaning of the metaphors and to what they allude will be known to all" (MT *Laws of Kings* 12:1). In a sense, deciphering metaphor is the defining feature of the messianic age. Aside from the political activism required to bring about universal peaceful coexistence, every reading of prophetic texts that is cognizant of their metaphorical content and that determines the meaning of such metaphor constitutes a step closer to this redemptive epoch. Hermeneutics is redemptive.

The time when all humanity will be engaged in one goal—the knowledge of God—is also tantamount to a universal engagement with the interpretation of metaphor. Messianic redemption is as much about hermeneutical activity as it is about political and theological activism. It is precisely for this reason that Isaiah casts this period as a new creation— "For behold I create new heavens and a new earth" (Isa 65:17)—since clarity of metaphor brings clarity of a "First Existence who has brought everything that exists into existence." Piercing through the veil of metaphor leads to understanding the origins of the world, which in turn lends permanence to the new world, heralded by the Messiah.[15] The metaphors that now conceal God will become transparent when the metaphors that now conceal the messianic period become themselves transparent. Maimonides sought to offer hermeneutical guidance so that one can fully appreciate "the key to the understanding of all that the prophets, peace be on them, have said, and to the knowledge of its truth . . . [that is,] an understanding of the parables, of their import, and of the meaning of the words occurring in them" (GP Intro., 9–10). During the course of his enterprise, he constructed his own "parables" out of the biblical and rabbinic fabric he inherited. The theme of this study is to show how this was accomplished with one piece of that fabric—namely, outsiders constructed as "parables," or metaphors. In this vein, Maimonides perpetuated the legacy of the prophetic hermeneutic.

To illustrate what awaits the reader, I offer here a sampling of two of the "outsiders" who are afforded comprehensive treatments in later chapters: the convert and the king. Both operate at the margins of society although at extreme opposite poles of the social spectrum. The convert, the alien who has joined the ranks but whose status remains legally distinct and who will likely never achieve full social integration,[16] becomes a parable about the authentic Jew. For Maimonides, this foreign import is, in essence, the only truly indigenous Jew. All biologically bred Jews are actually hampered by their genetic pedigree, and the standard by which their Judaism is to be judged is the convert's. The outsider, whose presence has infiltrated insider space, becomes the only genuine insider, relative to whom all insiders are edged outside.[17] Though Maimonides was constrained by his commitment to the rabbinic tradition to assign the convert a separate juridical status, he was able to escape that inequity by constructing a metaphysics of conversion. Maimonides' convert ultimately overcomes the rabbinic presentation of converts "as marginal beings, occupying the liminal space between the Israelite and the gentile communities."[18] God's personal love for the convert—for the biblical *ger* (stranger) in Deut 10:18, which becomes the rabbinic term for convert[19]—is a reflex of the convert's love for God, as the only one even capable of an unadulterated *amore dei*.

The king, as a figure who occupies the uppermost extremity of the social hierarchy, is also an outsider presence, but is one who can be so imposing and overwhelming as to leave no space for anyone else. While the convert's acceptance is always tenuous and his "orphaned" status leaves him vulnerable, the king's position may be so overpowering as to expose everyone beneath him to that same vulnerability. In a sense, he poses the danger of making all who perceive him as the ultimate authority into outsiders and therefore need look no further upward than him as the source of their sustenance and object of their fear.[20] Civilization has in fact experienced the logical outgrowth of just such a perception in the doctrine of the divine right of kings. To prevent the realization of such an idolatrous theology, Maimonides' juridical construction of the king consciously aims at lowering the king to the opposite end of the social spectrum where, in fact, the converts, the orphans, and the destitute reside. The result is an imperial image that projects the very extremes of humility, an ideal ethical posture codified as an exception to the ethical golden mean in Maimonides' *Laws of Ethical Traits (hilkhot de'ot)*. It is through the prism of the king that Maimonides informs us of the precise meaning of the formulations "lowly of spirit" *(shefal-ruah)* and "exceedingly base of spirit" *(ruho nemukho leme'od)* (MT *Laws of Ethical Traits* 2:3).[21]

No Maimonidean king could ever deify the throne as did King James (1566–1625) in an address to the English Parliament in which he proclaimed, "Kings are justly called Gods for they exercise a manner or resemblance of divine power on earth. For if you consider the attributes to God you will see how they agree in the person of the king. God hath power to create or destroy, make or unmake at his pleasure. . . . And the like power have kings."[22] Maimonides' king becomes the very embodiment of supreme humility, a metaphor for everyman, by directing his subjects' gaze downward rather than upward. The precedent for Maimonides' ideal monarch is the midrashic David, of whom it is said, "No man in Israel abased himself for the sake of the commandments more than David . . . [as he said:] Like the baby that has just come out of its mother's womb and is not too proud to suck at his mother's breasts, so is my soul within me, for I am not ashamed to learn Torah even from the least in Israel."[23] The extreme standard of humility that is assimilated by the king not only thwarts any Pharaoh-like image that "belongs not to the order of mankind but to that of the gods,"[24] but also inspires a universal awareness of the great divide between man and God.

CHAPTER 1

The Convert (*Ger*)

Metaphor of Jewishness

Our first outsider is the convert to Judaism, who, I argue, is for Maimonides the only true insider, the only authentic Jew to be found in the community of naturally born Jews he has joined. The naturalized Jew in the Maimonidean oeuvre stands as the exemplar of genuine Jewishness for the natural Jew. Within the long tradition of technical legal (halakhic) stare decisis, or Jewish responsa literature, one can find no more intricate a weave of law and philosophy than that crafted by Maimonides in response to an existential query by Ovadyah,[1] a Muslim convert to Judaism.[2] Ovadyah's conversion raised particular concerns within the arena of institutionalized prayer and the rabbinically standardized texts that were its mainstay. The liturgy that had evolved was replete with ethnocentric expressions that rendered it highly resistant to the entry of outsiders anxious to become full-fledged members of the club.

How can the convert utter the phrase "God of our fathers," referring to the biblical patriarchs Abraham, Isaac, and Jacob, when his biological ancestry belies its pronouncement? What right does he have to lay claim to a divine election, with the words "who chose us," a reference to the divine selection of Israel for the granting of the Law (Torah) that was motivated by a preference for one "nation" over others? Can he appeal to a God who is particularized as a national liberator, "who took us out of Egypt," when enslavement and exodus were confined to a specific locale and time within a national historical consciousness? And finally, God's intrusion into history on Israel's behalf, as He "who performed miracles for our fathers," is a shared collective memory about which the convert, having no blood line to the Jewish past, cannot reminisce. This was no mere halakhic question as to whether Ovadyah could legitimately adopt these communal liturgical expressions. The implications of this question went far beyond those regarding the niceties of Jewish law commonly posed to the halakhic experts of the day. Ovadyah was also revealing a deep existential suspicion that he would never be able to consider himself an authentic insider of the religious community he had joined, in all likelihood, at great personal risk.[3] Maimonides used this opportunity to effectively address the much larger issue of "Who is a Jew?" The full import of Maimonides' response is that not only can the convert consider himself fully Jewish for halakhic purposes, but the convert is also transformed into an ideal, a metaphor for the truly authentic Jew.

Because I offer a close reading of Maimonides reading of the letter to Ovadyah, the entire text of the letter is reproduced here for ease of reference.

> *Thus says Moses, the son of Rabbi Maimon, one of the exiles from Jerusalem, who lived in Spain:*
>
> *I received the question of the master Obadiah, the wise and learned proselyte, may the Lord reward him for his work, may a perfect recompense be bestowed upon him by the Lord of Israel, under whose wings he has sought cover.*
>
> *You ask me if you, too, are allowed to say in the blessing and prayers you offer alone or in congregation: "Our God" and "God of our fathers," "You who have sanctified us through Your commandments," "You who have separated us," "You who have chosen us," "You who have inherited us," "You who have brought us out of the land of Egypt," "You who have worked miracles to our fathers," and more of this kind.*
>
> *Yes, you may say all this in the prescribed order and not change it in the least. In the same way as every Jew by birth says his blessing and prayer, you, too, shall bless and pray alike, whether you are alone*

or pray in the congregation. The reason for this is, that Abraham our Father taught the people, opened their minds, and revealed to them the true faith and the unity of God; he rejected the idols and aboolished their adoration; he brought many children under the wings of the Divine Presence; he gave them counsel and advice, and ordered his sons and the members of his household after him to keep the ways of the Lord forever, as it is written, "For I have known him to the end that he may command his children and his household after him, that they may keep the way of the Lord, to do righteousness and justice" (Gen. 18:19). Ever since then whoever adopts Judaism and confesses the unity of the Divine Name, as it is prescribed in the Torah, is counted among the disciples of Abraham our Father, peace be with him. These men are Abraham's household, and he it is who converted them to righteousness.

In the same way as he converted his contemporaries through his words and teaching, he converts future generations through the testament he left to his children and household after him. Thus Abraham our Father, peace be with him, is the father of his pious posterity who keeps his ways, and the father of his disciples and of all proselytes who adopt Judaism.

Therefore you shall pray, "Our God" and "God of our fathers," because Abraham, peace be with him, is your father. And you shall pray, "You who have taken for his own our fathers," for the land has been given to Abraham, as it is said, "Arise, walk through the land in the length of it and in the breadth of it; for I will give to you" (Gen. 13:17). As to the words, "You who have brought us out of the land of Egypt" or "You who have done miracles to our fathers"—these you may change, if you will, and say, "You who have brought Israel out of the land of Egypt" and "You who have done miracles to Israel." If, however, you do not change them, it is no transgression, because since you have come under the wings of the Divine Presence and confessed the Lord, no difference exists between you and us, and all miracles done to us have been done as it were to us and to you. Thus is said in the Book of Isaiah, "Neither let the son of the stranger, that has joined himself to the Lord, speak, saying, "The Lord has utterly separated me from His people'" (Is. 56:3). There is no difference whatever between you and us. You shall certainly say the blessing, "Who has chosen us," "Who has given us," "Who have taken us for Your own" and "Who has separated us": for the Creator, may He be extolled, has indeed chosen you and separated you from the nations and given you the Torah.

> For the Torah has been given to us and to the proselytes, as it is said, "One ordinance shall be both for you of the congregation, and also for the stranger that sojourns with you, and Ordinance for ever in your generations; as you are, so shall the stranger be before the Lord" (Num. 15:15). Know that our fathers, when they came out of Egypt, were mostly idolaters; they had mingled with the pagans in Egypt and imitated their way of life, until the Holy One, may He be blessed, sent Moses our Teacher, the master of all prophets, who separated us from the nations and brought us under the wings of the Divine Presence, us and all proselytes, and gave to all of us one Law.
>
> Do not consider your origin as inferior. While we are the descendants of Abraham, Isaac, and Jacob, you derive from Him through whose word the world was created. As is said by Isaiah: "One shall say, I am the Lord's, and another shall call himself by the name of Jacob" (Is. 44:5).

The problem of a fixed liturgy geared to common origins is particularly acute for the convert for a number of reasons. First, it is the most pervasive and dominant feature of the Jewish ritual system of commandments (*mitzvot*). The Jew's entire daily cycle is measured in terms of prayer intervals and blessing opportunities. The observant Jew's calendar is governed by prayer frequency and appointed times. Second, the Rabbis considered prayer a "worship of the heart" (*b. Taanit* 2a), which replaced the most prominent feature of ancient Judaism, the Temple sacrificial cult (*b. Berakhot* 26b; MT *Laws of Prayer* 2:5; *Sifre Deut, Eqev* 41). Praise, supplication, entreaty, appreciation, contemplation—virtually every facet of one's relationship with God—are articulated through prayer (MT *Laws of Prayer* 1:2).[4] What the Rabbis had in mind by "worship of the heart" was philosophically identified by Maimonides as the apex of human religious activity, "setting thought to work on the first intelligible and devoting oneself exclusively to this as far as this is within one's capacity" (GP III:51, 621). Despite its esoteric formulation in the *Guide* as pure contemplation, concrete prayer is valued as a step in the evolution toward this realization.[5] To diminish access to its domain for any Jew within a Jewish context is, therefore, to impede the process of achieving the single-minded "devotion" Maimonides determined to be a perfected "worship of the heart." It would indeed strike at the very *heart* of a Jew's practice and faith.

Finally, Maimonides' response reflects Ovadyah's concerns regarding his role in the public sphere as well as the private. The response specifically makes no distinction between private prayer and prayer in the capacity of a *shaliah tzibbur* (prayer leader or, in contemporary terms, the cantor) (Iggerot, 233, line 13). No starker image of the convert's alienation could be drawn than one in which the prayers of the prayer group's appointed representative are at odds with the group. Assuming this role, for whatever reason, would lay bare the convert's *difference* in the community, an embarrassment for all to see. Such a situation also accentuates the problematics of exclusion from a ritual whose essential characteristic is in fact communal. Prayer functions ideally only within the group (*b. Berakhot* 8a; MT *Laws of Prayer* 8:1). Indeed, the primary focus of the rabbinic maxim "*Every act of sanctification requires not less than ten*" (*b. Megillah* 23b) is directed toward prayer and benedictions. The very verse from which this minimum quorum is derived places God within the group, "that I may be sanctified in the midst of the Israelite people" (Lev 22:32). The verse confines sanctity to the community (*b. Megillah* 23b; MT *Laws of Prayer* 8:6). What should qualify a *shaliah tzibbur* is his ethical and intellectual constitution, not his ethnic background (MT *Laws of Prayer* 8:11). Therefore, any mark of distinction borne by the *ger*, though otherwise halakhically irrelevant to his qualifications as an emissary of the group, would serve to spotlight his "otherness" and delegitimize his capacity to personify the group.[6]

Motivated by the ethics of acceptance, Maimonides extended a philosophical and halakhic welcome to Ovadyah that fully integrated him into the fabric of the community of Israel. The convert's ancestry can be conceptually traced back to Abraham by replacing the biological father–son model with a pedagogical teacher–disciple one. Abraham is the founder of Israel because he conveyed universal truths through the medium of reasoned instruction. Abraham's language was educatory, for "he taught the people, and enlightened them and informed them the true way and the unity of God . . . he gave them counsel and advice" (Iggerot, 233, lines 14–15; 234, line 2). Maimonides here drew on his own portrait of Abraham in the *Mishneh Torah* as the Socrates of his age who missionizes by "sowing doubt," "engaging in debate," "informing," "overpowering with demonstration," "accumulating a following," informing each follower "in accordance with his capacity," and ultimately "authoring treatises" (MT *Laws of Idolatry* 1:3).[7] Abraham's legacy of "conversion" to the truth by way of "speech and teaching" (Iggerot, 234, lines 5–6) extends to every future convert. A figurative father–son relationship is thus established in the sense offered by the *Guide* for the Hebrew term "son": "whoever instructs an individual in some matter and teaches him an opinion, has, as far as his being provided with this opinion is concerned, as it were engendered that individual" (GP I:7, 32).[8] Maimonides himself, in his own correspondence with his students, played out this paternity constructed by his role as teacher and addressed them as his sons.[9]

Ironically, what allows the convert to assume the ethnocentric language of his newly adopted faith is not his acceptance of its unique command structure *(mitzvot)*. That was never Abraham's legacy. Rather, it is the embrace of those universal truths discovered and propounded by Abraham that eases the convert's entry into the community of Israel. Abraham professed "the unity of God, rejected idolatry and abolished its worship" (Iggerot, 233, lines 14–15)[10]—that is, he promoted universal truths while discrediting popular ideologies of falsehood. This teaching is what attracted large numbers of people to be domiciled "under the wings of the Divine Presence *[kanfe ha-shekhinah]*" (Iggerot, 233, lines 14–15). Maimonides' introductory deference to Ovadyah is understandably then a verbatim quote of Ruth 2:12, originally addressed to Ruth the Moabite, the classic rabbinic archetype of all converts: "May the Lord compensate him for his work and may he be granted the perfect reward by the God of Israel under whose wings he has sought shelter."[11] Ovadyah's journey toward Judaism is quite literally a reenactment of the originating moment that ultimately gave birth to Judaism. The irrefutable demonstrations crafted by Abraham have traversed time and spoken to the convert; by virtue of this he becomes Abraham's disciple and, ipso facto, his descendant.[12]

The proof-text cited in Maimonides' response, Gen 18:19, is vital in its concise formulation of the substance of Abraham's teaching: "For I have known him, to the end that he may command his children and his household after him that they may keep the way of the Lord *[derekh YHVH]*." The "way of the Lord" propagated by Abraham was defined by Maimonides in his *Mishneh Torah* as instruction in the ethical golden mean, which, once inculcated into one's constitution, is the fulfillment of *imitatio dei* (see MT *Laws of Ethical Traits* 1:5–7.). Behavioral *imitatio dei* is merely concomitant to a philosophically pure conception of God and the world. Correct conduct mirrors those attributes we associate with the manner in which nature operates—that is, "attributes of action"—and not God's essence itself.[13] Repetitive conduct that is consonant with such traits as mercy, graciousness, and holiness serves to entrench within the mind a correct conception of God. In the language of Herbert Davidson's seminal analysis, the ultimate performance of "walking in His ways" is not the mere cultivation of intermediate character traits as tentatively proposed in the *Mishneh Torah*. Rather, it is "by performing acts, as God does, not through intermediate, or any other psychological characteristics, but wholly dispassionately."[14]

In this sense, the convert not only achieves parity with the naturally born Jew, but actually gains an advantage over him. Given the familial background of the naturally born Jew, his fulfillment of *imitatio dei* will always be tainted by an ulterior motivation. The emotional and psychological impetus for following in the footsteps of one's father is ever-present and is, in effect, an obstacle to acting in accordance with the dictates of pure reason. The convert, on the other hand, has no such ties. Like Abraham, he has "no one to teach him and no one to instruct him in anything" since his parents, as well as himself, practiced an alien faith (MT *Laws of Idolatry* 1:3). Maimonides' precise categorization of those who can be considered "disciples of Abraham" now becomes apparent. As a consequence of Gen 18:19 they are "all those who will convert in the future and all those who profess the unity of God's Name *as it is prescribed by the Torah*" (emphasis mine).[15] Mere loyalty to family and the identity of one's biological antecedents do not qualify one as a student of Abraham. Further, the *mitzvah* to declare God's unity that is outlined in the very beginning of the *Mishneh Torah* does not imply obedience to law. It actually entails piercing through the literal sense of Scripture, an exercise that can only be realized by way of a detached and reasoned Abrahamic conception of God. Biblical language rife with anthropomorphisms that literally describe an adulterated god must be reread to conform to a pure demonstrable notion of unity (MT *Laws of the Foundations of the Torah* 1:3–6). The biblical text must, in effect, be overcome to perfect one's notion of God. Likewise one must overcome the obstacle of family (parents) to be accredited as a "student of Abraham." The convert conforms to both of these requirements.

Maimonides quite consistently maintained a strict distinction between two relational models of Abraham and posterity. He concluded, "It follows then that Abraham, our father, is father to all his pious descendants *(zaro)* [that is, *only* those among his descendants who are pious] who walk in his ways and father to his students *(talmidav)* and they are every convert who adopts Judaism" (Iggerot, 234, lines 7–8). There are "students" and there are "descendants," and the former are singled out as forming the class to which the convert belongs. Only one who did not possess his own tradition qualifies as "student" since his attraction to Judaism could only have materialized out of detached and reasoned study. Even biological descendants do not automatically qualify as Abraham's children but must earn the pedigree by "walking in his ways." This latter phrase subtly draws attention to the disadvantage a direct descendant bears vis-à-vis the outsider in his relationship with God. The halakhic source for the primary directive of *imitatio dei* is the exact same phrase "and you shall walk in His ways" (Deut 28:9; MT *Laws of Ethical Traits* 1:5–7). What is crucial is that in this instance the referent is God, not Abraham. When the genetic descendant complies with this directive, Abraham is, in a sense, an obstacle to its accomplishment. That human link in the genetic chain can never be certain that what he is engaged in flows from some ancestral or tribal allegiance and not from a rational appreciation of how God operates in the world. The virtuous life appurtenant to "walking in His ways" is one that is played out in the theater of the mind. Included in the *Guide*'s crusade to cleanse the Bible of its anthropomorphisms is its figurative treatment of the "walking" of Deut 28:9, which is a means of advancing "without in any way moving a body" (GP I:24, 54). Only the convert's journey along this path originates in the mind. He, therefore, can be confident that his final destination will correspondingly also be of the mind.

The citation of Gen 18:19 to establish the convert's credentials further fortifies his induction into Abraham's nuclear family *(bne beto)*. Its relatively frequent appearance in the *Guide* (GP II:39; III:24; III:43; III:51) serves to reconfigure its contours when it is cited elsewhere. The chapter dealing with the concept of "trial" *(nissayon)* (GP III:24) culminates, of course, with the most powerful instance, the binding of Isaac *(aqedah)*. One of the purposes of this trial, we are told, is to validate the truth and certainty of prophetic revelation, which, for the prophet, is of equal status in clarity of perception "as that of all existent things that are apprehended through the sense or through the intellect" (GP III:24, 501). Otherwise Abraham would not have proceeded with such dispatch to implement that "which is repugnant to nature" (GP III:24, 502). Genesis 18:19 is then cited to demonstrate that Abraham communicates ideas by example as well as oral teaching: "just as they followed his correct and useful opinions, namely, those that were heard from him so ought one to follow the opinions deriving from his actions especially from this action." The *aqedah* is transformed into a parable conveying theoretical truths whose narrative crux is the relationship between a father and son. Those who can trace their lineage back to Abraham are more prone to interpret the trial in terms of its paternal–filial dimensions, a hermeneutical stance colored by their own emotional and familial bond to the central characters.[16] On the other hand, the convert, who lacks such a bond and is detached physically from the personalities involved, can more easily separate the theoretical from the existential. The absence of a father–son lens through which to view the story enhances its theoretical import. The convert's vantage point gains him more direct access not only to Abraham's oral teachings, but also to his behavioral teachings.

The figurative father–son construct enables the convert also to legitimately lay claim to those concrete benefits that flow from the promises made by God to Abraham. Because Abraham was granted the land of Israel (Gen 13:17), by virtue of the convert's constructed link to Abraham, that grant extends to the convert, empowering him to honestly declare, "who has allotted our fathers."[17] Prayers, however, that allude to post-Abrahamic historical interventions by God on behalf of Israel, pose more serious problems for the convert. Phrases such as "who took us out of Egypt" and "performed miracles for our fathers" are left to the personal prerogative of the convert. He can adopt or amend them in accordance with his degree of comfort in appropriating the Israelite national historical consciousness.[18] Ultimately though, for the sake of avoiding the ritual perpetuation of a convert's otherness, even these ethno-specific references need not be altered ("who took Israel out of Egypt"; "who performed miracles for Israel"). The convert's assumption of his new identity is consummate; since he has "come under the wings of the Divine presence and joined *[nilvetah]* God there is no distinction at all between us and you" (Iggerot, 234, lines 14–15).[19] To expressly distinguish himself would even contravene a prophetic affirmation of his unconditional assimilation into the fold: "Neither let the son of the stranger, that has joined *[nilvah]* himself to the Lord speak, saying 'The Lord has separated me from His people'" (Isa 56:3). Isaiah's pronouncement would be particularly comforting for Ovadyah since it is secured by the prospect of a universal pilgrimage to the Temple that is defined as a "house of prayer" *(tefillah)*. That house is welcoming to all who share a common belief entitling them to "rejoice in my house of prayer . . . for my house will be called a house of prayer for all nations" (ibid., 56:7). Prayer, which for Ovadyah was initially divisive, is, in Isa 56, transformed into a supreme symbol of unification both for the convert and ultimately all of mankind.[20]

The term *nilvah* (joining), chosen by the response for both its description of Ovadyah's unconditional attachment to Judaism and its choice of proof-text (Isa 56:3), is instrumental to its rationale. First, its object is consistently God, not the Jewish people (Iggerot, 234, lines 14, 16; 235, line 18).[21] Ovadyah's ability to fully participate in communal practices such as prayer is dictated by his acceptance of the universal—the unity of God. The foundations of the Jewish nation were in fact rooted in its universal message. Thus the goal of the evolutionary process of nation building, as charted by the *Mishneh Torah* originating with Abraham, is also a universal one. Jewish demographic growth conveyed by the term *nilvim*, by which is meant a swelling of the ranks with new members, continued to be promoted by Abraham's moral and intellectual heirs Isaac and Jacob:

> Isaac settled, teaching and restoring. He, in turn, informed Jacob and appointed him to teach and be settled down teaching and restoring all those who have joined themselves [*nilvim*] to him . . . and so it evolved and strengthened among Jacob's children and those who joined themselves [*nilvim*] to them and *there was formed in the world a nation that knew God* [emphasis mine]. (MT *Laws of Idolatry* 1:3)

The national cohesiveness of the Jews is grounded in a common intellectual enterprise that knows no ethnic or geographic boundaries. Their absorption of others by way of *nilvim* orients them toward an identity that actually transcends the parochialism normally associated with national aspirations. "Knowing God" is a universally accessible ideal that, at its inception, already contemplates the utopian messianic unity of purpose, and that, as envisaged at the end of the *Mishneh Torah*, will culminate when "there will no longer be any concern in the world but to know God" (MT *Laws of Kings* 12:5).[22]

The term *nilvim*, which already biblically expressed the assumption of Jewish identity by outsiders (Esth 9:27), determines that identity by its very absence of specificity. It is therefore particularly apt for Ovadyah's admission into the fold. Assimilation into a family that recognizes no distinction in terms of common practice, whether it is joy during festivals (MT *Laws of Holiday Repose* 6:17)[23] or prayer in times of sorrow (MT *Laws of Fast Days* 4:4),[24] is its Maimonidean definition. Adherence to the Jewish faith gains one recognition as a "brother," thereby attracting the status of a social unit with its concomitant rights and obligations. The entire nation is considered to consist of "children of God" (MT *Laws of Gifts to the Poor* 10:2).[25] Biblical precedent for the figurative use of familial terms paves the way for co-opting Ovadyah into the family. The effacement of any lines of division carries over internally to a pervasive equality among all individuals of Israel since "they have joined God and behave in the principle of religion" (MT *Laws of the Murderer* 13:14).

Maimonides' rationale for the parity between Jew and convert cannot be fully appreciated without considering the philosophical underpinnings of his position. These are of utmost relevance when addressing issues raised by prayer, itself philosophically problematic for its misleading God-directed language of attribution and personalization. The picture of God that is reflected in a being that is addressed, queried, adorned with human traits, and historically interactive is in fact a false one. The hallmarks of prayer, petition, and supplication, are based on a conception of a responsive and interactive deity. Response implies change, thereby violating the concept of simple unity. Whether two inconsistent notions of prayer—one traditional and dialogic and the other philosophical and contemplative—can ultimately coexist has been thoroughly canvassed in previous scholarly studies.[26] For the present purposes it is necessary not to enter into the debate but merely to point out that, regardless of which side of the debate one aligns oneself, traditional notions of prayer cannot be sustained at the cost of an idolatrous corruption of God's nature. The very minimum that every worshiper must be cognizant of during prayer is that, just like the language of the Torah itself, its anthropomorphic language is a concession to the limits of human understanding. What motivated the "men of the Great Assembly," the traditional authors of Judaism's core liturgical compositions, to standardize prayer in this way was both historical and psychological. The historical was a consequence of the decline in popular facility with Hebrew (MT *Laws of Prayer* 1:4),[27] and the psychological was the "necessity to address men in such terms as would make them achieve some representation—in accordance with the dictum of the Sages: *The Torah speaks in the language of the sons of man*" (GP I:59, 140). Once this maxim is operative within the canon of prayer, as it is in that of Scripture, then one is not confined to the narrow straits of literalism. Terms such as "father" can imply a pedagogical model, and the door has been opened to invite the outsider into its figuratively appointed domain.

From a philosophical perspective the same reasoning would hold true for recalling "the miracles performed on behalf of our fathers." Once again conversion blurs the lines of distinction to the extent that "no difference exists between you and us, and all miracles done to us have been done, as it were,[28] to us and to you" (Iggerot, 234, lines 14–15). Miracles, as traditionally understood, posed philosophical problems for Maimonides since they disrupt the stability of the natural order. They also undermine the integrity of the radical unity of God and all that it entails regarding His nature, such as immortality, eternality, and knowledge of universals. Their impact on the rigid requirements of absolute unity is softened by relegating them to the world of natural phenomena, distinguished only by their rarity of occurrence.[29] Such being the case, miracles are not to be considered as historically conditioned, divinely mandated lapses in the natural order. Since they do not signify a divine response to historical events, references to them in prayer and blessings are devoid of any temporal sense. They therefore can only be pronounced figuratively even by those born into the fold. Once the convert has "joined himself to God," which means he has subscribed to the oneness of God as formulated by the *Guide,* then he can just as legitimately adopt the figurative reminiscence of miracles. The "as it were" of the performance of miracles "to us and to you" refers in the same manner to both the outsider and insider pronouns of "us" and "you." Both must equally understand these phrases in an "as it were" fashion.

Maimonides then turned from expressions laden with national history and ancestry to those acknowledging Israel's ground of election. Liturgical refrains such as "who chose us," "who granted us," and "who separated us"[30] all relate to Judaism's foundational document, the Torah. It is the gift of the Torah that singled Israel out from the community of nations. As the convert has wholeheartedly decided to submit himself to the jurisdiction of the Torah's legal regime, he has tethered himself to the very source of Israel's chosenness. That source is universally accessible and issues an open invitation to all who wish to reenact the Sinaitic moment of "conversion."[31] At this juncture in the response Maimonides strategically retraced the spiritual and intellectual decline Israel experienced prior to its "election" at Sinai: "Know, that our fathers who exited Egypt were largely idolaters while in Egypt, they became assimilated with the nations and adopted their behavior until the point God commissioned Moses" (Iggerot, 235, lines 1–2).[32] For all intents and purposes the Israelites had become naturalized Egyptians, acculturating themselves to Egyptian religion and customs. With this statement Maimonides interrupts the straight line between Abraham and present-day Jews. The Egyptian debacle sets up a historical barrier between all post-exodus Jews and Abraham, their biblical forbearer. The Egyptian Jews had alienated themselves from their Abrahamic heritage to the extent that they could no longer legitimately lay claim to their ancestral roots.[33] As they were desperately in need of conversion themselves, the figure of Moses intervened in his capacity as legislator rather than that of persuader.[34] Israel's election is rooted in Law and the Jew's claim to his uniqueness is through his submission to the Law. This feature also signals the convert's transition to his newly adopted faith. His allegiance to the Law links him to Moses and Sinai and enables him to voice those prayers that give expression to that link through chosenness. His allegiance to the mind, however, overcomes the legislative barrier to Abraham as his father.

In support of the proposition that the giving of the Law at Sinai contemplated not just the audience at hand but all potential converts in the future, Maimonides cited Num 15:15, "One ordinance *[huqqah]* shall be both for you of the congregation and for the stranger that lives with you, an everlasting ordinance, *as you are so shall the stranger be* before the Lord." The last phrase is the operative one that renders the convert and the Jew equal before the law. The formal process of initiation into the Jewish faith is halakhically derived from this very verse (*b. Keritot* 9a.). Israel's performance of circumcision, ritual immersion, and animal sacrifice in anticipation of the reception of the Torah at Sinai is the model for all future converts, for "as you are so shall the *ger* be." Numbers 15:15 mandates a reenactment of Israel's historical transition from a state of almost total assimilation to one of normative uniqueness. Maimonides' halakhic codification of this requirement is prefaced by a historical account in which Sinai is, in a sense, phased in by these three rituals of acceptance (MT *Laws of Forbidden Intercourse* 13:1–4).[35] The trading of identities for the convert is realized by the summoning of a past and an anchoring in the present, thereby appropriating a common history.

Numbers 15:15 also provides the exception to the exclusive endowment of Israel with the Law granted by Deut 33:4, as a "heritage of the congregation of Jacob." This verse, according to Maimonides, singles out Moses' exclusive legacy to Israel, and Israel alone: "Moses, our teacher, allotted the torah and the commandments solely to Israel" (MT *Laws of Kings* 8:10).

However, he continued, that allotment is also available "to all who wish to convert from the other nations" by virtue of Num 15:15—"as you are so shall the stranger be." This verse establishes a juridical parity between all those within the jurisdiction of Judaism since, as the next verse continues, "there will be one teaching *[torah]* and one law *(mishpat)* for you and the stranger *(ger)* who lives with you."

The operative term *torah* mentioned in Num 15:15, under whose legal rubric the convert is subsumed, also determines the telos of law and the natural order. Though *torah, ḥoq,* and *mishpat* (biblical terms for laws) all refer to a concrete set of subjective conventions that constitute the *mitzvot*, they also reflect abstract notions about existence as a whole, to which the convert is attuned by his developed capacity to reason. The general aim of *torah* is to "offer guidance toward what is correct" to "all those who seek guidance" (GP III:13, 453). The convert certainly fits into this latter class of people. Maimonides' definition of *torah* forms an introduction to his understanding of the end of all of creation. That understanding is limited to all creation's constituent parts in their "conforming to its purpose," but not to its "final end" (GP III:13, 453, 454–55). To presume that one can discover the "final end of His volition" would be a futile endeavor for any existent consisting of inferior matter. The convert has already come to this understanding by his abandonment of any culture premised on the ability to determine "His volition" and therefore control him. His preference for the *torah* may be motivated by its primary telos to "put an end to idolatry, to wipe out its traces and all that is bound up with it, even its memory as well and all that is bound up with it" (GP III:29, 517).

The concomitant of acknowledging one's limits with respect to the final end of creation is the duty to discover that end for the Law. What affords the Law its integrity is its intelligibility. Primary principles of justice, morality, politics, and philosophy underlie the entire system of *mitzvot,* whether they are classified as *ḥuqqim* or *mishpatim* (GP III:31, 524). The only distinction between these categories of law is the relative ease with which their respective utilities can be discovered (GP III:26, 507).[36] Surely the lure of Judaism for the medieval convert—grounded, as it can only have been, in reason—would have included this feature of the Law as a whole. Once he rationally formulated the basic tenets of Judaism— existence and unity of God—he adopted all the *mitzvot,* which, in one fashion or another, act as their safeguards.[37] In this sense the convert, experientially and intellectually, mirrors the formative event that transpired at Sinai. According to Maimonides, everyone present at Sinai heard the first two commandments, since "the existence of the deity and His being one, are knowable by human speculation alone" (GP II:33, 364). On the other hand, the rest of the commandments were heard solely by Moses, who related them in turn to the nation, since "they belong to the class of generally accepted opinions and those adopted in virtue of tradition not to the class of the intellecta" (ibid.). The audience at Sinai, just like the convert, reasoned the fundamentals of religion and then accepted their conventional safeguards on the basis of Mosaic authority.[38] The convert, by his precise replication of the Sinaitic revelation, can, without reservation, consider himself "chosen" and a recipient of God's "giving."

Elsewhere Num 15:15 is also cited as the critical proof-text in support of the jurisprudential principle that the Law, in its promotion of general societal utility, caters to the majority. It does not, and cannot, contemplate those rare individuals for whom conformity to the Law is in fact detrimental. Just as it is invariably applicable to all its subjects, it is also not temporally or geographically contingent. The verse is cited to substantiate the immutability of the Law: "matters that are primarily intended in the Law ought not to be dependent on time or place; but the decrees ought to be absolute and universal . . ." (GP III:34, 535). Even within its own constituency the Law cannot address the needs of the wide array of human psyches and temperaments; nonetheless, those isolated individuals cannot deviate or absolve themselves from abiding by it. This proposition is drawn into the rationale of Maimonides' response by virtue of the common proof-text. It also argues for the convert's conformity to every detail of the Law, but from the perspective of the Law itself. Though on occasion the liturgy may not precisely fit the unique circumstances and human condition of the convert, it should not consequently be altered. The convert, then, contributes to the Law's integrity by minimizing exceptions that, if prolix, would lead to anarchic deterioration.

Maimonides' response then includes a note of encouragement to Ovadyah, which, though extralegal, is consistent with the tenor of his argument developed thus far. The preconceived roles of born Jew as insider and convert as outsider are now reversed. Lack of ethnic pedigree is actually superior to its presence, for "we [natural born Jews] can only trace our lineage back to Abraham, Isaac and Jacob—whereas you [convert] can trace it to *He who spoke and the world came to be*" (Iggerot, 235, lines 5–6). The natural-born Jew's faith is always suspect since one can never be certain whether adherence to the faith is not somehow motivated by familial allegiances. The convert's intentions, however, like those of his archetypical predecessor, Abraham, are not subject to challenge since he arrived at the essential truths of Judaism by reason. Tradition and upbringing play no role in the convert's acquisition of the truth of God's existence and oneness. Therefore his relation to God is direct and free of extraneous cultural and social factors.

The reference to God in this part of the response as the one "who spoke and the world came to be" is particularly apt, for it appears often in the context of a direct and unmediated knowledge of God. In MT *Laws of the Foundations of the Torah* 3:9, Maimonides fixed this referent as the contemplative object of the stars and spheres, who are unceasingly cognizant of He "who spoke and the world came to be."[39] A consequence of this cognition is a virtual compulsion to "praise and glorify their creator," adopting the human language of prayer to describe the heavenly bodies' activity.[40] The *Guide* credits the spheres with the ideal prayer mode, "praising God and making known His wonder without speech of lip and tongue," which is superior to verbalization in its purity of thought and pristine representation (GP II:5, 260). Aside from its connotation of direct knowledge of God, the *Guide* here has a significant effect on the issue of prayer for the convert. What is critical is that which the convert has come to understand nonverbally by reason alone. Translating it into audible form is merely a utilitarian distraction[41] from the ultimate goal of self-representation. Transition from thought to speech is born of expediency and signals a distancing from the perfection of representation. Prayer, like sacrifice, is a concession to the exigencies of human nature that cannot tolerate worship that consists exclusively of silent meditation.[42] Therefore, once the convert himself is plunged into that concessionary domain, words must be acknowledged as pliable and susceptible to the same kinds of configurations as biblical anthropomorphisms.

Another crucial reference to the one "who spoke and the world came to be" also appears within a context of direct knowledge of God arising out of philosophical reflection. Probing the vast expanses of all of creation in order to extract its limitless ingenuity and complexity fulfills the halakhic obligation to love God. MT *Laws of the Foundations of the Torah* 2:2 then attributes the same liturgical impulse to this enterprise as it did to the heavenly bodies. One who has undertaken this penetrating contemplation of the wonders of the universe is overwhelmed by the emotional desire to "praise and glorify" God. This path toward the love of God is consistent, said Maimonides, with the rabbinic maxim regarding love that "as a result you will acknowledge *the one who spoke and the world came to be.*" The reference to this divine epithet conveys to the convert that he in fact has aspired to the essence of prayer as it emerges from the longing to know God rationally.[43] In this he has also emulated his figurative ancestor, Abraham, characterized by Maimonides as the quintessential "lover" of God "who serves God exclusively out of love" (MT *Laws of Repentance* 10:2). Perhaps this provides the sense in which the specific commandment to love the convert (Deut 10:19) is analogized by Maimonides to the obligation to love God (Deut 11:1): "One is commanded regarding the love of the convert just as one is regarding the love of Him" (MT *Laws of Ethical Traits* 6:4).[44] Abraham as "lover" of God is personified in every convert who provides a concrete model for the route to follow toward the love of God. Loving the "lover" guides one toward the divine object of desire.

God, in His capacity as the one "who spoke and the world came to be," appears in two additional halakhic settings.[45] Both are instances in which Maimonides appealed to this divine force in order to provide additional impetus for fulfilling certain halakhic obligations. In the first case, the care and sensitivity with which orphans must be treated is ensured by the personal interest God takes in their condition, as evidenced by "the covenant *He who spoke and the world came to be* entered into with them" (MT *Laws of Ethical Traits* 6:10).[46] The second guarantees the almost boundless extremes to which children must go in caring for their parents, who warrant fear and respect from their children even at the cost of the child's personal humiliation and insult. If obedience to such standards of behavior were forthcoming had they been promulgated by royal decree, how much more would such obeisance be expected if they emanate from the "one who spoke and the world came to be" (MT *Laws of Rebels* 6:7).

The universal connotations of this divine characterization are foregrounded by its appearance in the context of the law demanding respect for parents. That is the one obligation that, according to Maimonides, straddles the convert's former life as a non-Jew and his present one as a Jew (ibid., 5:11). His ruling is jarring both for its disregard of the halakhic rupture of the convert from his heredity,[47] and for its lack of support in the halakhic sources.[48] The choice of divine characterizations to appeal to in the response to Ovadyah could not have been more suitable. Its juridical setting is of a law that is incumbent on both the Jew and non-Jew by virtue of their shared humanity. Directing Ovadyah's attention then to the "one who spoke and the world came to be" impresses upon him his ontological identity with his newly adopted co-religionists.[49]

In both instances this singular divine referent is invoked to address situations involving an absence or presence of parents. The comfort provided to the convert by its identification as his direct ancestor is significantly augmented by its halakhically charged nuance. The convert, like the orphan, is considered bereft of parents by virtue of being "born again."[50] God places Himself personally in locus parenti to the orphan in order to compensate for his particular vulnerability.[51] Tracing the convert's antecedents back to God Himself not only serves to console him for his ethnic deficiency but substitutes God for his biological parents as his protector due to his socially inferior station. Any slight against the convert, such as assigning him a kind of second-class status with respect to prayer, amounts to one against God, who is both the convert's lover and parent. The demands of parental fear and respect, imported into the response by the divine reference, are acute when one considers Maimonides' sentiments expressed in his third response to Ovadyah regarding behavior toward the convert. The gravity of the obligation to love and fear parents and obey the prophet pales in comparison to what one is burdened with when it comes to the convert, "since it is possible to respect a person and fear and listen to one who is not loved, however we are commanded to love the convert, an emotion consigned to the heart" (Iggerot 240, lines 7–9).

Curiously, it is only after Maimonides provided a theological and philosophical rationale for his decision that he resorted to concrete halakhic principles. The mandatory recitation that accompanies the donation of the first fruits *(bikkurim)* during the Temple period poses the same theological existential problems as prayer does with respect to the convert. The rare biblically mandated doxology reads as follows:

> A wandering Aramean was my father, and he went down into Egypt, and sojourned there, few in number; and he became there a nation, great, mighty, and populous. And the Egyptians dealt ill with us, and afflicted us, and laid upon us hard bondage. And we cried unto the Lord, the God of our fathers, and the Lord heard our voice, and saw our affliction, and our toil, and our oppression. And the Lord brought us forth out of Egypt with a mighty hand, and with an outstretched arm, and with great terribleness, and with signs, and with wonders.

And He hath brought us into this place, and hath given us this land, a land flowing with milk and honey. And now, behold, I have brought the first of the fruit of the land, which Thou, O the Lord, hast given me. (Deut 26:5–10)

It is genealogically and historically particular, charting, as it does, the development of Israel from its inception in the patriarchal period through the Egyptian enslavement and liberation and climaxing with settlement in the promised land "as promised by God to our fathers." Among those who are required to donate the first fruits but do not have the legal capacity to recite the requisite doxology is the convert (*m. Bikkurim* 1:4). Although this ruling is declared by an anonymous mishnah recording an undisputed opinion, and as a result would normally be definitive, Maimonides rejected its authority in favor of the Palestinian Talmud's opinion (*y. Bikkurim* 1:4)[52] to the contrary. That opinion reasons that Abraham's progeny, by virtue of Gen 17:5, is not restricted to his biological line but rather to all those "who seek protection under the wings of the divine presence" (MT *Laws of First Fruits* 1:3).[53] His codification of the Palestinian Talmud's stand in the *Mishneh Torah* is imported into the response to Ovadyah the convert, halakhically reinforcing what has been ideologically argued up to this point.

Menachem Lorberbaum has argued that Maimonides' response is structured to "show how the legal precedent naturally flows from his theological position and exhibits how positive law reflects broader religious values in Judaism."[54] I believe Maimonides went much further, both from a methodological point of view and from a philosophical one. His code, the *Mishneh Torah,* is notoriously silent regarding its talmudic sources.[55] For example, the law at issue regarding *bikkurim* simply adopts the Palestinian Talmud's ruling without reference to its Babylonian counterpart. Without the assistance of the code's seminal commentators such as Joseph Karo,[56] the untrained would be unaware that there is any discrepancy. On the other hand, the response makes a point of mentioning the Bavli's position and then, insouciantly, dismisses it with the words, "this is an undisputed mishnah according to R. Meir, however it is not the halakhah, rather it is as expounded in the Palestinian Talmud" (Iggerot, 235, lines 12–13). This explicit halakhic preference preceded by a theological prologue is meant to apprise the reader that a conscious rejection of one halakhic text over another has been achieved on the strength of overarching theological concerns. Written after the completion of the *Mishneh Torah*,[57] it is also intended by Maimonides as an explicative gloss to his ruling there and how he arrived at it. Indeed, it may present a key to unraveling his method underlying other rulings in the overall project that comprises Maimonides' code of law.

Other than providing an intertext by which to read the code, Maimonides, by prefacing *halakhah* with theology, invites us to read the *halakhah* philosophically. It is not a separate rationale but blends in with its theological foreground. The essence of the recitation over the *bikkurim* is, according to the *Guide,* the ethic of humility. The annual reminiscence of one's humble origins coupled with rabbinic regulations intended to accentuate sentiments of diffidence[58] are remedial "of the normal qualities that are generally acquired by all those who are brought up in prosperity— I mean conceit, vanity and neglect of the correct opinions" (GP III:39, 551–52). Reference is made to the biblical directive to "remember that thou wast a servant" (Deut 5:15; 16:12) as affirming the moral design of this type of memory (GP III:39, 552). Strikingly germane to our letter is the context of this obligatory act of memory, which is intended to encourage fair and equal treatment of the powerless and the vulnerable, among which are "the stranger *[ger],* the orphan and the widow."[59] The superiority that arrogance breeds leads to the exclusion of the outsider, and it is precisely the *bikkurim* rite that provides its antidote. Because of its placement in the structured response, the law of *bikkurim* transcends its technical juristic significance to secure the moral posture one must assume vis-à-vis the alien, the convert. The entire letter is one seamless theological, moral, philosophical, and juridical argument for the unfettered inclusion of the convert.

In concluding the discussion of our first outsider, I wish to revert to the proof-text cited immediately prior to the *bikkurim* section of the response, in support of the notion that the convert has established a direct link to God contra the natural-born Jew who relates to the divine by way of pedigree. Isaiah 44:5 delineates various proclamations of allegiance to the nation and faith of Israel: "This one will say 'I belong to YHVH,' another will declare in the name of Jacob, yet another will write YHVH's name on the hand and add the name of Israel to his own." Though numerous rabbinic sources divide this verse into four distinct classes of people (God-fearers; purely righteous; converts; repentants), to my knowledge none of them correlate the first declaration, "I belong to YHVH," to the convert[60] as Maimonides does. As to whether he consciously altered his source or possessed a variant reading we cannot be certain, but the convenience of the modification combined with the number of divergent sources to the contrary tends toward the former contention. Unlike the law of *bikkurim,* various other rulings in the *Mishneh Torah* preserve an inferior legal status for the convert in terms of membership in the community.[61] One in particular is justified by the disqualification of converts from constituting "a congregation of God" (*qehal YHVH*) (MT *Laws of Forbidden Intercourse* 15:7, based on *b. Qiddushin* 73a). The attribution, in the letter, of the first proclamation in Isa 44:5 to the convert attenuates the theological and moral implications of the *Mishneh Torah*'s banishment of the convert from God's dominion. Maimonides, I believe, did no less than explicitly distinguish himself from a position that emerges from his idealized and impartial code of law. When the opportunity arose to encounter the convert within a personal and existential context Maimonides consciously chose to subvert the pejorative implications of the code. His passion for life managed to displace the detachment of his text.[62] Not only is there a subversion of the normative convert status but the response exquisitely subverts the convert's existential status. The convert has moved from the outside to become the very embodiment of the inside. All of the major currents in Maimonides' thought converge in this short letter to Ovadyah to construct a model of the convert as the only authentic Jew.

CHAPTER 2

The Leper

Illness as Contemplative Metaphor

The Plainness of "Signs," "Wonders," and "Miracles"

The "leper" in Jewish law represents the second type of outsider I discuss in this book; but here, in contrast to the convert who moves from the outside in, we are presented with a category of outsider that is edged out from the inside. They move in opposing directions, and for Maimonides, from a philosophical vantage point, the leper reverses what the convert has achieved. While the convert traverses an intellectual path that takes him from ignorance and error to knowledge and truth, thereby becoming an insider exemplar for Judaism, the leper threatens to undermine those very truths discovered by the convert. The leper must therefore be forcibly pushed to the outside where that danger is neutralized, pending his rehabilitation and readmission to the community that is entrusted with preserving philosophically true beliefs. Though the terms "leper" and "leprosy" are technically misnomers, for ease of reference they will be used throughout this chapter.

Chapters 13 and 14 of Leviticus describe the disease (or range of diseases) that has come to be widely, though incorrectly, known as leprosy *(tzara'at).*[1] It confounded medieval Jewish exegetes because its various manifestations, as biblically described, did not correspond to any disease within their experience. Buildings and fabrics, as well as human beings, could become symptomatic. Nahmanides (Ramban, d.1270) judged the leprous afflictions of buildings and clothing to be "not in the natural order of things, nor does it ever happen in the world," and therefore concluded that these were "miraculous" phenomena rather than natural ones.[2] Rabbi Samuel ben Meir (Rashbam, d.1174), grandson of Rashi, the most popular of all Jewish biblical exegetes, extended this rubric over the entire range of diseases, to the point that he admitted he must abandon his project of literal sense *(peshat)* exegesis in favor of the midrashic when explicating this subject. His rationalization for this rare detour from his avowed project of methodical peshat exegesis was that, "when we follow the plain meaning of Scripture or the expertise gained through the ways of the human world, we have nothing to add concerning all these sections . . . rather the truth is found through the exegesis *[midrash]* of the rabbis, their laws and traditions that they received from the earlier rabbis."[3]

In his legal code, the *Mishneh Torah,* Maimonides as well *ostensibly* conceded that science cannot account for those symptoms that Scripture anticipates can appear in houses and clothing, since they "are not extant in the natural order" *(minhago shel olam)* (MT *Laws of Leprosy Defilement* 16:10). He then resorted to an unscientific account that considers leprosy to be a "sign and wonder," whose cause can be traced to the moral order rather than the natural one. It is exclusively endemic to the people of Israel "in order to ward them off of slander" *(lashon ha-ra)* (ibid.). The traditional link between leprosy and this particular sin is consistently maintained in the *Guide of the Perplexed,* where it is considered a "punishment for slander" and "a miracle that was perpetuated in the religious community" (GP III:47, 596–97). Since much of this chapter involves a close reading of the MT passage, I include the full text in its entirety, here in English translation:

> *Leprosy* is a comprehensive term covering sundry incompatible matters. Thus, whiteness in a man's skin is called leprosy; the falling off of some hair on the head or the chin is called leprosy; and a change of color in garments or houses is called leprosy.

Now this change in garments and in houses, which Scripture includes under the general term leprosy, was no normal happening, but was a portent and a wonder among the Israelites to warn them against slanderous speaking. For if a man uttered slander the walls of his house would suffer a change; if he repented the house would again become clean. But if he continued in his wickedness until the house was torn down, leather objects in his house on which he sat or lay would suffer a change: if he repented they would again become clean. But if he continued in his wickedness until they were burnt, the garments that he wore would suffer a change: if he repented they would again become clean. But if he continued in his wickedness until they were burnt, his skin would suffer a change and he would become leprous and be set apart and exposed all alone until he should no more engage in the conversation of the wicked, which is raillery and slander.

Now on this matter there is a warning in Scripture which says, *Take heed in the plague of leprosy . . . remember what the Lord thy God did unto Miriam by the way* [Deut 24:9]. That is to say, consider what befell Miriam the prophetess, who spoke against her brother, even though she was older than he and had nurtured him on her knees and put herself in jeopardy to save him from the sea. Now she did not speak spitefully of him but erred only in that she put him on a level with other prophets; nor was he resentful about all these things, for it is said, *Now the man Moses was very meek* (Num 12:3). Nevertheless, she was forthwith punished with leprosy. How much more then does this apply to wicked and foolish people who are profane in speaking great and boastful things!

Therefore, it is proper that he who would direct his way aright should keep himself far from their company and speak not with them, that he be not caught in the net of the wicked and their foolishness.

Now the way of the company of the scornful and wicked is this: In the beginning they are profuse in vain words, as in the matter whereof it is said, *A fool's voice cometh through a multitude of words* (Eccl 5:2). Thence they go on to speak to the discredit of the righteous, as in the matter whereof it is said, *Let the lying lips be dumb which speak arrogantly against the righteous* [Ps 31:19]. Thence they become accustomed to speak against the prophets and to discredit their words, as in the matter whereof it is said, *But they mocked the messengers of God and despised his words and scoffed at his prophets* [2 Chr 36:16]. Thence they go on to speak against God and to deny the very root of religion, as in the matter whereof it is said, *And the children of Israel did impute things that were not right unto the Lord their God* [2 Kgs 17:9]; moreover it is said, *They have set their mouth against heaven and their tongue walketh through the earth* [Ps 73:9]. What brought it to pass that they set their mouth against Heaven? Their tongue, which first walked through the earth.

Such is the conversation of the wicked, occasioned by their idling at street corners, in the gatherings of the ignorant, and in the feastings of drunkards. But the conversation of the worthy ones in Israel is none other than words of Torah and wisdom; therefore the Holy one, blessed is He, aids them and bestows wisdom upon them, as it is said, *And they that feared the Lord spake together every man to his neighbor, and the Lord hearkened and heard. And a book of remembrance was written before Him for them that feared the Lord and that thought upon His name.* [Mal 3:17][4]

Maimonides' concluding remarks to *Laws of Leprosy Defilement* comprise an inordinately lengthy digression from strict law to trace a series of increasingly insidious crimes that spiral out of the offence of slander. Engaging in slanderous conversation sets the stage for far more severe offences of an intellectual and philosophical nature, all having to do with speech and conversation. In addition to constructing the Maimonidean portrait of the leper who becomes the shunned outsider, my aims in this chapter are twofold. First, and more narrowly, they are to identify the precise nature of these offences, to understand what Maimonides meant by excluding leprosy from the natural order, and to determine how he rationalized the "miraculous" causal connection between slander and leprosy. Second, and more broadly, the close reading I give to this non-*halakhic* passage in the *Mishneh Torah* offers further evidence in support of Isadore Twersky's thesis that there is an intrinsic symbiotic relationship between Maimonides' philosophical and juridical works. As Twersky has argued, Maimonides' law code "reveals a vigorous intellectualistic posture usually associated with the *Guide*," and his image "as a philosopher insisting upon the superiority of the theoretical life . . . is, in fact, fully developed in the pre-*Guide* writings."[5] Finally, Maimonides weaved rabbinic and biblical sources to create an entirely novel construct of the leper that moves him from the ethical to the contemplative sphere. In this construct, the leper becomes a metaphor for a far more serious contemplative malady.

According to Maimonides, the range of symptoms and phenomena classified by Scripture as *leprosy* all share that diagnosis strictly in an equivocal sense *(shuttafut)* of the term (MT *Laws of Leprosy Defilement* 16:10). They "encompass many matters that are not comparable to each other" (ibid.), which may vary from skin discoloration to hair loss to changes in the appearance of inanimate objects like houses and clothing. As stated in his *Mishnah* commentary, "these [clothing, houses] are not natural and reason does not account for them at all for material and buildings are inanimate and changes that occur in them are not *tzara'at* except that the Torah called them such" (PM *Nega'im* 12:5).[6] The *Mishneh Torah*'s solitary use of the term *sh-t-f* (equivocal), in the sense of equivocal language, neutralizes any rationalist's empirical dilemma with respect to the phenomenon of building and clothing leprosy.[7] If what Maimonides had in mind by this Hebrew term is the Judeo-Arabic term in his philosophical works always translated as such by his most prominent Hebrew translator, Samuel ibn Tibbon (d.c.1230), then it is wide enough to encompass things that have absolutely nothing in common except name alone—that is, homonyms—as well as things that share some common feature.[8]

He then explicitly identified their nature as a "sign *[ot]* and wonder *[pele]*" as distinct from the realm of "the normal way of the world" *(minhago shel olam)*. This classification is strategically formulated to accommodate disparate audiences distinguished by lack or presence of a critical perspective. Although "sign" and "wonder" can be understood as miraculous or supernatural, both can also refer to events within nature. The term *pele* is often used by Maimonides in legal contexts to simply connote a rare, yet entirely conceivable, occurrence within the boundaries of the natural order. It is an exceptional circumstance, halakhically distinguished from those that "are likely to happen most of the time" (MT *Laws of the Murderer and Preservation of Life* 6:12).[9] *Ot* is also a term that can refer to both the miraculous and the natural. Though it serves to authenticate prophetic status, it need not consist of "a change in the order of the world" along the lines of a splitting of the sea. A simple prediction of future natural events qualifies as an *ot* as well (MT *Laws of the Foundations of the Torah* 10:1).[10] Each was considered by Maimonides to be a legitimate *ot*.[11] At the very outset of his digression, then, Maimonides crafted a classification of biblical leprosy to appeal to the widest possible range of religious sensibilities. The further qualification that these leprous outbreaks do not accord with "the normal way of the world" *(minhago shel olam)* can then be read as broadly as its antecedent terms to include not only the miraculous, but the simply rare or extraordinary.[12]

What all the various manifestations of leprosy share in common is the moral "virus" of slander that triggers them. They are distinguished by the escalating strength of their cautionary affects, which begins on walls, spreads to furniture, then to clothing, and finally to the physical person. Each manifestation is calibrated to signal danger and afford an opportunity to avert further harm by a remorseful change in behavior. Unless an ethical awareness is achieved, the leprosy metastasizes from building to chattel to clothing to body in a pattern of increasing exposure and isolation, culminating in quarantine that leaves the perpetrator "segregated and identified all alone" (MT *Laws of Leprosy Defilement* 16:10).[13] After failing to repent *(hazar)* in response to the call of these graduated leprous omens, the gossipmonger is forced into a situation brought on by the ritual defilement of the disease *(tum'a)* in which he can no longer exercise his freedom to determine his own conduct. He becomes ostracized to the point that "he can no longer engage in the conversation of the wicked which consists of mockery and *lashon ha-ra*" (ibid.).[14] For Maimonides the philosophically offensive gravity of this "conversation's" content is far more substantial than its moral offensiveness.

The route of graduated misfortune followed by the spread of this disease resembles that suffered by Job, from the tolerable loss of possessions to the unbearable experience of physical pain that "no one endowed with sensation can support [pain] patiently" (GP III:22, 487). The model of Job's suffering is instructive, according to Maimonides, for the extreme limit of the mind's ability to endure the body's deterioration without succumbing to viewing the world as lacking order and justice. At that point people can no longer restrain themselves from "complaining and repining either with the tongue or in the heart" (ibid.).[15] In Job's case, however, his condition allows for lengthy discourse in the company of friends, leading ultimately to correct knowledge, while the leper's condition rules out any social contact in a situation in which he is most prone to false conceptions of God and the world. Job's condition prompts him in the direction of wisdom, which is the point of realization that God's governance and knowledge share absolutely no common ground with that of men: "This is the object of the *Book of Job* as a whole" (GP III:23, 497). Those who contract the halakhic impurity of leprosy fail to heed the lesson of Job. Consequently, for them, each stage of affliction provides further evidence

The Case of Miriam

Miriam and the Seventh Fundamental Principle

Maimonides followed the rabbinic tradition that locates the source of the link between slander and leprosy in the biblical juxtaposition of the directives to be cognizant of the affliction of leprosy and the memorializing of what Miriam had endured "along the way when you exited Egypt" (Deut 24:8–9).[16] That is taken to be a reference to Miriam's bout with leprosy in Num 12:10. Miriam is singled out, according to Maimonides, for the didactic effect of a minor transgression that attracts severe consequences. His reasoning follows the standard rabbinic a fortiori logic: if Miriam suffered such grave repercussions then surely (*qal va-homer*—a fortiori) so will "the wicked and the fools" whose speech is malicious. First, Miriam's relationship with her brother Moses belies the possibility of her truly slandering him, for "she was older than him in years, had raised him on her knees and had endangered herself to save him from the sea" (MT *Laws of Leprosy Defilement* 16:10). Her previous behavior presumes something less than offensive slander. Selfless conduct that indicates a preference for Moses' life over even her own would be incongruous with asserting herself at his expense. Second, she did not disparage Moses but rather "erred in considering him of a kind with other prophets." Finally, Moses, described as "exceedingly humble" (Num 12:3),[17] could not have been insulted since he possessed no sense of self to be concerned about. In other words, there was no slur nor was there a victim who suffered the effects of the slur. Miriam's "crime," then, was more abstract and self-contained than an ethical insult of another human being. It consisted of an intellectual perspective regarding prophecy that blurred the distinction between Mosaic and other degrees of prophecy. Given the position of the *Guide* on Mosaic prophecy, Moses' mode of apprehension is so unique that it falls altogether outside the ambit of prophecy proper. Moses exceeds the very highest degree of prophecy, as calibrated in the *Guide*,[18] and occupies a separate category of his own. To identify Moses as a prophet, then, is to use the term in an "amphibolous" sense (GP II:35, 367).[19] Miriam's leprosy is a direct consequence of her innocent confusion as to the superior nature of Moses' prophetic prowess.[20]

In effect, Miriam had violated the seventh of Maimonides' renowned thirteen principles of faith, that of Moses' prophetic supremacy and uniqueness, a prerequisite for no less than membership in the community of Israel.[21] One method of preserving Miriam's credentials as a full-fledged Israelite rests on the basis of Menachem Kellner's well-reasoned distinction between the first five and the last eight of those principles. The first five, including such principles as the existence and unity of God, consist of metaphysical truths required for the integrity of a philosophical religion, the rejection of which cannot be tolerated under any circumstances. The remaining eight, which include beliefs about Moses and the Torah, form the dictates of popular religion about which inadvertence and innocent mistake are not decisively fatal.[22] Within its biblical context, Miriam's case is a Maimonidean locus classicus for determining the factors by which Mosaic prophecy is distinguished from others. Mosaic clarity is due to the absence of any intermediary in facilitating the reception of the prophetic message, signified by divine speech that is "mouth to mouth" (Num 12:8).[23] Knowledge is not filtered through a parable but is direct and lucid, conveyed "plainly and not by riddles and he sees the likeness of God" (ibid.). Moses remains fully conscious and aware, as opposed to the semiconscious dream or trance-like states of other prophets to whom "I [God] speak with in a dream" (Num 12:6) (GP II:35, 367; MT *Laws of the Foundation of the Torah* 7:6).[24]

Moses' prophetic superiority, the nature of which is individual and particular, is not a proper subject of philosophy and therefore not something one can rationally demonstrate. It is known because the Torah endorses it. Miriam's action itself is what prompts the Torah's teaching on this issue and is not a position she could have arrived at by speculation alone. She therefore maintains her status as a bona fide member of the Israelite community while, at the same time, posing an existential paradigm for all those who might in the future repudiate this or any other of the thirteen principles. Leprosy, and the quarantine it commands as part of its treatment, is the external physical analogue to disqualification from the "community" and loss of "portion" (world to come) warranted by rejection of a principle (GP II:35, 367).[25] Simply put, the body is itself a parable and riddle (*mashal* and *hidah*) to be read like the text. Once the term "leprosy" has been emptied of its fixed referents by identifying it as equivocal, then, as Paul Ricoeur has argued, textual hermeneutics become a model for interpreting even human actions and events: "Human action, too, is opened to anybody who *can read* [emphasis mine]."[26]

Miriam and Divine Anger

The Miriam reference in the *Mishneh Torah* can only be fully appreciated by importing Maimonides' interpretation of Miriam's leprosy in the first section of the *Guide of the Perplexed*. The citation of verses to demonstrate various nuances of biblical terms in the lexicographical sections of the *Guide* very often afford a glimpse of how Maimonides would want us to read the particular biblical context from which those verses have been extracted. One such example that is the concern of this chapter is the term "going" *(halikhah)*, the focus of GP I:24, which cites the critical verse Num 12:9 ("And the anger of the Lord was kindled against them and He went away *[va-yelekh]*)" to illustrate the figurative senses of the term. When the subject of the term "going" is an incorporeal substance such as God, it assumes one of two meanings: "either the spread of a thing or the withdrawal of providence" (GP I:24, 54). In the case of Num 12:9, the context of which is God's reaction to Miriam's slander of Moses, God's *going* connotes both senses of the term. Miriam contracts leprosy as a result of both a "withdrawal of providence" from her person *and* divine anger that "spreads" and extends to her body. In existentialist terms Miriam has experienced both the stark absence of God and His brute and crushing presence.[27] Maimonides language is sensitive to popular conceptions and needs of varying intensity for a personal God who, in this case, singles Miriam out for divine recompense.[28] In Maimonidean terms, however, God in fact has very little to do with Miriam's fate. The fundamental premise on which Maimonides' entire theory of providence is built is that "providence is consequent upon intellect and attached to it" (GP III:17).[29] As a result, providence is graded proportionately to levels of intellectual perfection ranging from supreme protection to utter abandonment and vulnerability to the forces of nature. On the Maimonidean providential scale, those who do not realize their intellectual capacities "are given over to whatever may happen to befall them. For there is nothing to protect them against whatever may occur" (GP III:18, 476).

The extreme implications of this providential theory inform the mechanics of Miriam's leprosy by virtue of Maimonides' identification of the withdrawal-of-providence sense of the term "going" with the biblical manifestation of that state known as "the hiding of the face," found in such passages as Deut 31:18. This verse appears again in III:51 of the *Guide* as a proof-text for the notion that man is abandoned to chance when he fails to tap into the intellectual overflow by way of exercising intellectual apprehension. Among those of the prophetic class such as Miriam, misfortune occurs when they are distracted from their contemplative focus on God, which automatically entails separation from Him (GP III:51, 625). What is crucial is that responsibility for the hiding-of-the-face phenomenon of Deut 31:17–18 is laid squarely on the shoulders of man. It is a euphemism for man's removing himself from the divine providential purview since the verses, according to Maimonides, make it "clear that we are the *cause* of this *hiding of the face* and we are the *agents who produce this separation*" (GP III:51, 626; emphasis mine). The operative phrasing here is "*we* are the cause" and "*we* are the agents," making it abundantly clear as to who is the active agent when God's face is eclipsed. God does not hide His face. Man removes himself from God's constant unaffected gaze. Therefore, the withdrawal of providence, signified by Num 12:9, is a self-inflicted state of vulnerability to the dangers posed by the natural environment due to Miriam's intellectual error or mental distraction.

The second meaning of "going," which is the "spread, diffusion and manifestation of a thing," modifies the term "anger." Once this signification is drawn, the precise definition of anger when associated with God must be determined. Although all emotions are ontologically false descriptions of God, one of the most misleading as to the divine nature is anger. It is one of only two traits, the other being haughtiness, for which Maimonides demands total banishment from the human psyche (MT *Laws of Ethical Traits* 2:3),[30] and is explicitly ruled out in his legal code as a divine emotion (along with every other) (MT *Laws of the Foundations of the Torah* 1:11). In fact, considering Maimonides' approval of the rabbinic dictum equating anger with idolatry (MT *Laws of Ethical Traits* 2:3; b. *Shabbat* 105b), if God were to vent anger, He Himself would be guilty of idolatry. However, divine anger as a reaction to disobedience is also qualified as a *necessary belief* "for the sake of political welfare" (GP III:28, 512). It serves as a practical deterrent against social instability, and so is pragmatically essential but philosophically false. By attributing Miriam's leprosy to divine anger and withdrawal of providence, Maimonides skillfully maintained the popular association of the two while preserving the *true* philosophical belief concerning providence. That which invites God's anger exactly parallels that which repels His providence; "those who know Him are those who are favored by Him and permitted to come near Him, whereas those who do not know Him are objects of His wrath.... For His favor and wrath, His nearness and remoteness, correspond to the extent of a man's knowledge or ignorance" (GP I:54, 123–24).[31] Just as intellect is the measure of providence, it can be said equally of anger that "anger is consequent upon the intellect."

Elsewhere Maimonides deepened his naturalistic account of divine anger by reducing it to an appraisal of natural calamitous phenomena rather than a phenomenon that is in any way related to God's being. Man projects an emotion onto God such as jealousy or anger, which humanly would induce catastrophe. Yet in doing so he is merely empathically describing how nature operates, for "He is called *jealous and avenging and keeping anger and wrathful,* meaning that actions similar to those that proceed from us from a certain aptitude of the soul ... proceed from Him ... but they by no means proceed from Him, may He be exalted, on account of a notion superadded to His essence" (GP I:54, 126). The anger, then, extended to Miriam is identical to the withdrawal of providence: she becomes exposed to the natural vicissitudes of life in the world, represented, in this instance, by the contraction of disease due to some intellectual decay.[32]

The introduction of anger into the discussion of leprosy raises a vexing problem with the Maimonidean exegesis of the term noted by virtually all of the major medieval commentators on the *Guide*. Elsewhere, Maimonides categorically stated that expressions of divine anger throughout the entire Hebrew Bible are exclusively reserved for the crime of idolatry (GP I:36, 82). However, there are passages in which divine anger plays a role and yet idolatry is nowhere evident, notable among them the anger directed at Miriam and Aaron in Num 12:9.[33] The Miriam episode, I suggest, is a model for the resolution of this quandary when examined in light of an integrative hermeneutic between the *Mishneh Torah* and the *Guide*. The excursus at the end of the laws of leprous impurities does in fact consider slander against God as a final stage in a sequential evolution that commences with idle chatter and simple slander. That defamation of God consists of a denial of a fundamental principle *(kofer ba-iqqar)*. The precise nature of this divine defamation can be determined by the verse cited in illustration of it: "And the children of Israel did impute things that were not right unto the Lord" (2 Kgs 17:9). Predicating of God qualifying attributes constitutes, according to the *Guide,* a metaphysical slander *(lashon ha-ra),* a "loosening of the tongue with regard to God," the propagators of which are identified by the very same verse (GP I:59, 141–42). Such talk strikes at the very heart of God's unity by corporealizing Him and perceiving Him as subject to affections. Since "attributes are deficiencies with regard to God" (ibid., 143), ascribing them to God's essence is tantamount to a kind of hyper-idolatry that is "more blameworthy than a worshipper of idols . . . [and when you] believe that one of the states of the body belongs to Him, you provoke His *jealousy and anger* . . . much more so than an idolater" (GP I:36, 84).

Miriam's case is instructive for the narrow problem of Maimonides' unequivocal statement regarding the context of divine anger within the entire biblical corpus. Her innocent yet imprudent assessing of her brother's prophetic status bears within it the seed of hyper-idolatry. Thus any outburst of divine anger, if not occasioned by conspicuous idolatry, must be examined for an implicit presaging of it.[34] In the following section, I chart the logic that dictates a straight line between Miriam and the heresy of *kofer ba-iqqar.*

Miriam on Providence

First, Miriam's error vis-à-vis Moses presents a physical paradigm for human error vis-à-vis God. By regarding Moses as of a kind with other prophets, she fails to grasp his unique status. According to Maimonides, Mosaic prophecy is so singular that "the term *prophet* used with reference to Moses and to the others is amphibolous" (GP II:35, 367). His modes of apprehension and activity are so extraordinary "that we are incapable of grasping [this] in its true reality" (GP II:35, 369).[35] This reflects a parallel error commonly made with respect to God, which fails to appreciate anthropomorphic language as metaphorical or equivocal, and therefore assumes some commonality between God and humanity. Second, and what is more important, to relegate Moses to a general prophetic class is to fail to appreciate the extreme proximity to God that makes it possible for Moses to communicate with Him, described by Maimonides at the end of the *Guide.* Moses achieves a God-centered intellectual focus of such a concentrated magnitude that his worldly preoccupations are virtually disembodied from his noetic consciousness, "so that in his heart he is always in His presence while outwardly he is with people" (GP III:51, 623).

What raises the stakes of Miriam's confusion regarding Moses is that his state of perfection is inextricably linked to Maimonides' theory of divine governance and individual providence. Stretching the furthest limits of the human mind, God, in response to Moses' plea of "Show me Thy ways" (Exod 33:13), exposes all His *goodness* (33:19) to him, which translates into a global apprehension of all existing things, "their nature and the way they are mutually connected so that he will know how He governs them in general and in detail" (GP I:54, 124).[36] In addition, immediately after describing Moses' radical state of cerebral disembodiment in GP III:51, in which his body goes through the motions of political involvement while his mind remains wholly focused on God, Maimonides launched into an extended discussion of the radical quality of providence secured by it. Consistent with the principle that the duration and gravity of providence are functions of intellect, "providence always watches over an individual endowed with perfect apprehension, whose intellect never ceases from being occupied with God," to the point where he will "never be afflicted with evil of any kind. For he is with God and God is with him" (ibid., 625).[37] Moses' uniqueness, then, lies in his being the supreme exemplar, both noetically and existentially, of the mechanics of divine providence in the human realm. Miriam's punishment of "withdrawal of providence" would then be most apt from a rabbinic "measure-for-measure" perspective, since the quality of her providence conforms precisely to Maimonides' antithesis of the perfect man just described, the one whom God has abandoned and "becomes in consequence of this a target for every evil that may happen to befall him" (ibid.). Moses is the human apogee of Maimonides' theory of providence, and any mistake about where he is situate in the human hierarchy is also a mistake about where he fits in the overall scheme of divine governance; this, in turn, would be a mistake about the nature of God.

Accelerating Degrees of *Lashon Ha-Ra*

A "Fool's Voice"

Miriam's case serves as a stimulus setting in place a gradation of links in a chain of verses. Each link signifies an escalating level of malfeasance—from the simple frivolity and vacuity of bad company all the way to theological heresy—and reflects misconceptions of increasing severity regarding providence. The vanity of the prattle that takes place among an assembly of "scornful and wicked" *(letzim; resha'im)* is contemplated by the verse "A fool's voice comes through a multitude of words" (Eccl 5:2).[38] The offensiveness of such babble, however, may not be simply confined to its inanity. The reason one must be sparing with speech is furnished by the preceding verse 5:1 in Ecclesiastes, "For God is in Heaven and thou upon the earth, therefore let thy words be few." This latter verse culminates the chapter of the *Guide* in which 2 Kgs 17:9 was cited ("impute things that were not right unto the Lord") as part of a tirade against those whose religiosity is measured by the number of attributes that can be predicated of God. For Maimonides, rather than indicating perfection, they imply deficiencies in God. The "few words," then, advised by the verse, refer to restricting predications of God to the absolute bare minimum. The reason supplied, "For God is in Heaven and thou upon the earth," is the scriptural equivalent of the philosophical assertion "that the meaning of the qualificative attributions ascribed to Him and the meaning of the attributions known to us have nothing in common in any respect or in any mode: these attributions have in common only the name and nothing else" (GP I:56, 131). The verse also appears as exhorting silence because God's presence is all-pervasive. Yet it is a pervasiveness that is only pertinent to those who have, in effect, brought themselves into its precinct.

In III:52 of the *Guide,* God's presence and concern for man is predicated on the intellect, the sine qua non of divine providence, "that overflows toward us and is the bond between us and Him.... Just as we apprehend Him by means of that light which He caused to overflow toward us ... so does He by means of this selfsame light examine us; and because of it, He, may He be exalted, is constantly with us" (ibid., 629). Divine providence is a reflex of human intellectual perfection. Therefore, when Maimonides referred in the *Guide* to those who conduct all their daily affairs with the utmost reverence because "we are always before Him and walk about to and fro while His indwelling is with us" (ibid.), he contemplated only those of the intellectually perfected who warrant this kind of abiding accompaniment. Economy of speech is the hallmark of the reverential behavior manifested by these individuals. This, as Maimonides pointed out, complies with the admonishment of Eccl 5:1 to "let thy words be few." The garrulous "fool's voice" of Eccl 5:2, then, is one that has no appreciation for the preconditioned metaphysics of the first colon of Eccl 5:1, "For God is in Heaven and thou upon the earth." Moreover, since the network of the "scornful and wicked" typified by the "fool's voice" is the antithesis of the group envisaged by Eccl 5:1, it itself is the existential embodiment of those who are excluded from God's presence and who are providentially abandoned.

"Lying Lips"

The next stage along the ignominious trail of *lashon ha-ra* is the slander of the "righteous" *(tzaddikim)* anticipated by Ps 31:19, "Let the lying lips which speak arrogantly against the righteous become mute." Their conversation mirrors their existential state, which is devoid of divine concern. Their anthropocentric weltanschauung impels them to project their own predicament onto the state of affairs they perceive to be that of the righteous. Within its original biblical context, the verse is a plea to God to vindicate His existence over the wicked. The silencing of the "lying lips" would be accomplished by an incontrovertible demonstration of justice that protects the righteous and punishes the wicked, as petitioned in the previous verse 31:18: "let me not be shamed . . . let the wicked be shamed, let them be silenced to the grave."[39] The content of the slander relates to the issue of providence, since the often sorry physical circumstances of good men offer the most compelling evidence that the world lacks order.

The conclusion drawn by the slanderers is that "He [God] is ignorant and that everything that is in this lowly world is hidden from Him and He does not apprehend it" (GP III:16, 462). Since the wicked have no concept as to the manner of divine governance, they determine that the righteous, like themselves, are not the subject of divine attention. This conclusion logically follows from their root mistake that "all that exists, exists with a view to his individual sake; it is as if there were nothing that exists except him" (GP III:12, 442). This philosophical egotism is echoed in the self-centered, arrogant behavior of unethical slander.[40] One could say that they have confused "the hiding of the face," which, as stated above, is a consequence of men's own actions cutting themselves off from providence (GP III:51, 626), with a world that is "hidden from Him."

Prophet Mockers

The next targets for disparagement are prophets and their messages, whose vilification is underscored by 2 Chron 36:16: "But they mocked the angels of God, despised his words and scoffed at his prophets." Once we take note of the *Guide*'s identification of the term "angels of God" *(mal'akhe elohim)* in this verse with prophets (GP II:42, 390), the proof-text once again indicates the nature and gravity of this particular derision of prophets. Maimonides considered the vision of Jacob's ladder to be a parable about the prophetic process whereby the angels of God (again, *mal'akhe elohim*) ascending and descending the ladder represent prophets. The ascent, which consists of an ever-increasing knowledge of the stable and constant Being that resides at the summit, is succeeded by a descent that distills that knowledge into "governing and teaching the people of the earth" (GP I:15, 41).[41] In its historical context the verse refers to the flouting of prophetic advice that consisted of an integrated blend of what moderns would deem political and religious, yet for the biblical mind would have been indistinguishable. For instance, verse 13 of 2 Chron 36 considers Zedekiah's rebellion against the authority of Nebuchadnezzar, in direct contravention of Jeremiah's exhortations,[42] to be perfidy against God.

Catastrophic consequences, including the destruction of the Temple and total loss of sovereignty, inevitably ensue (vv. 17–21). The prophet, as "angel of God," most likely connotes the process of tapping into the intellectual flow from the Active Intellect, itself considered an angel (MT *Laws of the Foundations of the Torah* 2:7; GP II:36, 369; II:41, 386), thereby communicating angelic knowledge.[43] An assault on the integrity of the prophet's counsel, then, is tantamount to severing the link between the ultimate source of that counsel and the prophet's communication of it. Once again the verse contemplates an offense that relates to the issue of providence, since the prophet is the liaison between God's governance and human governance. Denigrating the prophet therefore jettisons the denigrators out of the arena of providence, since they have detached themselves from their sole means of affiliation with it.[44] And again, following the measure-for-measure principle, they are abandoned to the vicissitudes of chance and nature realized historically in the destruction of the first Temple, as described at the end of the chapter in Chronicles.

Maimonides' appropriation of 2 Chron 36:16 elsewhere reinforces the notion, at this point, that heresy *(kofer ba-iqqar)* is the inescapable outcome of this "crime." It is cited as a proof-text that accentuates the gravity of maligning scholars *(hakhamim)* (the rabbinic successors of the prophets) by attributing the destruction of Jerusalem to such behavior (MT *Laws of Studying Torah* 6:11; its rabbinic source is *b. Shabbat* 119b). Maimonides therefore endorsed the rabbinic definition of an arch-heretic *(apiqoros)* as one who reviles scholars (*b. Sanhedrin* 99a–b) because they are the "teachers of His words." At this stage Maimonides had situated the leper on the cusp of the ultimate heresy.

The conclusion of the verse cited from Chronicles depicts prophet-scoffing as exhausting God's patience to the point where "the anger of *[hamat]* the Lord rose up against His people, till there was no remedy." The three verses cited thus far correlate to the series of junctures along the route traveled by the leprous scourge, previously plotted by Maimonides, from building to body, as follows:

Eccl 5:2	Walls of house
Ps 31:19	Furniture
2 Chron 36:16	Clothing

Maimonides designated each of these stages as an ominous signal, affording an opportunity for repentance. Each opportunity that is squandered, however, increasingly isolates the slanderer to the point of no return where the leprosy ultimately strikes his body. Once its appearance in clothing is ignored, repentance is no longer available to block leprosy's onslaught, which can now traverse to the body. Maimonides, in his MT *Laws of Repentance* 6:3, appropriated the end of 2 Chron 36:16, where there is "no remedy," to signify an irremediable state of moral deterioration from which there is no recovery even by way of repentance *(teshuvah)*. "No remedy" means, "they have sinned willingly and persist in their iniquity until they are necessarily deprived of repentance which is the remedy *[marpe]*."[45] While the verse captures the total depletion of penitential resources, it also considers this depletion to ensue from God's anger. As discussed previously, God's anger portends a necessary belief essential to the naturalistic reading of Miriam's leprosy. For Maimonides, the failure to respond to calamity with penance itself reflects a bankrupt, mechanistic view of a world governed by chance. The schema of the leper oblivious to the wake-up calls of the disease, as configured in the *Mishneh Torah*, correlates literatim to the *Guide*'s theory of *teshuvah:*

> If you consider that the calamities with which I cause you to be stricken are to be borne as mere chance, I shall add for you unto this supposed chance its most grievous and cruel portion. This is the meaning of the

dictum: "[And if ye] walk with Me in the way of chance [*qeri*] then I will walk with you in the way of an angry chance [*hamat-qeri*]" [Lev 26:27–28]. For their belief that this is chance contributes to necessitating their persistence in their corrupt opinions and unrighteous actions, so that they do not turn away from them; thus it says: "Thou hast stricken them, but they were not affected." For this reason we have been commanded to invoke Him and to turn rapidly toward Him and call out to Him in every misfortune. (GP III:36, 539–40)[46]

Again, anger accounts for the measured response to disregarding misfortune as an invocation of *teshuvah*.[47] In other words, Maimonides preserved the pragmatic biblical and rabbinic construct of leprosy as deterrence from slander while maintaining, at the same time, his philosophical position that sees providence or its lack as conditional on intellect. The following is a schematic of parallel readings available to disparate audiences:

	Necessary Belief	*True Belief*
Transgression	Ethical—slander (*lashon ha-ra*)	Intellectual—providence
Divine response	Anger	Reflex of intellectual error
Punishment	Affliction—leprosy	Exposure to natural forces
Human response	Oblivious to call for repentance	Sees no linkage between Providence and intellectual perfection
Divine response	Anger	Reflex of intellectual error
Punishment	Repentance unavailable	Total exposure to forces of natural environment

The final destination of idle chatter's metamorphosis is the slanderous targeting of God Himself, resulting in a denial of a fundamental principle (*kofer ba-iqqar*). All three verses cited in this grand finale, the first two of which represent this offensive speech and the closing its polar opposite, direct the reader once again to a critical chapter in the *Guide*'s discussion of providence, which determines the precise content of this "speaking against God." 2 Kgs 17:9, "impute things that were not right unto the Lord," has already been cited as standing for those whose religious vocabulary is replete with graphic, predicative God-talk (GP I:59, 142). In chapter III:19 of the *Guide,* the "things that were not right unto the Lord" are taken to refer to a philosophical position that denies God's omniscience, on the empirical basis "that the circumstances of the human individuals do not take a course that is in accordance with what, as every one of us considers, ought to happen" (GP III:19, 479–80).

The *Laws of Leprosy* then locates the stimulus for subscribing to this warped theology in another verse, "They have set their mouth against Heaven and their tongue walketh through the earth" (Ps 73:9)—"What caused them to set their mouths against Heaven? Their tongues which walked first on the earth." First, this verse discovers the source of their error in the drawing of analogies between the physical world and God. Second, it acknowledges the graduated path that led to this point, from speech between an assembly of fools, to defaming the righteous, to disparaging the prophets, all products of "tongues which walked first on the earth." Third, it acts as a preface to the following verses in the Psalm, also cited in GP III:19, adducing the specific content of the critique of God's omniscience uttered by the "mouths against Heaven." Psalm 73:11–13 provides the proof for concluding that God lacks knowledge of worldly affairs in the success of the wicked. This, in turn, engenders a pessimistic defeatism that "impels the excellent man to think that his inclination toward the good and the hardships due to the opposition of others that he endures because of it are useless" (GP III:19, 477). The concatenation of slander with delinquent views on providence logically culminates in its most abhorrent form, which qualifies as a "denial of a fundamental principle"; it literally violates the tenth of Maimonides' thirteen principles, "that God is aware of the deeds of men and that he does not ignore them."

Maimonides concluded his philosophical homily at the end of the laws of leprosy with a verse that typifies speech that is the antithesis of the discourse of ignorance whose course he had been tracking thus far: "Then those who fear the Lord have been talking to one another and God has heard it and listened to it and a scroll of remembrance has been written concerning those who fear God and value His name" (Mal 3:1 5). In the *Guide* III:19, this verse is one of a block of verses from the final chapter of

Malachi, commencing with 3:13, which forms a response to those who consider the seemingly anarchic state of the world exemplified by the suffering of the righteous and the success of the wicked as evidence of God's lack of omniscience. This is the group who, by virtue of the intellectual caliber of their discourse, are *listened* to and *heard* by God. They attract the providence of the intellectual overflow with which they have communed. They grasp what Job becomes privy to as a result of his ordeal, that "the notion of His providence is not the same as the notion of our providence; nor is the notion of His governance of the things created by Him the same as the notion of our governance of that which we govern" (GP III:23, 496).[48] It is primarily this negative conception of God that dispels any "doubts regarding the deity and whether He does or does not know and whether He exercises providence or manifests neglect" (GP III:23, 497). Those who fear God qualify for that designation only if they have complied with the strict definition of the term afforded by the *Mishneh Torah*.

Fear is a self-perspective gained subsequent to an appreciation of the infinite wisdom reflected in the creation, which leads to a sober realization of the minuscule role one plays in it. This philosophical/psychological consciousness is the precise antidote to the self-centeredness that perceives a world rampant with evil since everything is measured in terms of its own existence (GP III:12). They see a world devoid of governance that is oblivious to moral conduct or philosophical pursuit. Conversely, Malachi continues, the fearers will "come to see the difference between the righteous and the wicked" (3:18), since their measure of existence is not an egocentric one.[49] Slander is an offense in which the ethical and the philosophical mirror each other. A moral arrogance that allows for the besmirching of another succumbs to an intellectual arrogance that deprives God of knowledge.

It is no coincidence that the only two moral offences and ethical traits that Maimonides considered to be on par with *kofer ba-iqqar* are haughtiness (MT *Laws of Ethical Traits* 2:3) and *lashon ha-ra* (slander) (ibid., 7:3), since they both exhibit the same metaphysical position. The proof-text substantiating the gravity of slander considers it to be an expression of self-aggrandizement that does not acknowledge any superior authority to the self, "who said by our tongues we will overpower, with lips like ours, who is master over us" (Ps 12:5). The vacuum left by a perspective that sees no master who administers order and governance is filled by a narcissistic conceitedness that only acknowledges the self as master, often asserting its dominance at the expense of others. In fact, it is so pernicious that Maimonides considered it more heinous than the three cardinal sins in Jewish law—idolatry, adultery, and murder (MT *Laws of Ethical Traits* 7:3).[50] The simple ethical ramifications of slander were not sufficient for Maimonides to warrant the biblical/rabbinic trope tying it to leprosy. The digression from law at the conclusion of the *Laws of Leprosy* provides the requisite philosophical dimensions to slander so repugnant as to demand a belief in a miraculous deterrence. When the repercussions of what begins as idle chatter are understood to end in a denial of a fundamental principle of religion, only then does Maimonides' appraisal, "The utility of this belief is manifest" (GP III:47, 97), become a palpable one.

CHAPTER 3

Elisha ben Abuyah and the Hubris of the Heretic

In Maimonides' hands the convert and the leper were recast to transcend their own particular predicaments and become metaphors for serious philosophical issues of universal import. In this chapter we move from an outsider who has made his way inside (in the case of the convert) and an insider who has been forced out (in the case of the leper) to the heretic who has removed himself from the inside. In a manner similar to the first two instances, Maimonides appropriated the particular case of the most famous of heretics, the ostracized second-century rabbinic rebel Elisha ben Abuyah (Aher), as the archetype of intellectual degeneracy.

Elisha's reckless drive to gain knowledge of what in itself is the ultimate goal of man qua man ended not only in dismal failure, but in an overwhelming and inescapable mire of self-deception. His impetuous foray into esoteric fields of knowledge stands in marked contrast to the methodical and conscientiously programmatic approach of his rabbinic colleague who accompanied him on his esoteric journey, Rabbi Akiva. Their discrepant entries into the *pardes,* identified by Maimonides as the fields of physics and metaphysics (MT *Laws of the Foundations of the Torah* 4:13),[1] are reflected in the talmudic account of their respective aftermaths, with R. Akiva having "entered in peace and gone out in peace" and Elisha resorting to "cutting the shoots," a euphemism for heretical thinking and acting (*b. Hagigah* 14b).[2] The original talmudic characterizations are particularly apt for the Maimonidean paradigm, where caution and patience are realized in "peace" while aggressive zeal succumbs to the violence of "uprooting."

Elisha's theological rebellion was considered so egregious as to result in the rabbinic erasure of his name and its replacement with the anonymous and shameful sobriquet of Aher (the other). However, his personality and the theological issues he addressed proved too powerful to succumb to the rabbinic attempt to suppress his identity. There is no other *other* than Elisha and Aher is synonymous with him. Those who concern themselves with God's relationship to the world, His governance of it, and the incongruence of evil and injustice that seems to pervade world (and in particular Jewish) history are bound to encounter this legendary figure. Maimonides was no exception and his diagnosis of Elisha's behavior is that he slipped into a kind of madness, replete with delusions and hallucinatory figments akin to the apparitions that plague those who "persist in looking at brilliant or minute objects" (GP I:32, 69). Though we are informed as to Aher's flawed cognitive assumptions, Maimonides left us to guess at the speculative domain into which he ventured, as well as the nature of the conclusions to which he jumped. It is simply implausible that so egregious a conceptual felony as that committed by Aher would be entirely glossed over by the *Guide*. Its probative value would be immeasurable, both for determining the general pitfalls that are to be avoided in logical reasoning as well as pinpointing the specific issue that is particularly prone to those pitfalls and therefore more demanding of extreme caution when contemplated.

Consistent with what Leo Strauss has discovered to be a predominant septenarius feature of the *Guide*,[3] but not with his schematic structure, chapter I:32, the core Elisha chapter, forms part of a discrete unit of seven chapters beginning with I:30 and ending with I:36. Though we have encountered a smattering of chapters so far that do not, strictly speaking, deal with a particular equivocal term,[4] this unit constitutes the first lengthy and sustained interruption of the lexicographical section. It is launched by a chapter dedicated to the term *akhol* (eating), which is a metaphor for knowledge, and figures predominantly in the discursive unit that follows, particularly with respect to Elisha.

The equivocal terms that initiate this interregnum on knowledge and its limits are "eating" *(akhol)* and "water" *(mayim)*, terms that feature prominently in the Maimonidean presentation of the Akiva/Elisha polarity. Eating, as a physical activity, connotes sustenance and consumption, thereby lending itself as a metaphor for both endurance and destruction at one and the same time. The latter sense of destruction connotes a "putting-off of a form" while the former positive sense aptly conveys the acquisition of knowledge "through which the permanence of the human form endures" (GP I:30, 63).

Two of the four verses cited by Maimonides as illustrating the sense of eating as knowledge incorporate honey as an image, both in a negative and a positive sense. Proverbs 25:27, which surfaces in the Elisha chapter, warns against too much of a good thing: "It is not good to eat too much honey"; while Prov 24:13 qualifies honey as "good" and recommends its ingestion: " My son eat thou honey for it is good." The verse immediately following is also quoted, "so know thou wisdom to be unto the soul," to perfect the equation between "eating" and "know" and "honey" and "wisdom." As this dietary staple is absorbed by the soul *(nefesh)*, and as "soul" is "a term denoting the rational soul, I mean the form of man" (GP I:41), the combination of the two verses attests to the assertion that "eating" contributes metaphorically to "the permanence of the human form." The chapter then proceeds to consider the term "water" and its metaphorical connection with knowledge, which we are told has become so overpowering as to virtually usurp its primary meaning (GP I:30, 64: "it has become, as it were, the first meaning"). Parameters of metaphor have been established for the imagery of "eating," "honey," and "water," logically prefacing the Elisha chapter in which they have central roles to play. However, I argue that the assembly of proof-texts also sets the conceptual stage for what is to follow.

These introductory proof-texts for the equation between eating and wisdom provide the first, and possibly the pivotal, clue to a full appreciation of Elisha's fall. All the verses cited by Maimonides line up in a progressive argument as to what constitutes appropriate consumption. It is the *Leitwort tov* (good) that aligns all the verses into a discursive unit. Isaiah 55:1, "Come ye, buy and eat," establishes the primary mandate to perform the activity of eating. Isaiah 55:2, "eat ye that which is good," provides the criteria for what is acceptably edible — that is, "good" *(tov)*. Proverbs 25:27 and 24:13–14 identify the precise substance that qualifies as "good"—honey (24:13: "Eat thou honey for it is good *[ki tov]*"); they also qualify the manner of consuming the good that can result in "no good"—excess (25:27: "it is not good to eat much honey"). Elisha is accused in GP I:32 of violating the proscription of this last verse. The predominant concept that informs the entire excursus on evil in part III of the *Guide* is that God can be associated solely with the good, since "He only produces being and all being is good" (GP III:10, 440). *Tov* is what captures this notion, as evidenced by the almost daily evaluation in the first chapter of Genesis of each stage of creation as *tov* and by the final divine assessment of Gen 1:31, "And God saw everything that He had made, and, behold, it was very good *[tov me'od]*." This comprehensive perspective on creation as good is the verse that launches the *Guide*'s investigation into the root of the common error to which man is prone on this issue (GP III:10, 440). To gorge on what is good is to arrive at its opposite, the "not good" of Prov 25:27. Elisha overreacted and assimilated the "not good," which, as I argue in this chapter, plunged him into an irremediable state of confusion regarding the true notion of evil in the world.

Tov, a primary *Leitwort* of the biblical Genesis account, is for Maimonides a technical term for a particular design feature of all of creation. He dismissed the quest for telos for any aspect of existence as an exercise in futility. All that can ultimately be ascertained is that everything is simply a product of God's volition, a proposition also confirmed by the rabbinic tradition that "there does not exist a final end but only will alone" (GP III:13, 452). All judgments regarding the function and goal of existence are reduced to the proposition that "He brought every part of the world into existence and that it conformed to its purpose" (ibid., 453).

The repeated declaration at creation that "it was good" simply conveys the understanding that the particular facet of existence in question conforms to its purpose, for *tov* "is an expression applied by us to what conforms to our purpose" (ibid.). The all-encompassing finale of "very good" is merely an affirmation that "everything that was produced conformed to its own purpose, and nothing went wrong" (ibid.). Perplexity (ibid., 448) and restlessness (ibid., 456) await those who conduct the senseless search for "any final end for what has no final end except for its own existence" (ibid.). To determine a telos rather than to descriptively record the interconnection between all of creation's working parts is to elide the import of *tov.* *Tov* militates against a teleological nexus between one constituent of creation and another. Any biblical assertions to the contrary are "merely information about their nature" (ibid., 454). For example, the dictum in Gen 1:28 regarding man, "And have dominion over the fish of the sea," "does not mean that man was created for the sake of this, but merely gives information about man's nature with which He has stamped him" (GP III:13, 454).

Yehuda Liebes' masterful treatment of the *pardes* episode traces the "sins" of Elisha to a morally flawed personality. Arrogance and hubris frustrate any attempt to come to grips with the problem of theodicy and foment his downward spiral into decadence.[5] Liebes' reading, I believe, is so sensitive to the nuances of the primary rabbinic texts as to be instructive for what motivated Maimonides to choose Elisha as his archvillain. Misinterpreting *tov* as a teleological affirmation rather than a culmination of a functionally descriptive account of the creation is precisely what leads to an egocentrism regarding man's place in that creation. To view creation from the vantage point of man at its apex is to commit the cardinal intellectual transgression:

> Know that the majority of the false imaginings that call forth perplexity in the quest for the end of the existence of the world as a whole or the end of every part of it have as their root an error of man about himself and his imagining that all that exists exists because of himself alone, as well as ignorance of the nature of inferior matter and ignorance of what is primarily intended—namely, the bringing of everything whose existence is possible, existence being indubitably a good. (GP III:26, 506)

These concluding remarks to Maimonides' account of the affiliated issues of providence and evil are symmetrically linked to those initiating the discussion. The root of all intellectual turmoil regarding the problem of God and evil is located in anthropocentrism, for "every ignoramus imagines that all that exists exists with a view to his individual sake: it is as if there were nothing that exists except him. And if something happens to him that is contrary to what he wishes, he makes the trenchant judgment that all that exists is an evil" (GP III:12, 442). The egoistic caricature of Elisha portrayed in the rabbinic literature qualifies him, for Maimonides, as ineluctably bound for intellectual chaos on the issue of evil. His intellectual disposition rendered him incapable of constructing a coherent theodicy that entails philosophical presuppositions inimical to his egoism. Narcissism is concomitant to "ignorance of the nature of inferior matter," which, at the onset of the consideration of evil in GP III:11, is also a consequence of misconstruing the "very good" of Gen 1:31 as being exclusive, rather than inclusive, of "even the existence of this inferior matter" (GP III:11, 441).[6]

The second colon of Prov 25:27 poses an obscure parallel to the first colon, "eating too much honey is not good *[tov]*." In terms of its ethical connotations it is positioned well, as it constitutes an antidote to pride and egoism. Based on general rules of biblical parallelism,[7] the negative of the first colon of the verse should be read into the second, eliciting the reading, "and the search for their glory is not glory *[kavod]*." *Kavod* is not attainable by way of the pursuit for self-glorification. As we have seen, evil becomes problematic when one is possessed of a trait where all is judged in terms of the self. Moral weakness seeps into the world of thought and dooms the eternal quest for *kavod,* God's essence, to dismal failure. Prefacing Maimonides' discussion of *tov* as an essential ingredient of all creation is a unique interpretation of the verse "The lord hath made everything for His sake" (Prov 16:4) as "For the sake of His essence that is for the sake of His will" (GP III:13, 453). This is the equivalent of the proposition that all exists solely because of God's will and not for the sake of anything else.[8] Physical observation yields laws of natural causality where *A* must be prior to *B* in order for *B* to exist yet does not allow for the presumptuous conclusion that *A* exists *for the sake of B.* Maimonides' illustration of this logical axiom presages the discussion of the *tov* principle and the problem of evil that follows. A "will"-constructed world envisions a divine thought pattern that posits all existence as a product of essence: "I have created that first thing, as for instance matter, which must indispensably have come prior to everything material. Then I made in that thing which came first or after it that which I intended to bring into existence, without there being anything except will alone" (GP III:13, 453). Therefore, the second half of the verse translates into the gloomy forecast that when men investigate their own glory—that is, attempt to cultivate man as the end of creation—then what they acquire is not glory *(kavod).* Such an attempt is a misconstrual of divine will, essence, as the basic building block and end of all creation, lending a positive reality to evil, which is irreconcilable with God's *kavod*.[9] If man is the yardstick by which all is measured then all his personal misfortunes—illness and death—yield evils that defy theoretical reconciliation with God as the ground of all being.

The antonymous rabbinic pairing of Akiva and Elisha is anteceded by their biblical counterparts, Moses and the nobles of Israel, as configured by Maimonides. Moses, at the sight of the burning bush, is the very picture of intellectual humility, who hid his face (Exod 3:6) in a gesture of supreme restraint when confronted with the irresistible prospect of ultimate truth (GP I:5, 29). His biblical converse is represented by the nobles of the children of Israel, whose intellectual recklessness and impatience resulted in a corrupt apprehension of God tainted by anthropomorphism. Their revelation was diluted by the crass corporealisms of feet and sapphire (Exod 24:10) ensuing from "their overhasty rushing forward before they had reached perfection" (GP I:5, 30). Aside from the obvious parallel of temperament between this biblical pair and their rabbinic successors, there are two other instructive points of intersection: the imagery of eating and the sharing of a common proof-text.

Maimonides favors a *midrash* that conceives of a causal link between those who participated in this perverse vision (nobles and the sons of Aaron, Nadav and Avihu) and their untimely deaths.[10] They are accused of "feasting their eyes" upon God and casting a glance at God while dining, an object far too serious for such casual and lax attention. Maimonides subtly transforms the midrashic precipitation of sin into its consequences. "And they visioned God and did eat and drink" (Exod 24:11) suggests a cause-and-effect sequence: "because of the corruption of their apprehension they inclined toward things of the body" (GP I:5, 30). Arrogance regarding the sublime leads to a preoccupation with the base and an inability to penetrate beyond one's material situation. Once again, in the discussion proper of evil, dining habits reflect a balanced or distorted perception of evil in the world. Excess is the source of the most ubiquitous evil in the world, "those that are afflicted upon any individual among us by his own action" (ibid.; GP III:12, 445). Not only is gluttony physically harmful, it also distorts philosophical perspectives on evil. It confuses the means for the end and substitutes matter for form as human telos. If reality is measured by matter, and defective matter abounds, then the problem of evil is an overwhelming one (PM *Neziqin*; GP III:8; III:35, 537, reasons for the thirteenth class of commandments). However, man does not realize that he is the creator of his own misfortune and that a "concupiscence for eating, drinking, and copulation . . . is the cause of all corporeal and psychical diseases and ailments" (GP III:12, 445).

The common proof-text shared by both Elisha and the nobles is the Solomonic advice they are said to have ignored: "Guard thy foot when thou goest to the house of God *[bet elohim]*" (Eccl 4:17; GP I:5, 30; I:32, 69). The "house of God" refers to the Tabernacle or Temple, which must be approached with extreme caution. The rationale for the complex and strict regime of restrictions on entering the Temple is to inculcate a feeling of veneration and awe for the geographical focus of God's presence (GP III:47). The barrier set up by laws of ritual impurity allows for only rare opportunity to visit the Temple precinct so that "an impression leading to the humility that was aimed at will be produced" (ibid., 594).[11] Within the context of the nobles and Elisha, the verse imports this notion of humility into the world of thought, which demands restraint and sufficient preparedness prior to delving into the essential questions of being.

The verse that Maimonides attributes to Elisha's transgression addresses the perils of devouring excessive honey: "Hast thou found honey? Eat so much as sufficient for thee lest thou be filled therewith and vomit it" (Prov 25:16).[12] In view of my proposal that Elisha blundered over the quandary of reconciling God with what seems to be pervasive evil in the world, this verse epitomizes this problem on a number of levels. First, it presents a circumstance that appears prominently as the root cause of the most widespread of evils—those that are self-inflicted. Emblematic of this phenomenon is, as I have already noted, "concupiscence for eating, drinking, and copulation, and doing these things with excess in regard to quantity" (GP III:12, 445). Second, overeating is indicative of prioritizing food as an end rather than a means; and when that end is frustrated, God's omnipotence is called into question. Finally, the context of the verse leads us back into the domain of Temple sanctity. It is to be read in conjunction with the verse that follows, parallel in structure, theme, and language: "Let thy foot be seldom in thy neighbor's house lest he be sated with thee and hate thee" (Prov 25:17). Maimonides cited the rabbinic employment of this verse to establish the principle that "familiarity breeds contempt" with respect to the Temple (GP III:47, 593; *b. Hagigah* 7a). The more one frequents the Temple and becomes comfortable in its precinct, the less reverence for what it represents will ensue. Accordingly, restricted entry is guaranteed by the proliferation of sources of uncleanness, rendering the possibility of a clean individual the rare exception rather than the rule.

The dizzying array of restrictions on entering the Temple discourages carefree attitudes toward it and correspondingly encourages its veneration. This reading of Maimonides becomes slightly more refined when considered in light of the verse's talmudic hermeneutic to which he alluded. The verse is taken to inveigh against frequenting the Temple with "sin and trespass offerings." Abstention from sin is called for, thus dispensing with the need for these types of sacrifices. Structurally, the hate ensuing from the frequent visitation in Prov 25:17 parallels the vomit induced by the overindulgence in sweets of 25:16. Rashness of thought on the issue of evil, implicit in the imagery of 25:16, is mirrored in the crass links that would be formulated between sin and punishment should Temple visitation be sin-oriented. One would be prone to make a simplistic causal equation linking sin, suffering, and absolution granted by the sacrificial cult. In reality, although suffering is "due to divine will in accordance with the deserts of those people as determined by His judgments," full comprehension of how God's judgment operates "cannot be attained by our intellects" (GP III:17, 472).

The next verse cited, following in the vein of Prov 25:27 and 25:16, is Eccl 7:16, "Neither make thyself overwise; why shouldst thou destroy thyself." Moderation in contemplative matters is a corollary of the ethical "golden mean" espoused by Maimonides in MT *Laws of Ethical Traits*. The essence of the first colon of this verse—to not be overly righteous—is situated on the ethical scale at the extreme opposite end from the one having to do with the excess of too much honey. Whereas the latter discourages overindulgence, the former restrains inordinate abstinence. Self-denial beyond that restricted by law violates the rule of the golden mean; "included in this those who constantly fast are not along the good path" (MT *Laws of Ethical Traits* 3:1). Both an abstemious and a sybaritic character belie the same malaise—an obsession with the material. Though antipodes, both are overly engaged with matter and fail to grasp the *tov* of matter, which "conforms to its purpose."

The final biblical proof-text extracted from Psalms and, of course, assumed by Maimonides to be from the pen of King David, is an autobiographical disavowal by David of ever having committed intellectual trespass into domains beyond his capacity. David is the ideal whose model of behavior, "Neither do I exercise myself in things too great or things too marvelous for me" (Ps 131:1), Elisha failed to follow. David's intellectual chastity is directly preceded in the same verse with a declaration of ethical innocence of pride. As we have seen, vulnerability to the precipitous acquisition of esoteric knowledge is a consequence of this moral foible and so David denies ever being subject to its allure: "My heart is not haughty nor my eyes raised so high" (ibid.). Intellectual humility is a natural consequence of never having fallen prey to the delusions of grandeur that is a monarch's occupational hazard, about which there is much discussion in chapter 4.[13]

Elisha and his ilk are then accused of not paying heed to the counsel of Ben Sira, as quoted by the Talmud, "Do not inquire about things that are too marvelous for you; do not investigate what is hidden from you; inquire into things that are permitted to you; you have no business with marvels" (*b. Hagigah* 13a). Punctuating a long discussion about the nature and number of heavens, firmaments, and, in particular, a heaven known as *aravot,* as well as God's habitat, the context for this talmudic admonishment provides another clue to Elisha's blunder. Maimonides demonstrated an unusual attraction to the rabbinic figurative representation of the inner workings of *aravot,* which he took as a referent "solely to one heaven: that which encompasses the universe" (GP I:70, 172). It is this heaven that God is said to be "riding" *(rakhov),* an equestrian metaphor for "His instrument by means of which He governs that which is existent" (ibid., 173).

Aravot is closely associated with righteousness *(tzedeq)* both rabbinically and biblically. Among other ethereal substances such as souls and the dew that will revive the dead, it is the abode of "righteousness *[tzedeq],* right dealing *[tzedaqah]* and justice *[mishpat]*." Maimonides favors this *midrash,* which, by locating these entities within the highest heaven known as *aravot,* conveys a dimension of governance whereby "the forces generating the particular thing in question and safeguarding its order come from that heaven" (ibid.). *Aravot* has also been biblically established as God's throne because He rides in it (Ps 68:5) and because "righteousness *[tzedeq]* and justice *[mishpat]* are the foundation of Thy throne"(Ps 89:15). Ben Sira's exhortation is a strategic allusion to the all-encompassing sphere *(aravot)* as the destination of Elisha's journey. He has embarked upon a path that should eventually lead him to the source of "righteousness and justice" *(tzedeq* and *mishpat)* in the world; but instead, upon his arrival he is ensnared in an intellectual quagmire of confusion.

The idea that haughtiness and hubris are particularly associated with posing an obstacle to what *aravot* stands for is enhanced by an ironic reversal of that character trait. The verse that signifies God's supreme control over the encompassing heaven is Deut 33:26. The first colon of the verse, referring to "the rider of the heavens," establishes that God "moves it in virtue of His power and His will" (GP I:70, 175). The second colon, "and in His excellency [pride] on the skies," parallels the preceding colon in the sense that *aravot* emerges "in virtue of His pride." What is symbolized by *aravot* is a manifestation of God's pride. There remains no room for the assertion of any other identity that imposes itself as a result of intellectual boastfulness. God's pride can only be penetrated by a contraction of one's own pride, as typified by the restraint and humility of Moses' covering his eyes at the burning bush.

Once *aravot* has been identified as the throne of glory, the reader of the *Guide* is directed to Elisha's biblical precursor, the nobles of the children of Israel, for a more expository account of the error to which he succumbed. The vision to which this class was privy is described graphically in Exod 24:10 as "under His feet, as it were, a work of the whiteness of sapphire stone." Onkelos'[14] interpretation of "his feet" as the throne of glory is cited by Maimonides with some approval (GP I:28, 60). For Maimonides the term "foot" *(regel)* established a causal nexus with the substance below symbolized by the whiteness of sapphire stone. This gem, considering the transparency of its color, stands for "first matter," which, "in respect of its true reality, lacks all forms and on this account is capable of receiving all forms in succession" (ibid., 61). The object of the nobles' philosophical investigation, then, was "first matter and the relation of the latter to God, inasmuch as it is the first among the things He has created that necessitates generation and corruption" (ibid.). This last phrase is crucial to the Maimonidean theodicy, since the survival and perpetuation of all of existence is contingent on the quality of generation and corruption naturally inherent in matter. All that man identifies as evil is associated with this essential quality of matter. The nobles apprehended "the true reality of first matter" (ibid.). This assertion is reiterated during an appraisal of the Platonic position on creation, where the same vision of Exod 24:10 is reconfirmed as "the true reality of the inferior first matter" (GP II:26, 331).

What is most peculiar about Maimonides' account of the nobles' vision is the marked discrepancy between his evaluations of that vision in different sections of the *Guide*. What has just been canvassed in I:28 is a grasp of one aspect of creation—first matter—untainted by any deficiency, misconception, or intellectual arrogance. An earlier account, however, offers an incongruous assessment of the same vision as "corrupt," "imperfect," arrived at "overhastily," and tarnished by "corporeality" (GP I:5, 30). In fact, the very same metaphor of "under His feet, as it were, a work of the whiteness of sapphire stone," which represented "the true reality of first matter" in I:28, is "solely intended to present a criticism of their act of seeing" in I:5. If the biblical imagery was never intended as a literal depiction, then how can its literality be exploited to attribute anthropomorphism to the subjects of the vision? The accusation of corporeality clashes discordantly with the figurative hermeneutic applied in I:28. There a facet of existence and its relationship to the creator have been assimilated. What could possibly be objectionable about the commendable project of gaining insight into an aspect of being?

Maimonides' criticism of the nobles is directed at their level of achievement coincident with an event that could not be more opportune, the Sinaitic theophany. Though they procured a certain intellection, the nobles arrogantly set their sights much higher than they were properly prepared for. I propose that what is abhorrent regarding their attainment is the confusion between what was initially aimed for and what in the end was actually obtained. Success, according to Maimonides, would have been indicated by the curtailing of their vision from "the God of Israel [*Elohim*]" and "there was under His feet," and so on, to simply the "God of Israel." The latter is what they aspired to, but due to the impulsive assault toward this goal, their efforts culminated in a God of first matter, "inasmuch as it is the first among the things He has created that necessitates generation and corruption" (GP I:28, 61).

Given that the original quest was for the "God of" [*elohe*], which connotes "governance,"[15] the repercussions of associating God's governance with that which "necessitates generation and corruption" were catastrophic. The "corporeality" that is said to have undermined the integrity of their vision would have wreaked particular havoc for the Maimonidean theodicy, since it would implicate God in the process of generation and corruption. All evils associated with the latter process (death, illness, deterioration) are privations with which God can have no essential link. To confuse God's governance with the modus operandi of matter is to attribute an ongoing working relationship between Him and what is perceived as evil in the world. The nobles committed a category error that mistook the God who creates prime matter with the "God who governs," allowing for the warped assertion that He "produces evil in an essential act" (GP III:10, 440). Their haste to reach *aravot* (throne), or "His instrument by means of which He governs that which is existent" (GP I:70, 173), doomed them to confound their goal with its subordinate, first matter, for it is "in true reality under the heaven that is called the throne" (GP I:28, 61).[16] The ravenous aspirations of Elisha followed suit.

Underscoring this escapade as no minor mishap is Maimonides' characterization of the distinction between heavenly matter and terrestrial matter as "one of the mysteries of being and a mystery among the mysteries of the Torah" (GP II:26, 331). During the course of the exposition on the meaning of the whiteness of the sapphire stone, our attention is explicitly directed to a later chapter in the *Guide*. In II:26 the rabbinic equivalent to the precious material the nobles envisioned is the snow under the throne of glory from which earth was created (GP II:26, 331, quoting *Pirqe de-Rabbi Eliezer*, 3). Conversely, the heavens were said to have their origins in the light of His garment, thereby formulating a bifurcation of the universe into "two matters, a high and an inferior one" (GP II:26, 331). Elisha and the nobles confounded the two, attenuating God's involvement with a domain to which He is only accidentally related. Failure to maintain the distinct nature of heaven and earth will most certainly distort the measure of God's proximity to each domain, calibrated by "the sublimity of that matter [heaven] and its nearness to Him and the defectiveness of the other [earth] and also the place where it is located" (ibid., 332). Elisha's and the nobles' own existential remoteness from God mirrors the conceptual distance of the earth.

As for the consequences of their heinous act, Maimonides referred to a midrashic tradition that accords the nobles and Aaron's sons, Nadav and Avihu, a temporary reprieve until they are finally called to account, at *Taverah* and the *Tabernacle of the Congregation* respectively (GP I:5).[17] The reference to *Taverah* is to the devastating conflagration recorded in Num 11:1, "And the fire of the Lord burnt among them and ate them up." In the case of the *Tabernacle of the Congregation,* the reference is to the verse in Lev 10:2, "And a fire went out from before the Lord and ate them up." In both cases the punishment takes the form of a fire that consumes, literally performs an "eating" *(akhol)* of the perpetrators. Within the Maimonidean hermeneutic, the rabbinic standard of "measure-for-measure" retribution operates with striking precision. The perpetrator's offence constituted, as in the case of Elisha, a metaphorical eating or gluttony that appropriately invites a punitive response in kind—a divine eating. Numbers 11:1 is cited, among other verses, as illustrative of the figurative sense of eating as "destruction and undoing and, in general, to all putting-off of a form" (GP I:30, 63).

Considering the last phrase, the retributive measure addresses the substantive nature of the offence as well, which was a failure to reconcile defective reality with God's omniscience. Paramount in resolving the evil of destruction and death is a notional reorientation toward these phenomena as a vacating of form: "With regard to every living thing, death is the privation of form" (GP III:10, 439). Their botched theodicy incurs a personal "putting-off of form." Even the cardinal ingredient of Maimonides' theory of evil, which denies God any essential link with deficiency, is implicit in the retributive verse of Num 11:1. The punishment is provoked by divine auditory function, "And the Lord heard." Every instance of this function in a divine context, according to Maimonides, is expressive simply of "apprehension" (GP I:45, 96), with this verse being specifically cited as one example of such. Since God never acquires new knowledge, being a constant intellect in actu (see GP I:68, 165), God cannot respond to anything in these circumstances. He simply knows, and knows what He has always known.

The verse then recounts a natural "putting-off of form" that may have been causally precipitated by a prior maculation of form. Moses, on the other hand, is granted the ultimate in human form, if apprehension is considered the natural form of man (see GP I:1, 22), in return for his laudatory self-restraint at the burning bush (GP I:5, alluding to *b. Berakhot* 7a). Though the meaning of God's revelation of His "back" to Moses merits a comprehensive treatment on its own, there is one aspect of it that is of particular relevance to this study of the heretic as outsider and that starkly opposes his persona to that of the Elisha/nobles camp. God favors Moses' supplication "Show me now Thy ways" (Exod 33:13) with the revelatory gesture "I will make all my goodness pass before thee" (ibid., 33:19). This goodness conjures up the divine assessment of "very good" in Gen 1:31 at the summit of the world's genesis. Moses occupies the same vantage point as God at creation, from which he perceives all existing things, and "apprehends their nature and the way they are mutually connected so that he will know how He governs them in general and in detail" (GP I:54, 124). Once Moses is enlightened from a macroscopic perspective, he understands the good that inheres in all things insofar as they "conform to their purpose." His initial gesture of humility at the burning bush, an acknowledgment of his own material self-limitations, gains for him in the end a global awareness of how every bit of matter interconnects to produce an all-encompassing good.[18]

Elisha and his ilk were also faulted by Maimonides for ignoring the ominous mishnaic warning "He who considers four things, it would have been better had he not entered the world: what is above, what is below, what is before, and what is after [ahor]" (m. Hagigah 2:3). In his commentary to this *mishnah,* Maimonides did not focus on any inherent unknowability of these subjects, nor did he consider them to be categorically occluded from any reflection whatsoever. Rather, the target of the mishnaic vitriol is, once again, intellectual arrogance and the pursuit of lofty disciplines without the rigid prerequisite training they demand. He treated the *mishnah* as a criticism of those who "delve into divine matters with simple imaginings without having progressed through various levels of sciences" (PM *Hagigah* 2:3). The trenchant judgment that such a person is not worthy to have ever come into existence is suited to the particular issue that has been prematurely broached—God's governance. The consequence is the vacating of the person's humanity. He becomes subsumed under other species of animals that, individually, are specifically excluded from divine concern (see GP III:7).

Elisha and those who chose to be his acolytes were, according to Maimonides, also subject to the second mishnaic condemnation of "He who does not have regard [literally compassion] for the honor of his Creator." Once again these perpetrators were said to be subject to the censure of "it is better that he had not entered this world" (m. *Hagigah* 2:3). Maimonides in his commentary on this *mishnah* inventively identified the honor of the person's creator as the human intellect; since he "does not appreciate the value of this thing that was donated to him he becomes lost to his desire and becomes like an animal" (PM *Hagigah* 2:3). His offense jettisons him out of the sphere of humanity to that of the animal kingdom where God's governance is not evident. There is a double entendre in the choice of the term "honor" *(kavod)* here since it can allude to both the intellect with which man honors God by way of its perfection and the essence of God as was pleaded for by Moses (see GP I:64, 57 for both these connotations). Intemperate exercise of the former leads to a perversion of the latter.

To more fully appreciate Maimonides' incorporation of this mishnaic excoriation within the Elisha context, we must consider the particular term that has been translated by Shlomo Pines as "creator" in the phrase "honor of the creator." The Hebrew term, *qoneh,* means literally "possessor." Its potency is emasculated by the translation "creator." *Qoneh* is one of four terms that, according to Maimonides, biblically denote the "relation between heaven and God" (GP II:30, 358). Though it signifies God's mastery over heaven and earth, it is singled out as being somewhat misleading since "it tends toward the road of the belief in the eternity of a certain matter" (ibid.). Belief in eternity wreaks havoc with theories of divine governance in the world; it is what led Aristotle to deny its application to individuals of any species including man. No equitable principle can be discerned to operate within nature since, for the Aristotelian school, there is no difference "between an ox that defecates on a host of ants so that they die, or a building whose foundations are shaken upon all the people at their prayers who are found in it so that they die" (GP III:17, 466).

Because randomness and chaos prevail as far as individual man is concerned, they "exist by chance and not through the governance of one who governs" (ibid.). Reconciling apparent evil in the material world with divine justice is a futile undertaking insofar as the two do not, by definition, share any common ground of intersection. Maimonides understood this outlook to be an extension of the conviction that the world is eternal: "this is consequent upon his opinion concerning the eternity of the world" (ibid.). Therefore, "not having proper regard for the *qoneh*" also alludes to the failure to fully appreciate the relationship between God and the world as captured by this term. The implications are disastrous for perceptions of God's governance in the world. To have proper regard for the glory of one's *qoneh* is to avert its isolation from its sister terms such as *baro* (creating) and *asoh* (making) (ibid.). These creative terms must be read in conjunction. Maimonides' choice of this mishnaic reference correlates Elisha's perfidy with the realms of providence and governance.[19]

With this reference, the original "honey" metaphor has journeyed full circle. The closing point of Maimonides' commentary on the *mishnah* is that, commensurate with its absorption, disclosure of such esoteric subjects as the Account of the Chariot and the Account of Creation is also severely restricted. In support of maintaining a kind of gag order on this material, a verse from Song of Songs is cited that also incorporates the honey metaphor: "honey and milk are under your tongue" (4:11). This consummates the honey image, moving from eating honey, which is intrinsically good, to eating excess honey, which is not good. Once the good has been imbibed it cannot be dispensed liberally. A more fitting context would be difficult to find, since the next verse (12) repeats the terms for "locked" *(na'ul)* and "sealed" *(hatum)* three times, while verse 13 imports the rare term *pardes* into its garden imagery. The *pardes* is virtually impenetrable, both because of the formidable barriers the philosophical sophomore must overcome and because of the constraints imposed on dissemination of its material.[20]

Aside from its degree of obscurity, there is an additional reason why this material almost naturally becomes trapped under one's tongue. Its attainment is ultimately self-reflexive in purpose. In MT *Laws of the Foundations of Torah,* Songs 4:11 is quoted in conjunction with two other verses, mandating the shrouding of these disciplines in strictest confidence. One of them is most revealing for our purposes. Secrecy pertains to the esoteric feature of the sciences cultivated in the *pardes,* but it is also a natural consequence of its self-serving function. "They shall be only thine alone, not to be shared with strangers" (Prov 5:17) is cited here with Songs 4:11 to narrowly circumscribe public teachings of these sciences. However, the verse lands us once again in the ultimate chapter of the *Guide,* which expresses the preference for what constitutes the summum bonum for humanity. The summit of human perfection is reached intellectually with "the conception of intelligibles." It is considered so because it is purely self-directed, as opposed to the other three types of perfection—material, physical, and moral. "If you consider each of the three perfections mentioned before, you will find that they pertain to others than you, not you. . . . The ultimate perfection however, pertains to you alone, no one else being associated in it with you in any way: *They shall be only thine alone and so on* [Prov 5:17]" (GP III:54, 635).

Complementary to this latter verse are Jer 9:22–23, verses we have encountered previously, which exclude glory from the first three perfections and reserve it exclusively for rational perfection, or the end "that he understandeth and knoweth Me" (III:54, 636). This knowledge in turn is identical with that procured in response to the Mosaic supplication "Show me now Thy ways." The latter comprises divine attributes of action; specifically, "those actions that ought to be known and imitated are lovingkindness, judgment and righteousness" (ibid., 637). Behavioral assimilation of these as ethical virtues ineluctably flows from an all-encompassing view of how these qualities manifest themselves in creation as a whole—the appreciation of how all existence conforms to the *tov* previously delineated.[21] The location of these attributes in the earth by Jeremiah demonstrates that "His providence extends over the earth in the way that corresponds to what the latter is" (ibid.). The mishnaic reference, then, dispatches the reader on a route that meanders along a series of allusions and references, and finally situates Elisha within the context of God's providence. His lack of "regard for the glory of his *qoneh*" disaffects him of the ability to discern "loving kindness, judgment, and righteousness in the earth."

Maimonides took his leave of Elisha with a parting shot at those who "regard darkness as light and light as darkness," an allusion to Isa 5:20, where the full text reads, "Woe to those who call the evil good and the good evil, who regard darkness as light and light as darkness, who make bitter into sweet and sweet into bitter." Added to previous distinctions blurred by Elisha—good *(tov)* and evil, and sweet (honey) and bitter—is that of light and darkness. The distinction between these two is absolutely pivotal for Maimonides' penetrating investigation of perceived evil in the world. Failure to discriminate darkness from light translates into a failure to determine their respective origins and to discern how God relates to either.

Darkness, like evil, is a privation that does not require an agent and is therefore dissociated from God. To prove this proposition, Isa 45:7 is called upon, as the pairs darkness/light and evil/peace are contrapositioned. The terms are distinguished in the same verse by their modes of conception. Darkness and evil are products of "creating" *(bore)* while light is "formed" *(yotzer)*. *Bore* "has a connection with non-being" (GP III:30, 438), qualifying it for phenomena that are in essence privations. *Bore* is problematic, though, since it also connotes the bringing into existence of heaven and earth (see Gen 1:1 and GP II:30, 358). *Bore* seems to contain an implicit ambiguity that accounts for both being and nonbeing. Perhaps Elisha read *bore* as effectuating a varied existence of good and bad, as opposed to its genuine sense. All is *tov*. *Tov* emerges from the process of creation indicated by *bore*. Matter is *tov*, yet its volatility and requisite state of flux entail privations. Elisha failed to grasp the grand sweep of *bore*, where nonbeing is simply a natural concomitant of being while, at the same time, is bereft of any ontic status of its own.

The other principal indicator of the critical role *tov* plays in the Elisha debacle is R. Akiva's anticipatory warning to his colleagues not to mistake marble for water. According to Maimonides, R. Akiva identified what is most vexing about the second day of the creation: the division of waters by the firmament, and specifically, the overhead waters. R. Akiva's caution is taken as counsel to prevent confusing what is water in name alone with the liquid substance empirically known to man (GP II:30, 353).[22] Through sharing a common matter, water is divided into three entirely distinct forms that occupy the firmament, the earth, and the suprafirmament.[23] What is most conspicuous about the account of the second day in Gen 1 is the missing appraisal that it "was good," so characteristic of the other days. The omission, we are told, caters to public perception that cannot fathom the existence or the utility of this creation, for "it is a matter whose meaning is hidden and that, understood in its external meaning does not exist in such a way as to appear useful, what utility externally visible to the people at large could there be so that the words, *that it was good* could be said with reference to it?" Intrinsically good, yet extrinsically unpalatable, this water is a confounding substance. Assumedly, the failure of Elisha to abide by Akiva's advice landed him in the unsavory company rife with misapprehension. He remained at the level of the external where *tov* is absent. Once again, it is a *tov* that has not been absorbed; this, as we shall see, reflects both an ethical and an intellectual offence that are mirror images of each other.

Mention of a group whose confusion is marked by an incapacity to distinguish between light and darkness guides the reader back to R. Akiva's "water, water" forewarning. As pointed out, Maimonides construed that caution as a direct reference to the variant forms of water situated above and below the firmament. Their segregation, which transpires in Gen 1:7, sequentially follows the demarcation between light and darkness in Gen 1:4; both separations are realized through the same divine action of dividing *(va-yavdel)*. Consequently, Maimonides draws a parallel between the two: "Thus the phrase, *And he divided between the waters which were under the firmament, etc.,* is analogous to the phrase, *And God divided between the light and the darkness,* in which the division is in respect of a certain form" (GP II:30, 352).[24] The root error of the confused group of Isa 5:20 who mistake darkness for light and vice versa can be traced to a misapprehension of the primal division that distinguished the two in Gen 1:4. Division is the process of informing air with light and its absence leaves darkness in its wake. Light, though, being a product of *yetzirah* (forming), is an accident of shape as indicated by the verse cited above, "Who formeth *(yotzer)* the light" (Isa 45:7). Full appreciation of the process exemplified by Gen 1:4 is a prerequisite for the proper sense of the water's division in 1:7. Mastering the notion of *tov* requires a proficiency in the working of nature, its origins, and its rudimentary components of form, matter, essence, accident, and privation.

In the final analysis, we have yet to unearth what exactly Maimonides found so "most hidden" about R. Akiva's waters caution, nor what lends it the complexion of "extraordinary secrets" (GP II:30, 353).[25] Whatever the identity of this substance beyond the firmament, my concern is more conceptual than technical. Others such as Sarah Klein-Braslavy have competently surveyed the various schools of thought on this thorny issue.[26] My intention is not to enter that debate but rather to underscore the notional perils to which those like Elisha would be exposed upon scrutinizing this facet of creation.

One of the most insightful of the medieval commentators on this passage is Asher Crescas, who sensed the danger of exploring this level of existence in view of its ramifications for public perceptions of divine governance and providence. According to Crescas, the aura of mystery surrounding these waters is due to the real threat that "they [the general public] will imagine that the downfall of the rains are natural events and not the direct acts of God, and this will lead to the alienation of divine providence from their belief systems" (MN II:60a–60b).[27] He continued that because rain plays such a central role in the biblical reward/punishment paradigm, unimpeded disclosure of its natural origins and mechanistic formation at the suprafirmament stage would seriously threaten cardinal tenets of theological belief. This challenge to public perception is, I believe, hinted at by the light/darkness reference of Isa 5:20. Immediately after discussing the hiddenness of the second day of creation, Maimonides traced the causal progression from the spheres to the world of generation, and passing to its primary source—light and darkness. These interact to generate various "meteorological phenomena among which rain figures." The causal links are traced from that point to "the final composition being that of man" (GP II:30, 354).[28] Rain figures most prominently in both the origins and sustenance of man. Knowledge of sequential causation with its inception in the permutations of light and darkness and subsequent generation of rain may obviate the notion of an interested God who acts in the world. The naive, yet necessary, beliefs of the general public[29] may become unhinged as a result.

This potential danger is enhanced by another destination in the *Guide* to which the light/darkness reference leads. In II:5 Maimonides proposed that governance of all created beings is processed through the spheres, citing in support of this assertion Gen 1:18, "And to rule over the day and over the night, and to divide," which is then intricately linked to the jurisdiction of the forces emanating from light and darkness: "Now, the meaning of ruling is domination through governance: and this is a supplementary notion added to that of light and darkness, which is the proximate cause of generation and corruption. For the meaning of light and darkness is referred to in the words: *And to divide the light from the darkness* [Gen 1:18]" (GP II:5, 261).

The confusion regarding the light and darkness of Isa 5:20 is about origins; about natural causation conceived with the spheres and funneled through light and darkness and rain down to humanity; about form and privation of form; and about the drama of generation and corruption within the divine scheme of governance. Elisha's grandiose ambitions beyond his ability condemn him to a theological morass that fails to account for the remoteness to which God has been consigned by this scheme. He cannot extricate Himself from a world abandoned to the ravages of rampant and random evil.

In the end, Elisha and Akiva embody their respective theological perspectives on God and the world. Elisha's failure to situate evil within a context of overall *tov* philosophically distances God from the world and leaves Elisha alienated in turn from the ultimate source of all being. His sobriquet of Aher, the other, resonates with the sense of *ahor* (back, consonantally identical with *aher*) offered by the Aramaic translation of Onkelos, and positions him experientially within the same habitat to which he has relegated the rest of existence: "the beings from which I have, as it were, turned away, and upon which, speaking in parables, I have turned my back because of their remoteness from the existence of God, may He be exalted" (GP I:37, 86). This is the back *(ahor)* at which Elisha/Aher has arrived and is the consequence of God's hiding of the face in Deut 31:17–18. Exposure to this turning of God's back causes men to be, in the words of verse 17, "devoured, and many evil and troubles shall come upon them." Maimonides' interpretation of this hiding of the face aptly captures the existential predicament in which Elisha now finds himself: "the reason for a human individual's being abandoned to chance so that he is permitted to be devoured by the beasts is his being separated from God" (see GP III:51, 626).

Akiva, on the other hand, "enters in peace *[shalom]* and exits in peace." His warning about the waters above the firmament adumbrates the danger posed by this region from which he will be shielded because he bears the armor of peace. What does this *shalom* signify? If we revert back to the instrumental phrase in Isa 45:7, "who forms light and creates darkness, who makes peace *[shalom]* and creates evil *[ra]*," to which attention was summoned by the confusion-of-light-with-darkness citation, two problems arise. First, the natural polarity that would constitute a common contrasting pair is good *(tov)* and evil *(ra)*. *Shalom* appears instead. Second, what Maimonides found most appealing about this verse is the deliberate pairing of *bore* with privations of darkness and evil as opposed to "making" *(asoh)*, "for these are not existing things with which the word making would be connected" (GP III:10, 438). Furthermore, the term "making" connotes "specific forms that were given to them [heaven + earth]—I mean their nature" (GP II:30, 358). How, then, can "making" produce a conception or notion such as peace?

Shalom, the understudy for *tov* in this context, represents an accomplished appreciation of *tov* in the creation. *Tov* advances the principle of conformity to purpose, including the natural degeneration, corruption, and deficiencies associated with matter. Everything operates in tandem and purposefully, including that perceived as evil, yielding a pervasive harmony or peace. Once *tov* is procured, no conflict, tension, or friction exists between all the facets of existence, most certainly not on the plane in which *asoh* (making) is operative—that of natural, or essential, forms. The forms coexist idyllically. Guided by this outlook prior to embarking upon one's contemplative odyssey ensures a successful return with one's *shalom* intact.[30] One's robust grip on what *shalom* represents entrenches God's relationship with the world, however remote it seems. In contrast to Elisha, then, Akiva is the existential model of God's presence, since "he has rendered himself so worthy that the intellect in question overflows toward him, has providence attached to him, while all evils are prevented from befalling him" (GP III:51, 626).

This invincible state of being acquired by those who have achieved intellectual perfection is substantiated by a proof-text, Job 22:21, in which peace *(shalom)* is adopted as the chief trope: "Aquaint now thyself and be with Him and be at peace." The verse translates into the counsel "turn toward Him and you will be safe from all ill" (GP III:51, 626). Akiva, then, personifies this state of *shalom* attained as a result of perceiving how all existence, including the defects of matter, manifests a state of *shalom*. Preoccupied with *shalom* as an operative rationale for the creation, he personally embodies *shalom* that shields him from all evils, since they are gauged within the context of that rationale. God does not hide His face (Deut 31:17–18) from the likes of Akiva. Instead, Akiva is presented with the back that "has come to be like Me, and follows necessarily from My will" (GP I:38, 87).

The *tov* that Elisha failed to grasp is the *tov* omitted from the account of the second day of creation, not because it is not *tov*, but because it bears an esoteric doctrine regarding God and His relationship to the world. The missing *tov*, so mysteriously absent from the second day, lends the verse the identical format in which any esoteric matter is to be taught. Indeed, it parallels the very structure of the *Guide* itself. Maimonides' description of his own esotericism and that of the divine author in the composition of the second day's account are striking analogues:

Guide: "The seventh cause—In speaking about very obscure matters it is necessary to conceal some parts and to disclose others. . . . In such cases the vulgar must in no way be aware of the contradiction; the author accordingly uses some device to conceal it by all means." (GP Intro., 18)

Torah (regarding the missing *tov* of the second day): "If, on the other hand, the matter is considered according to its inner meaning and to what was truly intended, it is most hidden. For in that case it was necessary for it to be one of the concealed secrets so that the vulgar should not know it." (GP II:30, 353)

Elisha, in his haste, fell prey to the conspicuously missing *tov* whose reinsertion the text demands of its accomplished readers. Maimonides applied a creative hermeneutic whereby a novel construct of Elisha emerges out of a mélange of biblical and rabbinic proof-texts. Each reference draws the reader across the spectrum comprising the *Guide,* the *Mishneh Torah,* and the *Mishnah* commentary to present Elisha in an arrogant, hubristic, and premature attempt at forging a coherent theodicy. Failure is ruinous not only for a routed theodicy, but for whatever Elisha has previously intellectually accomplished. The pith of his egregious error has been tracked to the incapacity to assimilate the full purport of the *tov* of creation.

To conclude this chapter, I return to the core talmudic text in order to accommodate this new hermeneutical construct of Elisha in our rereading of it. Having dealt with the debacle of the *pardes* journey, my concern is how to approach its aftermath. For the purpose of this study of outsiders, there is one feature of the version in the Palestinian Talmud on which I wish to focus,[31] the series of encounters with Elisha's disciple, R. Meir, who remained inside the rabbinic fold while his master crossed the line. The first of these encounters consists of exegetical jousting between the former teacher and his pupil regarding the meaning of various biblical phrases. The final encounter is a posthumous one in which R. Meir becomes a compelling advocate for his master in the face of God's cruel punishment of Elisha in the afterlife.

What is quite striking is that these two confrontations, marking the beginning and end of the Meir/Elisha cycle, both pivot on the key term *tov*. In the former case the debate focuses on the meaning of the apothegm "The end of a thing is better *[tov me]* than its beginning" (Eccl 7:8). In the latter case, at the sight of Elisha's smoldering grave, R. Meir adduces a number of verses in a daring challenge to God's verdict. Exploiting Ruth 3:13, the sexually charged scene at the threshing floor between Boaz and Ruth, R. Meir assumes the voice of Boaz: "'Stay the night, then in the morning if he will redeem you, good *[tov]* [Ruth 3:13]'—this refers to the Holy One Blessed be He, who is good *[tov]*, as it says, 'He is good, to all, and His mercy upon all creatures' [Ps 145:9]. 'But if He does not want to redeem you I will redeem you myself, as God lives [Ruth 3:13].'" The Meir/Elisha cycle revolves around Meir, who remained on the inside, attempting to draw Elisha, who had moved outside, back in. According to his Maimonidean construct, Elisha was outside because of the missing or misconceived *tov*. Both the heretic and the leper find themselves on the outside because of the *philosophical* dangers they pose to the community, threatening to undermine its core beliefs, while the convert reinvigorates those beliefs.

It is appropriate, then, that Meir's encounters with Elisha are guided by attempts to refine the meaning of *tov*, and reintroduces the *tov* personified by the Deity Himself. In fact, Ps 145:9 is the very verse cited in the *Guide*'s discussion of evil to convey God's ultimate beneficence and munificence: "For His bringing us into existence is absolutely the great good" (GP III:12, 448). Redemption for Elisha rested in assimilating the full import of God as *tov*, to which Meir sagaciously resorted in order to quell his master's purgation. God, according to Maimonides, is imported into the world by way of a recognition of His "goodness" in the creation; once this was declared by Meir on his master's behalf, "the fire was extinguished."

CHAPTER 4

The King

The Ethics of Imperial Humility

In this chapter I consider another outsider—namely, the king. Unlike the convert, the heretic, and the leper, the king is an outsider by virtue of who he is and the office he occupies and not by virtue of what he does, thinks, or espouses. Just like the leper and heretic, his presence inside the group poses serious philosophical and theological dangers that threaten the theological fabric of the Jewish faith community. How the king acts and thinks can either diminish those dangers or bolster them. The power and stature of his office can be so overwhelming as to replace God with his own person. Maimonides carefully constructed the king in both his legal and philosophical works with an eye to preventing this danger from ever becoming real. This he accomplished by situating the king so far inside as to reach the very other extreme of the community spectrum, which itself lies outside the norm. Thus, although the king wields the power of an absolute sovereign, he assumes the demeanor of those on the other end of the social hierarchy who are absolutely powerless. His predicament is unlike those of the outsiders previously discussed in this study. He must both command the authority and respect needed to function in his sovereign role while at the same time avert any semblance of his being perceived as ontologically sovereign.

When dealing with the rules governing ethical conduct in the *Mishneh Torah*, Maimonides adopted the Aristotelian "golden mean" as the sole legitimate measure of all character traits, which he suggestively categorized as "opinions" *(deʿot)* rather than as moral qualities. Initially, he categorically endorsed this principle: "The correct path is the median *[middah benonit]* for each and every characteristic that is found in man" (MT *Laws of Ethical Traits* 1:3).[1] As he further developed his codification, however, this rule came to be inconsistently subject to exceptions. Humility, in particular, is specifically excluded from the application of the golden mean doctrine.[2] The only method of immunizing man from falling prey to his hubris is in fact to violate the norm of ethical balance and swing to the utmost extremes of self-abnegation. When it comes to the trait of pride or, literally, an "elevated heart" *(govah-lev)*, it is not only advisable to break with the norm of moderate conduct, it is actually forbidden to act in accordance with it: "There are those traits for which man is forbidden from following the mean but rather he should veer to the other extreme, and that is an 'elevated heart'" (ibid., 2:3). In this case the model is one of virtual self-effacement, rather than what is usually understood as common humility *(anivut)*. This recommended extreme is expressed by the key, yet undefined, phrases "lowly of spirit" *(shefal-ruah)* and "exceedingly base of spirit" *(ruho nemukho le-me'od)*.[3]

It is not my aim in this chapter to address these apparently contradictory principles advanced by Maimonides in very close proximity to each other, which have vexed scholars, both rabbinic and academic.[4] Rather, it is to determine what kind of exaggerated behavior these phrases convey and what dangers they are intended to combat.[5]

Maimonides did in fact define the parameters of this extraordinary humility, but chose to do so within the context of a distinct and concrete personality—namely, the king. This opportunity comes at the end of his legal code, in the tractate entitled *Laws of Kings and their Wars (Hilkhot Melakhim U-Milhemotehem)*, which is largely taken up with the prescribed conduct Israelite kings must follow. The nexus between his theoretical formulation of extreme humility at the beginning of his code and the specific political personage of the king at the code's end is formed by a shared terminology and a common biblical model. First, the assimilation of "lowliness" and the avoidance of an "elevated heart" are hallmarks of the king's rule. Second, Moses is presented as the archetype of uttermost humility, the model for both man in general and the king in particular. Finally, the conspicuous appearance of the phrase "lowly of spirit" elsewhere in Maimonides' code to capture economic dependence and political vulnerability is shown to direct the king to the very opposite end of the social spectrum in order to ascertain what ethical posture he must assume. These elements serve as pointers toward the concretization of Maimonides' extremist ethic in his halakhic construct of the king. The person who occupies the highest political office is that individual best suited to embody what, without him, would remain an ambiguous and largely abstract ideal. Occupying the most extreme limit of the social spectrum, the king is also most prone to whatever dangers pride poses. His administration of the royal office is limited by the ethical and philosophical dictates of humility, thereby offering a window into the distinction between its common *(anivut)* and extreme *(shefal-ruah)* manifestations.[6]

I aim to demonstrate that the Maimonidean monarch's definitive characteristics are aversion to pride and adoption of humility. On the one hand, the laws governing the throne legitimize the excesses of power normally associated with that institution. On the other hand, the king, who is informed by these laws, is also humility personified. Like the typical despot, the Maimonidean king's personage looms over every aspect of his subjects' lives. Its effect, however, is not intended to be that of crushing and overpowering concentrated power, but quite the reverse. The office is synonymous with power. The personality, though, is projected through the prism of extreme humility and lowliness.

Moses as Archetype of Kingship

The figure of the king is drawn into the main discussion of the ethics of humility by the identification of Moses as the existential model of a *shefal-ruach*. There is, for example, the description of Moses in Num 12:3 as being "very humble" *(anav me'od)*, rather than merely "humble" ("Now Moses was a very humble man, more so than any other man on the earth"). Moses, in addition to being a prophet and lawgiver,[7] was also identified by Maimonides elsewhere in his legal code as Israel's first official king (MT *Laws of the Temple* 6:11). The juridical context of this allusion to Moses as king[8] is critical for determining the limits the dictates of humility impose on absolute power. Moses' actions are here portrayed as the original halakhic model for all future Temple and municipal expansions related to the city of Jerusalem.[9] The rationale is rooted in the constraints imposed on the kind of absolute power usually associated with a monarch by the virtue of humility. There is a space acknowledged as "holy" within the king's domain, over which his supreme authority is curtailed. The borders of the Temple and Jerusalem cannot be tampered with lightly, since they occupy the uppermost limits of spatial holiness. Since other geographical spaces are less holy, any expansion of Jerusalem or the Temple would require an introduction of supplemental holiness. However, in the words of Maimonides, "the implementation of new holiness cannot be achieved without the supreme court" (PM *Sanhedrin* 1:5).

For halakhic purposes, the holiness that is immanent in the Temple and Jerusalem, unlike that in the rest of Israel, never lapses despite destruction and loss of sovereignty. This is so, stated Maimonides, because its holiness uniquely attaches "as a result of the divine indwelling *[shekhinah]* and the *shekhinah* never dissipates" (MT *Laws of the Temple* 6:16).[10] Though Maimonides adopted rabbinic categories, and reasoned accordingly in order to draw practical legal distinctions, "holiness" for him did not connote any sense of ontological otherworldliness. Once we consider the Maimonidean notion of holiness, it is evident that the single juridical identification of Moses as king is thoroughly suffused with the principle that the preeminent check on power is humility.

Holiness itself, for Maimonides, is a function of human conduct and not, as in anthropomorphically or mystically inclined currents in Judaism, of a tangible divine presence.[11] The sanctity of the Temple does not, and indeed could not for Maimonides, accrue as a result of God's having taken up residence in that location. Rather, its holiness and the strictly regulated entry to it are intended to instill a certain ethic. According to Maimonides' philosophical account in the *Guide,* previously discussed in chapter 3 regarding the study of the heretic, admission to the Temple's precinct is severely restricted so as to instill reverence for it. Most importantly, "fear will continue and an impression leading to the humility that was aimed at will be produced" (GP III:47, 594).[12] Any single-handed tampering with Temple sanctity would be incongruous with the very things the Temple's sanctity represents—namely, submission and humble servitude. All the rituals unique to the Temple, its utensils, and its services are geared, according to this account, toward neutralizing any illusions of self-importance, "for when one came there [the Temple] the soul was affected, so that hard hearts were softened and touched. For the deity . . . devised this gracious ruse in order that they be softened and become submissive when they came to the Temple, so that they accept God's guiding commands and fear Him" (GP III:45, 580).

The extraordinary requirement of consensus among all branches of government (legislative/sanhedrin; political/king; clerical/priest; prophet) prior to broadening the arena of holiness entails a public exercise of self-limitation by the king. The decision process mirrors its effect—the diffusion of holiness follows the diffusion of power. An independent executive decision by the king on this matter would amount to an exercise of power in a domain over which he has no jurisdiction. That very domain is designed to impress the virtue of humility on a national scale. Moses' self-limiting gesture with respect to this particular domain is consistent with its very telos. The fact that the assumption of humility is performed in his political capacity as king sets the standard of humility for all future monarchs, whose stature vis-à-vis the Temple is of a kind with their subjects.[13] In this instance, absolute power is shared to dispel any hint of motivations fueled by delusions of grandeur.[14]

The notion that the king's relationship to the Temple is, as initiated by Moses, grounded in humility is intensified in the Maimonidean scheme, once the reason that the construction of the Temple is solely a royal prerogative is taken into account. The *Guide* considers the construction of the Temple to be contingent on the appointment of a king as a practical measure in the restraint of human arrogance. It is necessary for the king to spearhead its construction in order to avoid power struggles. Should the precise location of the Temple have been disclosed prior to the establishment of a regent, violent conflict would have exploded among all the tribes and nations, attempting either to lay claim to it or to destroy its commanding prestige. Armed conflict is avoided by the king's development of the Temple Mount, since only he "would be qualified to give commands and quarrels would cease" (GP III:45, 576; MT *Laws of Kings* 1:1–2). The self-limitation that the king endures for the sake of widening the Temple's borders flows directly from his original link with constructing the Temple. The pairing of king and Temple signifies the containment of violence that would otherwise be unleashed by impulses of pride and arrogance.

Maimonides, in the course of his rationale for the king as Temple builder, cited an historical example of precisely the type of power struggle the king's mandate is meant to avoid. The king's involvement is instrumental in thwarting intratribal civil war and prevents the recurrence of sedition "such as happened with regard to the priesthood" (GP III:45, 576). This is an allusion to the biblical episode recounted in Num 16–17 of a mutiny by an Israelite noble, Korah, against the perceived unfair hegemony of Aaron and Moses in the desert. The exclusive hereditary claim by Aaron and his descendants to the priestly class was under attack by accusations of nepotism. The rebels' primary challenge to Moses and Aaron is an indictment of their alleged arrogance: "Why do you 'raise yourselves' [from the Hebrew root *nasa*] above the community of God!" (Num 16:3).

As noted previously, a large section of Maimonides' *Guide* is devoted to the explication of biblical terms that are problematic for their anthropomorphic applications to God. Throughout this lexicographical section, his method was to demonstrate that biblical language, and language in general, is equivocal and capable of different meanings in different contexts. One such term is "raise" *(nasa)*, and this very verse, Num 16:3, was cited to illustrate one of that term's equivocal, nonliteral meanings. In this context it bears the same meaning as it does elsewhere when referring to God: "elevation, exalted station, and great worth" (GP I:20, 47). Although Maimonides' primary aim with this proof-text was to dispel any theological anthropomorphisms, at the same time he afforded an analysis of the motivations fueling this rebellion. It concerned class and status, which revolved around the sense of inflated self-worth captured by the term *nasa*. By characterizing Korah's mutiny as the type of conflict that is suppressed when the king throws the power of his office behind the construction of the Temple, the ethical aspect of his role is deepened and overshadows any geopolitical motivations one might normally attribute to his actions.

Once Maimonides established the equivocality of a biblical term, his next step was invariably to cite verses in which the "offending" term appears in relation to God and to reread the verses in consonance with its appropriate sense. The case of the term *nasa* (raise) is no exception. What is particularly striking about the two verses chosen to illustrate the metaphorical sense of *nasa* when used as descriptive of God is that they are both set in the context of pride and humility manifested by God Himself. The first proof-text cited is Ps 94:2: "Rise [from the root *nasa*] up, judge of the earth." It is followed by the plea to "give the arrogant *[ge'im]* their deserts." In this verse, then, the "rising" of God is invoked as a remedy for arrogance. It reflects an ethical response, not self-exaltation. The second verse cited to corroborate the metaphorical sense of "raise" with respect to God is Isa 57:15: "Thus saith the High [He that is] borne on high." Once again, when read in their original biblical context, these words describe a God who, although *high* and exalted (root *nasa*), attends to the needs of the now familiar lowly in spirit (those who are *shefal-ruah*) by reviving them.[15] By alluding to the Korah rebellion, Maimonides mapped out a route whereby a parallel is ultimately drawn between the king and God.

The king, when erecting the Temple, is also performing a kind of *imitatio dei*. By doing so he first suppresses the "arrogant" *(ge'im)*, as God does in Ps 94:2. Once the construction is complete he needs to dispel any trace of self-grandeur that may accompany his reputation as Temple builder. That is accomplished by the continual projection of his own sense of "lowliness of spirit" *(shefal-ruah)*, in the preservation of the original perimeters of the Temple and the capital city. Both are symbols of power, and their circumscription is a reminder of the king's self-restraint in wielding his own power. To sum up:

Moses is the humblest man on earth.
Moses is referred to once in the Maimonidean corpus as a king.
That reference is in the context of self-limitations with respect to the Temple.
The royal prerogative to construct the Temple is intended to suppress arrogance.
The king–Temple nexus is a perpetual *imitatio dei* of divine humility.

Lowliness: An Existential Model for Majestic Humility

Since the notion of *imitatio dei* has been introduced, it is instructive at this point to determine what precisely this entails for Maimonides. Though he considered this a halakhic imperative and divine command (SM, Positive Commandment 8), in light of his negative theology, which denies the possibility of predicating any attributes of God,[16] what is there of God that man can in fact imitate? Maimonides effectively shifted the attempt to establish God's attributes from His essence to His actions. Whenever God is said to possess some moral quality such as kindness or compassion, what such a statement really amounts to is that a natural phenomenon has been observed that would, in the sphere of human actions, flow from some such quality. The meaning of such statements about God, however, "is not that He possesses moral qualities, but that He performs actions resembling the actions that in us proceed from moral qualities" (GP I:54, 124). Men normally exhibit moral behavior emotively, whereas God's actions strictly accord with what reason dictates to be appropriate.

Genuine *imitatio dei,* then, is, as Herbert Davidson has so ably argued, to act morally but dispassionately.[17] Moral virtue, for Maimonides, does not inhere in actions but rather in internal psychological traits. Such psychological virtue is particularly demanded of politicians and rulers and is, therefore, critical for our understanding of ideal monarchic governance. The ruler governs virtuously by approximating God's governance,

> so that these actions may proceed from him according to a determined measure and according to the deserts of the people who are affected by them and not merely because of his following a passion. . . . Sometimes with regard to some people, he should be *merciful and gracious,* not out of mere compassion and pity but in accordance with what is fitting. Sometimes, with regard to some people, he should be *keeping anger and jealous and avenging* in accordance with their deserts, not out of mere anger. (GP I:54, 126; emphasis mine)

The previous reference to Isa 57:15, "Thus saith the High, borne on high . . . with the lofty and holy ones I dwell and with the crushed and lowly of spirit *[shefal-ruah]* to revive the spirit of the lowly," is critical for its identification of a class of people who are halakhically defined as "lowly of spirit," a condition already seen to have been held out as the extreme ideal of humility. They are predominantly those who occupy the polar opposite of the social hierarchy in relation to the king—orphans, widows, converts (MT *Laws of Ethical Traits* 6:10; *Laws of the Megillah* 2:17), the impoverished (ibid.; *Laws of Gifts to the Poor* 10:5), and slaves (*Laws of Slaves* 1:7, 8:11). The verse appears as a proof-text for the proposition that treating members of this class with the utmost sensitivity to their needs qualifies as *imitatio dei,* "for whoever gladdens the hearts of these unfortunates is likened to the divine indwelling *[domeh le-shekhinah]* as it says 'to revive the lowly of spirit and revitalize the hearts of the downtrodden [Isa 57:15].'" The laws governing gifts for the poor also cite this verse as setting a divine standard of care for those who are destitute (MT *Laws of Gifts to the Poor* 10:5).[18]

The features shared by all those who need to be compensated for are their vulnerability and powerlessness. Orphans and widows are deprived of their source of support. The destitute cannot support themselves. Converts have abandoned their native religion and their society in favor of one in which they have no family ties, in effect orphaning themselves.[19] Slaves are chattels and exposed to the whims of their masters. Common among all such persons is their utter dependency on the magnanimity of others. The fact that these classes are all characterized by the expression "lowly of spirit" *(shefal-ruah)* allows us to focus on precisely what state of being this term captures—that of loss of autonomy and total reliance on others higher up in the social structure. A system that encourages a social hierarchy whose class divisions are maintained by ensuring that the lowly are constantly reminded of their status by the self-assertions of those higher up is not only behaviorally corrupt; worse still, it has dire philosophical consequences. Because it promotes dependence of the weak on the whims of the powerful, it fosters an arrogance that judges men to be merely either controlling or controlled. God is edged out, fostering an anthropocentric view of the world for both the oppressed and the oppressor. When the downtrodden look up and the tyrant looks down it is only man, and not God, who they perceive as ultimately in control of the world.[20]

This view is an outgrowth of the one that holds man to be the ultimate telos of the universe, a view emphatically rejected by Maimonides as leading to all kinds of confusion regarding the nature of the world, the nature of God, and God's governance of the world. In Maimonides' words: "It should not be believed that all the beings exist for the sake of the existence of man. On the contrary, all other beings too have been intended for their own sakes and not for the sake of something else" (GP III:13, 452). If everything is judged with reference to man, then God's omnipotence is undermined (GP III:12, 446). Man's inflated sense of self-worth and prominence in the hierarchy of being is a primary cause of philosophical confusion about God and His relationship to the world; this confusion could be avoided "if man considered and represented to himself that which exists and knew the smallness of his part in it" (ibid., 442). That is why the highest level of charity, according to Maimonides, consists of all efforts toward achieving a state of self-subsistence for desperate individuals, to the point where there is no longer any need for a "charitable" relationship—in Maimonides' words, "in order to strengthen his hand so that he will not be dependent on others and will no longer need to beg" (MT *Laws of Gifts* to the Poor 10:7).²¹ The notion that relationships with the powerless are informed by the dangers of anthropocentrism is reinforced by the concluding verse of Maimonides' laws of charity (ibid., 10:19), "'Blessed is the man that trusts in God'"(Jer 17:7).

The practice of self-abasement (becoming *shefal-ruah*) that is mandated by Maimonides as the ideal form of humility consists of replacing a human sense of autonomy with that of dependence. Once the ego is displaced, there is clarity regarding man's and the world's dependence on God. Those who have internally assimilated that trait gain no advantage over those who materially personify *shefal-ruah* because there has been an equalization of class. Benevolence toward the needy that aspires to "gladdening" them constitutes the rarified form of *imitatio dei* expressed as "likened to the Indwelling" *(domeh le-shekhinah)*. For Maimonides, just as "holiness" does not pertain to ontology, so God's Indwelling *(shekhinah)* is not the hypostasized presence of the mystical tradition. It is a notional referent to God's relationship with the world that draws on the figurative meaning of *shakhon*, dwell, another term dealt with in Maimonides' lexicography as "everything that is permanent and is attached to another thing" (GP I:25, 55).²² It thereby connotes "the permanence of providence with regard to a certain matter" (ibid.). As stated previously, divine governance, which translates into actions normally considered as kind or compassionate, actually "proceeds from Him, may He be exalted, in reference to His holy ones, not because of a passion or a change" (GP I:54, 125). God acts *dispassionately*, and it is for that very reason that His providence is "permanently attached." There is nothing that can affect Him to cause any change in His governance. The type of care for the less fortunate that microcosmically reflects this cosmic relationship is the kind that "gladdens" them because it is not tenuous or capricious. The phrase "likened to the Indwelling" *(domeh le-shekhinah)* already anticipates in the *Mishneh Torah* what Davidson has convincingly argued is the more cogently developed ethical theory of the *Guide*, which "directs the perfect man to crown his knowledge of God with dispassionate behavior in areas affecting others."²³

The only other use of the expression "likened to the Indwelling" in the *Mishneh Torah* corroborates this interpretation by its linkage with the ascetic behavior typical of the *hasid*—with respect to the trait of humility, the one who veers away from the mean to the extreme of lowliness *(shefal-ruah)* (MT *Laws of Ethical Traits* 1:5). Such asceticism leads to a holiness *(qeddushah)* of the soul, removed from bad character traits, and holiness of the soul causes one to be likened to the Indwelling *(le-hiddamot be-shekhinah)* (MT *Laws of Food Defilement* 16:12).[24] The only holiness that can resemble God's is one that is attained by way of the suppression of all corporeal desires, impulses, and emotions so that a constant pattern of ideal conduct ensues. Here again Moses provides the archetype of holiness, as one who disengaged himself from the world of desire to the extent that "his mind became fixated on the Rock of the world . . . and he became holy like the angels" (MT *Laws of the Foundations of the Torah* 7:6).[25] Moses disavows any attraction to the material beyond basic necessities, thus reducing himself to the state of lowliness of the "unfortunates."[26] This induces a state of dependency, but, since it is driven by the intellect, it is angelic in nature. "Angel" is another equivocal term dealt with by Maimonides in his *Guide,* whose meaning in this context is "separate intellect." The very term for angel, *mal'akh* (messenger), connotes absolute subservience; that is, "everyone who carries out an order is called an angel" (GP II:6, 262) They also "always do that which is good, and only that which is good with them" (GP II:7, 266). Analogously, Moses achieves a supreme angel-like dependency on God[27] through the practice of extreme humility, which has as a physical model the class of people that occupies the lowest end of the social spectrum. Moses cannot act any other way because he has internalized moral virtues.

Apart from the Mosaic paradigm of extreme humility, Maimonides' non-halakhic discussion of the virtues of charity once again imports the monarch into the context of the term "lowly of spirit" *(shefal-ruah).* Charity requires more punctilious attention and care "than any other positive commandment" because "the throne of Israel *[kisse yisrael]* will never be established nor will the true religion *[dat ha-emet]* be sustained except by way of charity . . . and Israel will never be redeemed *[nigalin]* except through the merit of charity" (MT *Laws of Gifts to the Poor* 10:1). Maimonides in essence tied the realization of the messianic period to the performance of the law most involved with remedying the human condition of the lowly of spirit. The benefits that flow from the fulfillment of this command are formulated in monarchic terminology. All biblical instances of the term "throne of Israel" refer to political kingship.[28] The expression "true religion" is almost exclusively linked by Maimonides to the king's mandate in universally promoting its principles (MT *Laws of the Hagigah Sacrifice* 3:1, 6; *Laws of Kings* 4:10, 12:1; *Laws of Leavened and Unleavened*

Bread 7:4).²⁹ Redemption is, of course, associated with the messianic period, when the monarchy and its political sovereignty over Israel will be restored (MT end of *Laws of Kings*).³⁰ The ultimate reward for the proper performance of charity is couched in monarchic imagery because, as shown below, the king's reign is assessed by his ability to command fear and respect while at the same time projecting a personal image of extreme humility *(shefal-ruah)*. It is most appropriate, then, that the ethical act of redressing the malady of *shefal-ruah* caused by material impoverishment should result in a redemption that is effected by one who has an abundance of wealth and power and yet has assimilated the character trait of *shefal-ruah* into his very being.³¹ The king is a symbol of a freely chosen internalization of self-effacement that is so strikingly at odds with his physical environment that it clearly reflects his liberation from it. His extreme humility, then, can only be interpreted as a manifestation of a purely abstract dependency on something that transcends the material. He is the mirror image of the "unfortunates" who must be liberated from their material dependency by way of the largess of halakhically prescribed rules of charity.

Torah and the Constriction of the Royal Heart

I now turn to Maimonides' specific formulations of laws governing the king that are critical for his achieving the psychological self-extirpation required by "lowliness of spirit." The king is appointed only by the joint decision of a court comprised of seventy elders and a prophet (MT *Laws of Kings* 1:3). His authority therefore derives from a combination of both law *(praxis)* and theory *(theoria)*. In other words, he is a living reminder that true governance takes into consideration both "welfare of the body and welfare of the soul" (GP III:27). The continuing restriction on his authority noted previously, which also requires a joint decision of prophet, court, and king with respect to the expansion of holiness in Jerusalem, echoes this original source of his claim to the throne and is a constant reminder of it.³² Though historically there was a division of powers between the king and other bodies of government (priest, prophet, court), the king's image, by virtue of both this continuing restriction and his origins, is permeated by that of the pristine king who was an amalgamation of the theoretical and the practical—Moses.³³

In light of this, we can better appreciate Maimonides' resolution of the dichotomy between what seems to be an unequivocal commandment to appoint a king in Deut 17:15 and God's later displeasure with the people's request of Samuel to do so, as recounted in 1 Sam 8. According to Maimonides, it was not the request per se but its manner and motivation that were troubling, "for they asked in a challenging manner, not in order to fulfill a commandment but because they rejected Samuel the prophet, as it says 'for it is not you that they have despised but me they have despised [1 Sam 8:7]'" (MT *Laws of Kings* 1:2).³⁴ The issue was not their personal rejection of Samuel but rather the rupture they introduced between prophecy and kingship. The grounding of the king's coronation in a prophetic prerogative informed his reign throughout with the *theoria* the prophet represented. The people wanted a monarchy that was divorced from the prophetic.³⁵

The king is considered a personal embodiment of the national ethos, "for his heart is the heart of the entire congregation of Israel *[q'hal yisrael]*" (MT *Laws of Kings* 3:6). Because of this unique identity between the monarch and his constituency, he is obligated to "attach himself to the Torah to a greater degree than the rest of the nation as it says 'all the days of his life [Deut 17:19]'" (MT *Laws of Kings* 3:6). The heart, which is the seat of the arrogance most closely associated with haughtiness (MT *Laws of Ethical Traits* 1:1, 2:2), must be confined as much as possible, so that it can be as expansive as possible in its capacity as the people's representative. The requisite attachment to Torah for sustaining this vital intimacy between the people and their king entails his perpetual engagement with Torah throughout his tenure as king. The public expression of this kingly bond to the Torah is the mandatory writing of a Torah scroll that surpasses the common obligation of every Jew to do so; this scroll accompanies his person at all times, even when he is carrying out his royal prerogatives. It must literally "never leave his presence" (MT *Laws of Kings* 3:1; *Laws of Phylacteries, Mezuzah and Torah Scrolls* 7:2).³⁶

The reading of the Torah "all the days of his life," which signifies his relentless dedication to it, appears in the *Mishneh Torah* as a prophylactic stricture against alcoholic and sexual indulgence (MT *Laws of Kings* 3:5, 6).³⁷ For Maimonides, abstinence on both these counts is singled out as constituting holiness *(qeddushah)*: "*qeddushah* consists in renouncing sexual intercourse, just as He also states explicitly that the giving up of the drinking of wine constitutes *qeddushah*" (GP III:33, 533).³⁸ The presence of this royal Torah thus reflects a holiness that is a function of the extreme rather than the golden mean, since it is associated with the utmost suppression of human desire. By minimizing his own natural appetites, the king maximizes his focus on others. His own "heart" is replaced with the "heart" of the "congregation of Israel." The dependency of the people on the king is enhanced by his obsessive concern for them. The theological danger, however, that dependency on man fuels anthropocentrism is checked by a royal asceticism signified by the holiness of the designated Torah—a holiness that we have seen is God-dependent.[39]

In the *Guide,* profligacy in matters relating to sex, alcohol, and food is the most explicit reflection of a weltanschauung that grants primacy to the body over the mind. If bodily concerns are paramount, then "cares and sorrows multiply, mutual envy, hatred, and strife aiming at taking away what the other has, multiply" (GP III:33, 532). The result of such behavior is the exact converse of what charity demands—providing the other with what he has not. It follows, then, that the proper exercise of charity entails the reverse of indulgence, or abstinence. In matters of sex, alcohol, and food, the *Guide* generally favors a near-monastic attitude. The king complies so as to project an image of selflessness whose sole concern is the other—his royal subjects.

The additional Torah, which signifies the curtailment of physical desire, is also associated with the same symbols that we have seen to place restraints on the king's power so that it is not perceived as unbridled. This Torah must be "copied from the book of the courtyard *[sefer ha-azarah]*[40] under the guidance of a court of seventy-one" (MT *Laws of Kings* 3:1).[41] The Temple courtyard, which we have seen cannot be legitimately enlarged single-handedly, defies the arbitrary power of the king. The supreme judicial body is a source of the king's claim to the throne. This extra Torah scroll is thus charged with symbols that preclude the king from being viewed as the ultimate source of power and sustenance by the people. It marks him as ultimately dependent, not just on God, but on other earthly organs of authority.

Another representative effect of the "additional Torah" arises, not merely as a result of its continuous accompaniment, but from the activity it commands. The part of the verse that is stressed repeatedly by Maimonides is not "and it shall be with him" but "and he shall read therein all the days of his life," which is analogous to the general command to study Torah based on the verse "and you shall contemplate therein day and night" (Josh

1:8). The latter directive is universally applicable "whether poor or rich, healthy or disabled, young or elderly and infirm, *even a poor person reduced to begging*" (MT *Laws of Studying Torah* 1:8; emphasis mine). The study of Torah is an equalizing factor, by which the king is incorporated as simply another member of the larger body politic.[42] Of the three crowns with which Israel has, in the rabbinic tradition, been exclusively coronated, the "crown of kingship" can be bestowed only on those of an exclusive pedigree, whereas the "crown of Torah" is "set in place available to everybody . . . anyone who is willing can come and acquire it" (MT *Laws of Studying Torah* 3:1).[43] This all-encompassing entitlement to the "crown of Torah" sweeps across the entire social spectrum, eliminating any divisions set up by economic or physical disadvantage. In this domain there are no classes determined by dependency. The presence of the royal Torah reverses the direction of royal ascendance downward to a domain where the king shares the same space as his people.

As noted previously, those among the populace who are independent must themselves assimilate an internal sense of dependency *(shefal-ruah)* so that no parallel sense of dependency is evoked in others. The study of Torah *(talmud torah)* is one of those commandments *(mitzvot)* the ideal fulfillment of which is contingent on internalizing just such an extreme of humility: "it does not exist among the haughty *[gase ruah]* or in the heart of those who have elevated hearts but only in him who is downtrodden and lowly in spirit *[shefal-ruah]*" (MT *Laws of Studying Torah* 3:9). The king's enhanced attachment to the Torah, signified by the royal Torah and his engagement with it "all the days of his life," has as a direct consequence the melding of his heart with the heart of the congregation of Israel, because the very manner in which the study of Torah must be carried out renders it the most appropriate vehicle for achieving that state of identity. Lowliness of spirit *(shefal-ruah)* is the deelevation of an "elevated heart," necessary for all hearts to operate on the same plane of existence.[44]

The empathetic relationship between the king and his people captured by the all-encompassing heart of the king also acts to preserve the clear bifurcation between office and person intended by the laws governing the extraordinary respect due to the monarch. These laws reflect the dangers inherent in the blurring of lines that divide the king's public persona from his private one. Though the general rule denies the king any authority to forgo the supreme respect his public position demands (MT *Laws of Kings* 2:5),[45] privacy demands common norms of respect from the king. The dissonance between private and public standards of kingly conduct is particularly stark when the king is in the presence of scholars or sages. Privately he must acknowledge his subservience to them; publicly he is forbidden from doing so, as this may undermine the fear his position must impose so that it can properly function, "in order that the fear of him be in the heart of all" (ibid., 2:5).[46] The inherent danger of an inflated royal ego resulting from the king's fearsome presence must be checked by an internal sense of extreme humility. Striking fear into the heart of all must be balanced by his heart's assuming internally a lowly and "pierced" state. Psalm 109:22 is cited in support of this psychological imperative: "and my heart is pierced within me" (MT *Laws of Kings* 2:6).[47] The first colon of that verse locates this kind of heart in the "poor and needy." Appropriately, a verse is chosen that offers the epitome of human lowliness as the standard the king must emulate in order to neutralize his self-importance. The external trappings of ultimate control are psychologically displaced by an internal sense of ultimate dependence and reliance.[48] Once again, perfect governance is characterized by an internalization of virtue.

Following the directive for self-diminution, the king is enjoined to be gracious and merciful *(honen u-merahem)* toward all his subjects, particularly those who are most vulnerable, to the extent that "he must preserve the dignity of the smallest of the small" (MT *Laws of Kings* 2:6). Such royal benevolence, however, is in fact a natural consequence of the cultivation of a lowly heart. Grace and mercy are the quintessential character traits that must be assimilated in the performance of halakhic *imitatio dei*, as dictated by the midrashic explication of the command to "walk in His ways" (Deut 28:9): "Just as He is called gracious, so you be gracious; just as He is called merciful so you be merciful" (MT *Laws of Ethical Traits* 1:6).[49] The king's ethical mandate is couched in the original language of *imitatio dei*, which, as noted previously, consists of the achievement of a mode of being whereby one acts ethically in a dispassionate manner. The extreme humility prescribed by Ps 109:22 is the means by which this is accomplished. Once he has assimilated this inner state of selflessness, the king's rule will resemble God's, which operates "according to the deserts of the people who are affected by them and not merely because of his following a passion" (GP I:54, 126). The mercy and grace he exhibits will be consistent with the God-like governance advocated by the *Guide*. These traits are to emanate "not out of mere compassion and pity, but in accordance with what is fitting" (ibid.). In addition to his obvious political role, the king is thus also a theological paragon in two senses. His lowliness tempers the imperial/subservient dynamic between him and the people that is a political function of his office, with the sense of dependence necessary to quell anthropocentrism. As a result, his governance mirrors divine dispassionate governance, thereby providing a practical model of *imitatio dei*.

Biblical Images of Humility: A Monarch's Manual

Moses and Manna

Maimonides presented a number of images that should be projected by the king when carrying out his official duties. Each image is drawn from a biblical precedent pertaining to some regal personality, and each challenges images of domination and subjugation commonly associated with the figure of the king. The king is advised to variously assume the demeanors of "brother," "servant," "nursemaid," and "shepherd," all of which emerge from the adoption of extreme humility. David and Moses are the subjects of these biblical precedents, where David is the biblical progenitor of the divinely elected Israelite royal line and Moses is, from the rabbinic perspective, the first king. I argue that the scriptural proof-texts advancing each of these humility types were chosen by Maimonides with, to borrow an expression from the *Guide* (Intro., 15), "great exactness and exceeding precision,"[50] in order to address the ethical and philosophical dangers the figure of the king poses for the public.

Just as he was the example of a life of extreme humility in *Laws of Ethical Traits,* Moses is presented as the example par excellence of the kind of humility that should be adopted by the monarch. Here, however, the biblical proof-text is different. For the general rule of extreme humility, Num 12:3, characterizing Moses as "very humble," was the text of choice. For the monarch's humility, the text chosen is Exod 16:8, which relates Moses' response to the complaints of the Israelites in the desert as to their lack of food and their foreboding of death by starvation. It is Moses' acerbic rebuke "what are we *[ve-anahnu mah]*, your complaints are not against us" that is cited as the Mosaic emblem of "exceeding humility" for the king to follow. Having been deprived of the basic necessities of life in the desert, the people look to Moses for their sustenance.

Their relationship with him is expressed, through their complaints, in terms of the destitute in need of a provider. It is precisely this situation that is most prone to the theological/philosophical error that dependence provokes, particularly when that dependence is concentrated on a solitary figure who wields ultimate human power. Exodus 16:8, then, is chosen for its capacity to address both the practical and the theoretical ethical concerns of the predicament that confronted Moses and that will inevitably confront all future kings. The self-effacing expression "what are we" *(ve-anahnu mah)* already appears in the preceding verse (Exod 16:7), but captures only the practical ethics of humility. Verse 8, however, concludes with an admonition that the people's complaints are, in the final analysis, against God. It therefore redresses the philosophical misconceptions of anthropocentrism that absolute dependence promotes, by shifting the focus away from Moses the man to God.[51]

Exodus 16:8 is also carefully selected for the significance of the response elicited from God by the people's complaints. That response comes in the form of manna from heaven. Once again we see Maimonides, the great demythologizer of biblical and rabbinic myth, at work. The mythical dimension of the miraculous food in the desert, manna from heaven, is replaced with a philosophical one. The *Guide*'s analysis of manna's philosophical import renders it an apt referent for majestic humility. First, it conveys the teaching "that those who wholly devote themselves to His service, may He be exalted, are provided by Him with food in an unthought-of-way" (GP III:24, 499). The king's sense of self-importance would thus be curbed by the acknowledgment that he, as provider, is supplanted by a higher provider; that the nourishment he supplies is superseded by another kind of food; and that a power transcending his own commands utter devotion. The allusion to manna directs the king's and the population's gaze elsewhere, to the true source of their sustenance. Second, the *Guide*'s analysis invokes the principal aim of charity: the elevation of those on the receiving end from their state of lowliness *(shefal-ruah)*, by way of nullifying any causes of class distinctions that engender feelings of inferiority or superiority.

Discrepancies between individuals of the same species arise, as Maimonides put it, only accidentally and not essentially, and therefore "there in no way exists a relation of superiority and inferiority between individuals conforming to the course of nature except that which follows necessarily from the difference in the disposition of the various kinds of matter" (GP III:12, 447). The manner of the collection of the manna, which resulted in a kind of miraculous equalized distribution among the people regardless of how much was actually recovered, suggests this principle: "And he that gathered much had nothing over, and he that gathered little had no lack; they gathered every man according to his eating" (Exod 16:18). This, according to Maimonides, vitiates the false conception that true imbalance is a function of material gain or lack: "He who has obtained these luxuries has not gained thereby an increment in his substance, he has only obtained a false imagining or a plaything. And he who lacks the superfluities of life is not necessarily deficient" (GP III:12, 447).

In fact, the *Guide* offers the king as the prime example of the most defective of perfections that are extant in man. Because the relationship between a man and his possessions is external and does not form part of his essence, it cannot be a measure of what distinguishes one individual from another; therefore, "when the relation referred to has been abolished, there is no difference between an individual who has been a great king and the most contemptible of men, though nothing may have changed in any of the things that may have been attributed to him" (GP III:54, 634).[52] Lowliness of class can only result if there is no awareness of this principle. Cognition of the essential equality of all individuals in a species precludes differentiation based on economics or politics.[53] Exodus 16:8 speaks particularly to the king's standard of humility by raising the philosophical connotations of manna. There are no destitute or wealthy in the world conjured up by the symbol of manna. The human form (image of God) shared by all individuals of the human species places them all on a level playing field in terms of their common human activity (intellectual) and common telos (the knowing of God).[54]

Nursemaid

It is fitting that the other image cited from the account of Moses' leadership in the desert also relates to the manna. In this instance, however, there is a rejection of the manna by the people. The king is admonished to "tolerate their troubles, burdens, complaints, and anger 'as a nurse carries an infant.'" The nursemaid image is culled from Num 11:12, where Moses' indignant description of himself in response to the people's contempt for the manna reveals a frustration with the onerous responsibility he has been delegated. By his appropriation of this image, Moses argues that he should not be expected to play the role of nursemaid, since he has not "conceived" or "given birth" to the nation. God accommodates Moses' rhetorical protestations against the assumption of unassisted political leadership with a diffusion of power among seventy elders (Num 11:16). This power distribution is accomplished through the drawing of "spirit" from Moses that is then bestowed on the group of seventy, resulting in wide delegation of national authority. To fully grasp the significance of the nursemaid exemplar for the king, one must see that its biblical context is also the source for the establishment of a quorum of seventy-one on the Israelite supreme court known as the Sanhedrin (MT *Laws of the Sanhedrin* 1:3, 6; *b. Sanhedrin* 16b). Admonishing the king to adopt this model thus reminds him that his regime is not an autocratic one. Moses was right in one sense and wrong in another. The dangers of an autocracy are the kinds of anthropocentric conclusions that can ensue and that are captured in the ideas of "conceiving" and "giving birth" to the nation. The presence of other institutions such as judicial bodies is needed to dispel any such misconceptions. On the other hand, the ethical posture that the nursemaid image engenders is endorsed in order to foster an internal sense of humility in the king.

The nursemaid model is one that the king in fact shares with anyone who occupies a position of authority. Elsewhere in Maimonides' code, those in authority are exhorted to "tolerate the troubles of the community and their burdens just like Moses our master of whom it is written, 'just as a nurse carries an infant'" (MT *Laws of the Sanhedrin* 25:2). Maimonides emphasized the same model in particular for the judiciary, who are adjured to "tolerate the community 'just as a nurse carries an infant'" (ibid.). The shared nursemaid ideal induces both the king and the judiciary to look to each other as a constant check on their supremacy when administering their respective functions. It also induces them to look back toward the Mosaic inception of the ideal: a rejection by Moses of totalitarian governance; a dispersion and sharing of power; and a diffusion of power that is clearly generated by God.[55]

Once again, a state of lowliness is an instrumental motivation for nurse-like tolerance. Those who wield power may be tempted to assert that power without regard for those who are subordinate to them because of their lower social status. Nonetheless, "although they are plebeian and lowly *[shefalim]*, they are the children of Abraham, Isaac, and Jacob and the hosts of God who liberated them from Egypt with great power *[koah gadol]* and a strong hand" (ibid.). Their lowliness is neutralized by common national origins (when all were relegated to serfdom)[56] and the acknowledgment of where real power *(koah)* is ultimately located. Both the king and the members of the court become historically and theologically submerged into the lowliness of their constituents. Elsewhere Maimonides considered the supreme court (Sanhedrin) to be the embodiment of "the assembly of Israel in its entirety," thereby expressing the national will in its decisions (PM *Horayot* 1:6).[57] Prompting the king to reflect on the Sanhedrin therefore promotes an equalization of classes because it is, in effect, another concrete instance of the identity between the governed and the governor. The model serves as a prototype for the requisite merging of hearts between the king and the people that we have noted previously.

Brother

Another model for royal humility is the "brotherhood" said to exist between the king and the people, a relationship that David proclaims in his parting speech when addressing the people as "my brothers and my nation" (1 Chr 28:2). He then offers a rationalization for not having built a Temple for God during his tenure as king, and entrusts its construction to his son and successor, Solomon. For Maimonides, this gesture of humility also pertains to the philosophical problems raised by the absence of a Temple during David's reign. The Temple is a spatial focal point whose raison d'être is the effacement of idolatrous notions of God and the establishment of "the existence and oneness of the deity" in its place (GP III:32, 526–27). Further, as discussed above, the royal prerogative to construct the Temple was itself an act of *imitatio dei,* in its quelling of the grand desires of those who would lay claim by violence to the Temple Mount to boost their own stature. Sharing space with the Temple also reflected the king's lowliness of spirit *(shefal-ruah)*. In considering the anthropomorphically problematic term "throne" *(kisse),* the *Guide* traces the evolution of this term from its meaning as a literal throne to a metaphorical one of rank, by way of its association with people of "great authority such as kings" (GP I:9, 34). Greatness and sublimity, therefore, are what is intended by the term whenever it refers to God.

"Throne," then, is a term that, though sharing a common notion of "rank," marks a clear divide between a king and God. The Sanctuary is called a throne in the Bible "because of its indicating the grandeur of

Him who manifested Himself therein" and is a place "singled out to receive His light and splendor" (ibid.). The reference to David's courteous salutation is not endorsed merely for its etiquette but for its contextual implications. The Temple is the throne of God. The throne of the king is a concrete metaphor for that being which occupies the highest rank in existence. Without the actual physical Temple, the king's throne is apt to be wrongly perceived as the seat of the highest authority. David's speech, in its explanation of the missing Temple, provides both the ethical and the philosophical precedents out of which the king must fashion his own image of humility.

Slave

The next verse cited by Maimonides encourages the king to assume the posture of a "slave" vis-à-vis his subjects. The context is the advice offered to king Rehavam, the son and successor to Solomon, by his council of elders as to how to manage the royal office. Instead of an iron-fisted approach, they urge him to be sensitive to the people's needs: "and if today you will be a slave *[eved]* to this people and serve them and respond to them and speak with them good words then they will be forever your slaves" (1 Kgs 12:7).[58] The slave model once again directs the king toward the adoption of lowliness when asserting his power over the people. In his codification of the laws of slavery, Maimonides offered a novel rationale for the law, not found in its original rabbinic source.[59] A master must not treat a Hebrew slave *(eved ivri)* as a slave but rather as a hired laborer. The traumatic effects of being sold as chattel are demeaning "because his soul has been lowered *[nafsho shefelah]* as a result of the sale" (MT *Laws of Slaves* 1:7).

The contrast to the much harsher treatment permitted by Maimonides in the case of a laborer who has not been purchased is most instructive in determining precisely what it is that constitutes this feeling of despair captured by the phrase "lowliness of soul." Imposing slave-like demands on the laborer is sanctioned "because he performs this work of his own free will and knowledge" (ibid.). Lowliness, then, is a consequence of the total loss of autonomy and of the ability to control one's destiny, and the inevitable sense of utter dependence on others. The adverse theological implications of surrender to the total control of others are neutralized by regulations that prohibit capitalizing on the profound lowliness of the slave. By projecting his own sense of enslavement to the people, the king promotes their experience of autonomy and inhibits the anthropocentrism that would be fostered if he were viewed as an autocrat.[60]

Shepherd

Finally, the humility of a shepherd is also held out as a role model for the king. Two verses support the particular affinity between shepherd and king. One demonstrates how the Bible in fact deems the king a shepherd, and the other defines what kind of conduct is to be expected by assuming the role of a shepherd. The former is a pastoral metaphor for the divine election of David to the throne, "to shepherd Jacob, His people" (Ps 78:71). Since this excerpted part of the verse is preceded in its biblical setting by (vv. 70–71) "And He chose David His servant and He took him from the sheepfolds, from following ewes *(alot)*. He brought him," Maimonides' proof-text draws the analogy between the founder, and thereby the paragon, of the Hebrew monarchy, and the shepherd.[61] The verse accentuates the source of David's (and therefore the monarch's) authority by a threefold repetition of his investiture by God: He "chose," He "took," and He "brought."[62] The king's subordinate status is conveyed by the references to his servitude to God (His "servant") and to his common origins ("sheepfolds"). The king's proprietorship over the people is denied by the acknowledgment of where ownership actually resides: "Jacob, His people" followed by "Israel, His patrimony."[63] Shepherding, according to Maimonides, has been the historical occupation of Israel from its inception, "all of us being shepherds from fathers and grandfathers" (GP III:39, 552). A metaphor and a verse were deliberately selected to convey a sameness between king and people, which transposes their immediate political context of sovereign/subject into a theological one.[64]

Conduct that is emblematic of the shepherd is "explicated in the tradition" and can be determined by the final of the series of verses encouraging royal humility cited at the end of chapter 2 of MT *Laws of Kings:* "Like a shepherd he shepherds his flock, he gathers lambs with his arm and carries them in his lap, he leads the ewes *[a lot]*" (Isa 40:11). This prooftext is critical because it is a metaphorical representation of God. Maimonides has seamlessly moved from a Davidic reference to a Godly one, thereby constructing a divine standard of humility that the king must emulate. The gist of divine shepherding is extraordinary care for the weakest part of the flock—the ewes and lambs—conveyed by a threefold repetition of the tending they warrant: "gathering," "carrying," and "leading." The shepherd simile articulates in pastoral imagery the extreme humility that we have seen to be mandatory behavior toward the lowly of spirit. The king is judged by the extent to which he is able to manifest this behavior, which in turn is a reflection of a prominent trope of God as shepherd.[65] The evocation of this image by the king's conduct prompts his subjects to follow the routes mapped out by the shepherd proof-texts that originate in God (He "chose," "took," "brought"), and leads back to the same source by its conception as a form of *imitatio dei*.[66]

Imperial Humility: An Existential Model of *Imitatio Dei*

In his adoption of the Maimonidean guidelines for extreme humility, the king, in addition to constraining his own natural inclinations toward aggrandizement, acts as the existential model par excellence for *imitatio dei*. Imperial governance, when filtered through the prism of Maimonidean humility, results in a regime that most closely resembles a divine one. Here, once again, the precedent of Moses is most instructive, especially in light of what he is said by Maimonides to discover at the very apex of human enlightenment. Though Moses' request for a vision of divine glory *(kavod)* is denied (Exod 33:18), his appeal to be shown divine "way" *(derekh)* is granted (Exod 33:13). Maimonides' distinction between the natures of these two requests is critical for our appreciation of the king's administration. The former, "apprehension of His essence," lies beyond human attainment, while the latter "way" consists of "pure attributes of action" (GP I:54, 124).[67] What is revealed to Moses is the manner in which God governs the world. That governance does not proceed from "moral qualities" or "aptitudes of the soul"; rather, "He performs actions resembling the actions that in us proceed from moral qualities" (ibid.).[68] All those actions we normally ascribe to passions—such as mercy, grace, jealousy, and anger—are all precisely and objectively calibrated "in accordance with what is fitting" (ibid., 126). Though Moses may have acted appropriately up until this point, his behavior may not have qualified as *imitatio dei,* since it might have been passionate behavior. From the moment God's way is revealed, the king's governance is more likely to be modeled on God's, and he will act "as it behooves a governor of a city . . .

so that these actions may proceed from him according to the deserts of the people who are affected by them and not merely because of his following a passion" (ibid.).[69]

Moses, in effect, perfects his monarchy and, at the same time, becomes the exemplar of that which Maimonides termed *de'ot,* or an ethics based on *imitatio dei.* This may account for the very word *de'ot,* coined by Maimonides in his legal compendium as a term of art for ethical traits. The traits Maimonides sought to be assimilated are those revealed to Moses as a result of his request in Exod 33:13 "let me know *[hodi'eni]* Your ways that I may know You." The term he used to characterize the laws of moral virtues is quite strategically one that is based on the same root as the term "to know." We now know why. Moral virtue is associated with the internal psyche, not with the external act. Ethical traits that truly emulate God's attributes of action constitute the knowledge granted to Moses in response to his entreaty to know. Passionless activity can only arise when there is no self to be impassioned, and that is the function of the self-effacement demanded by extreme humility. By tempering his governance with humility the king in some way fashions his administration along the lines of Moses and the Patriarchs, whose focus was solely on God, even as they "engaged in increasing their fortune . . . while they tended their cattle, did agricultural work, and governed their household" (GP III:51, 624).[70] All these activities that are normally perceived as motivated by self-interest are transformed into disinterested acts calculated to galvanize "a religious community that would know and worship God" (ibid.). When his subjects observe him, the king is seen to be a beacon of ethics that are intellectually grounded and God-oriented, transforming even "increasing fortune" into an integral aspect of emulating God. That observation, in turn, informs their own ethics, raising them from simple, albeit commendable, moral qualities, to the *imitatio dei* contemplated by Maimonides' *de'ot.*

The "Way" to the Utopian King

The legacy of the golden mean is the link between the inception of Jewish history by Abraham and its consummation by the messianic king. Maimonides assigned the phrase "the way of God" *(derekh YHVH)* to the teaching of the ethical mean because God Himself is scripturally characterized by those attributes that constitute the median path (compassionate, merciful, holy, and so on), "and it is what Abraham taught to his children" (MT *Laws of Ethical Traits* 1:7).[71] It is that very teaching that will mark the culmination of Jewish history, with its dissemination by the messianic king "who will arise from the seed of David, possessing more wisdom than Solomon, who will be almost as great a prophet as Moses, and therefore will teach the entire nation and instruct them in the 'way of God' *[derekh YHVH]*" (MT *Laws of Repentance* 9:2). All of Jewish history between these two critical junctures consists of a continuous series of the same teaching, beginning with Isaac and then Jacob, whose final legacy to his children shortly before his death was to "admonish them as to the unification of the Name and the 'way of God' *[derekh YHVH]* in which Abraham and Isaac his father walked" (MT *Laws of Reading the Shema* 1:4). The intellectual and ethical heritage of the patriarchs is then passed on by Jacob to all his sons; but it is Levi and his descendants in particular who are commissioned "to teach the 'way of God' *[derekh YHVH]*" in perpetuity (MT *Laws of Idolatry* 1:3).

Each king anticipates the ideal messianic king through the manner in which he rules his kingdom. By adopting the ethics of extreme humility he preserves the transmission of the core teaching of the way of God, which conveys an ethical *imitatio dei* that is anchored in intellect. A royal ethic that neutralizes grandeur and dominance with lowliness will naturally culminate in the utopian administration of the messianic polity, which minimizes control and maximizes freedom.[72] The notion that rabbinic and prophetic yearning for the messianic era was fueled by visions of domination is emphatically dispelled by Maimonides in a pointed denial of any such motivations. Their messianic longings arose "not in order to rule the entire world, and not so that they would subjugate the nations, and not so that the nations would exalt them . . . but in order that they would be free to pursue Torah and its wisdom" (MT *Laws of Kings* 12:4).[73] This freedom is nurtured by an environment in which all the social, economic, and geopolitical factors normally necessitating a king are absent, for "in that time there will be no hunger and no war and no jealousy or rivalry, goodness will be abundant, and all luxuries will be as common as earth" (ibid., 12:5).[74] The ethics of kingship intended to counteract the theological perils of dependence on the king reach their zenith in the messianic era, when the king can virtually be dispensed with. Kingship has weaned itself out of existence.[75]

The king is the most prominent exemplar of what is in essence the human condition. He must struggle to promote the integrity of his office while, at the same time, avert any public perception that the office is self-serving. Each stratum of the social spectrum, except the lowest, those halakhically characterized by Maimonides as the "lowly of spirit" *(shefal-ruah)*, finds itself faced with the same struggle. Most vulnerable to the allure of power and grandeur is the king, who must look to the *shefal-ruah* for guidance as to what constitutes the requisite degree of humility for counteracting that allure.[76] By internalizing the posture of extreme humility emblematic of the *shefal-ruah* class, he in turn becomes the existential model for a universal ethic of humility that trickles down through each successive level of society. It is only then that his kingship can strike the proper balance between supreme power and supreme submission necessary to project an image consistent with the essential Maimonidean definition of a king, "over whom no man from Israel can exercise any authority and above whom there is none in his kingdom except the Lord his God" (MT *Laws Sacrifices for Unintentional Sins* 15:6). Every gaze downward is a reflex of a gaze upward.

This ideal of monarchic governance is captured by the rabbinic legend of David's waking each night at the stroke of midnight to study the Torah until dawn, when he would attend to the affairs of state (*b. Berakhot* 3b). Considering the Maimonidean ethics of kingship examined in this chapter, he would have cited with approval Emmanuel Levinas' epitomization of this tradition as a portrait of "a double life in order to remake the unity of life. The political action of each passing day begins in an eternal midnight and derives from a nocturnal contact with the Absolute."[77]

CHAPTER 5

The Sage/Philosopher
A Solitude of Universalism

Maimonides' introductory letter to his *Guide of the Perplexed* is addressed to R. Joseph b. Judah,[1] thus personalizing the *Guide* as the fruition of a journey he embarked on, some years prior to its composition, as guide and teacher for a beloved disciple. Despite their physical separation, it is the cultivation of an intimate relationship between master and student that engendered a host of passions clearly transcending the pedagogical space of the classroom.[2] The master and his disciple are wrapped in an impenetrable intellectual embrace. Their classroom lies outside, not inside, the educational system. The solitude of the sage can be penetrated only by the student who desires the company of solitude himself and is prepared to lead the outsider life his master bequeaths him. In this chapter, I move from constructs of outsiders to the existential predicament of Maimonides himself. Any study of the sage is also a study of Maimonides' own personal ambivalence in finding a balance between the inside and the outside.

In Maimonides' letter to Joseph, he recounted how he was impressed from the beginning with his student's motivation for study ("I had a high opinion of you because of your strong desire for inquiry"), a motivation so consuming that its vitality could only be captured by the creative surge of poetry ("your poems of your powerful longing for speculative matters"). Those impressions momentarily gave way to a sober skepticism regarding the prospective student's qualifications ("perhaps his longing is stronger than his grasp"). A probationary period of preliminary text study revealed an "excellence of mind" and a "quickness of grasp," dispelling any remaining doubts regarding the student's intellectual abilities. Elated ("my joy in you increased"), Maimonides encouraged Joseph to pursue a course of independent study ("I let you train yourself in that science [mathematics]"), and had supreme confidence that his goals would be successfully achieved ("knowing where you would end"). The process is a propaedeutic one, all the while prodding the student to acquire knowledge through his own efforts ("read under my guidance texts"). The utmost care is required so as not to overwhelm the student with the master's formidable acumen, but to preserve the student's intellectual autonomy, thereby guaranteeing his ability to function when the inevitable day of separation arrives.

Maimonides continued to trace his teacher–student relationship with Joseph, relating how the joy over his student's progress led to an optimism that *this* student is indeed prepared for what *this* master uniquely has to offer. A standard curriculum of general science required a tutelage of simple scientific competence, not one also imbued with a prodigious biblical and rabbinic expertise. At this juncture, the student graduated to a qualitatively new subject. Philosophy offered a hermeneutical path into the student's sacred texts ("secrets of the prophetic books") necessitating a radical departure in pedagogical method ("[to] let you see certain flashes and to give you certain indications").[3] Along with academic progress had come maturity as a complete human being ("consider in them that which perfect men ought to consider"). The master was no longer faced with the disciple's intellectual curiosity, but confronted a far more serious challenge of existential turmoil ("perplexity"; "stupefaction had come over you"), in which the student is possessed by a compulsion for truth that originates at the very core of his being ("your noble soul demanded of you").

Joseph's education by this time had been transformed into a quest to resolve the apparent contradiction in his commitments to both "reasoned" and "revealed" texts. Choosing one over the other would entail a betrayal of either his intellect or his religion (GP Intro., 6).[4] Since, at this juncture, it was Joseph's encounter with his religious texts that was at stake,

Maimonides strategically articulated Joseph's longing for resolution in biblical language, to "find out acceptable words" (Eccl 12:10). Yet, in its original context the subject of this sentence is in fact the teacher, Ecclesiastes, whose communication skills excel because his words are attuned to his audience. The verse portends the student's evolving into a teacher himself, and the compulsion to teach is a reflex of the absorption of the master's teaching.[5] The "acceptable words" discovered by Solomon, the traditional author of Ecclesiastes, are the exposition of parables *(meshalim)* of the previous verse (12:9), which he subjected to close scrutiny *(izzen vehiqer)* in order to teach the people knowledge *(limed da'at et ha-am)*. He literally "fixed and righted" *(tiqqen)* these parables, which may mean deciphered them for the public[6] or taught by means of composing his own parables.[7] Either way, and leaving aside the question whether metaphysical truths can be conveyed by any means other than parable,[8] the projection of Joseph into the Solomonic enterprise prodded him to assume a different literary posture than he had been accustomed to assume with philosophy. The logic of argument receded but remained a backdrop for the logic of metaphor. Though the subject matter may remain the same, the verse signals Joseph's entry into the world of exegesis.[9]

His striving for "acceptable words" placed Joseph into the camp of that rare breed of person whom Maimonides, in the introduction to his thirteen principles of faith, identified (with this very citation) as mimicking Solomonic methodology. Such persons distinguish themselves from the literalists by their appreciation for parables and riddles, the preferred literary genre of the Bible and the Rabbis, and acknowledge that "all men of wisdom speak of the ultimate in lofty matters only by way of riddle and parable *[hidah u-mashal]*" (PM, introduction to the tenth chapter of *Sanhedrin*). Since membership in this group is a prerequisite to assimilating the thirteen principles, which in turn qualifies one for membership in the nation of Israel, Maimonides intimated that at stake in his writing of the *Guide* was nothing less than truly belonging to the community, to which Joseph may have assumed he belonged solely by accident of birth.

Once Joseph ventured off on his own, Maimonides filled a palpable absence with reminiscences of their private seminars. Yet it was only the memory of his student's struggling with biblical and rabbinic texts that decisively impelled Maimonides to compose the *Guide* for Joseph, "and for those like you, however few they are."[10] Any such text "in which there was a pointer to some strange notion" always elicited an explication from the master. The *Guide* replaces the classroom discussion about the "strangeness"[11] of their shared parochial tradition. The literary vehicle of that strangeness is the parable, constructed out of the "deviant discourse" of metaphor.[12]

The *Guide* is essentially a handbook for making sense of biblical and rabbinic equivocation, which is entirely concerned with teaching the semantics of parabolic language. Should any passage of the *Guide* be devoid of any explicit reference to the Bible, then it is to be taken as either "preparatory for another, *or* it will hint at one of the meanings of an equivocal term I might not want to mention explicitly in that place, *or* it will explain one of the parables *or* hint at the fact that a certain story is a parable" (GP Intro., 10). In its overarching engagement with a literary form that, by definition, is impenetrable to "ordinary" reading, and in his demand for a rigorous and scholarly accomplished "perplexity," Maimonides carved out an intimate space between his work and his audience. The book is further virtually hermetically sealed against any public accessibility beyond the private teacher–student relationship by his admonishment to *his* reader that "whatever he understands from this Treatise of those things that have not been said by any of our famous Sages other than myself should not be explained to another" (ibid.). Given his claim that nothing in his treatise can be found in "any book—written in the religious community in these times of exile" (ibid., 16),[13] nothing in it repeats what was formerly espoused by the rabbinic tradition. Therefore everything to be gleaned from it is novel, and everything so gleaned must not be divulged.[14] The hermeneutical orbit of the *Guide,* its author, and its intended reader is constricted to the periphery of their faith community at large. Wisdom has been isolated from the mainstream, and therefore the sage (philosopher *[talmid hakham]*) who is possessed of true wisdom finds himself living on the margins. When speaking of the writing that has taken place "in these times of exile," Maimonides may very well have had in mind not just a national geopolitical state of affairs, but his existential state as a writer and communicator of wisdom, albeit unrelentingly surrounded and besieged by his compatriots and patients, in his capacity as community leader.[15]

In this chapter I delineate more sharply the boundaries enclosing this marginal space in which Joseph and Maimonides interacted and, more broadly, in which the sage becomes increasingly absorbed by "wisdom" *(hokhmah)*. What did Maimonides mean, philosophically, by his conclusion that love of God and devotion to Him are perfected "in solitude and isolation," and what precisely are the existential dimensions of the sage who, consequently, "stays frequently in solitude and does not meet anyone unless it is necessary"? (GP III:51, 621).[16] Though this experiential dimension is by no means exclusive to Maimonides, or for that matter medieval Jewish philosophy, and certainly draws very strong parallels with thinkers in the Islamic tradition, particularly ibn Bajja,[17] I confine myself in what follows to its expression in the Maimonidean oeuvre.

Joseph, one of the "few," that "single virtuous man" for whose sake Maimonides was willing to suffer the derision of thousands,[18] was also singled out as one for whom alone the *Mishneh Torah* would have been worth writing. Joseph was considered by his teacher to be among the select "remnants who *call out to the Lord [YHVH]*" (Joel 3:5),[19] those whom Maimonides thought to be worthy recipients of his teachings.[20] The intent of the prophet Joel is to limit the survivors of a future apocalyptic conflagration preceding messianic redemption to those who "call YHVH" and, in the first colon of the verse, "who call in the name of YHVH." Calling in the name of YHVH constitutes the Maimonidean rallying cry to the core public teaching of Abraham's pioneering discovery (or rediscovery) of monotheism,[21] comprising "both the existence of the deity and the creation of the world in time by that deity" (GP III:29, 516).[22] Joseph is located along a chain of transmission bearing the philosophical underpinnings of monotheism stretching back to Abraham, each link of which has been, and continues to be, forged by those rare individuals who subject current norms to scientific scrutiny without regard to familial or societal pressures.[23]

Joel 3:5 was also cited by Maimonides to typify the exceptionality of those willing to undertake the lengthy and arduous program of "preliminary studies," from logic to mathematics, through the natural sciences, and culminating in divine science (GP I:34, 75), since there is "no way to apprehend Him except it be through the things He has made"—or what Maimonides called "the totality of existence" (ibid., 74).[24] In this endeavor, however, the acquisition of scientific knowledge is purposefully geared, in a sense, toward defeat. Its aim is a thoroughness of inapplicability in the realm of divine science, where all that has been demonstrated must now be vigorously denied (see GP I:60, 143–47). The name "YHVH" invoked by Joseph and his comrades is significant, for it represents the ultimate destination of all God-talk, the "clear unequivocal indication of His essence" (GP I:61, 147), "in such a way that none of the created things is associated with Him in this indication" (ibid., 148). All other names are derivative; they "correspond to the actions existing in the world," while "YHVH" is "divested and stripped of all actions" (ibid., 149). The protean demands of Maimonides' preliminary curriculum are paid off with its own divestiture, arriving at a point that is radically without analogy, the articulated name "YHVH." The religious disciple contemplated by Joel 3:5 is willing to embark on a path of scientific inquiry consciously directed toward its own deconstruction and utter failure to account for the God that he seeks.[25] He is thereby marginalized, not just from the uneducated masses, but from the scientific community as well.[26] His existential aloneness bears some resemblance to the ontological aloneness of the pristine divine essence conveyed by the articulated name, which, according to a midrashic tradition, preexisted the world and "alone is indicative of the essence without associating any other notion with it" (ibid.).[27]

Consolation for Joseph's scholarly solitude could be found in the inner tranquility he must have attained, qualifying him to graduate to the highly specialized program of the "garden" *(pardes)* studies. Within Maimonides' tripartite classification of Torah study into "written torah" *(torah she-bikhtav)*, "oral torah" *(torah she-be'al peh)*, and *talmud*, the esoteric disciplines of the *pardes*—the Accounts of the Chariot and Creation *(ma'aseh merkavah; ma'aseh b'reshit)*—are subsumed under the last (MT *Laws of Studying Torah* 1:11).[28] The study of Talmud is the final academic stage for which the other two classes of study are mere preliminaries. Graduation to this level of study entails an exclusive devotion to it, and restricts the preparatory subjects of the earlier two categories to mere review for the sake of memory retention: "after one has matured in wisdom and no longer needs to learn the Written Law, or be constantly occupied with the Oral Law, he should . . . reserve all his days exclusively for the study of Talmud, according to his breadth of intellect *[rohav libbo]* and serene state of mind *[yiššuv da'ato]*" (ibid., 1:12).[29] Intellectual broadness must be balanced by an ethical composure lest it become an intellectual arrogance fueled by unbridled curiosity to venture into areas that lie beyond one's capacity.[30]

The choice is between two opposing models of the limitations of human intellect: Moses' hiding of his face at the sight of the burning bush in an acknowledgment of his own limitations (GP I:5, 29) or Elisha ben

Abuyah's deluded rush into the domain of the *pardes* (GP I:32, 68–70).³¹ That composure attends an engagement with the Oral Law, the world of rabbinic behavioral restraints *(issur ve-heter)* whose accessibility cuts across all levels of society regardless of age, gender, or intellectual acumen (MT *Laws of the Foundations of the Torah* 4:13). Joseph's marginalized field of theoretical endeavor in the *pardes* is anchored practically in a shared space of common ritual. It must harness the impulse to abandon altogether the distraction of community obligation consequent to organized religion for the undisturbed focus of reclusion.

The sage's³² inward drive toward the margins and beyond is also restrained by his formal duty to orient his inner life outward through teaching. Each advance closer to the periphery anticipates its own retraction, necessary to impart what has been acquired to others, for "there is a *mitzvah* [command] on each and every sage of Israel to teach all students even if they are not his children" (MT *Laws of Studying Torah* 1:2).³³ "Tradition" *(mi-pi ha-shemuah)* (*Sifre Deut* 34, on Deut 6:7),³⁴ the very rabbinic source of this halakhic obligation, forms part of the curriculum envisaged by Talmud study, "to deduce what is permitted and forbidden from what one has learned from tradition *[mi-pi ha-shemuah]*." This contemplates an ongoing engagement with rabbinic hermeneutics for the sake of posterity. For Maimonides, teaching and learning are both integral constituents of the same *mitzvah*,³⁵ and so every personal intellectual advance portends the advancement of others.

Moses, once again, serves as the archetype for all sages: he reached the furthest extremities of human intellectual growth to occupy a plane of existence beyond the reach of his religious cohorts. Yet his supreme inner maturity is accompanied by an outward posture, notably indicated at those critical junctures in the *Guide* where Maimonides' formulation of Mosaic uniqueness might imply consummate social detachment. In his intellectual hierarchy represented by varying intensities and durations of light, Moses occupies the very apex, whose noetic clarity is captured by lightning that is flashing so rapidly that no lull in light can even be detected to the point where "night appears to him as day." Two verses are cited that convey the bidirectional movement of Mosaic knowledge. Given the metaphorical sense of the term "stand" in Deut 5:28 ("But as for thee, stand thou here by Me"), this verse connotes Moses' unique fixation on God, permanently and enduringly (see GP I:13, 40). The second verse, Exod 34:29 ("the skin of his face sent forth beams"), ostensibly signifying the same state of ceaseless illumination, depicts Moses as a source of light radiating outward. That light, or knowledge, is so intense that it cannot be contained and bursts forth in a flow of knowledge directed toward others. The etymology of the term "face" *(panim)* is traced by Maimonides to "turn": "since man turns his face toward the thing he wishes to take as his objective" (GP I:2, 26). Moses' orientation in view of the knowledge he has acquired is in the direction of its transmission.

Deuteronomy 5:28 appears again at the end of the *Guide* to express once again Moses' perpetual cognitive focus on God, while he still preserves a social dimension "in which he talks with people and is occupied with his bodily necessities while his intellect is wholly turned toward Him" (GP III:51, 623). Again, every rung of intellectual ascent heavenward on Jacob's ladder is, at one and the same time, a rung of instructional descent "with a view to governing and teaching the people of the earth" (GP I:15, 41).[36] God's "standing erect" at the summit of the ladder is paralleled by Moses' "stand[ing] erect upon the rock" (Exod 33:21), an *imitatio dei* of sorts where the constancy of God's being is matched by the constancy of Moses' mental absorption with the divine being (GP I:16, 42, where Exod 33:21 is an expression of *Rely upon and be firm in considering God as the first principle*).

What kind of wisdom is it that draws the sage into the exclusive company of Moses Maimonides and his biblical namesake? Here the life and career of Job, another biblical personality, is instructive, for his biography, according to Maimonides, largely consists of his evolving from a life absorbed with moral virtue to one dominated by rational virtue. The fact that Job begins his ordeal possessed only of moral perfection, yet lacking in wisdom, is "the most marvelous and extraordinary thing about this story" (GP III:22, 487).[37] Though I cannot here pursue all the intricacies of the allegorical imagery out of which the Jobian narrative is constructed, for our purposes it is sufficient to state that the dramatis persona of Satan represents an intrinsic component of Job's (and the human condition's) character. Satan is also identical with the "evil inclination" of the rabbinic tradition, which represents a given natural tendency with which man is born (GP III:22, 489).[38]

What is pertinent to this discussion is the correspondence Maimonides drew between the two inclinations of man, good and evil, and different stages in the intellectual an ethical development of a human being. While the evil inclination is biologically innate,[39] the good is acquired as a result of human effort. The biblical imagery chosen from Ecclesiastes to express this understanding conveys a sense of intellectual development that is attained at the cost of increasing social isolation. A rabbinic tradition, to which Maimonides refers (*b. Nedarim* 32b), treats Eccl 9:14–15 as an allegory of the interaction between various constituents and faculties of the human body: "There was a little city, and few men within it and a great king attacked it, besieging it and building breastworks against it. But there was found in it a poor wise man who saved the city by his wisdom. . . ." The city signifies the body over which there is a power struggle, where the formidable onslaught of the evil inclination (great king) succumbs to the resistance of the weak and impoverished good inclination (poor wise man). Though the battle for wisdom is waged internally, it takes its toll externally. Job, initially, had "known God only through the traditional stories and not by way of speculation," but at least he can find comfort in that he maintains friends and family, and blends into a society whose common ground is an uncritical acceptance of tradition and authority.[40] Tradition provides comfort but not true knowledge, and so to gain the latter one must move away from the former.[41]

The end of the parable in Ecclesiastes is daunting—"though nobody remembered this man"—for the process of acquiring wisdom may distance the sage from his community to such an extent that no memory of him lingers for posterity. Its negative impact may be somewhat alleviated by the manner in which wisdom, once acquired, is in turn transmitted. Here the sage must take his cue, as Maimonides did with Joseph, from Elihu, the only one of Job's friends to propose a philosophically tenable theory of providence. However, it must be sifted out of a barrage of discourse that merely parrots the discreditable opinions of all the other friends who preceded him. Here the strategy is to preserve political harmony among the vast majority, who it is futile to teach except by tradition, "in order to hide the notion that is peculiar to the opinion of each individual, so that at first it occurs to the multitude that all the interlocutors are agreed on the selfsame opinion; however this is not so" (GP III:23, 495). Regurgitation of well-worn ideas and sameness guarantee social acceptability. However, they also indicate a triteness that calls for either refinement or rejection. As in the Job/Elihu paradigm, the quest for the true teachings of the sage lies in filtering out the novel from the commonplace.

In Maimonides' signature deference to scriptural idiom, those who can independently reason their way to the truth without the assistance of tradition amount to the statistical anomaly of "one of a city or two of a family" (Jer 3:14) (GP I:34, 75).[42] As with every biblical proof-text, Maimonides undertook a rereading of its original context, wherein the prophet goes on to relate how these privileged individuals are being brought to Zion, where "I will give you shepherds after my own heart, and they shall shepherd you with knowledge and understanding *[de'ah ve-haskel]*") (3:15). First, in place of "tradition" these elite will be taught with "knowledge and understanding," the tools of trade of the intellect. Second, the metaphor of shepherd expresses the external demeanor the teacher must project lest he alienate himself from the community at large.

For Maimonides, shepherding historically was the predominant national occupation of the people of Israel, "all of us being shepherds from fathers and grandfathers" (GP III:39, 552). As indicated by the proof-text cited to corroborate this historical detail, shepherding itself carries with it the national ideology of monotheism. Joseph's family, in response to Pharaoh's query as to the nature of their livelihood, asserts "thy servants are shepherds, both us and our ancestors" (Gen 47:3). This, the biblical narrative tells us, distinguishes them from the prevalent pagan culture that would find this occupation an affront to their gods and therefore compel the Egyptians to segregate them (Gen 46:33–34).[43] The choice of the shepherd to represent the sage/teacher captures the double life he must lead. In one of those lives he must project the public persona of the shepherd who has assumed his ancestral trade, accompanied by a popular monotheistic theology that places him squarely along a continuum fueled by a unique national identity. In the other life he must be a shepherd to his disciples, elevating the continuum along another plane informed by speculation and demonstration.

The sage/shepherd is caught between two worlds—one where God is known and experienced by His audible word, and the other where the only audible sounds are those of man as he drives toward the ultimate silence in which God is known by His not being known. His goal is to guide his students out of a religious worship rife with God-talk that is the staple of all prayer and into a wordless service that Maimonides found captured by the Psalter's declaration "Silence is praise to thee" (Ps 65:2) (GP I:59, 139). Every verbal exaltation of God philosophically amounts to its opposite, and prayer is simply a psychological outlet provided by the rabbinic tradition to both accommodate and constrain the religious impulse to heap praise on God (ibid., 140–42).[44] Thus prayer, the quintessential act of religious community, becomes the forum in which the sage feels alienated most; he must, in a sense, disengage his mind from his tongue since "silence and limiting oneself to the apprehensions of the intellects are more appropriate" (ibid., 140).

Maimonides' appeal to a celebrated philosophical aphorism to endorse his ideal of contemplative silence is really a corollary of the lightning metaphor discussed previously: "We are dazzled by His beauty, and He is hidden from us because of the intensity with which He becomes manifest, just as the sun is hidden to eyes that are too weak to apprehend it" (ibid., 139).[45] Simply understood, the intensity of light in the lightning metaphor mirrors intellectual growth. Combined with this adage, the metaphor becomes more nuanced by the notion that intense light can also blind. Taken together, then, ignorance, paradoxically, is directly proportional to knowledge: the more one knows how much he cannot know, the more one knows.[46] The sage must be mindful of this paradox, particularly when participating in a prayer quorum, and disengage himself intellectually, not only from the words on the page of the prayer book, but from his co-religionists with whom he shares this experience.[47]

Every prayer assembly becomes a reenactment of the originating assembly at Sinai, where the disparity between the sage and his people could not have been more pronounced. The scale of intellectual gradation was so acute as to result in a great disparity between the sage and all others; the extent of this disparity led the Rabbis to describe it in terms adopted by Maimonides: "Moses is an enclosure apart and Aaron an enclosure apart" (GP II:32, 363, quoting the *Mekhilta de-Rabbi Ishmael* to Exod 19:24). Spaces that are sharply defined by respective understandings of God are bridged only by sounds whose articulation can only be made out by Moses: "they heard the great voice but not the articulations of speech . . . Moses being the only one who heard the words and reported to them" (GP II:33, 364).[48] The people were enveloped in a cacophony of sounds and so all future communications between the people and God, in a kind of *imitatio dei,* are modeled on this aural revelation. The sage, though, while partaking in the prayerful din that surrounds him, also cordons himself off by a mode of communication that mirrors Moses' reception of words at Sinai.[49]

God, possessing no organs of speech, is not capable of speaking audible words and therefore all biblical references to divine "saying" *(amirah)* or "speaking" *(dibbur)* "never signify that He, may He be exalted, spoke using the sounds of letters and a voice" (GP I:65, 159). The *imitatio dei* of the sage is modeled on the nonverbal experience, which segregated, indeed *enclosed,* Moses and Aaron from the rest of those who stood at the foot of the mountain. The very intellectual history of the multitiered experience at Sinai is itself reflective of this variegated communication being driven by a multitiered reception of it, since it "is a matter that is transmitted by tradition in the religious community *and* [emphasis mine] that is known to its men of knowledge" (GP II:33, 365). The religion's collective memory of its originating moment is shattered, since it is shaped by the sophistication of its recipient. The community traces its link back to Sinai through tradition, whereas the individual men of knowledge do so by knowing. The daily ritualistic public intrusion of prayer into the private life of the sage is a recurrent occasion in which the sage must drain its formalized language of its linguistic content, thereby preventing his worship from becoming idolatrous blasphemy.[50]

Maimonides urged the sage to retreat into a silence that would both liberate him from popular religion and confine him to an internalized state of isolation. His preference is for a silent endorsement of the unity of God over its public proclamation. He admonishes the sage not to be

> one of those who merely proclaim it with their mouth without representing to themselves that it has meaning. With regard to men of this category, it is said: *Thou art near in their mouth, and far from their reins* [Jer 12:2]. But men ought rather to belong to the category of those who represent the truth to themselves and apprehend it, even if they do not utter it, as the virtuous are commanded to do—for they are told: *Commune* [say, from the Hebrew root *amar*] *with your own heart upon your bed, and be still. Selah* [Ps 4:5]. (GP I:50, 112)[51]

"Communing with one's heart" is an expression that conveys "a matter to which a man does not give utterance and that he does not tell to somebody else" (GP I:29, 62). "Heart," in the Maimonidean biblical lexicography, is a term that signifies, among other meanings, the intellect (GP I:39, 89),[52] and "be still" is a form of the Hebrew root for *silence.* The sage is perpetually confronted with the choice between words and silence, between company and solitude, between action and immobility ("upon your bed").

Maimonides did not propose a physical withdrawal from society, but rather one that allows the sage to escape either/or alternatives by adopting a mode of being I term "functional contemplation." The silence called for is a state of mind like that of Moses, who "talks with people and is occupied with his bodily necessities while his intellect is wholly turned toward Him, so that in his heart he is always in His presence, while outwardly he is with people" (GP III:51, 623).[53] By insulating his intellect from his environment and his own physicality, man achieves the "likeness" to God that Maimonides asserted to be intended by the divine design for constructing man of Gen 1:26: "in our image, after our likeness." When exercising his sheltered intellect, "no sense, no part of the body, none of the extremities are used" (GP I:1, 23). Cultivating an inner solitude is a form of *imitatio dei* in which there is an absence of dialogue, of reaction, and of response that is typical of the sublime divine activity of "thought thinking itself."[54] Prayer is the ultimate normative expression of both communal and verbal worship of God, and traditionally is understood to have as its objective the eliciting of responses from God. It is a public performance thoroughly fraught with a distorted theology that must be privately neutralized with the "likeness" advocated by Ps 4:5, in a gesture of supreme estrangement from community and popular ideology. While in the synagogue, the sage must silence his own prayer by mentally transporting himself to the inner sanctum of his home.

One of the most avid proponents of the Maimonidean school, the thirteenth-century thinker Shem Tov ibn Falaquera, eloquently captures this existential dichotomy in his philosophical reinvention of Moses' anguished self-assessment "I am a stranger in the land" (an imprecise reference to Exod 2:22, 18:3). According to him, Moses articulated the deep-rooted sense of alienation shared by all those perfected sages, "for even when they are in their homes, among their brothers and families, they are strangers in their opinions, going in their thoughts to other levels which are their residences."[55]

Psalm 4:5 is a critical proof-text for the uncompromising nature of the silence that Maimonides felt the sage had to endure. It adjures an abiding silence that allows for lapses of speech in only two instances, teaching and establishing one's legitimacy as a teacher. Representations internal to the psyche constitute the only authentic praise of God, "whereas the words concerning it are meant to instruct someone else or to make it clear concerning oneself that one has had the apprehension in question" (GP II:5, 260). The words exchanged between Maimonides and Joseph, both textual and oral, were mere dispensations from the strictures of the silence demanded by "Commune with your own heart." The verse is cited in II:5 of the *Guide* to impose a standard of being that approximates that of the heavenly spheres, of whom the Psalter says, "The heavens tell of the glory of God... there is no speech, there are no words, neither is their voice heard" (19:2–4). Given that Maimonides believed the spheres to be endowed with intellect,[56] the verses can be read as indicating that their praise of God consists entirely of soundless thought. The depth of the sage's isolation is so profound that he is encouraged to adopt a mode of existence peculiar to another species of existence altogether. The model, though in all likelihood unattainable, is once again Moses, who aspired to a level where he "transcended the human species and reached angelic status" (see the seventh of Maimonides' thirteen principles in PM, introduction to chapter 10 of *Sanhedrin,* and his introduction to *Avot,* chapter 7 of the "Eight Chapters"; see also MT *Laws of the Foundations of the Torah* 7:6).

The anguish that accompanied Maimonides' pondering whether to write the *Guide* must have involved far more than the mere political and halakhic considerations of both the prohibition against public dissemination of esoteric knowledge and the fear of upsetting popular belief systems with a radically new teaching. To resort to speech is to suffer a relapse into nothing short of an entirely different species, to a kind of sphere-like existence. His deliberations were thus exacerbated by an existential anguish, which could only have been alleviated by another kind of *imitatio dei* that the speech of teaching entails, the natural "overflow" of perfection. Both philosophers and prophets can either be self-subsisting or "sometimes the measure of the overflow [intellectual] is such that it moves him of necessity to compose works and to teach" (GP II:37, 375).[57] The discourse of teaching is not chosen but is a compulsion of a perfected speechlessness that mirrors the very structure of the chain of being from God down to the lowest sphere, fueled by a cosmic perfection that compulsively overflows to perfect others.[58]

Teaching is a reflexive compulsion of knowledge because they are the earthly parallels to God's ethereal generative initiative to create man in His likeness and image. Once knowledge has been acquired by the abstract exercise of one's own intellectual faculties, a reenactment of the divine creative drama unfolds. Normatively, everyone is obligated to teach one's children, based on Deut 6:7, "and you shall teach your children." A sage, however, is required to teach regardless of biological attachment since, according to Maimonides, the oral tradition broadens the scope of "your children" to include disciples (MT *Laws of Studying Torah* 1:2, based on *Sifre Deut pisqa* 34, to Deut 6:7).⁵⁹ Philosophically and existentially, because the teacher contributes to the development of the student's own intellect, and therefore his human *form,* he also engenders an individual, as primal man Adam did, "in his own likeness, after his image" (Gen 5:3): "As for Seth, it was after [Adam] had instructed him and procured him understanding and after he had attained human perfection that it was said of him *And Adam begot a son in his own likeness, after his image"* (GP I:7, 32–33). It is only through teaching that a "genetic" continuum of image is established between Adam and Seth. As was argued in the discussion of the convert, however, a community of shared likenesses and images is not strictly speaking forged biologically or genetically. Nothing less than the perpetuation of *humanity* as opposed to the human animal species is contingent on the inculcation of ideas to which only very few have access. Adam's move away from *form* is marked by his move toward society and its concerns.⁶⁰ In thinking and teaching, this primal move is reversed by withdrawing from a social dimension concerned with the survival of the species (to which biological reproduction is essential) to a private dimension concerned with the transmission of absolute truth (to which academic reproduction is essential).

Every student is faced with the same choices as Adam vis-à-vis his teacher, God. He can opt to imitate his master at the cost of a constricted social space or broaden that space at the cost of severing the link to his master. It is ironic that choosing the former very often entails the replacement of a biological parent with an intellectual one. One of the principle reasons for intellectual confusion is "habit and upbringing" (GP I:31, 67)— that is, an uncritical acceptance of traditional teachings. Upbringing, then, is something that ultimately must be overcome. At the same time, the student must be willing to challenge the entire literary corpus on which one's cultural and religious heritage is based, since the veracity of belief is popularly determined by "people being habituated to, and brought up on, texts that it is an established usage to think highly of and to regard as true" (ibid.).⁶¹ Conversely, for the sage, the decision to teach is determined by a choice between "giving satisfaction to a single virtuous man" and "displeasing ten thousand ignoramuses" (GP Intro., 16). In other words, he can enjoy the safety of the collective where human form is scant or he can cultivate human form and suffer the vulnerability of a life in isolation.

There is another normative dimension to the sages' compulsion to teach, one that enables the student to fulfill his mandate to keep the company of sages. The sixth positive commandment, as calculated on the basis of Maimonides' unique tally of Judaism's traditional 613, enjoins all to ensure that sages are abiding presences in their lives regardless of the social context. One must exploit every opportunity for associating with sages, be it dining or business, "so that their behavior can be imitated and to believe in the correct opinions that they teach" (SM, Positive Commandment 6). The importance of this association is underscored by its enumeration among those commandments that concern the core tenets of Judaism, such as God's existence and unity. Given God's nature, the biblical injunction to "cleave to Him" (Deut 10:20, 11:22), cannot possibly be taken literally, thereby implying another object of "cleaving." Maimonides adopted the rabbinic version of this reasoning in which another biblical image of God as a "consuming fire" (Deut 4:24) rules out a literal cleaving, which leaves the sage as its metaphorically intended object.[62] Rabbinic logic proceeds in part on uncovering the inconsistency of two literal readings. A raging fire cannot be adhered to. The inconsistency is resolved by one verse (cleaving) surrendering its literal connotation and the other (consuming fire) maintaining it. For Maimonides, though, both must be read metaphorically since God is absolutely incorporeal. For the Rabbis, proximity to the tangible presence described in Deut 4:24 is physically impeded. For Maimonides, there is no presence that exists on any material plane, and therefore each biblical expression is independently incoherent from a literal perspective. Cleaving to the divine is no more or less problematic because of the consuming fire imagery and vice versa. Maimonides' position on the nature of God demands a metaphorical reading of both. Because he rarely cited rabbinic derivations for the legislation he codified,[63] those instances where Maimonides did so most likely signal some heightened interest in its rabbinic underpinnings. I believe, therefore, there is a philosophically tenable inconsistency between these two metaphors that is of particular relevance in appreciating the relationship with the sage.

A being that attracts cleaving is at conceptual, rather than literal, odds with one that is projected as a consuming fire. The latter, in its original biblical context, is a component of a threat, calculated by Moses, to guarantee an ongoing commitment to monotheism that would survive his death. The power of this image of God, philosophically false though practically effective, is conveyed by the *Guide*'s translation of the metaphor into the threat "that He destroys those who disobey Him as a fire destroys that which is in its power" (GP I:30, 63). It is prefaced by Moses' announcement of his impending death, followed by a warning not to abandon the peoples' covenant with God, for He is "a consuming fire, a jealous God." Moses' choice of images is intended to compensate for the inevitable absence of Israel's supreme sage. He realizes that his legacy of a true teaching alone is not sustainable without an underlying anthropomorphic belief in divine anger. Divine anger and jealousy, while philosophically offensive to a correct notion of God, are *necessary beliefs* exclusively and pragmatically constructed to deter the multitude from veering off into idolatry (GP I:36). Moses' wrathful description of God is geared toward the one who needs to accept truth based on "the authority of men who inquire into the truth and are engaged in speculation if he himself is incapable of engaging in such speculation" (ibid., 85).

Of course, the true disciple of the sage needs no motivation to maintain his loyalty to the truth other than the truth itself.[64] He certainly does not require false conceptions of God to do so. His cleaving to God operates on another level altogether, reflected by the doubling of proof-texts promoting cleaving as a normative endeavor. Though the norm is established by "and cleaving to Him" of Deut 11:22, "this command was already repeated when it said *to Him shall you cleave* [Deut 10:20]" (SM Positive Commandment 6). The performance of cleaving straddles the individual commandments of cleaving and of *imitatio dei,* which is also doubly reinforced by "and you shall walk in His ways" of Deut 28:9 and their shared verse, Deut 11:22, which encourages a faithfulness to God that combines "loving the Lord your God, walking in all His ways, and cleaving to Him." This common verse allows the sage's student to pursue a cleaving that is informed by the *imitatio dei* called for by "walking in His ways," which, for Maimonides, signifies "living the good life, without in any way moving a body" (GP I:24, 54).[65] That ethereal way contemplates the cultivation of intellectual apprehension, identified by Maimonides in the very first chapter of the *Guide* as the feature that man and God share, since "In the exercise of this, no sense, no part of the body, none of the extremities are used" (GP I:1, 23).

The true student's relationship with the sage consists of being drawn into the sage's space, which is primarily occupied by mind rather than body. Once he enters this space, his understanding of the consuming fire profoundly diverges from that of the common man, transforming it from a punitive threat to a description of the natural consequences of incorrect beliefs. As noted in the discussion of the heretic in chapter 3, Maimonides dealt with that metaphor in his chapter on the term "eating" (*consuming fire* is literally *eating* fire), where it is assigned its figurative meaning of "destruction and undoing and, in general, to all putting-off of a form" (GP I:30, 63). Since the natural form of man consists in his apprehension, any defect in that activity constitutes either a failure to actualize it or a deterioration of it. Perverse beliefs such as idolatry do not attract punishment from an external source, but are themselves tantamount to the natural self-destruction contemplated by "putting-off of a form." Maimonides' formulation of cleaving, then, accommodates the relation of the sage and his student, and of those who simply keep the sage's company, both in its substance and in its repercussions. The former has enrolled in the sage's program while the latter merely audits his classes.

Excursus 1. A Halakhic Consequence of the Sage's Loneliness: A Psycho-Philosophic Account

The following is Maimonides' legal formulation, in his codification of the *Laws of Prayer,* meant to govern the public Torah reading of the final eight verses of Deuteronomy recounting Moses' death: "It is permissible to read the final eight verses of the Torah in the synagogue in the presence of less than ten people. Even though it is all Torah and they were recited by Moses from the mouth of the Almighty, since their sense is that they were recited after Moses' death, they are different. And therefore it is permissible for an individual to read them" (MT *Laws of Prayer* 13:6). The general rule governing formal public Torah readings is that they must be conducted only in the presence of a minimum of ten Jewish males, the standard prayer quorum known as a *minyan* (ibid., 8:4, 12:3). Though this law has rabbinic origins, Maimonides' reading of its source to the effect that the quorum can be dispensed with is quite novel. Since this final Deuteronomic passage recounts Moses' own death and burial, its authorship was problematic for a theology that conditioned the authenticity of its divine content to Mosaic transcription. However, for both those of the opinion that Moses recorded these verses, though in a different manner from which the other verses were recorded, and those who attribute them to the pen of Moses' successor, Joshua, there is a consensus that its recital is governed by a unique regulation. Its talmudic formulation is "the last eight verses of the Torah are read alone" [*yahid*, which can also be rendered "by one person"] (*b. Menahot* 30b; *b. Bava Batra* 15a). Rashi and his school read this as prohibiting any division of these verses between different readers. One person must recite them continuously, with no interruptions.[66]

Maimonides' formulation incorporates the language of those who attribute even these final eight verses to Moses himself. According to this position, these verses are treated differently, not because of different authorship, but because of the exceptional manner in which Moses wrote them: "Up to this point God dictated and Moses recited and wrote, but from this point on God dictated and Moses wrote with tears" (ibid.). These last eight verses are imbued with the emotive passions of Moses, their writer. However, as Jacob Levinger points out, Maimonides dissociated himself in part from the precise nature of this "different" style of Mosaic script.[67] Levinger attributes this subtle distancing from "writing with tears" to Maimonides' endorsement of its psychological implications, though not necessarily its literal version. The portrait of the sage I have drawn in this chapter can valuably enhance Levinger's perceptive insight that draws our attention to the Mosaic psyche.

Since the subject of the final eight verses of Deuteronomy is Moses' death, it is instructive to consider how Maimonides conceived it in the *Guide*. Moses' death was "in true reality salvation from death," resulting from an intellect that had become so formidable as to overcome the body: "when a perfect man is stricken with years and approaches death, this apprehension increases very powerfully, joy over this apprehension and a great love for the object of apprehension become stronger until the soul is separated from the body at that moment in this state of pleasure" (GP III:51, 627). The singularity of Moses' intellectual maturity was, as we have seen, such as to be "occupied with his bodily necessities while his intellect is wholly turned toward Him, so that in his heart he is always in His presence" (ibid., 623). If Moses' body posed no impediment whatsoever to his focus of intellectual contemplation, then he had, in effect, achieved a Platonic liberation from the material, a death in life. The literal events of the last eight verses can be perceived as a figurative account of the absolute divorce between body and mind Moses had already achieved in life.

Though the literal is not totally displaced (Moses does die; is buried;[68] is mourned;[69] does not lead the people into Canaan; Joshua succeeds him), Maimonides hinted at another, parallel reading on the metaphorical plane, one that is incongruous with the literalist account of Moses' physical state at the point of death. Moses' erotic death by a divine kiss[70] indicates that the strength of his intellect was directly proportional to the declining strength of his body: "in the measure in which the faculties of the body are weakened and the fire of the desires is quenched, the intellect is strengthened, its lights achieve a wider extension, its apprehension is purified, and it rejoices in what it apprehends" (ibid., 627). This is at odds with the literal description of Moses' physical vitality at the time of death, which was intact: "And Moses was one hundred and twenty years old when he died, his eyes were not dimmed nor had his vigor diminished" (Deut 34:7). Maimonides led his readers to consider another dimension to this account that is normatively grounded in this peculiar law regarding the recital of this Torah passage. Since, by Maimonides' account, this verse cannot refer to Moses' physical vitality, it must be read in light of his lexicography of heterogeneous meanings offered throughout the *Guide*. The word "eye," for example, can have a number of different meanings depending on the context in which it is used: "state of affairs" is one such meaning. The biblical illustration of this is 2 Sam 16:12, "It may be the Lord will look in my eye," implying, according to Maimonides, that God will understand "my state" (GP, III:2, 421).[71] Similarly, the term "eye" in Deut 34:7 can signify that Moses' state overall has not deteriorated, though his eyesight may have. Further, if the use of "state" is understood to refer to a state of mind or internal disposition, then 34:7 can be descriptive of Moses' remaining intellectually intact while his body declined.

For Maimonides, the critical point in this biblical denouement is the utter inimitability of the prophetic stature of Moses, whose knowledge of God was grounded on a "face-to-face" relationship and the likes of whom "there has not risen a prophet since in Israel" (Deut 34:10). Here we have the sage at the very outer limits of solitude, with no one of his community, indeed of his species, capable of engaging with him in any kind of meaningful discourse. The only face he faces is the divine *face*, following the Plotinian flight path of "the alone to the Alone."[72] In this sense he has reversed the course set by primordial Adam, whose decline is captured, according to Maimonides, by the verse from Job: "He changes his face and Thou sendest him forth" (14:20). Once the term "face" *(panim)* is understood to be derived from the root "to turn," this verse depicts the quid pro quo of Adam's offense and God's reaction: "when man changed the direction toward which he tended and took as his objective the very thing a previous commandment has bidden him not to aim at, he was driven out" (GP I:2, 26).[73] Moses' face orients the face of Adam back toward its primordial focus.[74] It is an internalized turn of estrangement from his political/social/religious environment.

This internal uniqueness, however, is also accompanied by a corresponding uniqueness in the public sphere. Miracles performed by Moses are also inimitable in the sense of their universal acknowledgment as such by friend and foe alike. Deuteronomy 34:10–12 integrally links Moses' prophetic singularity to his singularity in his public persona, which "works signs before those who are favorably and those who are unfavorably disposed toward him" (GP II:35, 368). The size of Moses' audience dwarfs any known in the history of prophecy.[75] Ironically, his popular dimension expands in proportion to the intensity of his inner solitude. The more he edges to the periphery the more he is drawn back to the core to execute, to teach.[76] The *teaching* of the miracle doubles back onto itself. The miracle simply substantiates the prophet's acumen regarding the workings of the natural order that could only have been achieved by a programmatic solitude—"the sign of a prophet consists in God's making known to him the time when he must make his proclamation, and thereupon a certain thing is effected according to what was put in its nature when first it received its particular impress" (see GP II:29, 345). Structurally, the miracle itself is a phenomenological critique of spontaneity or any radical rupture of the natural order. According to Maimonides, miracles are historical contingencies, inherent in the natural order from the time of creation, which can be forecast by the prophet. The miracle is an extraordinary event that in fact vindicates nature rather than underscores its tenuousness. Moses did not "perform" miracles; rather, his appreciation of the workings of nature was so profound that he could predict these "miraculously" natural events just as a scientist's comprehension of nature allows him to safely do so with the daily rising and setting of the sun.[77] The miracle then is not a parochial event but attests to a universal wisdom of which no one is more superior an exemplar than Moses. It is in this sense that Moses' miracles are accessible to all peoples. The Deuteronomic epilogue depicts Moses as *man*, not Israelite, who has arrived at the pinnacle of *human* achievement.

Maimonides' halakhic rendering of the rabbinic rule, distinguishing these verses from the rest of the Pentateuch as dispensing with the requirement of a prayer quorum, is informed by his philosophical anthropology. Their narrative transcends the narrow confines of their historical context, their particular politics, and their limited audience defined by religion or nationality, in two senses. One is their universality. This is a teaching about *human* perfection and the very limits of *human* knowledge. Since miracles point back to creation, it is also a teaching about God's relationship to the *world* by virtue of His being its creator, rather than one about His interventions on behalf of a particular people. The necessity for a *minyan* is based on the halakhic rubric that "any thing that entails holiness must be conducted within an Israelite congregation *(edah)* as it says *And I will become holy in the midst of the children of Israel* [Lev 22:32]" (MT *Laws of Prayer* 8:6, 12:1). The teaching in this sense is thus muted within a quorum, whose necessity for prayer is rabbinically mandated by a verse that conditions anything of God, "holiness" or otherwise, on the presence of an Israelite assembly. The second sense is the existential teaching about the solitude of the sage, the prophet, the philosopher—the perfected individual. His knowledge of God and consequently his worship of God are not shared with his co-religionists nor are they articulated by standardized formulas replete with anthropomorphic platitudes. The silence of his inner voice must withstand the noise of the crowd.

For this very same reason the private space maintained by the sage within ritualized public worship is also halakhically preserved by unique dispensations granted exclusively to those who's "torah is their profession"*(torato ummanuto)*.[78] Generally mandated prayer times interrupt Torah study except in the case of one "whose Torah is his profession and who is not engaged in any occupation whatsoever." Such an exceptional scholar need not pause for prayer since "the command to study Torah is superior to that of prayer" (MT *Laws of Prayer* 6:8).[79] Standardized prayer historically is used to fill a vacuum created by ignorance and lack of linguistic proficiency (ibid., 1:2–6). It would be incongruous, therefore, for the scholar to interrupt an enterprise in which he is eminently qualified for the very ritual intended to compensate for lack of qualification. Likewise, the Torah professional is permitted to study Torah during the congregational Torah recital (ibid., 12:9).[80]

Once again, the very institution of public Torah readings was intended to ensure that everybody is periodically exposed to its contents (ibid., 12:1), a measure that would be superfluous for someone who is perpetually engaged with Torah. These are halakhic corollaries of the unique juridical status granted to the last passage in Deuteronomy. They cordon off a small space in which the sage can continue to "ply his trade" even within the legislated public space of a quorum. In fact, the very rabbinic definition of a quorum as constituted by a minimum of ten Jewish males is itself impressed with the singling out of exceptional individuals from the group, for "every ten of Israel is called an 'assembly' *[edah]*, as it says *How much longer shall that wicked* assembly *[edah] keep muttering against me* [Num 14:27], and they amounted to ten since Joshua and Caleb were excluded" (MT *Laws of Prayer* 8:5). The word "assembly" is taken to refer to the spies from whose discouraging counsel Joshua and Caleb dissociated themselves. The exegetical strategy that is determinative of the number ten arrives at that number by *excluding* those who have not conformed to the norm, those who have distinguished themselves in their perfected worship of God. Maimonides carved out a small halakhic space here for the individual to ponder and express the universalism of the solitary.

Excursus 2. A Festival for the Sages: A Halakhic Creation of Common Space

While the intellectual must carve out a space for himself within the religious public sphere in which he can worship properly, elitism of any kind always runs the risk of turning into self-absorption. Just as we have seen a halakhic space reserved for the sage to assert the private dimension of his worship, so there is a halakhic forum in which the sage must publicly declare his commonality with his co-religionists. The greatest expression of devotional joy takes place during the annual pilgrimage festival of Tabernacles *(Sukkot)*, a holiday that is itself particularly associated with joy. The "rejoicing at the place of the water drawing," a Temple ritual celebrated at the conclusion of the first day of Tabernacles, was considered by the Mishnah to be the very definition of joy, the extent of which is captured by its pronouncement that "he who has not seen the *rejoicing at the place of the water drawing* has never seen rejoicing in his life" (*m. Sukkah* 5:4; *t. Sukkah* 4:2).[81] Its celebratory mood was boundless, a virtual second Temple "Woodstock," with musical performance on a variety of instruments, singing, dancing, clapping of hands, and free form body movements (*m. Sukkah* 5:4; MT *Laws of Shofar, Sukkah, and Lulav* 8:13). It was a carnival of wide-ranging artistic freedom. According to the Mishnah, however, active participation in this celebration was severely restricted to the "pious *[Hasidim]* and men of deeds *(anshe ma'aseh)."* Maimonides codified the narrow class for whom this celebration was reserved:

> It was a religious duty to make this rejoicing as much as possible, but the ignorant and anybody who wanted to could not participate. Only the great scholars of Israel, heads of the academies, members of the Sanhedrin, pious men, elders, and men of deeds,[82] only they danced and clapped and made music and rejoiced in the Temple during the festival of Tabernacles. However, the rest of the people, men and women, all came to watch and to listen. (*Laws of Shofar, Sukkot, and Lulav* 8:14)[83]

In restricting public celebrations of *Sukkot* to the pious and the men of deeds, the Mishnah's qualifying characteristic for members of either category was the ethical. However, Maimonides' programmatic expansion of this class to encompass notable scholars, academic deans, high court judges, and senior sages programmatically changed its main constitutive feature from the ethical to the intellectual.[84] Since, for Maimonides, true devotion to God consists of perfected intellectual contemplation of Him, what singles out individuals from the crowd is not simply moral perfection but intellectual apprehension.[85] On the face of it, Maimonides presented the most festive occasion of the Jewish calendar as the exclusive preserve of the scholarly elite, from which the common people are shut out. However, when seen in light of Maimonides' general remarks about joy in the performance of commandments, what appears initially to be an obnoxiously pretentious religious event is actually a gesture of supreme humility.

After describing a particular instance of joy within the Jewish ritualistic framework, Maimonides concluded his *Laws of Laws of Shofar, Sukkah, and Lulav* with a general definition of normative joy in Judaism that is applicable to the performance of any commandment:

> The joy that a person experiences in the performance of the commandments and in the love of God who has commanded them is a great form of worship. Anyone who holds himself back from this joy deserves punishment as it says *Because you would not serve the Lord your God in joy and gladness* [Deut 28:47]. Anyone who is arrogant and apportions glory for himself and is egotistical in these places is a sin-

ner and a fool. This is what Solomon warned of when he said *Do not glorify yourself before a king* [Prov 25:6]. Anyone who belittles himself and humbles his person in these places, only he is great and respected and worships God out of love. And so David, king of Israel, said *I will dishonor myself even more and be low in my own esteem* [2 Sam 6:22] and there is no greatness or glory except to rejoice before God as it says *King David was leaping and whirling before the Lord* [ibid., 6:16]. (MT *Laws of Shofar, Sukkah, and Lulav* 8:15)[86]

For Maimonides, adopting a posture of extreme humility evidences true joy in religious performance. Here he imposed the exceptional ethical extreme of self-abasement, which he advocated as the general norm for humility in his *Laws of Ethical Traits* (the precise nature of which is discussed in chapter 4) onto the performance of all commandments. Any other conduct would reflect a worship that is in fact self-serving rather than directed outside of oneself to God.[87] The joy that is expressed at the water drawing festivity is reserved for the elite precisely because they are most prone, as a result of their office and the respect they command, to fall prey to their own sense of self-importance.[88] The intense physicality of song and ecstatic dance publicly demonstrates their camaraderie with their constituency. It is reserved for men of stature precisely because it is a humbling experience. The people are relegated to "watch and listen" not because they are shut out, but to confirm that those to whom they defer for guidance in their daily affairs are motivated by interests that transcend their own. They observe as their superiors joyously demean themselves to rule out self-importance as a source of their joy.[89]

The sage is also provided with a biblical model of this behavior in the person of King David. David's position on the scale of eleven degrees of prophecy constructed in the *Guide* is instructive because it features the lesson of the water drawing celebration. Maimonides identified the biblical expression "the spirit of the Lord" as the degree of prophecy that is characteristic of David, as well as of other kings and judges—a degree that is very loosely considered prophetic and more appropriately is a kind of divine inspiration where he "finds in himself something that moves and incites him to the action" (GP II:45, 396). The crucial point for appreciating David as the exemplar of the type of joy discussed here is that often the recipient of this type of "prophecy" seems to benefit only himself by his inspired actions. Joseph is the prime biblical example of one who personally gains stature and political power but whose private successes actually contribute to "great things that occurred afterwards" (ibid., 397). Such phrases as "spirit of the Lord" or the "Lord is with him," as in the case of Joseph's career advances (Gen 39:2), transform what appear to be self-interested actions into altruistic ones aimed at broader national interests. Personal gains may coincide with higher aims, but these expressions of divine accompaniment rule them out as motivating factors: "not everyone who has received divine help in some chance matter—such as the acquisition of property or the achievement of an end that concerns him alone—can be said to have been accompanied by *the spirit of the Lord*. . . . We only say this about one who has performed a good action of capital import or an action that leads to that result" (GP II:45, 397). David's career, then, when read in light of this "divine inspiration," parallels the public "reading" of the sages' celebratory performance at the water drawing festivity. These are not stories of self-aggrandizement; rather, they are about the selfless pursuit of matters beyond their private contexts.

The verses cited regarding David are excerpted from the narrative of an incident that concisely illustrates a confusion of perspectives with respect to the sage's behavior and status. 2 Sam 6 relates the story of David's repatriating the ark to its permanent rightful setting in the City of David. The ark is borne by a triumphant procession of dance and music remarkably similar to the mishnaic description of the water drawing festivity.[90] The narrative presents a situation that is rife with duality. It can be perceived as a devotional event dedicated to the honor of God as represented by the ark and its contents. Or it can be perceived as David's victory march with the ark as a trophy of his victory over the Philistines and a celebration of his own increasingly formidable reputation.

The two verses cited from this episode capture these two conflicting perspectives. The second cited, but first in the narrative sequence, is that of Michal, David's wife, peering out of her window at the spectacle below and viewing "King David leaping and whirling before the Lord." Her reaction is repulsion at the sight of her husband, the king, engaging in such undignified behavior (6:16), and she accuses him of cavorting with the rabble, thereby demeaning himself and his office. The first verse cited by Maimonides, but chronologically in response to Michal's indictment, is David's intention to stoop even lower and to diminish himself to the point where he shares the same space and "honor" as the "maidservants," the lowest class among the social strata. David, then, is the supreme exemplar for the sages at the annual water drawing festival, whose gyrations demonstrate his concern not for his office, but for God. What prompts him to humble himself even further is Michal's concern with the office of the monarch, which she believes to be demeaned by the king's dancing (6:16). David understands from Michal's reaction that his performance was not sufficiently intense to efface any hint that he might be celebrating his own kingship. He now realizes that his jubilatory expressions must be so thoroughgoing in self-abasement as to make it crystal clear that they are a celebration of God and His Law.[91] His willingness to intensify his self-effacement precedes Michal's reaction in Maimonides' citation because it reflects back on her misguided perception of David's ecstatic movements. They were never dedicated to personal triumph and self-exaltation.

Maimonides' highly selective use of proof-texts not only affords us his exegesis of this particular biblical narrative, but sensitizes us to the predicament of the sage. In the previous excursus, Maimonides allowed the sage his space within the normative framework to assert his individualism. With his unique exposition of devotional joy and its practical manifestation at the water drawing festival, Maimonides also delineated a space in which the sage and his co-religionists could share a common ground of religious worship.[92]

Yet, even the outward expression of supreme joy is itself a reflection of the sage's internal alienation from his religious cohorts. Joy is not only an essential component of halakhic practice, it is also essential to inner contemplative activity. One can only aspire to prophecy out of a joyous solitude:

> None of the prophets prophesize whenever they please, but rather, they must focus their minds and be calmly joyous and happy *[tov lev]* and isolate themselves *[mitbaddedim]* for prophecy does not alight out of sadness or laziness but only out of joy.[93] Therefore the "sons of prophets" [prophets in training][94] had lutes, drums, flutes, and lyres prepared when they wanted prophecy. (MT *Laws of the Foundations of the Torah* 7:4)

The joy necessary for the kind of perfection that attracts prophecy can only thrive in a forum that is the very antithesis of the place it is expressed at the water drawing festivity. There must be a retreat from the public and from an external physical display of stark physicality into solitude. But the solitude called for need not be an actual social withdrawal. It is a solitude induced by a focusing of one's mind that can, and indeed must, be realized within a social setting that includes the rhythms of the musical instruments at hand. The joy of the water drawing celebration and the inner joy that prepares for prophecy are not inimical but operate in tandem on two planes of existence—the social and the solitary. One joy draws them into community while the other prompts their withdrawal into the worship conducted in the inner recesses of their beings. In this way these two normatively configured joys combine to form the paradigm of sagacious solitude.[95]

Excursus 3. A Revolutionary *Sukkot*: The Transition from Priest to Sage

The previous excursus focuses on a Maimonidean transformation of a class of individuals whose membership was rabbinically defined by "deeds" and "piety" to an intellectual class. Though his rationale for this transformation can easily be determined from an internal analysis of Maimonides' thought, which values intellectual activity above all others, in this excursus I explore a biblical model that possibly inspired his halakhic reformulation. This is a valuable exercise for a number of reasons and is, I believe, encouraged by the Maimonidean enterprise.

First, as we have seen, his resolve to compose the *Guide* for his student Joseph was "aroused" by the memory of their live discussions regarding "a [biblical] *verse* or some text in the *Sages*" (GP Intro., 4). Consistent with that motivation is the avowed intention to devote his entire treatise to a microanalysis of "perplexing" biblical terms, which should set the stage for a macroanalysis of larger biblical units or parables. As for those passages in which no term, verse, or parable can be found, it would be a mistake to view them as addressing strictly philosophical issues, of no relevance to biblical literature. On the contrary, they too are concerned with the Bible, but covertly so, either preparing the way for or "hinting" at the elucidation of problematic terms or parables (ibid., 10). Though always cognizant of the universal, the overarching concern of the *Guide* is how to engage the foundational texts of a shared parochial tradition with its readers.

Second, the *Guide* is only an instructional manual intended to accompany the never-ending process of reading the verses and understanding the sages, whose simple exposure of narratives as parables is "like someone's removing a screen from between the eye and a visible thing" (ibid., 14). Every proper philosophical understanding of a biblical parable is thus, in some sense, a reversal of the regressive vision obtained by Adam and Eve, subsequent to their sin, whose "eyes were opened and they knew" (Gen 3:7). Gaining sight here is a metaphor for the psychological transition from thinking about universal truths to thinking about matters that are contingent and tenuous—"uncovering mental vision" (GP I:2, 25). Being oblivious to the parabolic in Scripture is tantamount to reading it through post-sin Adamic lenses—it remains historically, culturally, and ethnically contingent. Maimonides provided the reading strategies necessary to liberate the text from its contingent moorings and repatriate it to its pre-sin Adamic universalist perspective. His legacy is to spur readings of biblical narratives that are both philosophically tenable and that transcend their own simple historicity. One such narrative is chapter 8 of the book of Nehemiah, whose account of a unique fifth-century BCE celebration of Tabernacles is itself a parable about the timeless relationship between a Jew and his traditional texts.

One can (indeed, must), of course, dispense with any historicocritical method to appreciate how Maimonides may have understood a biblical text. Furthermore, any such text, for Maimonides as for any Jew firmly ensconced in the rabbinic tradition, would have to be filtered through a history of classical rabbinic exegesis. It is therefore not only the core text that must be subjected to the Maimonidean method, but its reception within the rabbinic corpus as well. The narrative of Neh 8 consists, in brief, of the following events: In approximately the middle of the fifth century before the Common Era[96] on the first day of the seventh month, the date of the traditional rabbinic Jewish New Year,[97] Ezra assembles the post-exilic community of Jerusalem for a mass public Torah recital. The "book of the Law of Moses" *(sefer torat Mosheh)* is read from "dawn until midday."[98] The next day, another opening of the book leads to the discovery of the festival of booths that is prescribed for that month. The people are advised to construct their booths and the holiday is celebrated for seven days; on each day there is a reading from the Torah scroll. Unlike its traditional role as the New Year, the ceremony on this day is staged as preparatory to the observance of the festival of booths. No mention is made of either the New Year or the biblically prescribed, intervening Day of Atonement scheduled for the tenth of the month. The keys to a Maimonidean unraveling of this account are the *Leitwörter* of *understanding (binah)* and *intelligibility (sekhel)* that anchor the entire chapter.[99] The appeal for Maimonideans lies in Ezra's vigorous endorsement of Torah (and, consequently, Judaism) as a process of understanding rather than one of obedient ritual.

The assembly is composed of "men and women and all who could listen with understanding" *(mavin lishmoa)* (Neh 8:2), a group whose members share the power of comprehension.[100] The defining characteristic of wisdom is repeated in verse 3 when the reading takes place in the presence of "the men, women, and those who could understand." The reiteration of "understanding" coupled with a concentrated attentiveness signified by "the ears of all the people were given to the scroll of the Teaching [Torah]"[101] convey the sense that this is not a mere ceremonial recitation of the Torah; rather, it is being *taught*. The scene's shift in religious orientation from one that is cultic, Temple, and priestly based to one that is textually and intellectually focused is particularly captured by the role of the Levites, who "cause the people to understand the Torah" (v. 7). The Levites' traditional role as assistants in the Temple service is replaced here by a new overriding role as *teachers*.[102]

For Maimonides, the Levites are reverting to their original ancestral legacy that originated with the commissioning of Levi and his descendants by his father Jacob as educators, "setting apart Levi, whom he appointed as head of an academy to teach the way of God and preserve Abraham's mandate. He commanded his sons that Levi would be in charge in perpetuity so that the teaching would not be forgotten" (MT *Laws of Idolatry* 3:3). The Levites ensure the perpetuation of an intellectual tradition as educators and not as cultic assistants and performers. Since true knowledge by definition cannot be the exclusive preserve of any particular class, Maimonides understood the Levites' dedicated life of learning and teaching to be a model to which all human beings can aspire (MT *Laws of the Sabbatical Year and Jubilee* 13:12–13).[103] Maimonides transforms even their particular Temple functions as singers and musicians who were a soothing accompaniment to Temple ritual, ancillary to the priestly role, to primary communicators in and of themselves. Their role is recast in direct contradistinction to the cultic function of the priests, since they "did not sacrifice and [were] not imagined as imploring forgiveness for sin as is stated with regard to the Priests" (GP III:45, 579). Instead, their task is entirely reduced to singing, "for the purpose of *singing* too is to bring about an affection of the soul by means of the words in question; and the soul can only be affected by means of pleasing melodies." Music is simply a means of communicating, and therefore the use of singers is wholly dependent on the tonal integrity of their voices, the essential medium of teaching (ibid.; MT *Laws of the Temple Vessels* 3:8, where qualification for Temple service is solely a matter of the Levite's voice remaining intact). Their portrayal as pedagogues in Neh 8 captures the purpose to which their cultic duties allude. They are purveyors of knowledge, not merely assistants to sacrificial rites.[104]

Ezra's educational campaign climaxes in verse 8, where the Torah reading is imbued with a multidimensional language of intelligibility— "they read from the scroll of the Teaching of God, *translating it [meforash]*[105] and giving *the sense [sekhel]*[106] so they *understood [mevinim]* the reading." Whether one parses this threefold phraseology as the Talmud does[107] or interprets it as many of the medieval commentators do,[108] the sense is of a profound noetic experience that demands an intense intellectual engagement with the text. Religious worship is no longer the precinct of the priests, but is democratized into the domain common to all men qua men—thought and mind. The scene consists of all those who are capable of doing so (understanding) expressing their true humanity and cultivating their divine image that, for Maimonides, consists of "intellectual apprehension" (GP I:2). Why is it, however, that this sublime Maimonidean moment is abruptly shattered by a peculiar outbreak of sadness and weeping (Neh 8:9)?

Gersonides, a loyal Maimonidean, attributes it to the recital at that moment of the Deuteronomic curses that promise to rain down on violators of the Law. For Maimonides, human nature matures and evolves but cannot shift gears instantaneously.[109] Gersonides' explanation is insightful, for it sees the people momentarily lapsing into a superstitious, fear-based mode of worship motivated by the anticipation of reward and punishment rather than the pure virtue of wisdom that Ezra has attempted to inculcate. The antidote lies in the teaching that true joy can only be experienced in the amassing of wisdom, as Maimonides so vividly conveyed with the restriction of the water drawing joy to the intellectual elite. The Levites, therefore, appropriately assert themselves again in their capacity of "making the people understand" (v. 9), to silence them by advising them that "rejoicing in the Lord is the source of your strength" (v. 10). The Levites are successful in consoling the people because they have managed to *explain* things. As the verse indicates, joy returns because the people have made the transition from fear to knowledge—"then all the people went to eat and drink and send portions and make great merriment *for they understood the things they were told*" (v.11).

At this juncture those who previously held positions of authority on the basis of heredity, clan leadership, or their being priests or Levites, attend to "fathom *[le-haskil]* the words of the Torah" (v. 13). Authority can no longer be maintained by tradition and lineage, but must be authenticated by understanding *(sekhel).*[110] What they discover is the commandment to celebrate the festival of booths *(Sukkot)* (v. 14), but this *Sukkot* celebration is unique in the annals of ancient Israel. They have "not done so from the days of Joshua son of Nun to that day—and there was great rejoicing" (v. 17). It is the joy of this extraordinary *Sukkot,* unprecedented in the previous six centuries of Israelite history, that may have inspired Maimonides to intellectualize the participants in the extreme joy associated with that holiday. That joy would not have consisted in the construction of booths of verse 16 but in the performance that follows, the reading from "the scroll of the teaching of God each day from the first to the last day" (v. 18). Every day of this singular event is defined not by a ritualistic Torah recital, but as one whose tenor is informed by the essential characteristics of the mass recital preceding it—wisdom and understanding. The notion that the relationship between man and God is mediated through wisdom and not ritual is also represented by the construction of booths everywhere in Jerusalem, including "in the courtyards of the house of God."[111] Encroachment into the priestly sanctum by the conspicuous symbols of this unique festival is a metaphor for a religion driven by intellect usurping one fomented by cult and mystery.[112]

Finally, since Ezra is the driving force behind the events recounted in Neh 8, his literary portrayal is consistent with his philosophical reconfiguration of this holiday and, more broadly, of Judaism. Ezra is described in this chapter alternately as a scribe *(sofer)* and a priest *(kohen).* He is identified as a scribe in verses 1, 4, 13, as a priest in verse 2, and once as a combination of both. The fluctuation between scribe and priest or both is a literary device conveying the sense that Ezra is neither purely scribe nor purely priest, but rather a blend of scribal priesthood—his priestly status is informed by his scribal (intellectual) proficiency. There are, however, two other mentions of Ezra in close sequence in which he appears as simply Ezra, without any title or official designation, during the dramatic opening of the Torah: "Ezra opened the scroll[113] in the sight of all the people, for he was above all the people;[114] as he opened it all the people stood up. Ezra blessed the Lord, the great God and all the people answered Amen, Amen" (vv. 5–6). This is the prototype for all future synagogue Torah recitals, which are preceded by a blessing.[115] A rabbinic tradition considers the "great God" blessed by Ezra to have been the Tetragrammaton *(shem ha-meforash)* (b. *Yoma* 69b).[116] Traditionally, it was only the High Priest who could ever utter this divine name, only once annually, and then only within the secret confines of the Holy of Holies in the Temple (see MT *Laws of the Yom Kippur Service* 2:6–7). Once again, the scene captures Ezra's policy of rendering man's relationship to God accessible to all by way of wisdom. His two titles merge and then disappear into the anonymity of simply Ezra, an Israelite, indistinguishable from his cohorts. Just as the booths were set up on sacred space, so Ezra usurps the private, rare, and mysterious utterance of the ineffable name by the High Priest and publicly pronounces it in dedication of the venture to understand Torah.

Even in the midst of this national joint effort to substantively comprehend the contents of the Torah there still remains that elite enclosed space cordoned off from its surroundings. Ezra's Torah-reading spectacle is the source of the rabbinic law mentioned previously that prohibits any conversation during a Torah recital, including discussions regarding *halakhah*. Between the two possible verses of Neh 8 proposed by different schools in the Talmud—verse 3 or 5—Maimonides chose verse 3, "the ears of all the people were given to the scroll of the teaching," as the biblical source for this rule. The rule contemplates unmitigated attention to the reading: "everyone listens and remains silent and pays attention to what he is reading" (MT *Laws of Prayer* 12:9).[117] The exception is the one "whose Torah is his profession," who is allowed to ply his trade even during the sacrosanct moments of public Torah readings. No mass endeavor, no matter how focused, can ever accommodate the intensity of the sage's focus; and so the halakhic legacy of Ezra's assembly is one that preserves the distinction between the sage and the people.

CHAPTER 6

God, the Supreme Outsider

Indwelling (*Shekhinah*) as Metaphor for Outdwelling

Physical or existential displacement is often the lot of the outsider who defies containment within the narrow confines of the societal norm. The convert's loss of family can never be fully replaced by his newly adopted family for its cohesion is still largely determined by ancestral roots. The heretic, though sharing those roots, travels in the opposite direction than that of the convert by rejecting the beliefs that help shape his lineage. The leper is halakhically ostracized and forced to assume an official mode of estrangement that is "outside the camp." The king, as we have seen, must resist the tendency of his office to situate himself beyond the reach of his people, which is accomplished by relegating himself to a place on the social spectrum accessible to all. One form of social estrangement driven by humility neutralizes another driven by arrogance. The sage fits comfortably within the social framework of his co-religionists, but only externally. Internally he practices a religion and worships a God wholly alien to those who surround him.

The Ontologization of a Placeless Presence

All these outsiders share a sense of spatial alienation, either internally or externally, from their surrounding religious and intellectual environments, and their physical spaces shift, either congruently or not, with their inner psychic spaces. The leper's expulsion from his home environment follows a diagnosis by the priest, and not by a medical practitioner, which indicates an inner dislocation serious enough to invite physical spatial dislocation. In Heideggerian terminology, one can only understand where any of these "outsiders" are situate in the world "in terms of the 'yonder' of the world that is ready-to-hand—the 'yonder' which is the dwelling place of Dasein as *concern.*"[1] For Maimonides, however, the "yonder" is the limit of intellectual reflection regarding the nature of God, or the ground of all Being. The predicament of these various outsiders serves to accentuate the authentic dwelling place of man in general, which is dwelling *as concern,* concern for that Being as creator that provided the dwelling place enabling man to create his own dwelling place saturated with concern.

This book would be incomplete without a chapter devoted to God, the one existence that ontologizes placelessness. God does not occupy space, but provides and governs space, as indicated by the midrashic translation of the verse "The eternal God is a dwelling place" (Deut 33:27): "He is the dwelling place of the world, but His world is not His dwelling place" (*Gen Rabbah* 68:9; quoted in GP I:70, 172–73).[2] The locus of God is pure perfection, and His *place* in the prophetic texts, for Maimonides, always signifies "His rank and the greatness of His portion in existence" (GP I:8, 33). As such, there is no greater model for the kind of place man must ultimately stake out for himself. *Imitatio dei* would consist of striving for, and eventually achieving, a place of rank and perfection. Man's destination is God, and the road he travels is thought; as he gets closer to his goal (as discussed in the case of the sage), he merges with placelessness. Since Maimonides' entire body of work can be said to be about God, in this chapter I limit myself to God as *shekhinah* (Indwelling), a "manifestation" of God particularly problematic for its later emergence in the mystical tradition as an actual divine hypostasis. That the notion of "place" must be thoroughly deconstructed is indicated by a particularly lengthy digression in the lexicographical chapter in the *Guide* on the term "place" *(me'onah),* which actually serves as a second introduction to the *Guide* as a whole:

Know with regard to every term whose equivocality we shall explain to you in this Treatise that our purpose in such an explanation is not only to draw your attention to what we mention in that particular chapter. Rather do we open a gate and draw your attention to such meanings of that particular term as are useful for our purpose, not for the various purposes of whoever may speak the language of this or that people. As for you, you should consider the books of prophecy and other works composed by men of knowledge, reflect on all the terms used therein, and take every equivocal term in that one from among its various senses that is suitable in that particular passage. These our words are the key to this Treatise and others; a case in point being the explanation we have given here of the term *place* in the dictum of Scripture *Blessed be the glory of the Lord from His place.* (I:8, 33–34)

Maimonides strategically chose the chapter on place to reiterate this introduction for both literary and philosophical reasons. First, it admonishes the reader not to be trapped by the chronological placing of his own composition. The meaning of every discussion dedicated to biblical terms is not confined to its particular place in the planned structure of the *Guide,* but radiates out across its entirety. It is also not restricted to the particular verses chosen as illustrations of a particular term's figurative senses but extends to any other verse cited in the *Guide* in which that term reappears. Philosophically, the notion of "place" permeates the entire enterprise of the *Guide* insofar as it reorients the relationship among God, man, and world from space to the ethereal, and reroutes the path along which proximity to God is gained.

Maimonides directed the reader to transpose the equivocal sense of the term "place" onto God's direction to Moses, "there is a place by Me" (Exod 33:21). The place God has reserved for man is "a rank in theoretical speculation and the contemplation of the intellect, not that of the eye" (GP I:8, 34), commensurate with the "place" He occupies. As His place is one of "rank," so is man's; as God's rank is so supreme that it surpasses anything with which man is normally familiar, man, in order to appreciate some semblance of that divine rank, must detach himself from his surroundings and *see* beyond them with a seeing that is "not that of the eye." Two inanimate natural objects, whose tangible dimensions disappear in his mind's eye, bracket Moses' journey toward this intellectual climax: the burning bush from which he "hid his face" (Exod 3:6) in a gesture of intellectual humility, restraining himself from what can be known but what he was not yet prepared to know (GP I:5); and the rock at Mt. Horev (Exod 33:21), which is the final destination of all knowing, the final *place* (= rank) to which one can intellectually elevate oneself.[3] Moses travels from a place he rightly perceives as nonspatial, while acknowledging his own limitations, to a place at which he must be apprised that he can go no further. In both instances, Maimonides preserves the literal sense of geographic location alongside the abstract sense, conceding the human penchant for the concrete. The intellectual metaphor, in the case of the burning bush, is not exclusive. It is "an additional meaning of the verse over and above the external meaning" of shielding his eyes from the light. Further, the theoretical degree of understanding indicated by the *place* of Mt. Horev is "in addition to the meaning alluding to a local place that was to be found on that mountain on which the separation and achievement of perfection came to pass."[4] These caveats are crafted to both accommodate a mass psychological need and relegate their relevance to a mere afterthought, without which the passage's integrity remains intact.[5]

Moses' reading of the world mirrors his existential condition within his community. Moses flees the burdens of his Egyptian social context, assumes the lonely profession of shepherding, and roams the desert in solitude, seeking self-fulfillment. His eventual return to his social commitments is actually enabled by his intellectual revelation at the burning bush. He comes to realize that self-perfection need not be achieved by ascetic disavowal of his surroundings but can be "in addition to" it. Just as his perceptions of the bush and rock are abstract and concrete, so he can sustain a speculative progression, fueled by solitude, alongside his social movements. He can be an insider and an outsider at the same time, heading his way methodically toward the mountain where he remains high above the people physically and metaphorically. His revelation at Mt. Horev is the culmination of what he embarked on at the bush, where "*separation* and achievement of perfection came to pass."[6]

Moses approximates, as far as humanly possible, the model posed by God Himself as the supreme outsider, and becomes, by his separation, a living corrective to any temptation for grounding God in the world.[7] That is why the Mosaic approach at the burning bush is presented in GP I:5 as a model for priests and anyone of the general public who nears the Temple. The priests are warned at Sinai to "sanctify themselves lest the Lord break forth upon them" (Exod 19:22), and the public is cautioned by

Solomon to "guard thy foot when thou goest to the house of God" (Eccl 4:17). Because the public tends to conceive the Temple as a residence, or a space, which God occupies, it is a location that must be approached bearing in mind Moses' restraint at the bush. The entire cultic apparatus must, in essence, negate itself, since its very raison d'être was a concession to a culture that could not possibly fathom abstract worship of an abstract God.[8] The emotional rush to embrace an insider God must be suppressed so that eventually the outsider God becomes the fulcrum for human thought. One of Maimonides' primary aims in the *Guide* is to methodically dismantle the scriptural and rabbinic edifice that promotes God's being drawn into the human sphere of existence, and then to fill the vacuum with a minimalist theology of the outsider God. To accomplish this he continued the deconstructive reading he applied to "place" with another major offending term, *shakhon* (to dwell), so that the common rabbinic term for God's presence that is derived from it, *shekhinah,* can assume its proper place within his theology.[9]

Deconstructing Biblical Dwelling *(Shekhinah)*

As was his usual course, Maimonides began his analysis of the term *shakhon* with its literal sense, supported with biblical illustrations. In this case the first literal construction of the term already contains within itself the seeds of its figurative expansion, since it means setting up a residence "by which either a general or a particular place may be meant" in which a person dwells "even if he undoubtedly moves within it" (GP I:25, 55). "Dwell" does not imply a stationary mode, nor is it confined to a narrow locale. It can encompass a wide area within which one has established residence. The literal sense of the term "Dwell," then, is distinct from another term often used to convey residence, *yeshivah* (sitting),[10] which suggests "a state of the most perfect stability and steadiness" (GP I:11, 37). With respect to residence, the term "dwell" has a wider range with greater flexibility than the rigid and narrow "sitting." Even at this level of external meaning, the term *shekhinah,* when God is its subject, need not be read as confining Him to one particular geographical spot, since it is not limited by a "particular place" or localized by immobility. In its literal sense it has already allowed for a roaming presence of God that is not circumscribed by the Temple.

Maimonides then carved out a figurative dimension to the term *shekhinah* by citing a verse in which its subject is lifeless (cloud) and its object is incorporeal (day)—Job's agonizing lament regarding his day of birth, "Let a cloud dwell upon it" (3:5). His proof-text, though, is no mere randomly chosen evidence for the proposition that "dwell" can be taken metaphorically. It is also an integral prologue to his next proclamation that whenever God is the subject of the term "dwell," it connotes "the permanence of His Indwelling" or His providence in whatever place they may subsist in permanent fashion or toward whatever matter providence may be permanently directed." He then concluded the chapter by reiterating, with some further clarification as to what is meant by "Indwelling," that with respect to God "it is used in the sense of the permanence of His Indwelling—I mean His created light—in a place, or the permanence of providence with regard to a certain matter."

From a literary perspective, Job's anguished regret at having been born is expressed as a negation of each of these metaphorical aspects of "dwell." First, the call for obscuring that day with a cloud is preceded by the plea "Let not God seek [from the root *darash*] it from above" (v. 4); in other words, God should have ignored that day or it should not have come within the ambit of divine providence. Second, Job wishes the day blackened to the point where "no light shine upon it," so that it is left enveloped in utter darkness. In sum, Job has called for an absence of directed providence and created light, the two metaphorical senses of "dwell," thereby lending some theological rationale to his incomprehensible suffering. This is the perspective of the pre-revelation Job worldview, a world devoid of wisdom, in which suffering is incongruous with moral virtue.[12] Job can only explain the lack of correspondence between practical morality and reward and punishment by conceding that "the deity has no knowledge of our actions merely from the fact that they see wicked people living in prosperity and abundance" (GP III:19, 477).

In his non-wisdom state, Job is a colleague of "philosophers" like Elisha ben Abuyah. They attribute a lack of omniscience to God because of their anthropocentric outlook, as they "consider that which exists only with reference to a human individual . . . and if something happens to him that is contrary to what he wishes, he makes the trenchant judgment that all that exists is an evil" (GP III:12, 442).[13] Job conveys this view of an ignorant God through the poetic expression of a day that is "darkened," which God does "not seek" and which is shrouded by a "cloud." Post-revelation Job, however, is apprised of the theory of providence Maimonides developed in the *Guide* III:17—namely, that "providence is consequent upon the intellect and attached to it" (GP III:17, 474). Maimonides intended this citation not simply as a proof-text but also as a philosophical preface to the metaphorical meanings of "dwell" and to the three verses cited as exemplary of these meanings.

The first verse cited as an illustration of the metaphorical meaning of *shakhon* in relation to God, "And the glory of the Lord dwelt" (Exod 24:16), is calculated as a direct challenge to Job's lament of Job 3:5. The divine "glory" of this verse manifests itself in a cloud, as its full context relates: "And Moses ascended to the mountain *and the cloud covered the mountain*. And the glory of the Lord dwelt on Mt. Sinai *and the cloud covered it for six days* and He called to Moses *from the midst of the cloud* . . . and Moses came *into the midst of the cloud*" (Exod 24:15–18). A biblical moment of supreme revelation chosen by Maimonides to represent the workings of divine providence is itself inundated with the image of the cloud. Job's cloud of confusion is subverted by Moses' cloud of clarity, both of which disclose conflicting understandings of divine providence. In each case the image of the cloud can maintain its poetic signification of obscurity, but the difference lies in the subjects and objects of that obscurity. For Job, the appearance of disorder in the world entails an ignorant God, for the world is obscured from the divine field of vision. For Moses, the cloud that envelops that which represents God's providence ("the glory of the Lord dwelt") signifies what is obscured from man's intellectual field of vision. Moses' cloud precisely corresponds to the post-revelation Jobian awareness that there is a limit to man's cognitive potential; "it is obligatory to stop at this point and to believe that nothing is hidden from Him, may He be exalted" (GP III:23, 496).[14] The cloud is that upper intellectual barrier that cannot be overcome, the recognition of which is attained by way of the realization that divine governance does not correspond to anything within the human experience. Maimonides went so far as to reduce the entire aim of the book of Job to this "knowledge," which refutes any conception that "His knowledge is like our knowledge or that His purpose and His providence and His governance are like our purpose and our providence and our governance" (ibid., 497). A cloud of informed ignorance remedies Job's predicament, for "if man knows this, every misfortune will be borne lightly by him" (ibid.).

The *Guide*'s deliberate selection of proof-text[15] is designed to lay the groundwork in the introductory lexicographical section for its radical theology of providence and governance, which determines the faith of the religious man by his efforts to distance God.[16] The further God is pushed outside the human physical and cognitive experience, the closer one gets to Him. Proximity to God entails a negative appreciation of Him as "outsider." As He is drawn inside, "you get further away from the knowledge of His true reality," and "you become more remote from Him" (GP I:59, 139). The literary strategy of the planned proof-text constructs the only authentic "Jewish" way of accomplishing that distancing—methodical and concentrated engagement with Judaism's primary formative texts.

I would like to advance another reason for Maimonides' choice of Exod 24:16 to illustrate figurative divine dwelling. It is embedded in a passage that sharply contrasts the Mosaic and the mass perceptions of the divine presence at Mt. Sinai. For Moses, it is the "cloud," a cloud I have argued to stand for the self-acknowledged limits negative theology imposes on the intellect, from which God beckons him and into which he enters for his ascent. For the people, it is a "consuming fire" *(esh okhelet)*, specifically identified as their perception alone: "And the appearance of the glory of the Lord *in the sight of the Israelites* was like a *consuming fire*" (24:17). Elsewhere Maimonides cited Deut 4:24, a key verse for his construction of the heretic, which also describes God as a consuming fire, to signify one of the two notions conveyed by the activity of eating. One is constructive, since the body is nourished by food intake, while the other is destructive, since the food ingested is broken down and disappears (GP I:30, 63). God as a consuming fire reflects the latter sense—"He destroys those who disobey Him as a fire destroys that which is in its power" (ibid.).[17]

The verse also equates God's image as a consuming fire with His being a "jealous God" *(el qanna)*. For Maimonides, these are pragmatically necessary representations of God reserved exclusively for the battle against idolatry.[18] Chapter I:36 of the *Guide,* which advances this proposition, explicitly condemns those who seek to excuse their idolatrous notions of God because of being misled by the external sense of Scripture. Although they cannot be held accountable for their lack of intellectual resources to logically demonstrate the veracity of negative theology, they can be held accountable for their lack of *belief* in it. That belief is achieved only by acquiescing to the sage's teachings, for "there is no excuse for one who does not accept[19] the authority of men who inquire into the truth and are engaged in speculation if he himself is incapable of engaging in such speculation" (GP I:36, 85). Exodus 24:16 then evokes this intellectual stratification at the very inception of Israel as a national religion, posing it as a paradigm for Israel's future viability. Moses is the man of authority who has attained a correct notion of God and whose stature demands obedience. He is also the sage as supreme human outsider, captured by the conclusion of this passage in verse 18 that has him situated alone at the top of the mountain "for forty days and forty nights." The majority of the people, who can never hope to transcend, on their own, corporeal notions of God, are compelled to believe in negation, in God as outsider, on the basis of Mosaic authority alone, and sanctioned by the threat of God as a consuming fire.

Moses, in this passage, is the perfect man of authority from whom the people learn, since his intellectual profile subverts the image of the consuming fire at the very same time that it exploits it to reinforce his teachings. His philosophical career is launched by the spectacle of an object ablaze but yet not consumed by the fire—"And there was a bush all aflame, yet the bush was not consumed" (Exod 3:2). Maimonides directed his readers back to that dedicatory phenomenon by his discriminating selection of the third proof-text corroborating the figurative sense of "dwell," "And the will of Him that dwelt in the bush" (Deut 33:16). For the rabbinic mind there can be no escaping the reference here to the burning bush encountered by Moses.[20] Moses represents those who are not in need of the anthropomorphic threat of a wrathful, consuming, fire-like God to sustain their beliefs in an incorporeal being. Their belief is maintained by the constructive notion of eating symbolized by the *non-eating* fire, since the food in this case does not deconstruct and disappear. Moses, therefore, directs the mind to the positive sense of "eating" as "knowledge, learning, and, in general, the intellectual apprehensions through which the permanence of the human form endures in the most perfect of states, just as the body endures through food in the finest of its states" (GP I:30, 63).[21] The metaphor rigorously works itself out with Moses' antithesis, the "nobles of Israel," whose conception of God is tainted by corporeality and who are appropriately punished by being consumed by fire themselves.[22] The manner of their demise preserves the necessary belief entailed by the image of God as consuming fire ready to retaliate against the idolatrous ideology of anthropomorphism.

As the Moses/Israel model at Sinai is the pedagogical model for the ongoing future of the belief in God's unity, the specific association of divine "will" with "dwelling at the bush" is critical. Maimonides acknowledged that the uniqueness of Mosaic prophecy and of the Sinaitic theophany poses a dilemma for the future of Judaism. What takes their place once they have expired? Subsequent prophets perpetuate the Sinaitic Mosaic model, since what transpired at Sinai "will not be a thing subsisting permanently with you, and in the future there will not be anything like it: and there will not permanently be *fire* and a *cloud,* such as those that are now *always on the tabernacle*" (GP II:34, 366–67). What this means is that all post-Moses prophets are commissioned to instruct the people by maintaining the delicate balance in their teachings between necessary and true beliefs, signified by the cloud and fire at Sinai that are no longer extant. More accurately put, they must preserve the message of the *metaphor* of the fire and cloud, which has a *literary* history of transpiring and then ceasing.

The very notion of prophecy also carries with it, from a popular perspective, a counterintuitive limitation on what is perceived to be an unbridled divine will. Only intellectually trained individuals qualify as recipients of prophetic communication. It is no more possible for God to transform an unqualified individual into a prophet than it is to "turn an ass or a frog into a prophet" (GP II:32, 362).[23] The corollary of Moses' gesture of restraint at the bush is that God Himself is restrained by the characteristics of the recipient that determine the quality of prophetic endowment. Theoretically, had the divine will at the bush wished to grant Moses some prophetic knowledge for which he was not prepared at that moment, it could not have done so. Properly understood, the very existence of a prophet attests to a "limited" divine will, the metaphor of "the will of Him that dwelt at the bush," which must replace popular notions of perfection. What the will at the bush also teaches is that limitation in certain instances is, from a philosophical perspective, perfection.[24]

Maimonides' remark about the transience of the fire and cloud that were "always on the Tabernacle" needs to be addressed. His reference is to the desert Tabernacle over which "a cloud of the Lord rested by day, and a fire would appear in it by night" (Exod 40:38).[25] What must be stressed here is that Maimonides was making a claim about the literary life of these miraculous phenomena, picking up on biblical narrative and language that are couched in metaphor. The metaphor has now migrated to another context, from Sinai to the Tabernacle, and presents a new conception of the Tabernacle's function. The continuity between the contextual metaphors of Sinai and Tabernacle provides the background necessary for understanding the choice of the final proof-text for the figurative sense of "dwell": "And I will dwell among the children of Israel" (Exod 29:45). Maimonidean exegesis here benefits from the biblical theology reflected in this verse. The verse is preceded by a singling out of the Tent of Meeting as a localized source for sanctity and oracular communications. Unexpectedly, it does not provide a residence for God. Rather, His dwelling jarringly finds itself among the people, so that a certain knowledge is conveyed about God who "brought them out of Egypt that I might dwell [from the root *shakhon*] among them" (v. 46).[26]

The citation of 29:45 picks up on this striking shift of anticipated place and accentuates the Tabernacle's lack of any palpable presence. God is a homeless presence consistent with His aloof state of being. The other two citations are capable of assuming either figurative meaning offered for "dwell." Given that the dwelling in this case is not localized but diffused among the population, unlike the other two proof-texts, one of its figurative connotations as "the permanence of His Indwelling—I mean His created light—in a place" can safely be ruled out.[27] The remaining option is to read the verse in light of its alternative meaning of "the permanence of providence with regard to a certain matter." What sense does the verse make now? What is the "certain matter" *(amr)* with regard to which the "permanence of providence" is directed?

Prior to answering these questions, I want to state my position that they are equally as relevant to the other two proof-texts for the following reason. Although the other two verses can be read plausibly with "dwell" as a signifier for "created light," this is intended only as a concessionary reading for those who cannot tolerate absolute abstraction. In the chapter devoted to the term "passing" *(avor)*, Maimonides exploited an opportunity to discuss the substance of the very apex of Moses' search for divine knowledge, captured by "And the Lord passed by before his face" at Sinai (Exod 34:6).[28] Pertinent here for our discussion of these proof-texts related to "dwell" is that Maimonides offered his audience a clear and free choice from among three alternative readings in deciphering what precisely "passed by": (1) the Mosaic encounter unfolded entirely within a prophetic vision containing "everything, namely, that which he had demanded, that which was denied to him, and that which he apprehended, being intellectual and admitting of no recourse to the senses"; (2) there was an empirical vision, that is, "there was, in addition to this intellectual apprehension, an apprehension due to the sense of sight, which, however, had for its object a *created thing*, through seeing which the perfection of intellectual apprehension might be achieved"; or (3) there was an auditory component as well as visual, that is, "there was in addition an apprehension due to the sense of hearing: that which *passed by before his face* being the *voice*, which is likewise indubitably a *created thing*" (GP I:21, 51). The second alternative is ascribed to Onkelos, whose exegetical signature, according to Maimonides, is to always fill in a subject for actions that in the Bible are directly attributed to God, thus avoiding anthropomorphisms.[29] These inserts can be alternatively "glory" or *shekhinah* or "word" (ibid., 50).

There is no reason why that same choice, between pure abstraction and some trace of empirical tangibility, would not be available in other contexts of divine action or revelation, especially when the option is expressed, as it is with "dwell," as either an "Indwelling" or "created light" or a pure conception like providence. In addition, when such choices are offered,[30] given Maimonides' overarching principle that true knowledge of God is proportionate to how much corporeality can be negated with respect to Him (in other words, how much He can be abstracted),[31] Maimonides' unqualified preference was for the nonsensory and cognitive. On one such occasion he articulated his preference, explicitly relegating the sensory option of created things to a dumbing-down of pure monotheistic theology.

The very chapter that deals with Moses' vision at the burning bush concludes with a general hermeneutic applicable to all ocular terms that have God as their object, which rules out sensory apprehension altogether. For those incapable of such an austere minimalism, he offered the following indulgence: "If, however, an individual of insufficient capacity should not wish to reach the rank to which we desire him to ascend and should he consider that all the words [figuring in the Bible] concerning this subject are indicative of sensual perception of *created lights*—be they angels or something else—why, there is no harm in thinking this" (GP I:5, 31). A theology of created lights is strictly an allowance to satisfy an anthropomorphic appetite, by deflecting it once removed from God. However, for the refined intellect, it is simply an intolerable falsity. Read in light of this concluding assertion, Moses at the burning bush, raised previously in the same chapter, could not possibly have confronted any empirical phenomenon like light. The fact that Moses' noetic experience is identified as "an additional meaning over and above its external meaning that indicates he hid his face because of his being afraid to look upon the light manifesting itself" now means that there is a hierarchy of meaning. The "additional meaning" is its only meaning for Moses and those like him, while the "external meaning" is unacceptable to them but *allowable* for mass consumption. Identification of the sensory reading as the "external *[zahir]* meaning" attunes the reader to an even more radical displacement of the narrative's literalness.

In his introduction, Maimonides adopted the rabbinic metaphor that analogizes the function of a parable to the lighting of worthless material in order to find lost valuables. Its role "in itself is worth nothing, but by means of it you can understand the words of the Torah" (GP Intro., 11, quoting *Songs Rabbah* 1:8).[32] So the hermeneutical structure of biblical parables consists of a valuable "internal *[batin]* meaning of the words of the Torah," embedded in a literal narrative, and an "external *[zahir]* meaning" whose value for "all parables *is worth nothing*" (emphasis mine). The application of that hermeneutic to our narrative of the burning bush thoroughly eradicates any "external" connotations of observable phenomena.

With this in mind I return to the question whether the biblical passage "And I will dwell among the children of Israel" (Exod 29:45) can bear the meaning (and, as the above argument demonstrates, the *sole* meaning) of "permanence of providence with respect to a certain matter." Once a verse is sifted out for citation and assigned meaning it cannot simply be read in isolation. It projects the reader back to its source, which informs its entire context. Since the primary aim of the *Guide* is to address the deep psychological trauma of those intellectually honest scholars of Torah and sophia who "must have felt distressed by the externals of the Law" (GP Intro., 5), failure to perform such an exercise betrays the author's intent. Here that aim is reflected in the connection between the establishment of a central locale for divine presence (Exod 29:43–44) (Tent of Meeting, Tabernacle) and a certain knowledge of a God who "took them out of Egypt to dwell among them" (v. 46)—the declaratory "I am the Lord their God" (v. 46). The narrative constituents of the Tent of Meeting (precursor of the Temple), dwelling as attaching providence, and the precondition of liberation from Egypt in order to dwell amidst Israel can now be read as a philosophical mini-treatise on the nature of divine providence. Such a reading can only be successful within the context of the treatise as a whole. To treat Maimonides seriously is to heed his admonitory preface on how to "grasp the totality of what this Treatise contains so that nothing of it will escape you," a task that eschews any atomistic reading of the work. It is, quite literally, the reader's obligation "to connect its chapters one with the other," and "when reading a given chapter . . . not only to understand the totality of the subject of that chapter, but also to grasp each word that occurs in it in the course of the speech, even if that word does not belong to the intention of the chapter" (GP Intro., 15).

Lexicographical chapters, like the one under discussion, among all others leave a trail of biblical verses that demand revisiting once the treatise has been completed, so that hundreds of biblical passages can be understood as Maimonides would have us understand them.[33] The chapter under discussion is particularly critical because it drains the term *shekhinah,* that is at the root of a rabbinically prominent expression for the divine presence in the world, of any sense of place.[34] For Maimonides, the Bible already deontologizes a term most prone to suggest divinely ontologized space in rabbinic and later kabbalistic theology.[35]

What Maimonides means by "dwelling" among Israel is contingent on what that dwelling has to do with the exodus from Egypt and the construction of a Tent/Tabernacle/Temple, as is indicated by the context of Exod 29:45. Much of the Maimonidean rationale for the commandments is driven by Israel's experience of assimilation in Egypt. The exodus is the beginning of an evolutionary process to wean the Israelites off the pagan theology and modes of worship they had become accustomed to. One of its main targets is the all-pervasive pagan vehicle of worship—the sacrificial cult.[36] Though Maimonides' entire edifice of rationalizing the commandments *(ta'ame ha-mitzvot)* rests on this principle, it suffices here to focus on how the exodus is perceived as a critical stage in this evolutionary process. Jeremiah's enigmatic reproof, "For I spoke not unto your fathers, nor commanded them in the day that I *brought them out of the land of Egypt, concerning burnt offerings or sacrifices*" (7:22–23), demonstrates to what extent the role of the paschal sacrifice, the exodus' foremost normative expression, is diminished. Since Jeremiah cannot have meant this literally (there is after all an inordinate amount of concern with the details of the paschal sacrifice), his aim is to redirect his audience to the Law's primary telos: "For he says that the first intention consists only in your apprehending Me and not worshipping someone other than Me. . . . Those laws concerning sacrifices and repairing to the temple were given only for the sake of the realization of this fundamental principle" (GP III:32, 530).

Ultimately the true significance of the exodus lies not in its introduction of sacrifice but in its radical displacement of sacrifice and cult as proper modes of divine service.³⁷ The exodus was a historical juncture marking the beginnings of the transition in religious ritual from primitive idolatrous sacrificial cult to unadulterated contemplation of God. Consequently, the paschal lamb was in fact intended to subvert rather than reinforce a belief in the efficacy of animal sacrifice. Slaughtering what the host culture considered a god and displaying its blood are now apotropaic rather than destructive omens. Sacrifice, for Maimonides, wreaks havoc with pagan theology and turns its cultic obsession on its head.³⁸

The road toward divine apprehension can be said, then, to be paved with the corpses of sacrificial animals that increasingly contribute to the sacrificial cult's own demise as a viable mode of worship. The closer it comes to its final eradication, the closer one gets to its "first intention," the apprehension of God. The hermeneutical fabric of the end of Exod 29 is woven out of these notions of exodus and cult. Its representational structure is reinforced by the metaphor of "dwell" as "the permanence of providence with regard to a certain matter." Since "providence is consequent on intellect," the more one dismantles the entire cultic infrastructure from its pagan moorings the more one comes within the orbit of providence.³⁹ Not only did Maimonides subvert the cult, he also subverted the text. Even though the passage mentions a place of holiness, there is no place where holiness or God are actually present. Although the exodus from Egypt was orchestrated *around* a sacrifice, it was not accomplished *through* it. And a site designated for ritual slaughter is disengaged from its practical functionality. The exodus undermines the cult even as it mandates it, since its memory serves to entrench the "truth of prophecy and reward and punishment" (GP III:39, 552, commenting on Deut 16:7), two prominent consequences of intellectual perfection.⁴⁰ The three verses that have been cited for the metaphor of "dwell" form a historical trajectory of divine placelessness, beginning with the burning bush (Deut 33:16), moving on to the exodus and the desert temple (Exod 29), and culminating at Sinai (Exod 24:16). Deuteronomy 33:16, the reference to the bush, is one facet of Moses' parting blessing to the people "before his death" (Deut 33:1). As such it looks back to his origins as it looks forward to Israel's theological future. Moses transports his individual realization of divine placelessness at the bush through the exodus and during the desert interval climaxing at Sinai, and now offers that notion of divine otherness as a posthumous legacy if it is to survive him.

Though the term *shekhinah* is not mentioned in the chapter on *shakhon*, Maimonides laid the groundwork for how his students were to understand rabbinic theology as reflected in their use of this term. Leo Strauss, quite correctly and insightfully, draws our attention to the anomaly of this absence of the Hebrew *shekhinah* from the chapter on *shakhon*. He attributes this to Maimonides' concern in the first section of the *Guide* with biblical as opposed to rabbinic theology. Since the term never appears in the Bible, Maimonides conspicuously avoided mentioning it precisely where it would be most expected.[41] Its common connotations of "presence" have been replaced with "providence," to which, we have seen, access is provided solely by intellect.[42]

In the first section of the *Guide,* in four out of the five occasions where the Hebrew term *shekhinah* (as opposed to the Arabic equivalent *sakina*)[43] does in fact appear, it is always in association with the phenomenon referred to as a "created" thing. Three of these occurrences also relate to the methodology of Onkelos' Aramaic *Targum*.[44] Onkelos' approach is commended for its shunning of anthropomorphisms, yet is clearly not the position to which Maimonides himself subscribed. Chapter I:21 offers Onkelos as an option that is explicitly distinguished from Maimonides' own interpretation of Exod 34:6, "And the Lord passed by before his face." While Maimonides radically intellectualized Moses' request and God's response—Moses demanded a certain intellectual apprehension and was granted an intellectual apprehension, albeit somewhat inferior to that which he intended—"admitting of no recourse to the senses," Onkelos allows for a sensual dimension where something is seen (created light) and something is heard (created voice) (GP I:21, 51). Though the reader can exercise his own discretion in choosing between the two approaches, Onkelos caters to those anthropomorphically inclined who are not yet capable of removing the *shekhinah* altogether from the realm of the senses.[45] The notion of the *shekhinah* as a sensual phenomenon that is distinct from God merely paves the way, pedagogically, toward a philosophically advanced understanding of it as encapsulating a thoroughly intellectualized theory of providence.[46]

Maimonides' deconstruction of the term *shekhinah* may also have been a pointed response to the medieval Jewish parochializing of it as the exclusive preserve of Israel, a practice most prominently undertaken by Judah Halevi (d.1141). Though there is scholarly debate as to whether Maimonides was exposed to Halevi's writings and whether Halevi exerted any direct influence on him, it is not unreasonable to assume that Maimonides was, at the very least, familiar with a school of thought associated with Halevi and its doctrines.[47] As is well known, a central tenet of Judah Halevi's exclusivist tendencies toward the Jews and the land of Israel is what he called the *amr ilahi,* translated variously as "divine decree," "command," "order," or just "thing," which uniquely accompanies the Jews or is conjoined to them.[48] As Diana Lobel observes, the phrase, with its source in the Quran and borrowed from Ismaili thought, "becomes a fluid term for the Divine or divine immanence, for God in interaction with creation."[49] She goes on to describe Halevi's penchant for the term *amr* as indicating his being "enamored with the word *amr,* whose protean character matches the mysterious quality of God's presence in Jewish history."[50]

In the chapter on passing, the *Guide* (I:21) offers a number of clear options from which to choose regarding the *shekhinah,* ranging from a compromise position regarding it as a substantive presence associated with the Onkelos school[51] to the purist intellectual position advocated by the true Maimonidean school. Having established those options, the *Guide* then proceeds, in the intervening lexicographical chapters dealing with terms of motion leading up to I:25 on *shakhon,* to effectively disqualify the former as a viable option for Maimonides' dedicated disciples. The argument develops along a subtext that is propelled by key proof-texts interspersed with the insertion of the Arabic *sakinah* and Hebrew *shekhinah.* Maimonides' goal, I believe, was to preempt what he feared current notions of *shekhinah* could evolve into and also that which historically did in fact take root, which Scholem has described as "the role of the *shekhina* as a mythical hypostasis of divine immanence in the world."[52] For Maimonides this would simply amount to substituting one anthropomorphic deity for another. As he put it when explaining the abandonment of a book project concerned with difficult *midrashim,* it "would, as it were, have replaced one individual by another of the same species" (GP Intro., 9).

CHAPTER 7

Deconstructing God's Indwelling

The Challenge to Halevi

In this chapter, I continue with Maimonides' radical deconstruction of God's presence in the world. As a direct corollary of the sort of austere presenceless *shekhinah* explored in chapter 6, Maimonides had to deal with a host of biblical terms commonly used with reference to God. On their face, they undermine his project to "banish" God from the human domain because they pose seductive lures for drawing Him back in. At the very heart of Aristotelian physics is the principle of motion, the operative feature of the cosmos. Associated with properties such as potentiality and actuality endemic to the workings of the natural world, the literal application of motion to God constitutes an offence of capital proportions. Leading up to the chapter on *shakhon,* Maimonides rationalized the biblical use of numerous terms connoting motion, such as "approach," "coming," "going," and "going out" with respect to God. While doing so, he also constructed an intricate preface to his avowedly antimythological conception of the *shekhinah*. What follows is an attempt to reconstruct that preface in pursuit of the acutely outsider God advocated by Maimonides.

God's "Coming"

Chapter I:22 of the *Guide* focuses on the term "to come" *(bo);* to eliminate any of its anthropomorphic connotations, alternative meanings for this term are suggested when its subject is God. Depending on its context, for example, it can allude to either "the descent of His decree or to that of His Indwelling *[sakinah]*" (GP I:22, 52). The latter sense is then illustrated by two verses: "I come to thee in a thick cloud" (Exod 19:9), and "For the Lord, the God of Israel, comes through it" (Ezek 44:2). No general guidelines are offered as to what context demands which figurative option. The only instruction is to take these two proof-texts as paradigmatic, so that "all passages similar to these signify the descent of His Indwelling." The task at hand, as I am convinced it always is, and one which the literature to date has largely neglected, is to return to the passages from which these verses have been excerpted and reread them in light of translating "to come" in this sense. Only then will it be possible to extrapolate to "all passages similar to these," for without this reading there can be no determination of "similarity."

Exodus 19:9 consists of God's informing Moses as to the manner of His appearance at the upcoming Sinaitic revelation. The destination of the divine coming "in a thick cloud" is Moses, so that "the people may hear when I speak with you and trust you thereafter." The *Mishneh Torah* cites this verse in attributing the steadfast conviction concerning the veracity of Mosaic prophecy to the people's unmediated witnessing of God's communication with Moses (*Laws of the Foundations of the Torah* 8:1).[1] Though not privy to the content of that divine communication, they did hear Moses' being addressed by God to convey that content publicly, a form of direct hearsay evidence.[2] The insertion of "descent of the Indwelling" into this event, as described by the *Mishneh Torah,* is consistent with its narrative logic. A more anthropomorphic reading, such as that of Onkelos (as established in the *Guide*'s previous chapter on the term "pass"), can accommodate something "created," like a *shekhinah* that emits sound or speech. On this reading, God has created something of ontological substance separate from Himself that descends and is enveloped by the "thick cloud" and from which speech emerges.

Once Exod 19:9 is subjected to the more philosophically refined hermeneutic of the *Guide,* though, this substantive Indwelling account, I argue, becomes untenable. Notably, the verse appears again in the *Guide*'s exposition of the mass revelation at Sinai (II:33) where initially its role and narrative context are consistent with the *Mishneh Torah* account. The verse is taken to specify that "it was him [Moses] that was spoken to and that they heard the great voice, but not the articulations of speech" (ibid., 364). However, that reading, which maintains the participation of a publicly audible divine sound, is quickly discounted by its relegation to "the external meaning *(ẓahir)* of the text of the Torah."[3] Playing with the rabbinic *midrash* in which the first two commandments issued directly "from the mouth of the Force" (*b. Makkot* 24a; *b. Horayot* 8a; *Songs Rabbah* 1:2; *Pesiqta Rabbati* 22:3), and taking this as reflecting the narrative's level of philosophical truth, Maimonides stated that the publicly heard "voice" is really a metaphor for a collective intellectual apprehension of the nature of God inherent in the first two commandments — namely, His existence and His unity, which "are knowable by human speculation alone." The chapter proceeds to emphasize the uniqueness of that voice apprehension, being "heard" (apprehended) only "one single time — the *voice* through which Moses and all Israel apprehended *I* and *Thou shalt not.*" This detail was forcefully reiterated by Maimonides, who cited the *midrash* as absolutely categorical "that they had not heard another *voice* coming from Him." The only voices subsequently heard in the narrative refer to the natural sounds of trumpets and thunder. Maimonides thus presented a clear alternative to the "external meaning" of the narrative in which some audible divine sound is substituted for apprehension. The divine sound the people actually heard was the internal sound of their own minds arriving at ultimate demonstrable truths about God.

Yet on the heels of an insistent dismissal of any sound at Sinai other than those belonging to man or nature, Maimonides jarringly concluded his nonexternal interpretation with what seems to be an incongruous, even self-contradictory, summation:

> As for the *voice of the Lord,* I mean the created voice from which the *speech [of God]* was understood, they heard it once only, according to what the text of the Torah states and according to what the Sages make clear. ... This was the *voice on hearing which their soul went out of them,* and through which the *first two commandments* were apprehended. Know, that with regard to that *voice* too, their rank was not equal to the rank of *Moses our Master.*

This assertion melds two wholly incompatible accounts of Sinai—created voice and pure apprehension—that simply do not logically cohere. If the first two commandments crystallized in the mind then there was no created voice that communicated them, and vice versa. As Alfred Ivry has quite rightly pointed out, "The 'created voice' is thus as much an embarrassment for Maimonides as the voice of God itself; like his view of the latter he must really regard it too only as a figurative expression."[4] Once again, Maimonides has preserved some semblance of objective reality for the Sinai theophany while, at the same time, thoroughly undermining it. The philosophically astute reader will be logically forced to exercise a choice that will render Maimonides' account coherent by banishing any divine creation from the precinct of Sinai. Others can cling to some hybrid account, preserving the concrete anchor they need to sustain their faith while keeping their distance from outright anthropomorphism.[5]

Maimonides' reintroduction of Onkelos at this juncture of the chapter on Sinai subtly drives the wedge even further between the two levels of audiences. He cited Onkelos' exegesis of the various communications at Sinai to make "clear to you the proposition that we have set forth in detail" (GP II:33, 365). Onkelos' appeal lies in his distinction between divine speech addressed to Moses and the "self-described speech" addressed to Israel. The former is rendered literally and directly as "And God spoke [*umallil* as in Exod 20:1]"; in the latter a medium of speech is interposed between God and Israel, transforming Israel's plea of "Let not God speak with us" (Exod 20:19)[6] into "[Speech] should not be spoken with us on the part of the Lord." What precisely is the "proposition" said to be supported by Onkelos in GP II:33? Here, I believe, the translations of ibn Tibbon, Kafih, and Friedländer replacing (or adding to in the case of Kafih and ibn Tibbon) "proposition" with "distinction" is more instructive. The proposition he endorsed did in fact distinguish between the rank of Moses and the people with regard to their understanding of the first two commandments. Yet, earlier on in the chapter the point was made that precisely with respect to demonstrable truths like these two commandments, "the status of the prophet and that of everyone else who knows it are equal; there is no superiority of one over the other." These two inconsistent propositions, one maintaining a distinction and one an equivalence, merge in the exegesis of Onkelos. Onkelos drew the same distinction as Maimonides between two audiences defined by their *perspectives* on the source of divine speech. The verses chosen to underscore this distinction contrast an objective account

(Moses) with a self-described one (Israel) to reflect the distinction between a true state of affairs and a *perceived* one. The fault lines have been drawn and reinjected back into Onkelos, so that Onkelos' position, so closely tied with the "created things" theology, always reflects them.

Exodus 19:9 has been bifurcated into an external and internal hermeneutic in which the internal belies the external and exposes its falsehood. Demonstrable truths, as at Sinai, are and were universally accessible. When intellects lapsed, as Israel's did at Sinai, into perceived truths such as those suggested by Indwellings or intermediate divine manifestations, a barrier was erected impeding that access. Exodus 19:9 also provides the rationale for the lapse. Elsewhere (III:9) the *Guide* adopts the verse's image of God enveloped in a thick cloud as a metaphor for the impenetrability of His true nature to the human intellect due to its physical confines. The thick cloud represents an insurmountable obstacle to the limitations of the human intellect, "for it draws attention to the fact that the apprehension of His true reality is impossible for us because of the dark matter that encompasses us and not Him, for He is not a body" (ibid., 437). Once again, the "great assembly" is raised, the essential feature of which is God's murky appearance obfuscated by "darkness, cloud, and thick darkness" (Deut 4:11) and the thick cloud of Exod 19:9. Misrepresentations of the divine essence are due to the cloudiness inherent in the human intellect. The belief in divinely created hypostases of sounds or light is a figment of faulty reasoning flowing from that darkness. For that reason Maimonides challenged those sensual notions of light with his own metaphor of light at the conclusion of chapter III:9.

All the darkness surrounding God at Sinai is not to be taken literally, "for near Him there is no darkness but rather perpetual dazzling light, the overflow of which illumines all that is dark." Maimonides mounted a frontal assault on distorted perceptions of divine light as sensory by inverting that light into darkness. True light is knowledge and divine knowledge seeps down to the world in a constant and steady flow by way of the hierarchy of the Intellects. This identification of light with divine overflow reinforces the challenge to the "created things" theology because it projects the reader into chapter II:12, which defines the overflow as a constant stream of pure intellect. It is precisely when justifying the term "overflow" as having best captured the purely incorporeal intersection between God and the world that Maimonides launched into a diatribe against those who correctly acknowledge God's incorporeality but who assert God's governance of the world to be mediated by tangible entities. In addition to contriving an angelology, some also subscribe to the belief that "He gives a command to a particular thing by means of speech similar to our speech—*I mean through the instrumentality of letters and sounds—and that in consequence that thing is affected.* All this follows imagination, which is also in true reality the *evil impulse*" (GP II:12, 280).

This explains the choice of proof-text that closes chapter III:9 to illustrate the light imagery radiating from God down to the world: "And the earth did shine with His glory" (Ezek 43:2). The first half of the same verse introduces the direction from which this "glory" *(kavod)* emanates and what it "sounds" like: "And behold, the glory of the God of Israel was coming from the east and its sound *[qolo]* was like the sound of mighty waters." First, Maimonides was motivated to choose this verse because it combines three pertinent terms whose traditional senses are targets of Maimonides' philosophical purification and reinvention: "sounds/voices," "glory," and "light." Once the chapter has established God's light as His intellectual overflow and defined darkness as resulting from weakness of human intellect, the verse is used to locate the source of that light in "glory," a term I have more to say about further on. The term "overflow" *(shefa)* was chosen because the simile of "an overflowing spring of water" best captured, in human terms, the mode of this intellectual contact between God and world (GP II:12, 279). The "sound of mighty waters" of Ezek 43:2 merely imports the full nuance of the metaphor of overflow, of pure thought as a body of water. Once the verse is informed by the metaphor of intellectual overflow, sound and light that radiate in all directions become components of the same metaphor, representing the influence and impact of intellect on the world. The verse also negates its alternative—sound and light and glory are decidedly *not* created entities.

Second, the glory's eastern direction observed from the prophet's vantage point "at the gate which faces eastward" (Ezek 43:1), as well as the use of the term "coming" to describe a divine movement, turn the reader's attention, with all its heightened philosophical sensibility, back to the chapter on "to come" and the second proof-text (in addition to Exod 19:9) illustrating "the descent of the Indwelling": "For the Lord the God of Israel comes through it" (Ezek 44:2). In its biblical setting, that entrance which God comes through is the gate "facing eastward": "Then He led me back to the outer gate of the Sanctuary that faced eastward" (44:1). The eastward gate of Ezek 43:1 bearing this highly purified notion of God's presenceless presence must be superimposed back on Ezek 44:2, which in its *Guide* context actually illustrated a presented presence—"the descent of the Indwelling." Once the sophisticated reader has returned to the chapter on coming, he realizes that his previous reading of a substantive presence indicated by Indwelling is no longer tenable. The mention of Indwelling at this point becomes a prompt for its abnegation. Maimonides signaled his readers to the following encoded message: "Whenever I mention Indwelling, you now know that I disavow any possibility of hypostatic manifestations of God, and Indwelling, for me, simply means God's presence as intellect."

Maimonides purposefully planted a reference to Indwelling early on, which suffices for the majority in distancing them from direct anthropomorphisms. On the other hand, he also faced the challenge of disaffecting his philosophically attuned audience from what must have been a popular alternative. He therefore resorted to the fifth cause of "contradictory or contrary statements," a pedagogical strategy that he acknowledged would be incorporated into the *Guide*. I quote it, with my own gloss, to show its application in this instance:

> For there may be a certain obscure matter that is difficult to conceive [a purely incorporeal God composed of pure thought who is incapable of any sensual manifestation and does not create any objective medium of His presence separate from His own being]. One has to mention it or take it as a premise in explaining something that is easy to conceive [that an anthropomorphic term, in this case *coming*, need not always be taken literally] that, by rights, ought to be taught before the former, since one always begins with what is easier. The teacher [Maimonides], accordingly, will have to be lax and, using any means that occur to him or gross speculation [the notion of "Indwelling"; "created things"] will try to make the first matter [figurative use of biblical terms to avoid anthropomorphisms] somehow understood. He will not undertake to state the matter as it truly is in exact terms [that there is no such thing as an Indwelling in the Halevian or Sa'adyan sense], but rather will leave it so in accord with the listener's imagination that the latter will understand only what he now [chapter I:22] wants him to understand. Afterwards, in the appropriate place, [e.g., II:33; III:9] that obscure matter is stated in exact terms and explained as it truly is. (GP Intro., 17–18)

The process of philosophically refining Scripture to sift out its anthropomorphic dross, including the slightly more palatable but still grossly anthropomorphic readings of those like Halevi and Sa'adya, evolves throughout the treatise, reaching its crescendo in a chapter like III:9 that revisits proof-texts, or alludes to such in its early lexicography. The "listener" must then reread the entire lexicographical section in the first part of the *Guide* in light of everything he has absorbed from the rest of the treatise.

God's "Going Out" and "Returning"

The chapter following I:22 offers the one instance in the first section of the *Guide* where *shekhinah* is referred to, unassociated with either Onkelos or a "created thing," and affords an unadulterated conception of the term. Chapter I:23 begins by dedicating itself to the term "going out" (*yetziah*) and its various shades of meaning, ending with a biblical reference to a divine exiting from *place*, "For behold the Lord goeth out of His place" (Isa 26:21; Mic 1:3). In addition to the term "going out," the term "returning" (*shivah*) is also addressed, with its figurative sense illustrated by a proof-text of divine returning to place, "I will go and return to My place" (Hos 5:15). Though these biblical references act primarily to exemplify the meaning of this chapter's particular designated terms, they must also be read in conjunction with the figurative meaning of "place" established in GP I:8.

As previously noted, the term "place" was also explicitly singled out as an example of the *Guide*'s method in general of not restricting the understanding of any term discussed to the narrow confines of the particular chapter dedicated to it. By juxtaposing the figurative sense of other terms with the term "place," chapter I:23 presents a model for the *Guide*'s programmatic extension of the lexicographical chapters' import beyond their own strict parameters. Since any association of God with place renders its signification exclusively as an utterly unique "rank of His existence . . . there being nothing like or similar to that existence" (GP I:8, 33), that meaning must be imported into the verses cited in I:23 alongside the metaphorical meanings of the terms "going out" and "returning." An uncalled-for insertion of the term *shekhinah* signals a subversion of its traditional association with divine locus in favor of divine placelessness. Man, in turn, as I make clear in what follows, must also himself become placeless to appreciate and obtain proximity to that new detached sense of *shekhinah*.

Of course, if the term "going out" has God as its subject, it cannot be taken literally; consequently, "the Lord goes out of His place" means "His decree, which at present is hidden from us, will become manifest" (GP I:23, 52–53).[7] In both Isaiah and Micah[8] God's going out portends destruction and retribution, respectively "to punish the dwellers of the earth for their iniquity" and to "trample upon the heights of the earth." Maimonides elaborated further on the precise nature of this "decree" as "the coming into being of something after its not having existed, for everything that comes into being from God, may He be exalted, is attributed to His decree. Thus *By the word of the Lord were the heavens made, and all the host of them by the breath of His mouth* [Ps 33:6]." The allusion to the creation here traces the punitive "decree" of both Micah and Isaiah to a design feature of creation itself. The punishment is merely an unfolding of that originating divine will that *decreed* the world's existence, not an historical reaction to human conduct. Micah 1:3 is in fact later cited as one of a series of prophetic cataclysms, whose radical upheavals of nature must all be read metaphorically in light of the rabbinic axiom *The world goes its customary way* (*b. Avodah Zarah* 54b).[9] In that same chapter, Maimonides extended this axiom to encompass even those aberrant phenomena regarded as miracles, which are essentially woven into the very fabric of nature at the point of creation.[10] God's going out is also listed as one of a series of prophetic idioms to express "states of anger with regard to men or communities" (GP II:29, 337). As God cannot possibly be subject to any emotions, and since divine anger is specifically identified as a necessary, but not a true, belief to ward off anthropomorphic conceptions of God, the phrase concerning God's "going out of His place" paradoxically means God "stays in His place" while nature runs its course. The coupling of place, going out, and creation radically negates any notions of time, space, and motion from the divine realm.

The reference to Ps 33:6, linking the originating moment of creation to a consequence of pure divine volition, further entrenches Maimonides' thoroughgoing naturalism in the discussion of "going out." In chapter I:66, naturalism is associated with a mishnaic tradition in *m. Avot* 5:6 enumerating ten miracles "created" at twilight of the sixth day of creation. Maimonides cited this as an endorsement of the notion that miracles were preprogrammed into nature at the time of creation.[11] Chapter I:66 is devoted to rationalizing the miraculous nature of the tablets on which were inscribed the Ten Commandments, biblically considered to have been "the work of God," "the writing of God" (Exod 32:16), and "written with the finger of God" (Exod 31:18). Maimonides understood these expressions to be highly fanciful metaphors for attributing natural phenomena to the divine will. They convey precisely what is conveyed by the idiom "by the word of God," in Ps 33:6, which could just as well have been formulated as *"written by the will of God,* I mean His will and volition" (GP I:66, 160). Concomitantly, "written with the finger of God" could be substituted for "by the word of God" with no resultant change in its philosophical nuance.

The analogy to Ps 33:6 is more significant, though, for what it imports into chapter I:23, the sole instance in the first section of the *Guide* of the term *shekhinah* unaccompanied by "created thing" or mention of Onkelos. After translating "finger of God" as simply "will of God," Maimonides, with no apparent urgency to do so, went on to question Onkelos' "strange interpretation" of "written with a finger belonging to God," the meaning of which is "that the finger is a created instrument that has cut into the tables through the will of God." He was at a loss to explain why Onkelos resorted to this anthropomorphically gross interpretation when the more palatable option of "written by the word of God, and indeed the option more consistent with Onkelos' own exegetical technique,"[12] is readily available. His critique of Onkelos is crowned by rhetorical sarcasm: "Do you think that the existence of writing on the tables is any stranger than the existence of stars in the spheres? For just as the stars came into being through the First Will and not through an instrument, so the inscribed writing came into being through the First Will and not through an instrument" (GP I:66, 161).

What is startling about this trenchant assault on Onkelos' interpretation of one verse, Exod 31:18, is that its logic equally applies to his exegetical strategy, as understood by Maimonides, throughout his Aramaic translation/commentary. Characteristically, whenever direct actions are ascribed to God, Onkelos supplies an implied intermediary existence, be it word, glory, or *shekhinah*,[13] which mediates those actions thereby effacing their anthropomorphic connotations. However, Maimonides' challenge on Exod 31:18 demands an abandonment of the sensual altogether in favor of pure abstraction. Why, indeed, does God ever need to resort to an "instrument" or a "created thing" to effectuate anything when there was no such recourse when inaugurating all of existence? While Maimonides undermined Onkelos' entire hermeneutical edifice, he did so at a crucial juncture that bridged his critique in I:66 with the mention of *shekhinah* in I:23 by way of the common proof-text allusion to Ps 33:6. God is relegated to the original inception of the world. Just as that moment materialized without any medium or tool or created thing, so all future history is informed by that very same sheer act of unabridged divine will. *Shekhinah* has been effectively drained of any connotations of presence or sensual objectification. That which, in the rabbinic tradition, most captures divine immanence and closeness with humanity is banished to the seclusion and remoteness of time (creation) and space as expressed by place *(maqom)*, a place we have seen to be utterly devoid of space.[14]

The deontologization of *shekhinah* is driven home and perfected from both a literary and a philosophical perspective by the shift in the chapter's concern from the term "going out" to its directionally reverse term of "returning" *(shivah)*. Their opposing movements signify metaphorically opposing phenomena: "Inasmuch as the term *going out*, as we have made clear, was figuratively applied to the manifestation of an act of God . . . the term *returning* is figuratively applied to the cessation of such an act likewise brought about in virtue of God's will" (GP I:23, 53). Maimonides distinguished the figurative referents of these terms as between natural phenomena that occur and those that cease to occur. It is merely a physically descriptive distinction without any qualitatively distinguishing philosophical features—in other words, a distinction without a difference. Both terms represent natural phenomena, both materialize as a result of the will of God, and both can be traced to a divine will that is located at the remotest end of the causally sequential chain of nature—the origins of the world. The proof-text cited in support of this sense of returning is "I will go and return to My place" (Hos 5:15), a literary reversal of the proof-text for the term "going out," "The Lord goeth out of His place," with the latter's starting point identical to the former's destination—the divine place. God starts off and ends up in the same place for the simple reason that He never leaves that place. Each term signifies natural events that are anchored in a pristine act of divine volition, issuing from the identical place that we have seen is no place and space that is no space.

This divine returning is thus a metaphor: "The *shekhinah* that had been among us is removed. This removal is followed by a privation of providence, as far as we are concerned." The term *shekhinah* is strategically imported and integrally identified with privation of providence, which, as

Maimonides went on to define, "leaves one abandoned and a target to all that may happen and come about, so that his ill and weal come about according to chance." Rather than the comforting *shekhinah* of the rabbinic tradition, which accompanies Israel in its exilic wanderings,[15] or the "created things" of Onkelos and Sa'adya, Maimonides consciously drew the equation between *shekhinah* and the random and arbitrary forces of nature.

God's "Going"

The choice of Hos 5:15, "I will go and return to My place," as a metaphor for the movements of the *shekhinah* deepens even further the deontologization of that term by its juxtaposition of the term "returning" with the term "going" *(halikhah),* the subject of the following chapter I:24 of the *Guide.* The metaphorical referent of *shekhinah* is "the spread and manifestation of a certain thing even if the latter *were in no way corporeal*" (GP I:24, 54; the emphasis is mine). Without exception, when related to God, "going" assumes this abstract meaning: "I mean that with respect to what is incorporeal, it is used to denote either the spread of a thing or a withdrawal of providence." The *shekhinah,* as the subject of Hos 5:15, bears no physical manifestations, and its spread or removal are ethereal processes. The two terms, "returning" and "going," also share the identical biblical metaphor that illustrates what is intended by withdrawal of providence — the hiding of the face of Deut 31:17 – 18. Not only is the sense of *shekhinah* as some sensual medium dispelled, but this graphic biblical allusion also radically subverts the rabbinic sense of *shekhinah* as symbol of divine immediacy, concern, and empathy of God for His people, especially in the most trying of times. In GP III:51, "hiding of the face" is taken as merely a metaphorical reflection of the human condition. It is the state of vulnerability to the arbitrary forces of nature in which those who are intellectually disengaged find themselves, a state characterized by abandonment and exposure. This was, as discussed in relation to the leper, Miriam's condition of divine abandonment. As described in GP I:23, Maimonides identified the existential deterioration of ignorant man as "a target for every evil that may befall him" (GP III:51, 625). An equation was therefore formulated between *shekhinah* and providence whose location, so to speak, is a function of human choice and endeavor, for "[i]t is clear that we are the cause of this *hiding of the face,* and we are the agents of this separation" (ibid., 626). The *shekhinah* was thus demythologized, dehypostasized, decorporealized, and reduced to a mirror of man's internal psyche, an existential reflex of his intellectual predicament.

Herbert Davidson has shown that Halevi draws a close association between the "divine thing" *(amr ilahi)* and the *shekhinah* in which both "are collective animating principles within the Jewish nation, but the *amr ilahi* is more spiritual, whereas the Shekina is more tangible."[16] More importantly, Davidson has also posited one unifying philosophical principle that accounts for at least three seemingly disparate uses of the phrase *amr ilahi:* "as an internal principle possessed by select individuals who represent the highest degree of sub-lunar existence; as a divine aura enveloping the Jewish nation and the Holy Land; as a divine attribute or perhaps God Himself."[17] Fundamental to each of these is the notion of direct divine causality.[18] Maimonides would have considered this anathema to the divine nature he advocated, which postulated a God who is an efficient cause of everything occurring in the world, but strictly in the sense that all worldly phenomena can be traced back to God's being the efficient cause of the world, the one who started the ball rolling.[19] It is therefore precisely when discussing Hebrew terms that could be the analogues of *amr,* such as *amirah* (saying), *dibbur* (speaking), *tzivvui* (commanding), and *qriyah* (calling), that he contended vigorously against ascribing to them the sense of direct divine causality or intervention.

Every single phenomenon in the world, ranging from ocean waves to animal impulses to any exercise of human volition to pure chance, can be ascribed to God's command or direction, but only in the sense that He is the original cause of the world. When the prophets ascribed any such event directly to God's decree they poetically omitted the entire causal chain linking God's original move to create the world and the particular occasion at hand.[20] The beginning of chapter II:48, where these terms are dealt with, drives home the point using the postulate of an infinite regress that ultimately threads its way back to God. Everything has a proximate cause, and "in its turn that cause has a cause and so forth till finally one comes to the First Cause of all things, I mean God's will and free choice. For this reason all those intermediate causes are sometimes omitted in the dicta of the prophets, and an individual act produced in time is ascribed to God" (GP II:48, 409–10). By situating these terms that recall the *amr ilahi* in a chapter that locates God only at creation, Maimonides mounted a frontal assault on the Halevian proponents of the direct divine causality they take this term to signify.

The tangibility of the *shekhinah* in Halevi[21] offers a kind of visual testament to the spiritual *amr ilahi,* concrete evidence of divine intervention and special attachment to the Jewish people. That concept of *shekhinah* is also dismantled in the mini-treatise I:23 on "going out" and I:24 on "going." God's "going out of His place" of Isa 26:21 refers to "His decree"; we have seen this refers, by way of analogy with the proof-text "By the word of the Lord were the heavens made" (Ps 33:6), to the pure incorporeal act of divine will at creation. In I:24, the term "going," so instrumental in identifying the root cause of Miriam's leprosy, means either "the spread of a thing or the withdrawal of providence." Pines astutely felt the need here to justify his translation of *amr* as "thing" rather than the equally or more plausible philological alternative of "command," with the brief rationale that "other passages in this chapter seem to indicate that in this case the word should be translated 'thing' or 'matter.'"[22] However, I believe Kafih captures its sense more appropriately with the Hebrew equivalent of what Pines consciously rejected as an alternative—namely, *pequddah* (command or decree).

Considering the number of discordant translations of the term, whether French, English, or Hebrew,[23] it would seem to have a built-in ambiguity that is resolved by each reader for himself. The translation of *amr* here as "decree" maintains its literary consistency with the metaphorical meaning offered for its sister term "going out" as the manifestation of God's "decree," thus drawing "going" into the same vortex of meaning. At the same time it discloses itself as a scathing subtextual critical engagement with the Halevian school of divine immediacy. The "spread of the thing," then, is tantamount to the realization of a divine decree whose divine attribution is limited to God as the efficient originating cause of the world. The paradigmatic instance of going that assumes both meanings of "spread of a thing" and "removal of providence" is God's expressed anger at Miriam's slander in Num 12:10, "and the anger of the Lord was kindled against them and He went away," a verse whose Maimonidean sense is examined in chapter 2 on the leper. It needs to be restated here only that by identifying God's anger as the "thing" that spread, Maimonides, in the very same breath, indicated that nothing in fact has spread. God is philosophically incapable of any emotion, let alone anger. Brilliantly, a highly graphic narrative of divine anger and retribution veils a devastating critique of Halevian metaphysics, and forms a kind of preface to chapter I:25 on *shakhon* that follows, where the subtextual rejoinder to Halevi continues. From God's perspective nothing has transpired, no reaction has been evoked, and nothing new has been created. From man's perspective, he has brought on himself a state of abandonment and alienation, has exposed himself to the vicissitudes of nature, and suffers the physical repercussions of the uninformed life.

Once the Halevian personal, responsive, and somewhat sensual God is banished from the theological scene, what remains for the religiously committed disciple of Maimonides? How and for whom does Maimonides' Jew express his faith once something like the *amr ilahi* is eliminated as a viable presence? The answer lies in the literary structuring of the two chapters I:23 and I:24, its intricate weave of proof-texts, and the sharp turn the conclusion of I:24 takes in its analysis of the term "going." The chapters are bracketed by excerpts from the very same messianic vision at the beginning of the second chapter of Isaiah, exemplifying the terms' metaphorical referents. At the beginning of I:23, Isa 2:3, "For out of Zion shall the law *[torah]* go out," corroborates the assertion that "going out" can refer to an incorporeal movement, since here it is information and knowledge (law) that is disseminated (going out). In its biblical context, this verse is part of Isaiah's messianic vision of events that will occur "at the end of days" *(aharit ha-yamim)*.[24] The most striking facet of this redemptive prediction, however, is its universalism. Isaiah 2:3 is the rationale for the magnetic attraction the Temple mount in Jerusalem[25] ("the Mount of the Lord's house") will hold internationally. Because Zion is the source of the *law,* "all the nations shall gaze on it (the Temple mount) with joy and the many peoples shall go and say 'Come, let us go up to the Mount of the Lord, to the House of the God of Jacob; that He may instruct us in His ways and that we may walk in His paths'" (Isa 2:3). The chapter that prominently features *shekhinah* at its end, a term historically linked with exclusivist theologies, launches itself with a pointed reference to a utopian state that envisions its very antithesis, when the *torah* will be universally acknowledged and not the exclusive preserve of one people.[26] In this way Maimonides began to dislodge *shekhinah* from its particularistic moorings, from its *amr ilahi* associations.

Chapter I:24 concludes with an excerpt from the very same Isaianic vision with which I:23 commenced. After discussing the figurative viability of the term "going" when related to God, the chapter shifts to its metaphorical application within a human context, where it can assume the meaning of "living a good life, without in any way moving a body." That sense is then corroborated by a series of three verses, the first two of which—"and thou shalt go in His ways" (Deut 28:9), and "after the Lord, God shall you go" (Deut 13:5)—are the biblical sources for the halakhic obligation to perform *imitatio dei* (SM Positive Commandment 8; MT *Laws of Ethical Traits* 1:6). The juridical formulation of this obligation in the *Mishneh Torah* mandates the adoption of the ethical golden mean, by way of assimilating divine conduct that always follows the mean. It is this principle, known as the "way of the Lord," which is identified as the pristine teaching that "Abraham our father taught to his children" (MT *Laws of Ethical Traits* 1:7). Abraham's mission, as opposed to that of Moses, was directed to humanity as a whole.[27] The core of his legacy was that *man* can achieve Godliness by knowing Him and subsequently emulating Him. The halakhic formulation of *imitatio dei* finds its philosophical complement in the *Guide*'s equation between image of God and the essence or form or definition of man as intellect. Man's function is to cultivate that form that he shares with God, in the exercise of which "no sense, no part of the body, none of the extremities are used" (GP I:1, 23). This is true of man qua man. This universalist quashing of *shekhinah* chauvinism is embedded in the very locution of the nations' motivation to advance toward the Temple mount, "so that He may instruct us in His ways *[derakhav]* and that we may walk in His paths."[28] God's way is the path that traverses two universalistic historical upheavals beginning with the Abrahamic legacy at one end and culminating with its messianic retrieval at the other.[29]

Maimonides disposed of the *shekhinah*'s ontologically parochial tendencies by sandwiching it between two expressions of a universalistic teaching that views all humanity as bound by a single characteristic and a single telos. The final proof-text, "Come ye and let us *go* [from the root for "going"] in the light of the Lord" from Isa 2:5, which illustrates going as man's nonphysical movement, deals the Halevian *shekhinah* its mortal blow for two reasons. First is its reversion to the prophetic vision of Isa 2 with which chapter I:23 of the *Guide* opened, thereby closing the universalist thematic circle. Second is its particular choice of light imagery and where this fits in the original literary structure of the vision. The prophet turns his attention from the nations and addresses this invitation to the "house of Jacob" in particular. Philosophically, what the prophet conveys, as suggested by the intertextual positioning of the verses in the *Guide*, is that Israel has been assigned a particular role in the natural realization of the messianic universal redemption of mankind as just understood. This is achieved by Israel's spearheading the way through a going defined as "without in any way moving a body," the ethereal going of intellectual apprehension that involves "no sense, no part of the body." This incorporeal movement is led by the light of God precisely so that the biblical imagery of light associated with divine revelations is wholly desensualized and intellectualized. This verse has been chosen for its subversion of the "created lights" phenomenon, a corollary of the Halevian ethnically elitist *shekhinah* theology.

De-Glorifying God

The Approach That Never Arrives

Another biblical term that is integrally bound to the theology of *shekhinah* and created things is "glory" *(kavod)*.[30] In discussing the term's nuances, Maimonides concentrated his exegetical energies in part on disaffecting it of its created-entity connotations. From his initial interpretation of Moses' request to "Show me thy glory" (Exod 33:18) as a longing for "intellectual apprehension and in no way to the eye's seeing" (GP I:4, 28), he built his case by leaving a trail of proof-texts that defy the created-entity tradition. In I:8, the very chapter of the *Guide* with which we began our discussion of the deontologization of God's presence with respect to the term "place," Maimonides exegetically identified the location of the divine glory in Ezekiel's praise, "Blessed be the glory of God from His place" (3:12), with the *place* of God's response to Moses' request of Exod 33:18, directing him to where God can truly be found: "Behold there is a place by Me" (Exod 33:21). If "place" is restricted to God's rank of existence and Moses' request to be privy to God's glory was denied (I:54), then, following the exegetical logic, God's glory inheres in its unknowable, unseen surpassing of the human intellect's utmost capacity. Though man cannot have knowledge of God's glory, His essence, the end of this proof-text juxtaposition indicates that man can in fact know where that glory is.

Maimonides' location for that place that houses God's glory is given in the second half of Exod 33:21, "and you shall stand erect upon the rock," which alludes not to a geographical space, but to an activity of the mind that appreciates God as "the principle and efficient cause of all things other than himself" (GP I:16, 42). He classified this notion of God as "the entryway through which you shall come to Him, as we have made clear when speaking of His saying 'Behold there is a *place by me*'" (ibid.). A bold hermeneutic transforms parochial space where divine glory can be discovered and visualized into a universal space, because every natural object or space within the creation, when considered philosophically, reflects the metaphysics of a Being as an ultimate efficient cause. The Exodus verse now indicates that every spatial encounter anywhere instigates an intellectual process that determines the precise relationship between that space and God as a causal one. Ironically, what might first appear as a "cold" and austere theology results in a kind of sanctification of all of existence, because "all things other than himself" constitute God's place. Man endows physical space with divine *glory* by drawing the philosophical link between all things created and God.

The phrase "glory of God" reappears in the chapter of the *Guide* most adamant in dissociating God from space. Here the terms "approaching" and "coming near," which have God as their destination, are metaphors for intellectual estrangement or proximity, "as the abolition of incorporeality entails that space be abolished; so that there is no nearness and proximity, and no remoteness, no union and no separation, no contact and no succession" (GP I:18, 44). Maimonides emphasized the point that in all such biblical instances these terms reflect cognitive movements: "cognitive apprehension is intended, not nearness in space." One of the most prominent biblical references cited in support of this metaphorical reading is critical to the thesis of this book, in that the relationship between God and the sage is defined by loneliness. Though Moses is accompanied by an entourage of elders at Sinai, access to God is restricted to him alone: "And Moses alone shall *come near* unto the Lord, but they shall not come near" (Exod 24:2). The intellectual process narrowing the cognitive distance between man and God entails its social converse. The gap between man and others widens as the disassociation of God from concrete space deepens. God and the sage embrace each other in a dance of marginality. Moses' movement toward God is propelled by the strength of his grasp of God's infinite remoteness. As he moves closer by pushing God farther away, he finds himself increasingly socially isolated.

Maimonides then slipped in his usual acknowledgment of the Onkelos/Halevi school, conceding the possibility of Moses' approaching a concentration of light—"I mean the *glory of God*" (GP I:18, 45)—that has "descended" onto the mountain. He immediately reverted, however, to the metaphorical account asserting that distance from God is measured in terms of intellectual magnitude, which accounts for "very many gradations in being near to Him or far away from Him." The next appearance of Exod 24:2 is occasioned by the need to biblically illustrate a graded scale of prophetic prowess (GP II:2, 363). Inserting a reference to "glory of God" in this context is a tactic intended to present the Sinaitic distinction between Moses and other *sages* (I stress sages here as Moses is contrasted to the seventy elders, Aaron, Nadav, and Avihu) in terms of their respective conceptions of this glory. Maimonides thereby instructed his audience that hypostatic notions must be abandoned in order to approximate Moses' level of cognition and, therefore, closeness to God. On the other hand, he also forewarned them that such a move may cost them the company of their fellow sages, as it did Moses. They must choose the company they wish to keep.

The difficulty in categorically renouncing the Sa'adya/Halevi/Onkelos position is that it also severs any relationship with the masses, with whose sensual biases they will no longer share any common ground. Maimonides offered a kind of consolation for the supreme sacrifice entailed by the pursuit of intellectual (and, ipso facto, "spiritual") perfection. He enlisted Exod 24:2 a third time to capture another unique feature of Moses' level of achievement, which in fact allows for a coexistence of the social and the intellectual: "he talks with people and is occupied with his bodily necessities while his intellect is wholly turned toward Him so that in his heart he is always in His presence while outwardly he is with people" (GP III:51, 623). What is critical in this description is the clear bifurcation between inner and outer, corresponding respectively to God's presence and the people. The only place where God is present is in the mind, as opposed to where people reside—"outwardly." The sage has attracted God's presence with his knowledge and conversely the people have access to that presence by learning from the sage. The locale of God's presence in the world has been transferred from spatial manifestations of divine glory and *shekhinah* to the acquisition and transmission of knowledge.[31]

After driving home the point that proximity to God cannot be measured in terms of spatial distance but rather "consists in apprehending

Him," Maimonides then proceeded to analyze the term *"touching,"* another problematic anthropomorphic term similar to "approaching" and "coming near." The chapter deals jointly with all these terms since touching, actual contact, is the final extension of the movements connoted by the other two terms. With this term, he mounted another challenge to the Halevian/Sa'adya school by occasionally importing the term *amr* into the discussion, thereby infusing it with his new purified intellectualist theology. Two verses are cited to illustrate the meaning of divine touching. The first is "Touch the mountains that they may smoke" (Ps 144:5), which figuratively translates into "Let Thy decree *[amr]* come to them." One of the *Guide*'s rare instances of the use of the term *amr ilahi* (divine decree) results in its demystification as some divine substantiation. In II:10 Maimonides defined "nature" as the generation and preservation of sublunar existents by the forces of the spheres. These natural, predetermined, and continuous forces are euphemistically said to "govern" the world with "wisdom." Then, almost gratuitously, Maimonides further equated that mechanistic process with "the divine decree *[a-amr al-ilahi]* from which these two activities derive through the intermediary of the sphere" (GP II:10, 272).[32] In light of that equation, the Psalter's plea, from a literal perspective, falls on deaf ears. In the end, the Psalm is poetically appealing for nature to unfold in accordance with its predetermined manner.

When combined with the second cited verse, "And touch Thou him himself" (Job 2:5), this discussion crystallizes into a vigorous attack on the Halevi doctrine. The verse is introduced as similar to the first one from Ps 144, and its meaning is cryptically rendered "let Thy infliction come upon him." The two verses intersect on the common theme of punishment and human suffering. The Job quotation consists of Satan's challenge to God to test Job's loyalty by a final assault on his physical person. God responds favorably, with the caveat that Satan must "spare his soul" (2:6). For our purposes it suffices to import the Maimonidean distinction that this verse conveys regarding what Satan controls. Since the soul "is applied to the thing that remains of man after death; this is the thing over which Satan has no dominion" (GP III:22, 488). The aspect of man that survives death is, in particular, the "rational soul," the sum total of man's perfected intellect during his lifetime (GP I:41, 91). "Satan" is merely a metaphor for all those natural elements to which man is exposed by virtue of his being composed of matter.[33]

Psalm 144:5 was traditionally understood as a call for punitive measures against the wicked.[34] The psalm is premised on the ephemeral and inconsequential view of man espoused by the preceding verses beginning with "What is man that Thou takes knowledge of him" (v. 3). That view in turn echoes the insignificance of man in Ps 8:5, "What is man that Thou art mindful of him."[35] This is cited to endorse the principle that punishment can be linked to God only in the sense that it materializes naturally as a result of the intrinsic composition of man and the world, "the reason being man is too insignificant to have his actions visited and to be punished for them were it not for the pre-eternal will." The two verses join to posit a doctrine that locates God's contact with the world in intellect and that wholly removes Him from the material world. The chapter then concludes with a new metaphorical definition of "touching," utilizing *amr* as its operative *terminus technicus,* as "union through the cognition and apprehension of a certain thing *(amr).* For one who apprehends a thing *(amr)* that he did not apprehend before has, as it were, approached a thing that previously had been remote from him." Maimonides has effectively drained the Halevian *amr ilahi* of its tangible qualities by appropriating *amr* as a purely abstract thing, as thought.

The Vacuum of "Filling"

The following chapter 1:19, which focuses on the term "to fill" *(male),* continues the relentless attack on the specious theology of created entities. Its particular target is the popular conception of the Temple as an area in which some divine presence is contained. The metaphorical sense of the term "to fill" is "the achievement of perfection in virtue and of the latter's end" (GP I:19, 46). Of the three verses cited to illustrate this metaphorical sense, two relate to the original construction of, respectively, the Tabernacle in the desert and its permanent replacement, the first Temple of Solomon. The eminent qualifications of the Tabernacle's architects are poetically captured by "Them hath He filled *[mille]* with wisdom of the heart" (Exod 35:35), while the coppersmith's expertise in constructing the pillars of the successor Temple is expressed similarly as "He was filled *[va-yimalle']* with wisdom, and understanding, and skill" (1 Kgs 7:14). In both cases the verses figuratively indicate the supremely skilled craftsmanship involved in the construction of these buildings. These verses attracted Maimonides for their association of the Temple with wisdom, particularly a perfected wisdom implied by the designers being *filled* with it. Maimonides thus embarked on a demystification of the Temple that progressed with an odd sequencing of the next two verses cited to corroborate this metaphorical sense of "fill."

The first verse chosen as an exemplar of the use of that term "in this sense" is "The whole earth is full of His glory" (Isa 6:3), which translates into the rational affirmation that "the whole earth bears witness to His perfection, that is, indicates it." That verse is followed up by the further example, simply introduced as "similar is its dictum," "And the glory of the Lord filled the tabernacle" (Exod 40:34; repeated in v. 35). Considering the fact that the first two verses cited both involved the construction of Tabernacle and Temple, one would expect the next supporting verse prefaced by "in this sense" to be Exod 40:34, which also deals with the Tabernacle. The intervening verse from Isa 6:3 strategically interrupts the orderly flow of verses to dispel any ontological sanctification of this sacred space.

The progression of verses itself formulates an argument against the Halevian doctrine in the very sequencing of their citation:

1. These are naturally developed structures, the products of human skill and expertise.
2. Their uniqueness is a function of human input, extraordinarily advanced, but human all the same.
3. "Glory of God" is interjected so that its Halevian/Sa'adyan overlay can be dispatched.
4. Isaiah 6:3 universalizes the glory and imposes itself on a reading of the verses about the construction of the Temple: the Temple and Tabernacle cannot be places that confine a presence, since that presence is diffused over the whole earth. The Temple was in fact constructed to confirm the principle of Isa 6:3.
5. The same glory that fills the earth also fills the Tabernacle (Exod 40:34, 35).
6. God's glory cannot refer to any sensual or spatially confined presence.

The now familiar concession concluding the chapter that allows for identifying this glory as a created light, since "there is no harm in it," signals its total unacceptability to the philosophically adept. The very raison d'être for composing the *Guide* was to guide its serious readers toward leading a life that did not compromise their religion or their intellect. One of the existential dilemmas it addresses is the feeling that "imaginary beliefs" cannot be abandoned without renouncing religion; and so the solution, prior to the *Guide*'s teaching, was to preserve them at the cost of "perceiving that he had brought loss to himself and harm to his religion" (GP Intro., 6). No harm would come only to those who never experienced such existential anguish, whose intellectual level could comfortably accommodate the credibility of an imaginary belief such as created entities. For those few sincerely theologically perturbed individuals whom Maimonides had in mind, though, the harm would be intolerable.

The Anonymity of Naming

When the *Guide* directly deals with the phrase "glory of God" in chapter I:64, the two verses Isa 6:3 and Exod 40:34 appear again, this time exemplifying the meaning of that phrase rather than the pertinent term "to fill" of chapter I:19. Moreover, this time they are specifically separated and distinguished in their metaphorical referents, whereas in I:19 those referents were clearly meant to operate in tandem. The primary focus of chapter I:64 is the significance of the name of God, YHVH, referred to as the "articulated name" or the Tetragrammaton, which can refer alternatively to a literal name, God's "essence and true reality," or to a divine commandment that in turn translates as "an instrument of My will and volition" (GP I:64, 156). The discussion then seems to veer sharply to the expression "glory of God," which occupies the remainder of the chapter. Two biblical illustrations of its meaning as "the created light that God causes to descend in a particular place in order to confer honor upon it in a miraculous way" are then cited, this time combining Exod 40:34 ("'And the glory of God [YHVH] filled the tabernacle'") with Exod 24:16 ("'And the glory of YHVH dwelt upon Mount Sinai, and [the cloud] covered it' and so on"). Maimonides' concern from that point on was to elaborate an alternative philosophical meaning of "glory of God" that essentially designates it as a product of human, not divine, activity. It is fundamentally a euphemism for that which results in "honoring" God, the principal vehicle of which is "apprehension":

> In fact all that is other than God honors Him. For the true way of honoring Him consists in apprehending His greatness. Thus everybody

who apprehends His greatness and His perfection, honors Him according to the extent of his apprehension. Man in particular honors Him by speeches so that he indicates thereby that which he has apprehended by his intellect and communicates it to others. Those beings that have no apprehension, as for instance the minerals, also, as it were, honor God through the fact that by their very nature they are indicative of the power and wisdom of Him who brought them into existence. For this induces him who considers them to honor God, either by means of articulate utterance or without it if speech is not permitted to him. (GP I:64, 157)

This last sense of "glory of God" is said to be captured by Isa 6:3, "The whole earth is full of His glory," a verse that formerly complemented Exod 40:34 but now stands in stark contrast to it. Chapter I:64 is both structurally disjointed and exegetically inconsistent. The following are some of the difficulties posed by it:

1. Why did Maimonides launch into a lengthy digression on the meaning of "glory of God" in the chapter devoted to the name of God? The difficulty is compounded by the fact that there is already an encounter with the phrase earlier on in chapter I:19 where it is dealt with briefly.
2. Why are the two verses Isa 6:3 and Exod 40:34 explicitly distinguished in I:64 when they were treated as bearing a common meaning in I:19?
3. Why is Exod 40:34 singled out as indicating a "miraculously" "created light" endowed on a "particular place" when that very same interpretation was dismissed as an inferior alternative in I:19?

The choice of where to examine the meaning of the expression "glory of God" may have been determined by the arguments of Maimonides' theological opponents. Halevi's doctrine of created lights and a sensual glory is closely tied to his conception of God's names, in particular the Tetragrammaton. Halevi's sharp distinction between the superiority of empirical evidence over purely abstract propositions leads him to consider the Tetragrammaton a special name entrenched in the particular prophetic tradition of Israel because it was *revealed* by God.[36] It is a *personal* name to which philosophers are not privy because of their conception of an impersonal supreme being: "None of them applies a distinct proper name to God, except he who hears His address, command, or prohibition, approval for obedience, and reproof for disobedience."[37] Each successive generation of prophets from Adam to Moses became acquainted with this name both by means of tradition and by personal revelation anchored in concrete experiences: "they comprehended Him by means of intermediaries called: glory, *shekhinah,* dominion, fire, cloud, likeness, form."[38] Halevi's Tetragrammaton signifies a particularistic relationship with Israel alone, substantiated by a history of visual and aural experience to which biblical terminology such as *shekhinah* and "glory" attest. The peculiar structure of chapter I:64 of the *Guide* can be appreciated as an integral part of the ongoing polemic Maimonides conducted against the Halevian doctrine. Because Halevi's divine name is conveyed by way of these entities, Maimonides had to respond to them as two sides of the same theological coin.

Maimonides' notion of the Tetragrammaton is the polar opposite of Halevi's. It conveys a "clear unequivocal indication of His essence," "the essence of which is not derivative," and "essence without associating any other notion with it" (GP I:61, 147–49). This name is decidedly not particularistic or exclusive to Israel. Indeed it cannot reflect any relationship whatsoever to anything outside of itself. In deference to a *midrash* that understands God and the specific name "YHVH" to preexist the world, the Tetragrammaton is isolated from nature and history, "divested and stripped of all actions" (ibid.). Halevi's YHVH is Israel's friend; Maimonides' YHVH is the supreme outsider resistant to any familiarity or personal rapport. The *Guide*'s purpose in turning to the "glory of God" immediately after an exposition on the name "YHVH" developed in the previous three chapters (I:61–63) and concluding in I:64 is to prod the astute reader into subjecting it to a rational microscope.

First, that reader will be struck by the three problems listed above. Second, he will attempt to translate "glory" of the phrase "glory of YHVH" as a "created light" and YHVH in accordance with one of its available designations, and find that there is no coherent fit. If YHVH indicates an essence that is "divested and stripped of all actions," it is incapable of association with any material manifestation or spatial coordinates. The only alternative is that it is "sometimes intended to signify His commandment so that when we say *the name of YHVH,* it is as if we said *the word of YHVH* or *the speech of YHVH*" (GP I:64, 156). Divine saying and speaking are defined in turn in the next chapter (I:65) to "denote either will and volition or a notion that has been grasped by the understanding having come from God, in which case *it is indifferent whether it has become known by means of a created voice or through one of the ways of* prophecy" (ibid., 158–59; emphasis mine). This sense of YHVH must be ruled out as well, since the glory has been ostensibly identified as a created light and not as a created voice.

Third, our ideal reader will notice what I believe is an intentional ambiguity in the formulation "created light that God causes to descend in a particular place in order to confer honor upon *it.*" The ambiguity, as reflected in the scholarly debate on this matter,[39] is that "it" can refer either to its antecedent "God" or to "place." Each alternative caters to a different intellectual palate. The latter would appeal to the Halevian sensibility with its attraction to divinely ontologized presences. The former appeals to one who already appreciates the Tabernacle as a microcosmic symbol of a God that is reflected in all of existence by virtue of the previously drawn correlation between "the glory of God filled the tabernacle" and "the whole earth is full of His glory," as "the whole earth bears witness to His perfection" (GP I:19). The Tabernacle and its successor, the Temple, are focal points that direct the mind toward ultimate Being in the same sense that any facet of existence does.

Finally, the parallel drawn between two glories, the glory of the Tabernacle (Exod 40:34) and the glory on Mt. Sinai (Exod 24:16), will alert the reader to the multipronged strategy of its hermeneutic. It has already been noted during the analysis of chapter I:25 on *shakhon* that Exod 24:16 captured Moses' perception of the Sinaitic epiphany as opposed to that of the people as expressed in 24:17: "And the appearance of the *glory of God* appeared *in the eyes of the Israelites* as a consuming fire on the top of the mountain." Exodus 24:16 therefore imports the idea of a stratification of perceptions, of different audiences, of the philosophically mature (Moses) and immature (Israelites), into the current discussion. All these factors will prompt our reader to a literary dissonance that ultimately collapses the distinction between the glories of the Tabernacle and the whole earth. The concluding verse of chapter I:64, "And in His temple all say Glory" (Ps 29:9), demonstrating that God's glory resides in informed philosophical discourse, is chosen to consolidate that collapse. This verse merges the glory associated with the Temple and that associated with speech to indicate that the former is synonymous with the glory of the whole earth. The verse displaces the objectified glory of God thought to occupy the Temple space and fills the vacuum with a human endeavor. The

Temple has been converted to a focal point for the stimulation of thought about God.

The diverse exegetical postures with regard to these verses mirror the original rationale for the Temple and its attendant sacrificial cult, aimed at both accommodating and reining in the idolatrous mentality of ancient Israel. Through these, "it came about that the memory of idolatry was effaced and that the grandest and true foundation of our belief—namely, the existence and the oneness of the deity—was firmly established, while at the same time the souls had no feeling of repugnance and were not repelled because of the abolition of modes of worship to which they were accustomed and than which no other mode of worship was known at the time" (GP III:32, 527). These very same considerations determined Maimonides' own strategies in offering a bold new biblical hermeneutic, although it is Sa'adyan/Halevian doctrine and not primitive idolatry that posed the contemporary threat to Maimonidean monotheism. God as YHVH is an isolated reality beyond the ken of human consciousness. The Tetragrammaton merely accentuates the theological dilemma of how to worship a remote, unknowable, and unapproachable deity. Maimonides' resolution for his students is to establish God's presence in the world by knowing God to the very depths of His remoteness, by maintaining a rigid divide between creator and creation. Those true students must sift through a language of compromise sensitive to the psychological needs of the larger community, which refrains from a categorical "abolition of modes of worship," in this case Halevian-like modes.

The Temple serves to perpetuate the revelatory monotheistic legacy of Sinai by subverting idolatrous ideology from within. The very decision as to the Temple's location and western direction is a reaction to the direction of sun worship, the reigning pagan cult of its time. Abraham's groundbreaking reversal of the prevailing religious practice from East to West forever ritualizes the ideological battle with idolatry: "Therefore Abraham, our father, turned, when praying on Mount Moriah—I mean in the Sanctuary—toward the West, so as to turn his back upon the sun" (GP III:45, 575). The direction of the Holy of Holies, a space most prone to conceptions of God on earth, was determined in terms of its conceptual assault on idolatry. Maimonides bolstered his redefinition of *shekhinah* by co-opting a rabbinic tradition that "The Indwelling *(shekhinah)* is in the West" as an endorsement of this notion of the Temple (ibid.).[40] West is no longer a spatial coordinate; rather, it is not East—that is, it stands for everything that opposes the East and confirms its opposite, the existence of God and His unity. Since knowledge is not a function of locale, West, as a symbol of universals, transcends its own spatiality.

The laws governing intention and direction in prayer legislatively complement its philosophical rationale. The association of Jerusalem and the Temple with the *shekhinah* is geared to command an appropriate intensity of intellectual focus during prayer. The requisite intention consists of "clearing his heart [= mind] of all thoughts and consider[ing] himself as if he were standing before the *shekhinah*" (MT *Laws of Prayer* 4:16). Though technically prayer must be conducted toward Jerusalem and the Temple, if one is incapable of determining their coordinates, "he must direct his heart [= mind] toward the *shekhinah* and pray" (ibid., 5:3). Halakhically the *shekhinah*'s relevance for prayer is to inculcate a state of mind and not to determine a physical orientation. And finally, the halakhically mandated physical posture for prayer captures the human dichotomy of mind and body, neither of which are exclusively definitive: "and his eyes should look below *as if* he were staring at the earth, and his mind should be directed above *as if* he were standing in heaven" (ibid., 5:4).[41] Prayer is an *as if* activity in both realms, since it is incomplete in either, providing a forum to act out humanity's bifurcated identity of matter (earth/body) and form (heaven/mind). Divine presence is contingent on a "clearing of the mind" and a double movement downward and upward, an inescapable reflex of the human predicament. Only posthumously, when there are no corporeal barriers, can there be an exclusive engagement with the *shekhinah*. Even then, it is reserved solely for those who have pursued it during their lifetimes.

Maimonides understood each facet of the rabbinic formulation of the ultimate reward—"the righteous sit with their crowns on their heads and enjoy the radiance of the *shekhinah*" (*b. Berakhot* 17a)—metaphorically: "The phrase 'the righteous sit' is allegorical and means that the souls of the righteous exist there without labor or fatigue. The phrase 'their crowns on their heads' refers to the knowledge they have acquired for the sake of which they have attained life in the world to come. This is their crown . . . so 'the crown' of which the Sages here speak, is not to be taken literally but refers to knowledge . . . 'they enjoy the radiance of the *shekhinah*' means that the righteous attain to a knowledge and realization of the truth concerning God to which they had not attained while they were in the murky and lowly body" (MT *Laws of Repentance* 8:2–4). The *shekhinah* that can be conceived during one's lifetime is a faint image of that which can be apprehended in the afterlife; but a lack of any sensuality maintains the continuity between the two. One could say that this eternal state of bliss is the crowning achievement of a lifetime dedicated to preserving the broadest possible distance between the *shekhinah* and the world.

The Confluence of Light and *Shekhinah*

We have seen how Maimonides fought back the anthropomorphic challenges of Halevian doctrines by replacing them with an entirely new vision of God and, consequently, with a new religious pursuit. Localized presences, hypostases, and created entities may satisfy elemental cravings, but they stunt human growth. Because they are confined they also confine by limiting, restricting, and parochializing the religious gaze. Maimonides recast light imagery to illuminate not a fixed place but rather that which guides a fluid way. There is nowhere that God is not, so there is nowhere that He is. He resides in the human effort to declare that God is and then to comprehend Him. The Halevian light is simply there; the Maimonidean eludes as it draws.

Toward the end of the *Guide,* light and *shekhinah* appear in a final powerful subversion of the old theology. God, providence, ethics, and epistemology all converge in a verse that is to become the motto of the new theology, "In Thy light do we see light" (Ps 36:10). Maimonides cited this verse as an endorsement of his root premise that the only link between humanity and God is the intellectual "overflow": "Just as we apprehend Him by means of that light which He caused to overflow toward us . . . so does He by means of this selfsame light examine us" (GP III:51, 629).[42] A constant stream of knowledge replaces the temporal and spatial light characteristic of an interventionist God of history. Knowledge, providence, and presence are all reflective of human thought, not divine endowment. Maimonides enlisted Ps 36:10 as part of his ongoing polemic with Sa'adya, who views the very same verse as an attenuation of his "created light" theory into the realm of the "world to come." For Sa'adya this light is a "fine substance" "that will shine for the righteous but not for the sinful, whilst it will burn the sinful but not the righteous." It is described as a unique substance that operates "by means of an accident whereby the ones will be protected against the heat and the others will be screened from the light."[43] Maimonides' "light" used as a metaphor for knowledge rolls back a theology that would extend the life of created lights to the world to come. It would have been intolerable for him to compound a this-worldly deception with one that would endure eternally, so he set about usurping a previous hermeneutic with his own.

Anticipating an accusation of arrogance for venerating human reason above all else, Maimonides asserted, on the contrary, that being aware of the operative meaning of "In Thy light do we see light" stimulates supreme humility: "they achieve such humility, such awe and fear of God, such reverence and such shame before Him—*and this in ways that pertain to true reality, not to imagination*" (emphasis mine). These last words take aim at the Halevian/Sa'adyan school that postulates divine essences that are actually products of the human imagination. As Elliot Wolfson has noted, the imagination for Halevi is key for religious rituals that "demand some iconic representation of God located in sacral space. It is the imaginative faculty that fulfills this critical role of allowing that which is spiritual to be materialized in space. The Temple and Synagogue assume a talismanic function for Halevi in providing receptacles to draw down the divine matter, but in the absence of human imagination that spiritual force would not be apprehended."[44] Religious worship focused on "iconic representations" of the imagination constitutes the very height of arrogance for Maimoinides. An iconic representation can be seen and approached. This closeness, though, captures God in a moment and at a place, in effect making Him a prisoner of human consciousness. The God of Maimonides— elusive and distant, unknowable and incomparable, unseen and unseeing, who defies the hubristic control of the "talismanic"—promotes far greater humility. The inherent limits of human capacity always accompany the supremacy of reason.[45]

"The whole earth is full of His glory" (Isa 6:3) enters the scene once more, "firmly to establish the notion that I have mentioned to you, that we are always before Him, may He be exalted, and walk about to and fro while His Indwelling is with us." Of course, the Indwelling is not a localized presence. Maimonides then cited two modes of behavior rabbinically inspired by the notion of an all-encompassing presence. The first is that the sages "avoided uncovering their heads because man is covered about by the *shekhinah.*"[46] The very same awareness encourages the second—the virtue of silence.[47] He then identified Eccl 5:1, a verse we have already seen to be critical to an understanding of the leper's profile, as the biblical source discouraging unnecessary speech: "For God is in heaven and thou upon the earth; therefore let thy words be few." At the very same moment that man has been clothed with the *shekhinah* ("covered about by the *shekhinah*"), he is also, by Eccl 5:1, removed from her precinct. That verse was previously cited in the *Guide* as a stricture against the human penchant to heap praise and accolades on God, especially during prayer, in the belief that it pays tribute to His existence. Ecclesiastes 5:1 advocates extreme restraint on this instinctual impulse because God defies any earthly qualification or common attribute.

Every human description of God is false and therefore increasingly constructs a false divinity. Garrulous glorification of God, an indulgence thought to be a means to "c[o]me nearer to God," actually "constitutes *unintended obloquy and vituperation* on the part of the multitude who listen to these utterances and on the part of the ignoramus who pronounces them" (GP I:59, 141–42). The verse advocates near silence because "God is in heaven and thou upon earth"; that is, God is not here, God is not immediately present, and there is no common ground between the world and Him. They each occupy two wholly separate realms. Maimonides presented his notion of *shekhinah* through a clash of biblical perceptions; on the one hand "the whole earth is full of His glory" and therefore humanity is encompassed by the *shekhinah,* and on the other, "God is in heaven and thou upon earth," thus segregating humanity and God from each other. Neither verse can be read in isolation from the other. All language about God, in particular about His presence in the world, consists of parables, riddles, and metaphor—literary devices constructed out of what Paul Ricoeur has coined as "semantic collision"[48] of terms that cannot logically coexist. If taken literally, their "meaning would be annulled by incompatibility." In this case the Ricoeurian paradigm applies to a collision between two verses created by their juxtaposition. The product of that collision is a new *shekhinah* that is nowhere because it is everywhere. Maimonides fashioned a "surplus of meaning"[49] out of his sacred Scripture, a text replete with semantic nonsense and logical absurdities, where God's everywhereness is felt in His nowhereness.

CHAPTER 8

Sabbath

The Temporal Outsider

In the previous chapters of this book, I have focused on types of outsiders, both human and divine. Each was shaped by Maimonides to transcend its own particularity, pointing to some universal philosophical offense or virtue, as the case may be. In this chapter, I turn to a different outsider, the Sabbath, which interrupts the natural rhythm of time and normatively addresses only one people to the juridical exclusion of all others.[1] However, its message is a universal one—namely, belief in the creation of the world in time.[2] The Jewish obligation to refrain from work on the seventh day publicizes a common worldwide truth: "For this reason we are ordered by the law to exalt this day, in order that the principle of the creation of the world in time be established and universally known in the world through the fact that all people refrain from working on one and the same day" (GP II:31, 359).[3]

Strict observance of the laws of Sabbath generates, by its strangeness, curiosity among people to determine the reason for such seemingly peculiar behavior. Investigation will ensue to determine why an entire people would weekly cease and desist from productive labor for one full day. Discussion will ultimately lead to the discovery of its textual source in the Bible, thereby inculcating a belief in creation: "If it is asked: What is the cause of this, the answer is *For in six days the Lord made* [Exod 20:11]" (GP III:31, 359). The Torah must be explicit about the Sabbath's rationale, in contrast to most other commandments, because it is instructive for all of humanity. Abstention from work signals a temporary, but necessary, move from reason to the text, from objectivity to encounter and faith.

Creation is also an issue in which intellectual discovery is supplemented by scriptural authority, since the former on its own cannot reach a definitive conclusion. According to Maimonides, there is no philosophical proof that persuasively demonstrates the eternality of the world, nor, for that matter, is there any that does for creation. Such being the case, the question "of the eternity of the world or its creation in time becomes an open question . . . it should, in my opinion, be accepted without proof because of prophecy, which explains things to which it is not in the power of speculation to accede" (GP II:16, 294). There is "openness" to a fundamental principle of Jewish belief, indeed "the most important fundamental of the Torah of Moses our Master,"[4] which renders the entire religious enterprise tentative. On this issue, Maimonides obliged his readers to bow to religious authority, a source of knowledge he normally considered vastly inferior to reason and reserved for those who are incapable of philosophical inquiry and must rely on tradition for their beliefs (see GP I:33, 72; I:50, 111).[5]

All discussion about creation will eventually end in deference to the founders of theoretical (Abraham) and normative (Moses) Judaism:[6] "Be therefore always suspicious in your mind as to this point and accept the authority of the two prophets who are pillars of the well-being of the human species with regard to its beliefs and its associations. Do not turn away from the opinion according to which the world is new, except because of a demonstration. Now such a demonstration does not exist in nature" (GP II:23, 322). The space reserved for the Sabbath, which interrupts the temporal continuum, also signals an interruption in the human intellectual continuum, where tradition trumps philosophical inquiry by having the final say. The Sabbath draws attention to the prophetic text as authoritative. Maimonides did in fact offer "speculative proofs" for preferring creation over eternality, but they do not measure up to the certainty of demonstration. Rather, they amount to showing that no matter what the problems are with creation in time "an even greater disgrace attaches to the belief in eternity" (GP II:16, 294). While reason endorses the superiority of creation in time over eternity, it also emphasizes, by way of its inadequacy, reason's own shortcomings on this issue. No matter how far one has penetrated the precincts of the imperial palace of knowledge in Maimonides' parable concerning the palace, the Sabbath marks the perpetual retreat from the antechambers, where speculation has led them, back to wandering at the periphery. There, they join company with those "who believe true opinions on the basis of traditional authority and study the law concerning the practices of divine service" (GP III:51, 619).[7]

In one of the boldest assertions of the *Guide,* Maimonides confided how far his commitment to the sovereignty of reason would take him had Aristotle convincingly demonstrated the eternality of the world. His preference for creation is not motivated by scriptural teaching but by extra-revelatory considerations:

> Know that our shunning the affirmation of the eternity of the world is not due to a text figuring in the *Torah* according to which the world has been produced in time. For the texts indicating that the world had been produced in time are not more numerous than those indicating that the deity has a body. Nor are the gates of figurative interpretation shut in our faces or impossible of access to us regarding the subject of the creation of the world in time. For we could interpret them as figurative, as we have done when denying His corporeality. Perhaps this would even be much easier to do: we should be very well able to give a figurative interpretation of those texts and to affirm as true the eternity of the world, just as we have given a figurative interpretation of those other texts and have denied that He, may He be exalted, is a body. (GP II:25, 327–28)

Two reasons, external to the sacred text, prevented Maimonides from resorting to figurative interpretation so that the text and Aristotle could coincide: the eternity of the world had not been adequately demonstrated; and belief in eternity and necessity "destroys the law in its principle," doing away with the possibility of miracles or reward and punishment.[8]

Maimonides offered a glimpse into his internal deliberations and startlingly admitted that, theoretically, had eternity been cogently demonstrated, he would have been forced to disavow the Torah's most fundamental teachings of miracles and reward and punishment. Though his commitment to revelation would have remained unflinching, its teachings would have had to be revamped. Accordingly, his thirteen principles of faith would have had to be drastically pared down, possibly dispensing with all but the very first three—God's existence, unity, and incorporeality.[9] Even a medieval commentator such as Shem Tov could be unreservedly frank in his understanding of Maimonides' disclosure: "and even if it destroyed the law entirely, should eternity be demonstrated, we would have interpreted the verses in accord with eternity" (MN, 51).[10] The Sabbath, then, is a testament to both the limits of reason (neither creation nor eternity can be demonstrated) and the boundless freedom of interpretation for the preservation of the rational integrity of revelation. Its disruption of the temporal continuum signals also the fluidity of the literary continuum. The Sabbath is a cyclic reminder that "the gates of figurative interpretation" are never shut.

The uniqueness of the seventh day of creation lies in its being the day God *rested (shavat)* (Gen 2:2) and *reposed (nahah)* (Exod 20:11). Since this is anthropomorphically offensive insofar as it depicts God as fatigued, it is no surprise that there is a chapter in the lexicographic section of the *Guide*, I:67, dedicated to rendering the description figuratively palatable when speaking of God. What precisely God did (or did not do) on the seventh day is critical for any appreciation of Maimonides' conception of the Sabbath and, more importantly, for his conception of God's ongoing relationship to the world from that point on. I say "ongoing" because the divine activity that ceased on the seventh day never resumed, and therefore ceased for all time thereafter. In other words, God does not rest periodically every seventh day, but from the primal seventh day onward God perpetually rests and reposes. God's relationship to the world, once the primordial creation process was completed, is defined by rest. The obsessive attitude of the early rabbinic master Shammai, who appraised every encounter with the world in terms of the Sabbath, reflects the conceptual reality of a world that is perpetually in a state of Sabbath.[11] All time, then, is captured by a break in time, by the temporal outsider. As was the case with other outsiders I have considered, with the Sabbath the interruption of the norm becomes a metaphor for the norm.

Chapter I:67 opens by drawing an analogy between saying *(amirah)*, the dominant activity of the first six days of creation, and resting *(shevitah)*, the operative divine activity of the seventh and final day: "As the term *to say* is figuratively used for the will in regard to everything that has been created in the *six days of the beginning*—with reference to which it is said: *He said, He said*—the term *to rest* is derivatively used with reference to the Sabbath as there was no creation on that day. It is accordingly said *And He rested on the seventh day* [Gen 2:2]." Maimonides here picked up on the meaning he assigned in a previous chapter to the divine saying of the creation account as exclusively "will and volition"; and so "[i]n all cases in which *He said, He said,* occurs in the *Account of the Beginning,* it means He willed or wanted" (GP I:65, 158–59). The analogy proposes reading the term "rest" not as a description of a state of being but rather in apposition to the saying of the preceding days—that is, God stopped saying or God no longer willed. The term "rested" supplies no information about God and implies a reversion to the disengaged state prior to creation when God was not involved with anything outside Himself. Once the sense of "rested" is understood in this way, the sequential logic of the series of chapters on God's names (GP I:61–64) preceding divine saying, speaking, and resting can be fully appreciated. All the names of God except the Tetragrammaton (YHVH) are only meaningful in terms of the creation. They do not capture God's essence, but rather His attributes of action: "all the derivative names have come into being after the world has come into being . . . for all these names have been laid down so as to correspond to the actions existing in the world" (GP I:61, 149).[12] In other words, rather than describing God, they describe how God acts in the world.

Without delving into the complexities of "attributes of action,"[13] it will suffice for present purposes to point out that only the ineffable name, YHVH, conveys "a clear unequivocal indication of His essence," while "all the other great names give their indication in an equivocal way, being derived from terms signifying actions" (ibid., 147).[14] Maimonides seized on the *midrash Pirqe de-Rabbi Eliezer* (chap. 3), "Before the world was created there were only the Holy One, blessed be He, and His name," as an endorsement of this position. The chapters on divine names then form a preface to the divine speech and resting of creation, since the derivative names and the one articulated name match up with the two stages of the creation process. Each divine saying during the original six days introduces the possibilities of derived names, since they all indicate willed acts from which these names are in fact derived. On the other hand, the nonwilling God indicated by the resting of the seventh day offers a semblance of that pristine God "divested and stripped of all actions," which preexisted the world. Our appreciation of the import of the Maimonidean Sabbath is significantly enhanced by this sequence of chapters because, as a normative weekly lived day, it provides a periodic jolt out of a notion of God suffused with attributes and into a notion of attributeless oneness, of absolute simple essence.[15] Exposure to the myriad of divine names manifest in the creation leaves man prone to misconceiving God as possessing attributes.[16] The Sabbath's turn toward the divine nonwilling of resting immunizes God from the misconceptions of attributes (and therefore divine multiplicity), since it directs the mind toward the truth of divine existence, which is wholly separate from the creation. The Sabbath is crucial for keeping humanity on track with respect to the nature of God's essence.

Maimonides corroborated the meaning of resting in Gen 2:2 as "refraining from speech" by drawing attention to a verse in the book of Job where the term "rest" appears in the context of speech and unquestionably means refraining from speech. After delivering lengthy discourses attempting to come to terms with Job's tragic predicament, each reflecting, according to Maimonides, a different position on divine providence, Job's friends' desistance from further speech is indicated by the verb *shavat* (to rest): "So these three men ceased [rested] *to answer Job*" (Job 32:1). Although Maimonides' choice of proof-text may have been motivated by the rare instance of "rest" in the context of speech, I believe the reference to Job in general, and this juncture of Job in particular, is far more than just textual substantiation of a wider range of meaning for the term "rest" than its most literal. The reference also draws Job's metaphorical context into the definition of the term and deepens the metaphorical meaning of the primary text regarding divine resting at the end of creation. The pivotal hermeneutical key for unlocking the philosophical meaning of the Job parable is Satan and his role in the unfolding of the narrative. At the very heart of Job's and his friends' muddled responses to the bewildering predicament of innocent suffering is their delusion "that God had done it Himself and not through the intermediary of *Satan*" (GP III:22, 487).[17] Maimonides went so far as to consider that once he had presented his detailed analysis of what the various dramatis personae of Satan represent, he had "analyzed and explained the story of *Job* up to its ultimate end and conclusion" (ibid., 490). Correspondingly, Elihu, the fifth participant in the debate after Job and his three friends, offers a novel philosophical antidote to their confused view "when he speaks of the intercession of an angel" (GP III:23, 495). For the purpose of sharpening our understanding of divine resting on the seventh day of the creation, I here concentrate solely on the message of these two angels—the Satan of Job and his friends, and Elihu's "intercessor"—as conveyors of the core philosophical subtext of Job.

In order to fully appreciate the relevance of this cryptic reference to an initial misconception as to the roles of God and the angels in the Job ordeal and Elihu's corrective thereto, a short précis of Maimonides' angelology is in order. Briefly, Maimonides broadened the meaning of the Hebrew term "angel" as "messenger" to encompass virtually every causal force or act, whether animate or inanimate, throughout the world. He appealed to the expansive range of the biblical term "angel" as a metaphor for such disparate items as the separate intellects, animal movements, the elements, human beings, prophets, and psychological impulses, to conclude that all "individual, natural, and psychic forces are called *angels*" (GP II:6, 262–64). Maimonides drained every biblical or rabbinic usage of "angel" of its mythical connotation as a substantive entity created by God to carry out some particular mission or appointed as a guardian, radically naturalizing the term to the extent that it could even signify biological stimuli for erections and orgasms (ibid., 264). There is no more striking attestation to the Maimonidean enterprise of demythologization than the reduction of angels to a metaphor for any link along the natural chain of causation.[18] His theory of angels is also an implicit critique of the *kalam*'s occasionalist doctrine that understands God's constant and immediate intervention as the driving force of all natural processes.[19] God's role in the ongoing unfolding of the world is concisely captured by the following matrix between God, angels, and natural phenomena: "Accordingly everyone who carries out an order is an *angel;* so that the movements of animals, even when these beings are not rational, are stated in the text of the Scripture to have been accomplished *through an angel,* if the motion was produced in accordance with the intention of the deity, who put a force in the living being that moved him according to that motion" (ibid., 262). In terms of the creation, "angels" cover all those components introduced into the natural schema during the first six days of the creation.

Prior to Elihu's entrance on the stage, Job and friends erroneously subscribed to a *kalamic* theology. By attributing Job's circumstances to God and not Satan, Job and company have acquiesced to a theology of a directly interventionist, responsive, and changing God. Embedded in their perspective toward creation is a failure to assimilate the divine resting of the seventh day. They live in the shadow of the previous six days where they experience the God who primordially willed every day, a God who once was but is no more. For them, the creative process has never ended and all natural phenomena continue to be products of a perpetually active divine will. To be blind to the immediate source of Job's circumstances is to be blind to the nature of God's governance of the world, whose mechanics really hinge on one's perspective regarding angels. Job's thought is initially dominated by one angel, which is the imagination, for "the imaginative faculty is also an angel" (ibid., 264–65).[20] Elihu prompts him to intellectually subordinate himself to another angel—the Active Intellect. This existential/intellectual transition from the predominance of one angel (imagination) to another (rationality) also mirrors a transition in Job's thinking about angels. The former view attributes every natural occurrence to some direct angelic manifestation of divine will, while his later view understands God's participation only in the sense of the angels (that is, natural forces) that are the building blocks of the natural order constructed in the first six days of the creation.

A direct consequence of Elihu's teaching is the revelation at the end of Job that basically consists of a scientific awareness of all of nature and the limits of that awareness: "The purpose of all these things is to show that our intellects do not reach the point of apprehending how these natural things that exist in the world of generation and corruption are produced in time and of conceiving how the existence of the natural force within them has originated in them" (GP III:23, 496). Once the newly developed metaphor contained in the term "angels" is accounted for, Job's revelation translates into a perception of a world governed by natural causation (angels = "natural forces" within "natural things"), whose origin during the primordial act of creation (first six days) are beyond human ken. Job has finally assimilated the meaning of the Sabbath. Maimonides' citation of Job 32:1 functions as a philological, exegetical, philosophical, and literary marker:

Philological: it corroborates the meaning of "resting" on the seventh day of the creation as "refraining from speech."
Exegetical: it provides an additional dimension to the story of Job and his intellectual maturation from the beginning of the story to the end.
Philosophical: it cross-references the notion of the Sabbath as the cessation of divine willing and the beginning of the natural order with

Maimonides' notion of the angel as a metaphor for the ongoing workings of that order.²¹

Literary marker: it structurally mirrors the transition marked by the Sabbath from the creation process to the final product.

Job and his friends represent the *kalamic* school that rejects the independent causal order represented by angels in favor of persistent divine intervention. The cessation of this school's speech, indicated by Job 32:1, signals the commencement of Elihu's advocacy of an angelology that represents natural causality and therefore the transition from a world governed by an unremitting divine will to one that was conceived by that will but operates on its own.

Shavat is not the only Hebrew term used in the Bible to describe what transpired on the seventh day of the creation, and so Maimonides proceeded to deal with these terms in the same manner as *shavat*. One such term, which appears in the Decalogue's formulation of the Sabbath ordinance, is *nihah* (reposing)—"And He *reposed [va-yanah]* on the seventh day" (Exod 20:11). Here again, Maimonides argued, the term is not used in the sense of some state of being that is susceptible to fatigue; rather, it "occurs in the sense of refraining from speech."²² He then cited a proof-text in support of this meaning featuring an incident in the life of King David, who sends messengers to a landowner named Naval with a request that is insolently rebuffed: "They spoke to Naval according to all those words in the name of David and reposed *[va-yanuhu]*" (1 Sam 25:9). Maimonides ruled out the possibility that "reposed" might convey rest from fatigue because there is nothing in the narrative that would indicate tiredness; nor is there any compelling literary reason for informing the audience of any such act of relaxation. On the other hand, there is a literary motive for punctuating the end of the messengers' communication, which is to underscore the offensiveness of Naval's response. That the messengers reposed emphasizes their faithfulness to David's polite and concise request, adding nothing further that could have warranted Naval's insulting behavior, "for the purpose of the story is to give an account of [Naval's] blameworthiness and to make it clear that it was extreme."²³ Like the Job reference, as is often the case, Maimonides' proof-texts act as proof and text, supplementing meaning rather than just substantiating it. This reference to the Naval passage in Samuel is another instance of his proof-text technique. The previous proof-text, confirming the meaning of *shavat* (to rest), drew Maimonides' view on angels into a fuller appreciation of the Sabbath, and the Naval citation continues in the same vein.

Those sent by David to convey his message to Naval are identified further on in the narrative as *mal'akhim* (1 Sam 25:14), the term commonly used to designate angels, but whose biblical sense is broadly configured as "messengers." It is the latter sense, devoid of supernatural connotations, which provided Maimonides with the underpinnings of his naturalist theory of angels. While the Job reference introduced angels within a theologically positive role, inspiring the perception of any causal agency as always pointing toward an originating divine will, the Naval reference raises its theological flip side. Angelic naturalism carries with it the inherent danger of losing sight of that original will. It can easily slip into an Aristotelian perspective that sees the functional independence of nature as reflecting divine abandonment. The narrative structure of the Naval reference mirrors just such a theological turn.

Naval's response to the messengers is to dismiss the principal behind their message and mission: "Who is David? Who is the son of Jesse? There are many slaves nowadays who run away from their masters" (1 Sam 25:10). His initial rhetorical insult can be read literally as a refusal to acknowledge the power that set these "angels" in motion. Though the second half of his taunt is aimed at demeaning David's stature, it can also be taken as an empirical observation regarding the pervasive phenomenon of slaves breaking away from their masters. The metaphysical equivalent of that sociopolitical assessment translates into a severance between nature (angels = causation) and its origins at the inception of the world. The emphasis on the break between master and slave reflects the philosophical rejection of a world informed by the Sabbath, which evokes an ultimate grounding in divine will, in favor of a mechanistic world that dismisses and ignores that will. The two proof-texts provide much more than mere philological corroboration of a biblical term's meaning. Their literary contexts mirror the philosophical dimensions of the debate surrounding the origin of the world and the link between the origin and its endurance, which converge in Maimonides' Sabbath formulation.

Maimonides then proceeded to offer various alternative meanings for the term "repose," corresponding to the number of roots from which the term *nihah* (reposing) derives. In addition to *nvh,* the root can also be either *ynh* or *nhh.* All of them, however, are capable of taking the world as their object—referring to what was done to the world—rather than describing a transition in God's activity from willing to not willing (saying to not saying). This alternative is first applied to Exod 20:11, normally translated as "And He [God] reposed on the seventh day." It now becomes "creation ceased on that day." Maimonides then cited a *midrash* in support of this interpretation that reads Exod 20:11 as "And He let His world repose on the seventh day" (*Gen Rabbah* 10:12). The problem one confronts regarding this particular *midrash* is identical to that which challenged Maimonides—namely, that of reinterpreting biblical language anthropomorphism. Various opinions within that *midrash* preceding the one cited by Maimonides struggle with the anthropomorphic connotations of divine resting in Gen 2:2, offering solutions that de-anthropomorphize the verse. Maimonides' excerpt enjoys the particular advantage of employing the term "repose" in Exod 20:11 to elucidate the meaning of "rest" in Gen 2:2, rendering them synonymous indicators of God's activity on the seventh day of creation.

The transformation of "rest" and "repose" into transitive verbs responds to the philosophical error reflected in the Naval narrative where God was denied any role in the durability of the world. In this midrashic sense, God endows the world with the quality of rest—that is, its resting is dependent on an originating act of God. The Sabbath, then, is a perpetual testament to the "basic principle of all basic principles" that God "brought every existing thing into being. All existing things, whether celestial, terrestrial, or belonging to an intermediate class, exist only through His true essence. If it could be supposed that He did not exist it would follow that nothing else could possibly exist" (MT *Laws of the Foundations of the Torah* 1:1–2). This chapter on the meanings of resting on the seventh day serves as an appropriate preface to chapter I:69, which defines God as both the "efficient cause" of the world *and* the form of the world, or "the ultimate form and the form of forms" (GP I:69, 168–69).[24] The sense of resting as the cessation of God's will conveys the idea of a being who is the efficient cause, so that every event in the world reflects a series of proximate natural efficient causes that ultimately trace back to God as the final efficient cause.[25] The Sabbath, understood as God's ceasing to will, entrenches the proposition that "every action that occurs in Being is referred to God . . . even if it is worked by one of the proximate efficient causes; God, considered as efficient cause, is then the remotest one" (ibid., 168).[26] On the other hand, the Sabbath that conjures up the

God who endowed the world with rest signifies the God who is the form of the world, without whom the world would, in a sense, stop resting. It would then be reminiscent of the God who is "that upon which the existence and stability of every form in the world ultimately reposes and by which they are constituted."

Another meaning emerges from alternative root forms of the term *nihah,* "reposing," that conveys that "He established existence, or He made the latter endure as it was on the seventh day." All the scientific laws governing the world, as we know it, crystallized on the Sabbath, introducing the framework of naturalism within which man confronts and encounters the world. The Sabbath signals the radical transition from chaos to order since, during the embryonic stages of the preceding six days, "events occurred that did not correspond to the established nature that exists at present in the whole of existence, whereas on the seventh day the state of things became lasting and established just as it is at present." Here Maimonides denied the Sabbath any metaphysical status that might be intimated by rabbinic designations of it, such as that it is a taste of the world to come (*b. Berakhot* 57b), or that it preexisted the creation in the mind of God along with other such supranatural phenomena as Hell, the waters of the flood, the second set of tablets, and the light of the world to come (*Pirqe De-Rabbi Eliezer* 3). It is also diametrically opposed to what was to become a dominant mystical motif of the Sabbath as "a rupture, a break in the unidirectional procession of history."[27] Maimonides ruled out the possibility of experiencing the Sabbath as, in the words of Mircea Eliade, "primordial mythical time made present."[28] The Sabbath, while recollecting a primordial event, aims at demythologizing the import of that event.

The Maimonidean Sabbath reverses the mystical direction of normal to mythic time, jolting man out of the mythic mode to which he seems so attracted into natural reality. It is precisely on the issue of angels, with which Sabbath is so bound up, where the lure of the mythic over the natural is most prominently expressed. Maimonides found that those who see material beings lurking behind every natural process are motivated by a warped sense of religiosity, which regards such a natural process "as a manifestation of greatness and power on the part of the deity, and also of His wisdom" (GP II:6, 263). However, if those processes were rendered intelligible by way of a scientific account of angels as natural causation, these same people "would shrink from this opinion." The Sabbath is an intermittent safeguard against falling prey to a mythical view of time and space. Sabbath signifies "established existence" in direct contradistinction to the mythical existence of the primordial six days, which defy intelligibility. Maimonides' Sabbath is meant to inculcate an overarching view of a world that has emerged from chaos into order, from governance by divine decree to the laws of physics. What remains without the Sabbath is the entropy of the first six days—a physical world suffused with the miraculous and, consequently, not subject to scientific scrutiny. This worldview is expressed in the far more attractive angelology that accounts for such biological processes as conception and pregnancy in terms of "the Deity sends an angel, who enters the womb of a woman and forms the fetus there," where the "angel is a body formed of burning fire and that his size is equal to that of a third part of the whole world" (ibid.).[29]

The Sabbath-oriented weltanschauung provides roles for God and the angels in that same process, but circumscribes God's role to the primordial six days and relegates "angel" to a literary trope. The result is a *religious* natural account of the development of a fetus, in which "God has placed in the sperm a formative force shaping the limbs and giving them their configuration and that this force is the *angel.*" For Maimonides, this account is a religious one because only an ordered world can disclose knowledge of its creator[30] while nothing but chaos can be extrapolated from an anarchic one. Man may be inclined toward the latter because of its undemanding requirements, while the former imposes an effort of near-Herculean proportions if any knowledge of God is to be gained.

At this juncture in his terminological analysis of divine resting in I:67, Maimonides preempted any critique of a linguistic nature that might undermine his own proposals. First, without delving into the morphological complexities of Hebrew, he explained that there are "irregular" grammatical conjugations of a verb that might not always strictly conform to the general rule. Second, and more importantly, the "doing-away with the notion in question, which gives rise to vain imagining, should not be negated because of the rules of conjugation obtaining in the [Hebrew] language, for we know that today we have no complete understanding of the science of our language and that in all languages rules merely conform to the majority of cases." Just as there are no obstacles to the exegetical freedom to harmonize Scripture with demonstrated truth on the issue of *creatio ex nihilo,* so there are no syntactical impediments to ascertaining the meaning of the end of that creative process represented by the Sabbath and its related divine activity of resting. Truth, not text, is determinative, especially since the "science of our language" has been lost.[31]

The credibility of the universal thesis that the Sabbath stands for cannot be impugned by the trivial niceties of Hebrew grammar. Law (Sabbath observance) and language (Hebrew) point beyond their own parochial confines because the Sabbath inherently aims toward the human collective with its message of the miraculous being superseded by nature. Conceptually, Maimonides also established a parallel between language and law. Grammatical rules are never sacrosanct since they can only presume to "conform to the majority of cases." Likewise, the law "does not pay attention to the isolated. The law was not given with a view to things that are rare" (GP III:34, 534). There are always exceptions—for example, when the application of the law would result in damage rather than benefit, since it can only account for the general norm: "only the universal interests, those of the majority, are considered in them" (ibid., 535).

Drawing attention to this particular principle that law and language share, precisely during the course of an excursus on the meaning of divine resting, is for Maimonides both formally and structurally strategic. The Sabbath itself conceptually operates in accord with this rule. By its delineation between the first six days of creation and all of subsequent history, it orients one's perspective both backward and forward. It looks back at the exception, the miraculous, and forward to the universal norm—nature. Just as language and law can only hope to provide for the norm, always admitting of exceptions that resist their application, so the Sabbath signifies the inception of the norm *and* the exceptional that preceded it. Though it represents the cessation of divine will, its emergence out of the previously miraculous process indicates the exception as an integral constituent of the fabric of nature. The Sabbath normatively underscores the distinction between Aristotelian and Jewish belief, which hinges on mere *possibility*. The advent of the Sabbath as harbinger of willed creation recurrently evokes the notion that "all the miracles become possible and the law becomes possible" (GP II:25, 329).

The Sabbath conjures up a hybrid of Aristotelian religion where everything is enduring and immutable and yet, at the same time, everything is *possible,* including termination and change: "we believe that what exists is eternal *a parte post* and will last forever with that nature which He, may He be exalted, has willed; that nothing in it will be changed in any respect unless it be in some particular of it miraculously—*although He, may He be exalted, has the power to change the whole of it, or to annihilate it, or to annihilate any nature in it that He wills*" (GP II:29, 346; emphasis mine). The Sabbath, then, also portends ultimate redemption, or the messianic era, which is located along the same trajectory of normal historical time that the primordial Sabbath inaugurated. The interminability of nature, suggested by the Sabbath, suppresses any false hope of an apocalyptic upheaval of nature leading to utopia with the notion that the end of time is really more of the same time and causality. In this sense, the observance of the Sabbath is also the normative safeguard against the cardinal misunderstanding of the messianic era warned of at the end of the *Mishneh Torah*: "Let no one think that in the days of the messiah any of the laws of nature will be set aside, or any innovation be introduced into creation" (MT *Laws of Kings* 12:1).[32] The Sabbath, looking backward and forward in this way, encourages man to pick up where God left off. The divine will was the original catalyst of history while the human will charts its course toward and into the messianic era.[33]

The Sabbath raises another radical Maimonidean conception of law, in this case Jewish law, that operates in consonance with the linguistic rule of conforming "to the majority of cases." In essence, Maimonides constructed his philosophical anthropology of *ta'ame ha-mitzvot* (rationale for the commandments) on the principle that the exigencies of human nature dictate the formal content of the law.[34] Virtually all of the rituals legislated at Sinai assume the form they do because of the law's need to take into account its ancient audience's character and psychology shaped by its surrounding pervasively idolatrous culture. It speaks to that collective mind geared to the majority of cases—the norm—by adopting the language and symbols of its host culture, such as sacrifices, and subverts it from within. However, the law's primary aim, what Maimonides termed its "first intention," is to eradicate all traces of idolatry and inculcate the belief that "there is a deity who is the Creator of all this" (GP III:29, 518), and, in the final analysis, "consists only in your apprehending Me and not worshipping someone other than Me" (GP III:32, 530).[35] The Torah's rituals are largely historically contingent means of achieving that overarching aim.

What is pertinent to the discussion of the Sabbath is that rabbinic tradition has actually offered a glimpse of what a stripped-down law, whose sole concern is "primary intention" with no need to address historical contingencies, might look like. The *midrash* provides Maimonides with just such a law that preceded Sinai at Marah, identifying the "statute *[hoq]* and judgment *[mishpat]* revealed there" (Exod 15:25) as "the Sabbath and civil laws."[36] For Maimonides, this is an illustration of a law that concerns itself exclusively with first intentions: "I mean the belief in correct opinions, namely, in the creation of the world in time. For you already know that the foundation of the law addressed to us concerning the Sabbath is its contribution in fortifying this principle" (GP III:32, 531).[37] Of course, beliefs can only thrive in a socially harmonious environment, so the first intention "also included the abolition of mutual wrongdoing among men." Maimonides seized on this as a utopian legislative code that, although supplemented by the Sinaitic code for pragmatic reasons, holds out an abstract ideal that informs the normative telos of Sinai.

The Sabbath then serves a dual function of stimulating contemplation regarding both metaphysics and jurisprudence. Not only does it look back at the creation to define the contours of God's ongoing relationship with nature, it also looks back to a normative ideal that antedates Sinai. In both cases its task is to constrain and circumscribe. In the first place, it confines God's interaction with the world to those primordial six days. In the second, by minimizing its intrinsic value, the Sabbath safeguards the ritual from becoming an end in itself and losing sight of primary intentions. Vis-à-vis the creation, it rationalizes nature, and vis-à-vis Sinai, it rationalizes the law, by extending a dimension of that nature, in this case human nature, to account for its statutory formulations. Every commandment originating at Sinai must ideally be performed while cognizant of its "first intentions." One could formulate this notion of command *(mitzvah)* performance as follows: Perfect fulfillment of a *mitzvah* is contingent on the knowledge that the Sinaitic formulation of it is a historical dilution of the pristine law revealed at Marah. To lose sight of Marah is to reduce the *mitzvah* to a relic of a remote past out of whose historical context it was the product. Every *mitzvah* must be informed by the Sabbath.[38] The Sabbath is both the normative and noetic way back to the truth about the nature of God and His governance of the world.

Maimonides then concluded his excursus on the term "repose" *(nihah)* with a flurry of verses corroborating its meaning as establishing something for a period of time rather than as a response to tiredness. His point here is that the Bible itself does not always consistently follow strict formulaic rules of grammar, and the term *nihah* is one of those words that can, at times, break the mold. Despite grammatical rules to the contrary, its context in certain verses clearly rules out translating it as resting from fatigue. Three such verses offer isolated illustrations of *nihah* as "established" or fixed, but when taken together their contribution to Maimonides' argument rises from mere philology to pith and substance:

1. "And *she shall be set* there" (Zech 5:10).
2. "And she suffered neither the birds of the air *to be established* on them" (2 Sam 21:10).
3. "That I might be *established* in the day of trouble" (Hab 3:16).

The subjects referred to by the term "established" are, respectively, an inanimate object (*efah*—measuring stick?), birds, and a person. Maimonides here selected three verses that cover major facets of the creation as a whole modeled on their original sequential order—inanimate, animal, and human. He literally reinforced his philosophical transformation of the term "resting" into a grand assertion about the steadiness of nature and its design. The combination of proof-texts reasserts the proposition that all of creation had been fixed on the Sabbath.

The third choice of proof-text listed above strengthens the plausibility of this reading, since its introduction seems somewhat intrusive and its interpretation goes against an overriding consensus. Virtually every major commentator preserves the most common meaning of "rest" for the verbal form of *nihah* in Hab 3:16,[39] acknowledgment of which is evident in Maimonides' prefatory remark to his unique reading: "In my opinion the verb has this meaning also in the verse *That I might be established in the day of trouble.*" Though it is far from clear precisely how Maimonides construed this verse, I understand him to have read it as an expression of stalwartness in the face of trouble; or, "My being is so fixed that it cannot be disturbed by suffering."[40] A verse was purposefully introduced, within the context of Maimonides' discussion of nature being fixed on the Sabbath, that affects any account of God's concern for man from that primordial Sabbath onward. Maimonides' account of divine providence is a logical extension of the divine resting that established nature's mechanics for the first and last time.

In sum, the relationship between man and God parallels that between God and the creation, both being a consequence of divine endowment or "overflow": "inasmuch as it had been demonstrated . . . that the universe is an act of His and that He is its efficient cause . . . it has been said that the world derives from the overflow of God and that He has caused to overflow to it everything in it that is produced in time. In the same way it is said that He has caused His knowledge to overflow to the prophets" (GP II:12, 279). The bridge between man and God is this overflow, access to which is a function of human preparation so that one "is receptive of the permanently existing action" (ibid.). Maimonides' providence is "consequent upon the intellect and attached to it"; "[a]ccordingly everyone with whom something of the overflow is united, will be reached by providence to the extent to which he is reached by the intellect" (GP III:17, 474).[41] The attribution of human predicaments to divine providence is a metaphorical personalization of what is essentially a permanent feature embedded in the structure of creation on that first Sabbath. The verse from Habakkuk points to the logical culmination of Maimonides' theory on providence at the end of the *Guide,* where the notion that abandonment to pure chance and its converse, attraction of divine providence, are functions of human activity vis-à-vis God's immutable primordial will. The height of providential achievement is a natural fruition of human effort, where "if a man's thought is free from distraction, if he apprehends Him, may He be exalted, in the right way and rejoices in what he apprehends, that individual *can never be afflicted with evil of any kind*" (GP III:51, 625; emphasis mine).[42] Whether this invincible state refers to physical existence or to a perfected intellect that survives the body, it is a natural finale of human achievement.[43] Habakkuk 3:16 ("I will endure [be protected] at the time of trouble"), rendering the term *anuah* as "established" (fixed or undisturbed), already portends Ps 91:7 cited at the end of the *Guide* to capture this supreme state of immunity: "A thousand may fall at thy side, and ten thousand at thy right hand; it shall not come nigh to thee." It is planted in an early key chapter dealing with the meaning of the Sabbath because Maimonides' theory of providence is rooted in his theory of creation and the institution of the natural order that reached its zenith on the seventh day. The Sabbath reverberates with both creation and providence, thus maximizing its significance.

Va-yinnafash is the third biblical synonym, in addition to *shevitah* and *nihah,* to describe the divine resting on the seventh day of creation. Once again, its etymology from the root *nefesh* (soul) dispels any possible connotation of a response to tiredness. Maimonides referred to his analysis of the term *nefesh* presented earlier in I:41 as indicative of "purpose and volition" whenever it relates to God, and concluded: "Accordingly it means that His purpose was perfected and all His will realized." Here too Maimonides cemented the notion of Sabbath as nature succeeding divine participation developed thus far. There has been, to import Hegelian terminology, an unfolding of Absolute Spirit for a very limited time. It unfolded for six days and ceased after reaching its apex, not in eighteenth-century Germany, but on the seventh day of the world's first annum of existence.

Exodus 31:17, where the term appears in relation to the divine activity of the seventh day, reads literally as follows: "For in six days the Lord made *[asah]* heaven and earth, and on the seventh day He ceased from work *[shavat]* and was refreshed *[va-yinnafash]*." Within the Maimonidean lexicon, the term *asah* stands for a technical component of God's original creative process.[44] Once heaven and earth are brought "into existence out of nonexistence,"[45] the second phase of making *(asah)* "is applied to the specific forms that were given to them—I mean their natures" (GP II:30, 358).[46] The verse in its Maimonidean guise then translates into "For in six days God willed the heaven's and earth's natures to be fixed and on the seventh day He ceased willing and His purpose was perfected and all His will was realized." In contradistinction to "refreshed," which anticipates renewed activity after a brief respite, "perfected" and "realized" render any further activity of no use. *Va-yinnafash* categorically asserts, as the other two terms subtly implied, the final resolution of all divine activity in respect of the creation, for all time.[47]

The reference to the lexicographic chapter on *nefesh* (I:41) serves more than just to offer one figurative sense of the term in order to disqualify any possible anthropomorphic reading of Exod 31:17. Though the Sabbath demarcates nature from divine will, this particular term for divine resting establishes a Maimonidean theology of the Sabbath. Apposite to God, it connotes will and purpose, but apposite to man it can also bear the meaning of "the rational soul, I mean the form of man" (GP I:41, 91). The other two terms, *shevitah* and *nihah,* could be distilled to the notion that nature succeeds divine will. The term *nefesh,* however, points up a corollary of that notion: man succeeds divine will. Man, by virtue of his "natural form"—intellectual apprehension—in a sense constitutes a remaining trace of God's involvement with the world since, by exercising the *nefesh,* he manifests the *image of God* in which he was created (GP I:1). By cultivating his natural form, man also triggers the sole activity that can even remotely be said to bridge God and the world. The kind of void left by the original Sabbath is filled by human activity that draws

God's attention: "Just as we apprehend Him by means of that light which He caused to overflow to us . . . so does He by means of this selfsame light examine us: and because of it, He, may He be exalted, is constantly with us examining from on high" (GP III:52, 629). Man generates the light that links God to the world by exercising his *nefesh,* which succeeds the fully accomplished divine will of the seventh day of creation. The *va-yinnafash* of the seventh day, indicating the end of God's *nefesh,* anticipates the replacement *nefesh* of man whose responsibility it is to preserve the bond between God and the world permanently set in place at the seventh day. God retires, only to pass the torch over to man in his capacity as the sole living creature that can somehow retrieve that divine presence that so overshadowed the first six days of creation.

Once the true meaning of divine resting on that primordial Sabbath has been established, the double rationalization of Sabbath observance proposed by Maimonides in II:31 of the *Guide,* practical and philosophical, can be seen to mirror the double movement that first Sabbath indicated. Here Maimonides located his two explanations in the two different rationales explicitly offered by the first and second versions of the Decalogue in Exod 20 and Deut 5. The first version attributes the cause of the Sabbath to the six days of divine creativity that preceded it: "For in six days the Lord made" (Exod 20:11). The effect of that original cause is "to regard that day as noble and exalted. As it says *Wherefore the Lord blessed the Sabbath day and hallowed it."* The blessing and hallowing (also translated as "holiness") of the Sabbath (Exod 20:11) are a direct consequence of the events preceding it—six days of creation and resting on the seventh—recounted in the very same verse. The Sabbath's holiness encourages human perception of the Sabbath as a "noble and exalted" day. Maimonides' definition of the word "sanctity/holiness" *(qodesh)* in the *Guide* is essential for grasping the mechanics of how holiness inspires reverence. He considered it an antonym, not of *hol* (profane) as is usually thought, but of *tum'ah* (uncleanness). Whatever *unclean* is, *qodesh* is its opposite (GP III:47, 595–96). *Tum'ah* is a normative category that is functional only vis-à-vis the Temple, barring any entry into its precinct: "*uncleanness* and *cleanness* concerns only the *Holy Place* and *holy things,* nothing else" (ibid., 594). The ultimate aim of the intricate *tum'ah* legislative regime is to curtail frequenting the Temple to an absolute minimum so that "*fear* will continue and an impression leading to the humility that was aimed at will be produced" (ibid.). Fear of the Temple constitutes a formal positive commandment; but Maimonides was emphatic, both in his *Book of Commandments* and in the *Mishneh Torah*, that the target of that fear is not the Temple space or location but rather "Him who commanded that we fear it" (MT *Laws of the Temple* 7:1; and see SM Positive Commandment 21).[48] The Herculean demands of cleanness imposed by holiness are all aimed at directing the mind toward the metaphysical truth that the Temple represents.

For the present discussion, it is critical that we appreciate Maimonides' analogy drawn between fear of the Temple and Sabbath observance both normatively and philosophically. A halakhic *midrash*, cited approvingly by Maimonides, considers the commandment to fear the Temple to be perpetually in force even after the Temple's destruction. That normative ruling is based on the biblical proximity between the directives demanding fear of Temple and of Sabbath observance. Their appearance side by side within the very same verse, "Observe my Sabbaths and fear my Temple, for I am YHVH" (Lev 19:30), provides the midrashic impetus for their correspondence: "Just as Sabbath observance is forever so is fear of the Temple forever" (*Sifra, Qedoshim* 7:8, cited by Maimonides in SM Positive Commandment 21, and MT *Laws of the Temple* 7:7). The purpose behind coupling these two unrelated commands, according to the *Guide,* is to "strengthen *fear of the Sanctuary*" (GP III:45, 577–78). A closer look at Maimonides' rationalization of the Temple and its role in the evolution of the ideal religion and its attendant proper conceptions of God reveals that this coupling of Sabbath and Temple is no mere excuse for halakhic prescription. The meaning of both Temple and Sabbath are substantively enhanced by their tactical juxtaposition.

As is the case with many commandments, virtually every normative detail governing the construction and daily operation of the Temple is aimed at subverting the then-prevailing idolatrous rites. For example, the altar must be built out of earth and not hewn stone because "the idolaters used to build altars with hewn stones" (ibid., 578). Priestly clothing addresses particularly offensive modes of worship associated with specific cults. Priestly trousers "to cover the flesh of their nakedness" (Exod 28:42) undermine the *Pe'or* cult, which mandated bodily exposure as a form of service (GP III:45, 578; see *m. Sanhedrin* 7:6). The very locus of the Temple and the directional coordinates of prayer are fixed in opposition to pagan practice, replacing the east with the west as its new orientation. Here we have a substantive attack on pagan theology involving much more than mere formalistic reversal. Spatial reorientation also accomplishes a theological reorientation, replacing a false object of worship with an authentic one: "as at that time the opinion generally accepted in the world was to the effect that the sun should be worshipped and that it is the deity, there is no doubt that all men turned when praying toward the east" (GP III:45, 575). There is a substantive philosophical underpinning to the analogy between the Temple and the Sabbath beyond its technical halakhic ramifications. The aggregate of subversions of pagan theology by the location, construction, and inner cultic practices of the Temple undermine, among other facets, the pervasive control exercised by the gods over human affairs. The sun virtually dominates human existence, which depends for its survival on the sun's daily and seasonal rhythms. The Temple, in its representational attack on worship of the sun and other heavenly bodies, is dedicated foremost to eradicating the religious impulse to worship physical entities that project overwhelming presence. In its place, it encourages a minimalist theology of divine presence by its deflection and redirection of that impulse.

Maimonides' conception of the Temple and its cult radically subverts the common practice that seeks to *establish* a divine presence on earth in favor of one that minimizes as much as possible a diffuse presence, confining it to one locale on its way to being detached altogether from the world. The Temple's restriction to one particular location, one building, and one family (priests or *kohanim*) who can officiate is pragmatically "intended to restrict this kind of worship, so that only the portion of it should subsist whose abolition is not required by His wisdom" (GP III:32, 529). The Sabbath strengthens the fear of the Sanctuary because it reinforces its theological raison d'être. Observing the Sabbath provides the framework for the disentanglement of God from the world, of spiritual entities from physical ones, as a prime religious duty. It inculcates the notion of a Being whose absence, rather than presence, is the true locus of reverence. The less trace of God there is linked to space, the greater is one's comprehension of His nature.

Sabbath observance, as a religious norm, is an aid in the pursuit of Maimonides' negative theology, a mandated "occasion on which it becomes clear to you by means of a demonstration that a thing whose existence is thought to pertain to Him, may He be exalted, should rather be negated with reference to Him" (GP I:60, 144).[49] In the case of Sabbath, what is negated is the possibility of any traversal of strict ontological boundaries between God and the created world other than the "bridge" of origins. Every Sabbath conceived of in this way becomes an opportunity to build a theological edifice of negation whereby "you undoubtedly come nearer to Him by one degree" (ibid.). The halakhic coupling of Sabbath and Temple, then, forces the religious adherent to retrieve the Temple's original intent—to *minimize* God's presence in the created world to one single spatial locus as the final theological stage toward its ultimate expulsion from created space altogether—and to restrain the ever-present impulse to ontologize space with a divine presence resulting in a self-defeating paganization of the Temple.

Historically, it did not take very long before Israel lapsed into just such an idolatrous conception of the Temple and its sacrificial cult. Addressing himself to the problematic assertion in Jer 7:22–23 that there were no commandments regarding sacrifices at the time of the exodus from Egypt (clearly belying the Pentateuchal accounts), Maimonides interpreted these verses as capturing this very confusion regarding the function of the Temple: "For he says that the first intention consists only in your apprehending Me and not worshipping someone other than Me. . . . Those laws concerning sacrifices and repairing to the Temple were given only for the sake of the realization of this fundamental principle. It is for the sake of that principle that I transferred these modes of worship to My name so that the trace of idolatry be effaced and the fundamental principle of My unity be established. You, however, came and abolished this end, while holding fast to what has been done for its sake" (GP III:32, 530). That the mandate to fear the Temple even in its physical absence should be derived from the Sabbath is now apparent. The Temple was never intended to confine any palpable presence, but rather to represent an idea. That idea, the attributeless God who bears no relation to the world, is ever-present regardless of the subsistence of any physical structure. A universal truth survives any physical structure. Therefore, as far as inculcating that truth, that locus in Jerusalem remains just as potent whether it bears an actual structure or not. The Sabbath, as representative of God's separateness from the world, is the temporal theological analogue to the spatiality of the Temple. The Sabbath, in fact, captures the very essence of a Temple that has disappeared—a divine presence that presents itself by virtue of its absence.

Immediately preceding Maimonides' reinforcement of the command to fear the Sanctuary by noting its biblical juxtaposition with observance of the Sabbath (Lev 19:30), he addressed the significance of the two sculpted cherubim that must be fixed over the ark in the Holy of Holies, or innermost sanctum of the Temple. Maimonides' rationalization for placing angelic forms where one would least expect such material images[50]—anathema to the notion of a unified incorporeal Being that this sacred space points to—augments our previous discussion regarding the critical role angels play in appreciating the full meaning of the Sabbath. Since belief in angels is "consequent upon the belief in the existence of the Deity and that thereby prophecy and the law are established as valid," the purpose of the commandment to place the cherubim over the ark is

> so that the belief of the multitude in the existence of angels be consolidated; this correct opinion, coming in the second place after the belief in the existence of the deity, constituting the originative principle of belief in prophecy and the law and refuting idolatry, as we have explained. If there had been one image, I mean the image of *one cherub,* this might have been misleading. For it might have been thought that this was the image of the deity who was to be worshipped—such things being done by the idolaters—or that there was only one individual angel, a belief that would have led to a certain dualism. As, however, *two cherubim* were made and the explicit statement enounced *The Lord is our God, the Lord is one* [Deut 6:4], the validity of the opinion affirming the existence of angels was established and also the fact that they are many. Thus measures were taken against the error that they are the deity—the deity being one and having created this multiplicity. (GP III:45, 577)[51]

Although the term "cherubim" here is used in a generic sense for all angels, Maimonides' appropriation of this term throughout both his philosophical and rabbinic works is much more complex and variegated. They can represent alternatively one of the ten heavenly Intelligences,[52] the human intellect,[53] or the heavenly spheres[54]—a profoundly nuanced manipulation of the term deserving a scholarly treatment of its own. However, its use here, and specifically in reference to the housing of the cherubim in the inner sanctum of the Temple, serves to sharpen the distinction between unity and multiplicity. Angels serve to inculcate correct knowledge of God's nature by their presentation as a kind of a foil for God—a representation of everything that God is not. The emphasis here is on angels as "many," as "multiplicity," whose purpose is to prevent any confusion between them and the absolute unity of God. At their most elemental level is their role in promoting "the belief of the multitude in the existence of angels"—that is, a realm characterized by multiplicity as opposed to the divine realm of unity. The knowledge of God's absolute and simple unity is dependent on the knowledge that He bears no resemblance whatsoever to anything corporeal that allows for "parts and dimensions," normatively realized in the daily pronouncement "The Lord is our God, the Lord is One" (MT *Laws of the Foundations of the Torah* 1:7). The angels, then, elevate this utterance from mere ritualized lip service to an enhanced knowledge of God's unity. Understood in this sense, though, angels are well on their way to self-abnegation, for if angels connote multiplicity they can have nothing whatsoever to do with the unified existence of God. The multivalent use of the term in the Maimonidean corpus and its link to the Sabbath by way of the Temple drive it toward the ultimate goal of overcoming its primitive sense of independent entities.

Angels served a purpose in the development of Israelite theology in much the same way as Maimonides claimed sacrifices did. Just as divine legislation accommodated the religious penchant for sacrifice, then "generally accepted and customary in the whole world and the universal service upon which we [Israelites] were brought up" (GP III:32, 526),[55] for the sake of realizing its primary goal of belief in unity of God, so it does with angels. Ultimately, by directing all attention toward the Temple and its innermost recesses (invisible to all but the High Priest), primitive beliefs are refined to the point where they self-destruct and are replaced by their very antithesis. The term "angels" was originally intended as a blurring of the divine and human realms, a kind of filling up of the empty space between them thus bridging the two and allowing for a closer proximity between them;[56] Maimonidean angels in the end maintain their strict segregation.[57] He reversed the trend by having angels revert to signifying the very problem they were meant to resolve. They transform themselves from bridges to theological barriers between God and the world. What were Maimonides' textual strategies in achieving this transformation?

The angel, which plays a vital role in the flow of prophecy, signifies in the Maimonidean lexicon the imaginative faculty. During the course of his discussion on the wide net of meaning cast by the term "angel," Maimonides cited a *midrash* that corroborates the identity of angel and imagination as follows: "*When man sleeps, his soul speaks to the angel, and the* *angel to the cherub.*⁵⁸ Thereby they have stated plainly to him who understands and cognizes intellectually that the imaginative faculty is likewise called an *angel* and the intellect is called a *cherub*" (GP II:6, 264–65). If, as Maimonides made clear, the sequential path of prophetic signals always follows from the "Active Intellect, toward the rational faculty in the first place and thereafter toward the imaginative faculty" (GP II:36, 369),⁵⁹ then this *midrash* follows those signals in their reverse direction.

Without further pursuing Maimonides' complex theory of prophecy, it is critical for present purposes to note that in this context cherub is distinguished from angel. Mosaic prophecy, however, is fundamentally distinct from all others in that this angel (imagination) is dispensed with: "to every prophet except Moses our Master prophetic revelation comes through an *angel*."⁶⁰ The Mosaic reference is relevant to how one perceives the cherubim in the Holy of Holies, and ipso facto the impact of that perception on angels in general. They are placed there to "consolidate" belief, for they play a unique role in the symbolic representation of the mechanics of Mosaic prophecy. The supreme biblical image that captures this essential distinction between Moses and all other prophets is in fact that of divine communication emanating from between the cherubim on the ark: "For a prophet can hear only *in a dream of prophecy* that God has spoken to him. Moses our master, on the other hand, heard Him *from above the ark cover, from between the two cherubim* [Exod 25:22] without action on the part of the imaginative faculty" (GP II:45, 403). Just prior to citing this proof-text, Maimonides reiterated the principle that all prophets with the sole exception of Moses hear speech through the intermediary of an angel. Once again, on this occasion within the context of the cherubim over the ark, cherub is distinguished as something other than angel.

Ultimately the cherubim in the Holy of Holies are integrally linked with Mosaic prophecy where they are decidedly not angels and where they are associated with the workings of pure intellect, undiluted by imagination. The result of this analytical digression that traces the path of cherub symbolism is that the end of that path radically subverts its beginning. The pedagogical journey of the cherub is launched at its most basic level "so that the *belief of the multitude* [emphasis mine] in the existence of angels be consolidated." Identification of a belief with one held by the multitude immediately signals its philosophical impoverishment, intended only as an initial position from which one departs as quickly as possible to a more refined and correct one. In light of the popular conception of existence only in terms of corporeality, "the minds of the multitude were accordingly guided to the belief that He exists by imagining that He is corporeal" (GP I:46, 98). Likewise, those same unsophisticated minds are guided to correct beliefs about prophecy and God's contact with the world by a primitive belief in angels. Moreover, just as that belief in divine corporeality must gradually undermine itself to the point of its utter negation, so a belief in angels as supernatural entities must progressively self-destruct into their signification as nature and the natural. Maimonides strategically achieved this radical transformation of belief by distinguishing cherubim from angels and then having those cherubim that are positioned in the Holy of Holies designate a process in which only intellects are involved, both human and separate.[61] Increasingly the reader's attention is drawn away from beyond nature to nature culminating in a reorienting reading of Exod 25:22.

One of the distinguishing features of Mosaic prophecy is its arrival while Moses was sensually intact. For all others, prophecy arrives at the cost of highly diminished sensual capacity and in a semiconscious trance or sleep-induced state. The proof-text Exod 25:22, in none other than the seventh of Maimonides' thirteen principles, refocuses the object of what is between the two cherubim from God or divine presence to Moses. Moses hears divine speech physically upright and standing between the two cherubim: "as for Moses, divine speech came to him by day and he was standing between the two cherubim as was guaranteed to him by God, *And I will meet with you there and I will speak with you etc.* [Exod 25:22]" (PM 4:213).[62] The Moses situated between the cherubim is a Moses who has achieved such a superior intellectual state as to be on par with the angels, who "remains pure intellect and on account of which it is said of him that he speaks with God without the intervention of angels" (GP I:51, 112–13). In a remarkable reversal, what started out as representative of angels (cherubim) for mass consumption ends up as representative of an existence (Moses) and a locale (Holy of Holies) that are completely divorced from and indeed absent of any trace of angels whatsoever. Maimonides prodded the targeted reader, his disciple Joseph and his intellectual compatriots, along a complex hermeneutical weave of text and tradition, from its beginning with cherub as angelic creature of the popular religious imagination to its final destination as a radically demystified cherub. The cherub is so thoroughly stripped of its ontic mystique that the popular imagination is exposed for what it is—imaginary and illusory.

The halakhic *midrash,* "Just as Sabbath observance is forever so is fear of the Temple forever," can now be fully appreciated as a union of *halakhah* and philosophy. Just as the Sabbath's holiness lies in its normalization of the creation, a space restricted to the natural and immune to divine intrusiveness, so the core of the Temple is a space where the natural inheres, a holiness defined by the absence of any divine presences, God or angels. In this way, Maimonides anticipated and attempted to preempt what later would become a prominent Kabbalistic motif of identifying both Temple and Sabbath with the hypostatized feminine aspect of God known as the *shekhinah,* or the lowest of the ten spheres. Familiar with Halevian teachings, as shown in chapter 7, Maimonides must already have sensed the stirrings of what was for him a dangerous regression to mythic notions of the Godhead. The Maimonidean Sabbath, just like the Maimonidean *shekhinah,* is painstakingly formulated to scuttle the movement toward what would eventually culminate in a Sabbath that would become, in Scholem's words, "*the* day of the Kabbalah," when "the light of the upper world bursts into the profane world in which man lives during the six days of the week."[63] Maimonides' conception of the Sabbath was a vigorous (and, as it turns out, unsuccessful) battle to suppress it from becoming hierophanic time, as it indeed became for many mystics—a time experienced "as a moment of the transfiguration of the entire reality, which is then permeated by the divine presence."[64] Whereas for the kabbalist the equation set up by Lev 19:30 between Sabbath observance and fear of the Temple concretizes each as in some way containing a divine presence *(shekhinah),*[65] for Maimonides the equation serves to vacate both of that presence.

The rabbinic Sabbath that foreshadows the world to come *(olam ha-ba)* by being definitive of it[66] is not rejected by Maimonides but is reconfigured in light of a thoroughly intellectualized conception of that anxiously expected world. If what survives man's physical tenure on earth is the intellect he has nurtured during that period,[67] the proper cultivation of that intellect is conditional on liberating itself of myth, of a world populated by divine beings in favor of one that operates in tandem with natural causation—the world most prominently represented by the Sabbath. For present purposes, it is of note that for Maimonides angels are the most appropriate analogy for the intellectual immortality to which human beings can aspire. Their joy of pure contemplation is the measure of the postmortem existence awaiting man, "where our souls will attain to the knowledge of the Creator as do the higher bodies [that is, angels or the separated intellects], or more."⁶⁸ One cannot attain that ultimate state of intellectual bliss where one becomes, in a sense, an angel, without fully appreciating what angels are while laboring toward that state—a labor driven by a Sabbath-oriented weltanschauung.

It would be no exaggeration to offer, as a prescription for celebrating a Maimonidean Sabbath, the polar inversion of what Elliot Wolfson has described as the Sabbath of theosophic Kabbalah: "The six days of the week represent the exile in which male and female are separated and the demonic has dominion over the world, whereas the Sabbath is the moment of redemption in which the sacred coupling of male and female is realized and the letters of the Tetragrammaton are reunited such that *the providential care over existence is entrusted solely to God*" (emphasis mine).⁶⁹ For Maimonides, that last state of affairs is in fact characteristic of the six days that are terminated by the Sabbath and not of the Sabbath itself.

A critical chapter devoted to the rationale for the Sabbath's holiness and halakhic impositions (II:31) is unexpectedly found in the second part of the *Guide* sandwiched between a philosophical exegesis of the Account of the Creation (II:30) and the beginning of the treatment of prophecy (II:32). The Sabbath gains its uniqueness because divine history and human history correspond to the theoretical and practical rationales for its observance. The reason assigned to the laws of Sabbath observance varies between the two versions of the Decalogue in Exodus and Deuteronomy, the former linking it to divine creation (Exod 20:11) and the latter to the memory of the period of enslavement and liberation from Egypt (Deut 5:15). There was divine disengagement from the world, since all nature had been permanently fixed, no longer in need of "miraculous" intervention. Almost as a reflex of that divine movement, human engagement took over, for temporality and fluctuation can only be encountered by a being that is of a kind with them—that is, itself temporal and ever in flux.⁷⁰

There are two facets to the Sabbath, the first of which is the holiness and blessedness conferred on it as a consequence of the transition from divine activity to its cessation: "For the Lord made the heaven and earth in six days . . . and He rested on the seventh, therefore God blessed the Sabbath day and sanctified it" (Exod 20:11). The second is its normative demand of human abstention from labor because of a transition in the human condition from slavery to freedom: "And you shall remember that you were slaves in Egypt . . . therefore God commanded that you perform the

Sabbath" (Deut 5:15). The first of these two facets reflects a vertical orientation of the divine vis-à-vis His creation, while the latter suggests a horizontal framework within which humanity is expected to engage it: "Accordingly the Sabbath is, as it were, of universal benefit,[71] both with reference to a true speculative opinion and to the well-being of the state of the body." What follows is an attempt to recover in part what must have been Maimonides' programmatic outline for the *Guide* at this particular juncture so that chapter II:31, rather than digressing, can be seen to fall neatly into place. In addition, I show that the practical rationale of the Sabbath based on the preservation of a historically particular national memory (Egyptian slavery) complements, rather than is at odds with, the universal dimension of the Sabbath's speculative rationale (creation).

The unexpected appearance of a discussion on the Sabbath's rationale seems esoteric to the reader. Its presence in chapter II:31 is intrusive, especially in light of the Sabbath's reappearance at a far more appropriate juncture of the *Guide*—III:43—where it is logically situated within the larger context of commandments in general.[72] The reader's puzzlement is compounded by the attribution of an entirely different rationale in that third section not afforded in the second section. Though its "speculative" dimension, "the assertion that the world has been produced in time," is reiterated, its practical dimension substantially deviates from its original formulation. A simple juxtaposition of the two sections illustrates the divergence:

II:31	III:43
"However, the order given us by the law with regard to it and the commandment ordaining us in particular to keep it are an effect consequent upon the cause that we had been slaves in Egypt where we did not work according to our free choice and when we wished and where we had not the power to refrain from working."	"for it is known how great a rest it procures. Because of it the seventh part of the life of every individual consists in pleasure and repose from the fatigue and weariness from which there is no escape either for the young or for the old."

The essential constituents of II:31—a particular historical memory, slavery, Egypt, and unfettered control over one's life—play no role whatsoever in the rationale provided by III:43. Alternatively, the physical benefits of a weekly respite, the utilitarian rationale of the Sabbath offered by III:43, is absent from its textual precursor in II:31. Their respective objectives can account for their differences. Chapter II:31 concludes Maimonides' running philosophical exegesis of the first chapter in Genesis offered in the previous chapter (II:30). If the Sabbath is the demarcating line between divine activity and nature, as we have claimed, then rest, in the sense of inactivity, is only a salient metaphor for God's posture in respect to the world. If, however, as a corollary of the previous assertion, human activity picks up where divine activity left off, then rest as "repose from fatigue and weariness," or inactivity—its assigned utility in III:43— is the very converse of that mode of being Sabbath signifies for humanity vis-à-vis the world. The third section of the *Guide* is concerned with law, therefore "repose from fatigue and weariness" must be introduced as the Sabbath's definitive worth if it is not to undermine its entire halakhic construction. The primary subject of the second section of the *Guide* into which the Sabbath is seemingly interpolated is God as creator and the precise manner in which to understand how the world came about. The Sabbath is of course the dénouement of that process and is therefore the concluding chapter of this section, after which the *Guide* moves on to the subject of prophecy. Any focus on man in this lengthy excursus, which really stretches all the way back to the very beginning of the second section, is solely for the sake of perfecting our understanding of the creation and God's continuing relationship with it.

In II:31, rest is the external halakhic means of preserving the Sabbath's core *practical* teaching—human freedom. The historical model of exodus is a mirror image of the Sabbath's theoretical teaching—the creation. If the Sabbath represents the termination of a period when the world had no independent existence outside of God's incessant molding of it, then it also marks the commencement of man's creative role within it, which can only be a function of his freedom to act, choose, and control his destiny. Without entering into the thorny debate over whether Maimonides endorsed a libertarian or determinist view of man,[73] every instance of reasoned human choice manifestly reflects a space from which God has receded. Ironically, the Sabbath in its truest sense, as reminiscent of the exodus, actually represents man's worldly engagement that succeeds God's disengagement. The Israelites as puppets of the Egyptians parallels the creation at the hands of God in the first six days; while liberation from Egypt and freedom to exercise control over one's life, an offshoot of which is the choice of when to work and when to rest, parallels the world "going its customary way" on the Sabbath. The Sabbath's commemoration of the exodus itself reflects its speculative dimension of creation. The world gained its independence from God and the Israelites gained theirs from the Egyptians.

Once chapter II:31 is understood in this way, the overview of the first six days in II:30 becomes far more of a substantive logical point of departure for it, rather than merely forming a chronological continuum with it—first, six days, and then capping it off with an unrelated discussion about Sabbath merely because the Sabbath follows the order of creation. First, Maimonides reiterated the point that no fixed natural order prevailed during the first six days, going as far as to cite the *midrash* that has the entire Garden of Eden episode transpiring on Friday in support of that assertion (*b. Sanhedrin* 32b). The lack of any established order accounts for such fantastic phenomena as talking serpents that defy current zoological data; "for this reason, none of these things should be judged incongruous; for as we have said, up till then no permanently established order had come about" (GP II:30, 355). Second, Maimonides read the "placement" of Adam *(va-yannihehu)* in the garden (Gen 2:15) in the same sense that he read the *va-yanah* of the world on the Sabbath as discussed previously in the exposition of Exod 20:11. He cited *Gen Rabbah* 16:5 on Gen 2:15, "And the Lord God took the man—[that is] raised him—and put him in the garden—[that is] He gave him rest," as conveying, not a change in spatial coordinates, but rather an ontological status: "He raised the rank of his existence among the existents that come into being and pass away and established him in a certain state" (GP II:30, 357).[74]

The ontological transition of the world on Sabbath from a fluid state to a fixed one, signified by the *va-yanah* of Exod 20:11, is precisely mirrored by the same transition of man captured by the *va-yannihehu* of Gen 2:15. Both were *established* in their natural states of being—both were accorded their independence. Third, chapter II:30 ends off with an etymological analysis of the various biblical terms connoting divine creativity, of which *qanoh* (possessing), one of four such terms, is its final focus. This term alone captures a kind of master–slave relationship between God and the world, "because He, may He be exalted, has dominion over them just as a master has over his slaves." This is the term that preserves the relation between God and the world extant for those first six days, when the world, like the slave, was at the beck and call of God and had not yet emerged as a self-subsisting entity governed by its own laws. This appropriately leads into the discussion of the significance of the Sabbath, which also signals the emergence of the Jew from a state of total subjugation to one of independence and self-regulation.

That *qoneh* signifies this primordial relationship of divine intervention is further substantiated by its specific distinction from another of the four terms singled out—*El*. The verse emblematic of the latter's usage, to which Maimonides was almost obsessively partial,[75] is "God of the World" (*El olam* or God of eternity) (Gen 21:33), the very verse cited as a preamble to each of the three sections of the *Guide*. The connotation of this term is pointedly distinguished from that of *qoneh*, differentiating between a relationship of dependence as maintained by *qoneh* and that of supreme ontological uniqueness. "God of the World" is "used with respect to His perfection, may He be exalted, and theirs [heaven and earth]. He is *Elohim*—that is, He who governs—and they are those governed by Him, not in the sense of domination—for that is the meaning of *qoneh*—but with respect to His rank, may He be exalted, in being and in relation to them. For He is the deity and not they—I mean heaven" (GP II:30, 359).[76] I believe Maimonides here contrasted, on the one hand, the God of the primordial six days in His capacity as *qoneh*, when the world was His "slave," and on the other hand, the God demarcated by the Sabbath, when the world is governed by its own inherent mechanisms and its relationship to God is characterized simply by radical otherness and inferiority. Abraham's philosophical quest toward a firm grasp of divine nature reflects both these facets of God's relationship with the world, which are expressions of his public teachings about God as creator.

Maimonides, in an earlier chapter, identified the Mosaic opinion on creation with Abraham's public declarations "in the name of the Lord God of the World" (Gen 21:33) and "Possessor of heaven and earth" (Gen 14:22) as follows: "It was Abraham our father, peace be on him, who began to proclaim in public this opinion [bringing into existence out of nonexistence] to which speculation had led him. For this reason he made his proclamation *in the Name of the Lord, God of the World;* he had also explicitly stated this opinion in saying *Possessor [qoneh] of heaven* and earth" (GP II:13, 282).

These passages in the *Guide* warrant the application of the critical reading strategy prescribed by the author himself in order to "grasp the totality of what this Treatise contains." Each chapter forms part of an integrative whole that defies a purely linear, sequentially progressive reading and demands that "you must connect its chapters one with another." A slavish allegiance to chapter division and resistance to liberating words from their particular contexts fragments the totality of meaning constructed by Maimonides; for "when reading a given chapter, your intention must be not only to understand the totality of the subject of that chapter, but also to grasp each word that occurs in it in the course of the speech, even if that word does not belong to the intention of the chapter" (GP Intro., 15).[77] Abraham's innovative dissemination of his autodidactically acquired truths as articulated in the two divine epithets of *El olam* and *qoneh shamayim va-aretz* can only be appreciated in light of the *Guide*'s later distinction between *qoneh* and *El*. What, on an earlier tentative reading, as every reading of every chapter must remain, seemed synonymous expressions of *creatio ex nihilo* ("he had also explicitly stated this opinion in saying") now reflect the two phases of creation that are of course vital to Maimonides' theory of creation as a whole. Abraham has set the precedent for all future teachers of esoteric truth. Their public pronouncements must be couched in a language that can accommodate a wide disparity of audiences. For the general public both *qoneh* and *El olam* indicate existence out of nonexistence. For the intellectual elite *qoneh* expresses the interventionist God operative during an unfolding and provisional process, while *El olam* is the God of Sabbath, who is relieved of His duties by the course of nature.

The very historical narrative in which Abraham's entreaty to God designated as *qoneh* is embedded reflects its metaphysical connotation. Abraham had just battled to liberate relatives, including his nephew Lot, from forced captivity. The king of Sodom offers him property in exchange for their remaining his slaves. Abraham rejects that offer in the name of God the *qoneh* so that no mistake can be made crediting Abraham's fortunes to any other's doing. *Qoneh,* we have seen, analogizes the master–slave relationship to that between God and the world. In this passage, Abraham's mission is to free slaves as well as to maintain his own absolute independence from others. His destiny will not be said to be shaped or controlled by anyone else, "Lest you say, 'It is I who made Abraham rich'" (Gen 14:23). The appeal to *qoneh,* in this context, constitutes the ethical mirror of its metaphysical dimension. God, as supreme master at the world's formative stage, vitiates domination over any aspect of that world by any other aspiring "masters." The metaphysics of creation doubles as a model for *imitatio dei*. Just as the world endured a six-day period of serfdom at the hands of its divine taskmaster and was then released to its own natural devices on the Sabbath, so must all human servitude end with autonomy. In a sense the Sabbath encodes the first Kantian categorical imperative that enslavement is a violation of the order of creation and that its imposition on others plunges them into an unnatural state of being.

Maimonides' halakhic construct of the Sabbath cannot escape the implications of his philosophical one. The locus classicus for the overarching halakhic rubric that human life takes precedence over religious observance is the Sabbath. The verse "You shall keep my norms and laws which man shall perform and live by them" (Lev 18:5) is understood by the Rabbis as a teleological statement about the law—it serves man, not vice versa; man "*shall live by them* and not die by them."[78] This general sacrosanct rule is postulated by the Rabbis within the context of normative discussions regarding the Sabbath, and is formulated by Maimonides in his *Mishneh Torah* thus: "It is forbidden to delay such violation of the Sabbath for the sake of a person who is dangerously ill, for Scripture says, *which if a man do, he shall live by them,* that is to say, he shall not die by them. Hence you learn that the ordinances of the law were meant to bring upon the world not vengeance, but mercy, loving-kindness, and peace" (MT *Laws of the Sabbath* 2:3).[79] If the telos of divine law is to promote a moral weltanschauung that is essential to the perpetuation of human life and not simply to express abject fealty to God, then what better framework in which to anchor that telos than the Sabbath, which itself represents the independent sovereignty of life and creation. Every breach of law for the preservation of life is itself a normative expression of the notional Sabbath, which conjures a realm of creation apart from God.

One of the rabbinic rationales underlying the mandate of violating the Sabbath for the sake of preserving life is also offered as a rationale for the emergency powers granted the courts to temporarily suspend divine law when the long-term viability of the law as a whole is at stake: "This is in keeping with what the early Sages have said: *Desecrate on his account one Sabbath, in order that he be able to observe many Sabbaths*" (MT *Laws of Rebels* 2:4).[80] Here Maimonides' unique appeal to a Sabbath norm as an endorsement of extraordinary judicial discretion carries more weight once supplied with what we have determined to be the Sabbath's philosophical significance. If the Sabbath represents independence of both nature and man from the divine vise of the first six days, then what greater expression of human autonomy exists than the authority to override God's very legislation should the court deem it necessary to do so.

Maimonides' closing remarks to his *Laws of the Sabbath* in the *Mishneh Torah* must now be read against the backdrop of the thesis developed in this chapter. After placing the gravity of the Sabbath on par with the strictures against idolatry and going so far as to consider the public violator of the Sabbath an idolater, he ended on a positive note regarding the virtue of Sabbath observance. As an incentive to encourage scrupulous Sabbath observance, Maimonides stipulated the reward in store, but remarkably accentuates its this-worldly component over that of the world to come: "With regard to him who observes the Sabbath in full accordance with the rules thereof, and honors it and delights in it to the utmost of his ability, the Prophet describes explicitly his reward in this world, over and above the reward laid up for him in the world to come in the following verse, *Then shalt thou delight thyself in the Lord, and I will make thee to ride upon the high places of the earth and I will feed thee with the heritage of Jacob thy father; for the mouth of the Lord hath spoken it* [Isa 58:14, emphasis mine]" (MT *Laws of the Sabbath* 30:15).

Although this peroration is based on rabbinic sources, none specifically highlights the attraction of a future reward compounded by one that is here and now.[81] In fact some of those sources cite the very same verse to prove the converse of Maimonides' emphasis, that the present benefits pale in comparison with those to come: "Moreover, whatever benefit you derive in this world, is but the fruit thereof, but the stock will remain for you in the World to Come as it says *and I will feed thee with the heritage of Jacob etc.*" (*Exod Rabbah* 25:12).[82] However, Maimonides' accent on this-worldly recompense is perfectly apparent. If the Sabbath represents nature, causality, and the exercise of human autonomy within those parameters, then the promise of natural recompense for its celebration serves to reinforce its vital naturalist symbolism.

Notes

Introduction

1. On esoteric writing and how "secrets" are communicated, I have been strongly influenced by the numerous studies of Elliot Wolfson who, while focusing on the Jewish mystical tradition, has found that the figure of Maimonides, notwithstanding his "rationalism," looms large in Jewish mystics' formulations of their own esoteric enterprise. For but one recent example, see his "Beneath the Wings of the Great Eagle," where he demonstrates the strong influence of Maimonides' hermeneutical rhetoric regarding secrets and parables on kabbalistic esotericism.

2. Fackenheim, *Metaphysics,* 4–5, nicely captures the predicament of Maimonides' "perplexed" audience who may cling to traditional beliefs, despite their rational untenability, as a life of "pragmatic make-believe." Though addressing what Fackenheim sees as a modern phenomenon, it is just as applicable to the medieval bad faith choice envisioned by Maimonides. Fackenheim's diagnosis of the current faith malaise is that "man, caught in skepticism, seeks escape from its paralyzing consequences. Unable to believe and yet seeking a purpose, he falls to pretending to believe, hoping that a pretended might do the work of an actual faith." He then continues with a dismal prognosis of failure: "For a pretended faith is no faith at all. Pragmatic make-believe collapses in self-contradiction."

3. Maimonides relied on the opinion in the Talmud (*b. Hagigah* 13a) that the teaching of the Account of the Chariot is to be restricted to the communication of only chapter headings and is to be revealed only to a chief justice *(av bet din)* who is troubled *(libo do'eg be-qirbo)*. In GP I:34, 77–78, this expression is also synonymous with a contrite spirit, signifying "obedience, submission and great piety joined to knowledge." There is no magic to the position of a head of court; rather, it indicates a high level of scholarly proficiency that must be accompanied by a humbling distress and perplexity. For the expression *libo do'eg* (his heart is troubled) in a halakhic context, see MT *Laws of Holiday Repose* 6:24, where it is identified as a state of mind that is an impediment to joy *(simhah)*.

4. Knowledge, for Maimonides, is determinative for ritual honors and privileges, and he considered the widespread perception that priests *(kohanim)* enjoy privileges because of their intrinsically superior status to be a pervasive "malaise" that has "absolutely no basis whatsoever in the Torah, and is not mentioned at all in the Talmud . . . and I have no idea where this defective custom originated." See PM *Gittin* 5:8 and also MT *Laws of Prayer* 12:18.

5. See Kugel, *The God of Old,* 16, who argues that Old Testament theology does not perceive a clear distinction between two domains, one of heavenly, spiritual beings and the other earthly and human, but rather that the former "is perfectly capable of intruding into everyday reality." Much of Maimonides' efforts can be said to have combated this "primitive" theology and constructed an impenetrable barrier between the two domains. My only disagreement with Kugel is his description of our modern age as "one in which God is axiomatically remote" (45). It seems to me that Maimonides' project to accomplish just this state of affairs largely failed to withstand the onslaught of mysticism, fundamentalism, and new age movements that have restored precisely this biblical view of the permeable division between the two domains.

6. See Goitein, "Moses Maimonides, Man of Action," and the bibliography listed in S. Harvey, Maimonides in the Sultan's Palace," 47 n. 3.

7. This is referring to the incident related in *b. Hagigah* 14b of the "four who entered the garden *(pardes)*": Ben Azzai, Ben Zoma, Elisha ben Abuyah, and R. Akivah. Only the last returned successfully.

8. This is the obscure term in the Massoretic text, but the Septuagint, Vulgate, Peshitta, and numerous Hebrew manuscripts all have "garden" here. The only other biblical appearances of *pardes* are Eccl 2:5 and Neh 2:8. The latter also presents *pardes* as a private reserve of the king, access to which would be severely restricted.

9. See Harris, *How Do We Know This,* 33–43, for a discussion of the axiom's phrase "language of the sons of man." Maimonides transformed this phrase, originally a rabbinic rule governing exegetical expansiveness, into an Aristotelian formulation that views biblical language as mythological. See Aristotle, *Metaphysics* XII (Barnes, 1698), where Aristotle makes the following observation regarding the anthropomorphist views of the ancients: "Our forefathers, in the most remote

ages have handed down to us their posterity a tradition, in the form of a myth, that these substances are gods and that the divine encloses the whole of nature. The rest of the tradition has been added later in mythical form with a view to the persuasion of the multitude and to its legal and utilitarian expediency; they say these gods are in the form of men or like some of the other animals . . . these opinions have been preserved like relics until the present." For a good discussion of the Platonic attitude toward myth, see Tate, "Plato and Allegorical Interpretation." Even though myth may contain truth, there is no way of determining the correct method to derive those truths; therefore, "to waste time in ingenious guesses at the meaning of myths or other passages where the poets do not speak plainly, is unworthy of the serious philosopher" (154).

10. *b. Avodah Zarah* 54b, adopted in GP II:29, 345.

11. *Gen Rabbah* 5:5. See also PM *Avot* 5:5.

12. This central characterization of the natural historicity of the messianic period is reiterated with the same maxim *The world goes its customary way* in MT *Laws of Repentance* 9:2.

13. As Ravitzky puts it, "the hope of redemption points toward the universal actualization of man as he was meant and ought to be, according to the original archetype" ("'To the Utmost Human Capacity,'" 233).

14. Much is made of the singular addressee in the Ten Commandments. See M. Kasher, *Torah Shelemah,* vol. 16, 13, and Nahmanides on this verse, who takes it as impressing on each individual their personal responsibility, which cannot be left to others.

15. See GP II:29, 341–42 for Maimonides' interpretation of this new "creation." A corollary of this hermeneutical clarity is the ethical balance and harmony contemplated by the Isaianic metaphor "the wolf shall dwell with the lamb," for through cognition of the truth, enmity and hatred are removed and the inflicting of harm by people on one another is abolished." (GP III:11, 441).

16. For the legal disabilities that attach to the convert in Judaism, see chapter 10 of S. Cohen, *Beginnings of Jewishness.*

17. For a good description of the normal insider/outsider relationship between a convert and his new Jewish home, see ibid., 325: "The gentiles can change their religion, convert to Judaism, and join the community of Israel, but within that community they remain legally and socially distinct, because they are not absolutely equal with natives under the law and because their foreign extraction prevents them from becoming true 'insiders.' They become 'insiders' only when they have Israelite (Jewish) blood—either an Israelite mother, an Israelite father, or 'our fathers.'"

18. See Porton, *Stranger,* 215.

19. See MT *Laws of Ethical Traits* 6:4, and R. Shimon b. Yohai's position in *Mekhilta de-Rabbi Ishmael, Mishpatim* 18.

20. See, e.g., Laqueur's description of Mussolini's popular image as "the greatest man who ever lived, the highest incarnation of the Italian race. He was

alone and sad, a colossus, a titan, a cyclope, a giant—he could and should not be measured by ordinary standards" (*Fascism,* 32).

21. MT *Laws of Ethical Traits* 2:3.
22. See McGovern, *From Luther to Hitler,* 53–54.
23. *Num Rabbah* 4:20 (Slotki, 137).
24. See Frankfort, *Kingship,* esp. 11, for the ancient Near Eastern theology of kingship.

Chapter 1   The Convert (*Ger*)

1. Ovadyah may have been a name of choice for converts to assume, as there was a talmudic tradition that the biblical prophet Ovadyah was an Edomite proselyte (*b. Sanhedrin* 39b). I thank Tibi Judah for this reference.
2. The letter is one of a series of three responses on different issues to Ovadyah and was most probably written in Hebrew. They appear in both Teshuvot, nos. 293, 436, and 448, and vol. 1 of Iggerot. Shailat believes they all form parts of the same correspondence. The English translation reproduced here is available in Twersky, *A Maimonides Reader,* 475–76. Kellner's well-developed thesis regarding Maimonides' nonessentialist view of the Jewish people (as opposed, for example, to Judah Halevi and the *Zohar*) forms the basis out of which my study has grown. See Kellner, *Maimonides on Judaism,* esp. chap. 6.
3. Under Islamic law conversion from Islam to another faith was considered to be an act of apostasy, punishable by death. Though there could be many motivations of a utilitarian nature to convert to dominant ruling religions such as Islam or Christianity, there was usually only one motivation to go the other way—sincere belief. As Wasserstein points out ("A Fatwa," 179–80), the draconian penalties for apostasy in countries under Islamic rule "made all reasons except one for conversion to a different faith totally irrelevant. That one exception was, of course, sincere belief." For documented instances of the hardships and persecution endured by converts to Judaism in the Middle Ages, see those culled from the Genizah by Goitein, *Mediterranean Society,* vol. 2, 299–311, and especially his observation on 304 that "Maimonides' favorable attitude toward proselytizing is echoed in the Geniza documents, in which converts to Judaism are mentioned far more frequently than Jews adopting Islam."
4. For a Hasidic formulation of prayer as an expression of Being, see Pinhas of Koretz, *Midrash Pinhas,* no. 52: "Prayer itself is God, for it is written 'Your prayer is your God' (Deut 10:21)." For two modern perspectives by thinkers who occupy polar extremes on the plane of Jewish observance, see the excerpt from Abraham Isaac Kook's commentary on the Siddur, *Olat Re'iyah* (Agus, 217–20): "Man uplifts all creation with himself in prayer . . . uplifts and exalts the All to the source of blessing and the source of life"; and Martin Buber, *Meetings,* 44: "If to believe in God means to talk about Him in the third person, then I do not

believe in God. If to believe in God means to be able to talk to God, then I do believe in God."

5. This is Fox's position ("Prayer," 135–36): "Ordinary prayers and fulfillment of mitzvoth serve as a propadeutic, a discipline which guides and prepares us for the life of true worship."

6. Community as a vital feature of prayer is captured in his customarily elegant fashion by Heschel, "Prayer," 45–46: "What we do as individuals is a trivial episode; what we attain as Israel causes us to become a part of eternity. . . . We never pray as individuals, set apart from the rest of the world. The liturgy is an order which we can enter only as a part of the Community of Israel."

7. For a parallel passage in the *Guide,* see GP II:39, 379, where Abraham is described as having "assembled the people and called them by way of teaching and instruction to adhere to the truth that he had grasped . . . attracting them by means of eloquent speeches and by means of the benefits he conferred upon them."

8. This parallels another analogy drawn between Abraham and his followers, that of a rock hewn from a quarry, in GP I:16, 42. See also MT *Laws of Studying Torah* 1:2 for the same model of teacher as parent and the same prooftext as the *Guide.* The rabbinic source for the halakhic identity of students and children is *Sifre Deut Va-Et'hanan* 33.

9. This notion actually manifested itself on a personal level when Maimonides addressed his students as his sons. See, e.g., his letter to his student Joseph ben Judah in Kafih, *Iggerot,* 125.

10. These are precisely what Maimonides mandates all prospective converts to be informed of in MT *Laws of Forbidden Intercourse* 14:2.

11. See *b. Yevamot* 47b. Maimonides adopts the phrase *kanfe shekhinha* as the destination of all authentic converts in MT *Laws of Forbidden Intercourse* 13:4, as well as that of the captive woman who is sincere about switching faiths, in MT *Laws of Kings* 8:5. See also GP I:43, 94 for the citation of Ruth 2:12 as an illustration of a figurative sense of "wing" *(kanaf).* The case of the biblical Ruth is paradigmatic of the diametric opposition between the rationalist camp typified by Maimonides and that of the kabbalistic school on the status of the proselyte. A recurrent theme in the latter is its ontological inferiorization of the proselyte, often ascribed to a different origin of his soul on the sefirotic hierarchy from that of the naturally born Jew. Ruth is but one example of this view, which has her introduce her ontological Moabiteness into the metaphysical genetics of Israel upon conversion. See the general discussion by Wijnhoven, "The Zohar," and on Ruth in particular at 60–62. Another popular conception of the proselyte among kabbalists maintained that they were in fact "Jews" all along. At some point in the past their souls were exiled due to some ancestral apostasy or foreign captivity. Conversion was therefore perceived as a repatriation of a Jewish soul to its proper place. See Halamish, "Some Aspects," 56–57.

12. The essential thesis of this chapter also accounts for Maimonides' nonessentialist view of circumcision. For him, as opposed to others, circumcision,

unlike baptism, is merely another commandment without which the Jew remains a Jew albeit a transgressor. See Shaye Cohen's recent discussion of Maimonides' position in chapters 6–7 of his *Why Aren't Jewish Women Circumcised?*

13. See the discussion of divine attributes in GP I:51–52.

14. Davidson, "The Middle Way," 67.

15. On this excerpt, some of the standard English translations, such as appears in Twersky's in *A Maimonides Reader,* collapse what I take to be two classes of people—namely, converts *and* gentiles who profess the unity of God, into one class of converts who profess the unity of God, by omitting the second "all" *(kol)* in the clause. For a cogent argument in support of my reading, see Kaplan, "Maimonides on the Singularity," xix–xx nn. 26–28. I am also in total agreement with his interpretation of the phrase "as it is written in the Torah" as descriptive and not prescriptive.

16. Such a stance would make them more amenable to readings of the story concentrating on its ethical dimension, such as Kierkegaard's and his "teleological suspension of the ethical"; these, I believe, would be anathema to Maimonides' view. See GP I:54, 125 for the essential bond between a father and son, "that is attached to compassion, pity and an absolute passion." When God is described in terms of father–son relationships, though, one must view the manifestation of these emotions as arising dispassionately.

17. This phrase appears in the postmeal blessing, the *birkat ha-mazon.* See also MT *Laws of First Fruits* 4:3. For a halakhic opinion disagreeing with this position, since the convert has no share in the land, see Tosafot's cite of Rabbenu Tam's ruling in *b. Bava Batra* 81a (s.v. *le-maāote*).

18. Nehorai, in his "Review" of Kellner, *Maimonides on Judaism,* 129, points this out in criticism of Kellner's general thesis. He claims that this part of the ruling can be interpreted either way; "however, it is impossible to refute one who claims that the Rambam, despite all the love he manifested for Ovadyah the convert, still did not entirely erase any distinction between him and the naturally born Jew." To my mind this part of the ruling in no way weakens Kellner's thesis. First of all, Maimonides immediately went on to assert that "there is absolutely no difference between us and you for any matter." Second, Kellner's thesis can admit of some halakhic differences, even according to Maimonides; however, they are not grounded in ontological difference. This particular dispensation for a discretionary altering of prayer merely caters to the particular comfort level of the convert. I do not believe there is any way in which this can be read to endorse an essentialist view of the convert.

19. Faur, interestingly, traces the scriptural roots of this concept to the obligation of a proselyte to offer a Paschal sacrifice just like the native Jew in Exod 12:48–49 (*Homo Mysticus,* 232 n. 21).

20. See GP III:45, which discusses where the original location of the Temple was concealed to prevent divisiveness on a global and tribal scale. III:46 also

suggests that one of the reasons for the annual Temple pilgrimages was to promote "fraternity."

21. For a contrasting expression capturing the nationalist element of the conversion, see the end of the third response to Ovadyah regarding Islam at 240, line 13: "and has attached *(nidbaq)* himself to this nation."

22. See also *Laws of the Sabbatical Year and Jubilee* 13:13, which renders God and ultimate reward, both in this world and that to come, universally accessible "to each and every individual who has entered the world." The only prerequisites are an all-consuming dedication to God and detachment from material concerns. For the most recent comprehensive treatment of kabbalistic attitudes toward alterity and otherness, see Wolfson, *Venturing Beyond,* 165–85. Wolfson cites several zoharic sources that are so negative with respect to the convert that one of the hallmarks of the messianic era is the cleansing of the Jewish people from the pollution of converts, indicating that the "purity of the Jews depends on sealing the borders so that no foreigners enter the covenant" (173–74). See also 56 n. 70, where Wolfson points out that the critical difference between Maimonides and "all streams of medieval kabbalah" is that the latter maintain an ontological distinction between Jews and non-Jews. This "anti-kabbalistic" distinction is precisely what is vigorously advanced by Maimonides in his letter to Ovadyah.

23. "Every man is obligated to rejoice in them, including him, his children, his spouse, his family members, and all those who have joined themselves *[nilvim]* to him."

24. Those qualified to pray during public fasts are those whose "children, family members, and all close to him who have *joined* themselves to him" are ethically pure.

25. "All of Israel and those who have *joined* themselves to them are like brothers." Clearly, his inclusion of outsiders on this score negates an essentialist view of moral traits. To be charitable is to act charitably. There is no inborn Jewish trait of charitability. See Kellner, "Maimonides on the Normality of Hebrew," 9–10.

26. See, e.g., two opposing positions represented by Fox, "Prayer in the Thought of Maimonides," and Benor, *Worship of the Heart.* There are basically three approaches to the problem, typified by the following scholars: Fox—dialectical tension; Benor—unified coherence; and Reines—esotericist incompatibility (Reines, "Maimonides' True Belief").

27. See Blidstein's discussion, *Prayer in Maimonidean Halakhah,* 34–48.

28. Shailat's preferred reading (in Iggerot) over another version that changes one letter to render the phrase "as it were" to "in these."

29. See Maimonides' PM commentary to *Avot* 5:6 and chapter 8 of the "Eight Chapters" regarding ten miraculous events "created" during the twilight hours of the sixth day of creation. According to Maimonides, these are particularized by their specific time of input but are emblematic of all miracles, having

been pre-programmed at creation, only at different intervals of the Genesis account. However, in GP II:29, 345 he seems to accept the occurrence of miracles but limit their duration: "For although the rod was turned into a serpent, the water into blood and the pure and noble hand became white without a natural cause that necessitated this, these and similar things were not permanent and did not become another nature." Some scholars have argued that Maimonides shifted his position on miracles from the maximalist one taken in the PM to a more moderate view in the GP. See H. Kasher, "Biblical Miracles"; Langermann, "Maimonides and Miracles"; and Seeskin's discussion of miracles in *Maimonides on the Origin of the World*, 160–65. Whatever his position is on miracles, though, it cannot entail some change in God. Even in the chapter quoted from the GP it is not *history* that accounts for temporary anomalies in nature but rather it is God's *wisdom* that accounts for them. As Seeskin so aptly frames it, it is the distinction between a "willing change and changing one's will" (163). The convert's perspective vis-à-vis the Jew's can be no different in this respect.

30. It is not clear to which blessing or prayer this particular phrase alludes. See Iggerot, 233 n. 6.

31. The polarization between the Maimonidean and Halevian positions can be no more conspicuous than on this point. The special *amr ilahi* (the ontological sign of election) that attaches to the nation of Israel can only be transmitted hereditarily, as Halevi makes quite clear in his *Kuzari* I:27: "Anyone from the nations of the world who accompanies us and converts, may the Lord be gracious to him as He is to us, is not brought to our level." It is on this basis that Halevi disqualifies the convert from ever achieving prophecy, since "he is not comparable to an Israelite from birth. For only an Israelite by birth is eligible to become a prophet" (I:115). For a discussion of the opposing schools, see Frydman-Kohl, "Covenant." For Halevi's position in particular, see Lasker, "Proselyte Judaism," 90, who conjectures that the rabbinic statement in *b. Qiddushin* 70b confining the *shekhinah*'s domain to the native-born Jew influenced his position.

32. Haim Hillel Ben-Sasson has characterized this segment of Maimonides' historical survey as a transformation of Israel into "a nation of converts, as it were," for the second time in their historical development ("The Uniqueness of Israel," 186).

33. The historical breach with Abraham is captured by MT *Laws of Idolatry* 1:3, where the result of Israelite apostasy was that "the principle which Abraham planted was uprooted and the children of Jacob reverted to the error of the nations and their waywardness." Moses then arrives on the scene to "crown them with *mitzvot*"—that is, to impose the law and its sanctions. See also GP II:39 for the distinction between Abraham the instructor and Moses the lawgiver. See also the last chapter of my *Maimonides and the Hermeneutics of Concealment*, 159–62.

34. For the argument that Moses is quite literally the author of the Law (including its particulars and conventions), whereas its divine origin is informed by its purpose and aims, see Bland, "Moses and the Law."

35. As an example of Maimonides' theology of conversion being perpetuated by future generations of his disciples, see Ben-Sasson, "The Uniqueness of Israel," who cites the thirteenth-century exegete David Kimhi's comment to Gen 17:1 that "those foreigners who enter into the covenant of Abraham and the teaching of God are considered Abraham's progeny and are included in *hamon goyim*, that is Abraham is father to them." I would still note, however, that even such a staunch adherent of Maimonidean teachings expressed some ambivalence on this point, for in the beginning of his comments to this very same verse he offers the following rationale for the timing of Abraham's circumcision: "and he was commanded to undergo circumcision prior to conceiving Isaac in order that Isaac should originate from a seed that is more *kasher*."

36. Here *mishpatim* should be read as "utility is clear to multitude"; *huqqim* as "utility not clear to multitude."

37. See MT *Laws of Forbidden Intercourse* 14:2, where Maimonides directs that the prospective convert be introduced to Judaism first and foremost with the principles of divine unity and prohibition against idolatry. Only these philosophical teachings are conveyed to him "at length." Once the philosophical groundwork is laid, he is advised in stages as to the particular *mitzvot* and the consequences of their violation.

38. Kellner, "Chosenness," makes essentially the same point.

39. See also GP II:4, 259, for the notion that "all spheres are living bodies, endowed with a soul and intellect, having a mental representation and an apprehension of the deity," adopted by the MT.

40. See MT *Laws of Prayer* 1:2–4 where praise *(shevah)* is the core sentiment expressed in prayer.

41. Ibid. Praises through speech "are meant to instruct someone else or to make it clear concerning oneself that one has had the apprehension in question."

42. See GP III:32, 526, where prayer is the rabbinic analogy to the "divine ruse" of sacrifice.

43. As Kreisel has argued ("Love and Fear of God," 147), the reason the second book of the MT is titled the *Book of Love* is "in order to let it be known that these *mitzvoth* are merely the *Jewish* framework in which the Jew aspires to *human* perfection." The latter is a universal goal of all mankind—namely, knowledge of what can be known. The ideal *love* of God, as defined in MT *Laws of the Foundations of the Torah* 2:1, is formulated as the goal of man qua man and not of the Jew in particular. The fact that a large portion of the MT *Book of Love* is taken up with laws relating to prayer and blessings is instructive for the Jew seeking to Jewishly cultivate his humanity. To distinguish the convert in these rites would be to promote an elitist view of them. This would ultimately be self-defeating.

44. See also SM, Positive Commandment 207. MT *Laws of Ethical Traits* 6:4 concludes with a biblical proof-text establishing God's personal love for the convert. The reciprocal relationship I have outlined here corresponds to the philosophical construct of reciprocity in the *Guide*, GP III:52, 629: "[T]he king who

cleaves to him and accompanies him is the intellect that overflows toward us and is the bond between us and Him, may He be exalted. Just as we apprehend Him by means of that light which He caused to overflow to us . . . so does He by means of that selfsame light examine us."

45. The expression also appears in the MT as the object of a blessing by Maimonides at the very end of the MT, for having been afforded the opportunity to see his great code *(ha-hibbur)* through to its intended completion. Other than that it is also part of the standardized daily liturgy, as recorded in the *Seder Ha-Tefillot Kol Ha-Shanah.*

46. Of relevance to our response is that Maimonides attributed particular divine receptivity to the orphan's prayers to this covenant.

47. He is considered to be *ke-qatan she-nolad dami* (like a newborn child). See *b. Yevamot* 91b.

48. See Joseph Karo's comments on this ruling in his "Kesef Mishneh" commentary to MT, regarding his difficulty in finding a source for it.

49. See Blidstein, "Parents and Children," who argues that this ruling demonstrates Maimonides' view of parental respect as a universal norm. However, his awareness of the paucity of halakhic sources manifests itself in his narrow construction of its scope for converts. He states that the standard for them is only partial respect *(miqtzat kavod).*

50. See note 47.

51. See also Moses ben Nahman's (Nahamanides') reasoning as to the severity of the consequences for maltreating proselytes and orphans, in his commentary to Exod 22:20. Their lack of natural protectors is compensated for by God's personal guardianship.

52. Maimonides was partial to citing the Palestinian Talmud in his code. His resourcefulness in its use is aptly described by Twersky, *Introduction to the Code,* 10: "Maimonides' reliance upon it in his *Mishneh Torah* is unusually bold and extensive."

53. Also in PM *Bikkurim* 1:4, where the formulation is that "Abraham is the father to all who enter the world since he has taught them the true belief and religion." See Kafih, 417 n. 13 of PM volume *Seder Zera'im,* which suggests that this may have been inserted consequent to the response to Ovadyah since the entire reference to the Palestinian Talmud is missing from the first edition of the PM.

54. See M. Lorberbaum, "Maimonides' Letter," 64.

55. This was a common criticism leveled against the MT. For but one early example, see Rabbi Abraham ben David of Posquieres in his *Hassagot* to the introduction of the MT: "He meant to improve but did not improve, for he abandoned the method of all authors who preceded him. They always cited proof for their statements and wrote the statements in the name of those who authored them."

56. See the comment of the "Kesef Mishneh" on MT *Laws of First Fruits* 4:3. For a list of various rabbinic scholars who either endorse or take issue with Maimonides' position in their respective novellae or responsa, see S. Cohen, *The*

Beginnings of Jewishness, 335–36 nn. 60–61. As expected, there was virtual unanimity of endorsement among subsequent Sephardi authorities, whereas the ruling was hotly debated in Ashkenazi circles. For an example of such debate regarding *bikkurim,* see that conducted between the twelfth-century tosafists Rabbenu Tam and R. Isaac of Dampierre in *b. Bava Batra* 81a, s.v. *le-ma'ote.*

57. Reference is made to *hibbur ha-gadol* in the second of his responses to Ovadyah. See *Iggerot* 236, lines 9–10.

58. The *bikkurim* must be transported on the shoulder of the donor (*m. Bikkurim* 3:4). The *Guide* singles out this requirement as a supreme symbol of humility.

59. In Deut 5:15, it is to allow them rest on the Sabbath and in Deut 16:12 it is to ensure their participation in the joy of holidays. Of course, the term *ger* here does not bear the formal characteristics of later rabbinic converts, but it does contain its seeds.

60. See Rashi's comment on the verse, where he adopts *Avot de-Rabbi Natan's* set of correspondences; tractate *Gerim* 4:3; *Mekhilta de-Rabbi Ishmael, Mishpatim* 18; and the relevant Targumim. A contemporary biblical scholar suggests that all four components of the verse allude to proselytes; see Blenkinsopp, *Isaiah 40–55,* 233.

61. See, e.g., MT *Laws of the Second Tithe* 11:17; *Laws of Forbidden Intercourse* 12:17; *Laws of Gifts to the Poor* 8:17–18; *Laws of Kings* 1:4. M. Lorberbaum, "Maimonides' Letter," deals with the inconsistency between these laws and the letter to Ovadyah by distinguishing between the different genres of responsa and codes. I find the most troubling of those laws to be that of *mattenot oniyim,* which sets up a hierarchy of descending priority with respect to the supreme social obligations of charity and ransoming from captivity. The scale of humanity peaks with the priestly class and bottoms out with the convert and manumitted slave. However, the opprobrium of this "caste" system is immediately neutralized by the addendum that what is determinative of priority is "wisdom"; it is only in the event of equivalence of wisdom that the hierarchy is operative. However, none of the laws that relegate the convert to a separate legal class are grounded in an essentialist view of the non-Jew as inferior to the biological one. For instance, the law in MT *Laws of Kings* barring the convert from holding any political office can be rationalized by very practical considerations. Its biblical source, Deut 17:15, is simply, according to Maimonides, a pragmatic directive aimed at staving off tyranny, since power in the hands of an outsider is more prone to abuse: "For no individual has ever been the chief of a religious community to whose race he did not belong, without doing it great or small injury" (GP III:50, 615). This is the moral of the biblical episode of the foreign kings who ruled over Edom (Gen 36:31), the result of which was tyranny and humiliation. See also H. Kasher, "Preferential Concern," 120.

62. Haym Soloveitchik's analysis ("Rupture and Reconstruction") of what he perceives as the recent shift in Judaism from a "mimetic" culture to a "text-based" one is instructive. In the latter, common practice "needs to be squared

with the written word." The *Letter to Ovadyah* was penned by the hand of a master of texts who was also a community activist closely attuned to the existential needs of his constituents. That sensitivity liberated him from the tyranny of the written word to whose theoretical demands he was not always obliged to surrender. In a similar vein and more pertinent to the discussion here, see Soloveitchik, "Maimonides' Iggeret Ha-Shemad," esp. 305–19, where he characterizes this letter more as a work of rhetoric addressing an urgent situation than a strict halakhic work.

Chapter 2 The Leper

1. As a result of a mistranslation of the Greek term *lepra*, these skin diseases have been mistakenly identified with Hansen's disease. The biblical term *tzara'at* covers a wide range of skin diseases as well as discolorations in inanimate objects such as buildings, clothing, and furniture. Milgrom, for instance, renders the term more appropriately as "scale disease" (*Leviticus 1-16*, 768–889).

2. See his comments on Lev 13:47 (Chavel, vol. 3). Nahmanides further corroborates this point textually, since its appearance in buildings is directly attributable to God in Lev 14:34: "and I inflict an eruptive plague in a house." Even Gersonides, who located these phenomena within the natural realm, was constrained to deal with the direct intervention of God indicated by this verse. See his prefatory comments to Lev 13:47 and his comments on 14:34 (Levi, vol. 3).

3. See his comments on Lev 13:2 (Lockshin, 72).

4. Danby, *Code*, vol. 10, 203–4.

5. Twersky, "Some Non-Halakhic Aspects," 95. For a more recent example of the interdependence between the *Guide* and the *Mishneh Torah*, see Stern's novel and convincing treatment ("On an Alleged Contradiction") of the seemingly contradictory positions on the commandment of "chasing the mother bird from the nest" *(shiluah ha-ken)*.

6. Maimonides went on to say that even physical symptoms that are deemed by the Bible to attract ritual impurity defy any classification of current diagnostic science, since conditions that medicine considers to be the very extremes of this disease are deemed ritually pure by the Bible and are therefore "legal things" (*sharia*, translated by Kafih as *devarim torani'im*). This is confirmed by the fact that what is determinative of a leprous sate of ritual impurity is the pronouncement of a priest *(kohen)* and not that of a medical expert. See *m. Nega'im* 3:1 and MT *Laws of Leprosy Defilement* 9:2. It is not a scientific/natural category but a legal/theological one.

7. In the discussion that follows I owe much to Twersky's incisive analysis of this passage in the *Mishneh Torah*, though I disagree with his conclusions (in fact arriving at an opposite one) that "leprosy in clothing and homes absolutely transcend nature" ("Halakha and Science," 147–49).

8. See, e.g., his translation of the very first instance it appears, in the introduction to the *Guide* in MN, 8. There are numerous examples of terms that are classified as "equivocal" *(sh-t-f)* of which the following is only a sampling: *face* (I:37); *air* (I:40); *soul* (I:41); *eye* (I:44). See also ibn Tibbon's definition of *shem meshutaf* in his *Perush Ha-Millim Ha-Zarot,* MN 85–86. Maimonides' *Treatise on Logic* (Kafih), 168–72, lists six different meanings of the term *meshuttaf.* See also Baneth, "Philosophical Terminology," part 2. Davidson ("The Authenticity of Works") has concluded that the *Treatise on Logic* was in fact a work produced by a Muslim and not, as has long been thought, by Maimonides. Even if this is the case it is still most instructive to look at what the Hebrew translator, in this case Moses ibn Tibbon, considered *sh-t-f* to mean.

9. For other instances of this meaning, see MT *Laws of the Murderer and Preservation of Life* 6:3; *Laws of Sale* 19:5 (a rare circumstance that is not governed by the terms of a private contract since it is considered not to have been contemplated by the parties); *Laws of Evidence* 16:4; *Laws of Rebels* 6:3 (an unusual name); *Laws of Sanctification of the Month* 5:2; 9:8. For the term as descriptive of the entire natural order, see *Laws of the Foundations of the Torah* 2:2. For its use as descriptive of a scholar possessing extraordinary legal acumen, see *Laws of the Sanhedrin* 4:8, 10.

10. Here the types of "signs" performed by Moses and Elisha are classified as *shinui minhago shel olam* (change in the nature of the world) and distinguished from signs that are mere predictions. For a list of miraculous signs, see MT *Laws of the Foundations of the Torah* 8:1. Signs can also be the result of "sorcery" (ibid., 8:2; 9:5), which, for Maimonides, can only mean a manipulation of nature that effects an illusion of the supernatural (MT *Laws of Idolatry* 11:16). See also GP III:37, 540–43. Another type of *ot* that most likely also falls within the natural is that performed by an established sage who is not technically a prophet. His *ot* is defined by the difficult expression "there is something in it" *(devarim bago)*—that is, problematic or questionable. (For the talmudic use of this expression, see *b.* Ketubbot 111a; *b. Qiddushin* 44b). Even "miracles" like the splitting of the sea can all ultimately be considered as natural in the sense that they were pre-programmed into nature at creation. See GP II:29, 345–46; PM *Avot* 5:5; and Reines, "Maimonides' Concept of Miracles." Even the "spectacular" signs like the splitting of the sea would end up as natural confirmations of a prophetic prediction, which "consists in God's making known to him the time when he must make his proclamation, and thereupon a certain thing is effected according to what was put into its nature when first it received its particular impress" (GP II:29, 345–46).

11. It is interesting to note that the first appearance of the term *ot* in the Hebrew Bible, Gen 4:15—the sign of Cain—is midrashically taken to indicate leprosy. See *Gen Rabbah* 22:15.

12. It is important to note that he does not describe this strange leprosy as a "change" *(shinui)* in the natural order as he did with Mosaic signs (see note 10). For phenomena that are not *minhago shel olam* and yet still within nature, see MT

Laws of Idolatry 2:1 (such heavenly bodies as sun and moon do not degrade like the *minhago shel olam*); *Laws of Forbidden Intercourse* 21:9 (unnatural sexual intercourse that is not reproductive); *Laws of Mourning* 13:1 excessive grief and mourning). For these reasons my analysis here and thus far is in disagreement with that offered by Twersky, who argues that the combination of *ot* and *pele* that are not *minhago shel olam* demonstrates that leprosy is indeed quite literally miraculous, and it can be legitimately considered as such "both from a philosophical and halakhic perspective," without any need to interpret it metaphorically "against the *peshat*" ("Halakha and Science," 149).

13. This picture of leprosy fits well with Sontag's analysis of "diseases encumbered by the trappings of metaphor," and particularly with how the leper was perceived in the Middle Ages: "a social text in which corruption was made visible; an exemplum, an emblem of decay" (*Illness as Metaphor*, 5, 58).

14. This is clearly Maimonides' exegesis of Lev 13:46, which forces the leper to "dwell alone in a habitation outside the camp." The rabbinic tradition views this state alternatively as either curative or punitive. Rashi, for example, cites both points of view when explicating the term "dwell alone" *(badad):* (a) "so that others who are ritually defiled do not dwell with him"; (b) "since he caused separation by *lashon ha-ra* between man and wife and between fellow human beings so he becomes separated." Maimonides' rationale for the leper's isolation is consistent with the curative (a). *Lashon ha-ra* ceases because the leper can no longer keep the company of others guilty of the same crime.

15. This "expected" behavior finds its antithesis in the *tzaddiqim* (righteous), who "endure insult without reacting and act out of love and *are joyous in suffering*" (MT *Laws of Ethical Traits* 2:3).

16. For the rabbinic sources on this association, see *Tanhuma*, 5:10; *Midrash Ha-Gadol*, Num 12:1; *Sifre Zuta*, Num 12:1; *Sifre Num* 12:1. Further midrashic corroboration of this is provided by taking *metzora* (leper) as an anagram for *motze shem ra* (defamation) in *Lev Rabbah* 16:1. See also *b. Arakhin* 16a.

17. In his commentary in PM *Avot* 4:4, during a lengthy excursus on the virtues of extreme humility, for which Moses is the exemplar as indicated by this verse, Maimonides pronounced leprosy to be a punishment for haughtiness and arrogance. In this light, Miriam's leprosy is apropos to her assault on the very personification of humility.

18. There are eleven degrees of prophecy, the eleventh of which attests to the pinnacle of human intellectual perfection "provided one exempts Moses our Master" (GP II:45, 402). Elsewhere Maimonides proclaimed him to have actually achieved a separate intellect status ("angelic"); see his introduction in PM to *Avot*, chapter 7 of what is known as the "Eight Chapters" (volume *Neziqin*, 393–96). See also MT *Laws of the Foundations of the Torah* 7:6.

19. Guttman succinctly categorized the distinction as not "a difference in degree, but a difference in kind" (*Philosophies of Judaism*, 172). See also Bland, "Moses and the Law," 51.

20. See also Rashi's commentary on Num 12:1, which draws the same a fortiori lesson from Miriam's inadvertence, though the substance of her "slander" concerns Moses' desertion of his wife rather than his prophetic capabilities.

21. The principles can be found in his PM, commentary to chapter 10 of *Sanhedrin*.

22. See Kellner, "Could Maimonides Get Into Rambam's Heaven?" esp. 240–42.

23. The unique case of Moses, according to Gruenwald, demonstrates that "there is one element in the area of prophecy that unequivocally points beyond the cognitive framework of prophecy itself." See his discussion of Mosaic prophecy in "Maimonides' Quest," esp. 152–57.

24. The other distinguishing sign of Moses is that he receives prophecy resolutely, without fear, and is in a perpetual state of readiness to do so.

25. These are the consequences Maimonides stated after formulating his list of principles.

26. Ricoeur, "The Model of the Text," 155.

27. One can imagine Franz Rosenzweig appropriating Maimonides' language.

28. This is most evident in the way many of the medieval commentators on the *Guide* understood the dual meaning attributed to "going" in the Miriam story. Typical is Isaac Abravanel, who reads the phrase "went away" of Num 12:9, in the sense of spreading, as modifying God's anger "which extends until Miriam becomes *leprous as snow* as a result and afterwards providence left them and therefore *va-yelekh bam* has both senses together." For similar interpretations, see Shem Tov and Efodi. Asher Crescas elaborates that the removal of providence implies "being cast to accidents" *(meshulah la-miqrim)*. It does not connote "an intentional evil from Him, however what happened to Miriam was intended by God as a punishment," as, he tells us, is often the case with the punishment of rebels in the Torah. For all these commentators, see MN 41a.

29. His position on providence is fully developed in chapters III:17–23. There is a large body of scholarly literature on the subject of providence in Maimonidean thought from which I offer only a sampling: Lebowitz, "Divine Providence"; Ivry, "Providence"; Nuriel, "Providence"; C. M. Raffel, "Providence," 25–71; and Reines, "Maimonides' Concepts of Providence and Theodicy." As Reines sums it up (187), "as a function of the human intellect, the providence men receive is entirely a natural event."

30. See D. H. Frank, "Anger as a Vice."

31. On the issue of anger, I am indebted to the incisive analysis of Hannah Kasher, "Mitos Ha-El Ha-Ko'es," which probes the precise meaning of God's anger as a necessary belief. Pertinent to my argument is her conclusion (105) that "the assertion *God is angry with someone,* does not describe a divine reaction but rather the epistemological state of that individual. Therefore, even though 'God' is the textual subject of the sentence, the conceptual subject is the individual who persists in his ignorance."

32. It is of interest to note Maimonides' analysis of Moses' sin that prevented his entry into Canaan—that demonstrating anger with the public led them to extrapolate that God was in fact angry with them at the waters of Meribah (chapter 4 of his "Eight Chapters").

33. See H. Kasher, "Mitos Ha-El Ha-Ko'es," 105–11, for a discussion of this problem. The following is a sampling of solutions offered by medieval commentators:

Efodi: (a) Maimonides does not mean literally all places but merely a majority. (b) Any error as to the nature of God amounts to a form of idolatry. (This is the opinion cited in the name of Joseph ibn Kaspi.)

Shem Tov: (a) Instances of divine anger such as Num 12:9 (Miriam) or Exod 4:14 (Moses) appear on the basis that even minor transgressions of the righteous are treated as severely as idolatry. (b) Maimonides means that nowhere other than idolatry will a combination of all three terms "wrath," "anger," and "jealousy" appear.

Abravanel: Maimonides' assertion is confined only to those instances where these terms describe only God and does not apply to those that describe recipients of divine anger (e.g., Miriam, Moses).

All these can be found in MN 56a–b.

34. Since some of the most prominent examples of divine anger are directed at such figures as Moses and Miriam, Maimonides tactfully omitted them from his list in GP I:37, leaving it to his readers to form their own conclusions based on statements elsewhere in his writings (e.g., GP I:24; MT), as I have done. This is simply to apply the method Maimonides himself recommended, to "grasp the totality of what this Treatise contains" by "connect[ing] its chapters one with the other," and grasping every word "even if that word does not belong to the intention of the chapter"(GP I, 15).

35. W. Z. Harvey has noted that III:51 is "a chapter whose ambience is more Sufi than Aristotelian" ("Crescas versus Maimonides," 122).

36. See Kaplan, "'I Sleep, But My Heart Waketh,'" esp. 138–40, who argues on the basis of this chapter I:54 that out of this noetic experience arises Moses' *imitatio dei* par excellence in his capacity as a lawgiver—that is, Moses formulates a perfect code of governance rooted in his understanding of God's governance.

37. What exactly Maimonides meant by this perturbed many of his commentators and was the subject of a comprehensive treatment by Samuel ibn Tibbon, in a letter addressed to Maimonides relating to inconsistencies between the general theory of providence in part III of the *Guide* and that of specific providence set out here in I:51. See Disendruck, "Samuel and Moses ibn Tibbon." For a useful summary of ibn Tibbon's account, see C. M. Raffel, "Providence," 29–35.

38. That Maimonides' concern for avoiding unnecessary conversation was paramount can be seen from his comments on the saying in *m. Avot* 1:17, "nothing is better for the body than silence," in which this verse appears as a primary prooftext and to which he dedicated one of his lengthiest treatments in the PM on *Avot*.

The verse appears again in MT *Laws of Ethical Traits* 2:4 to endorse the virtues of silence. For a full treatment of Maimonides' attitude toward speech, see R. Weiss, *Maimonides' Ethics,* 51–58.

39. Both David Kimhi and Rashi see this as a call for the death of the wicked—that is, the grave silences them.

40. See Broadie, "Maimonides on Divine Knowledge," 49, who sums up this opinion as "a product of a certain arrogance, by which a narrowly human perspective is treated as if sufficient to ground a universal truth."

41. The parallel between the parable of the ladder and the Platonic parable of the cave is inescapable. Strauss already pointed out the correspondence, but with Maimonides' hierarchy of light sketched out in the introduction to the *Guide.* His analogy fits the ladder just as well: "Just as according to Plato the perfect state can only be realized through the philosopher who has ascended from the cave into the light, who has gazed upon the idea of the Good, so according to Maimonides and the Falasifa, the perfect state can only be realized through the prophet for whom the night in which the human race gropes has been illuminated by lightning bolts from on high, by direct knowledge of the upper worlds." See Strauss, *Philosophy and Law,* 105.

42. See, e.g., Jer chaps. 27–28; 2 Kgs 24:20. See also GP II:40, 383–85. According to Maimonides, Jeremiah's compulsion to "address a call to the people" was so overpoweringly dictated by the strength of the intellectual overflow he tapped into that it overwhelmed his own personal urge to suppress his prophecy to avoid "the contempt he met with at the hands of the disobedient and unbelieving people" (GP II:37, 375).

43. See also the definition of prophecy in the sixth of the thirteen principles in PM *Sanhedrin* chap. 10. Pines, "The Philosophical Purport," 3, points out that this dogma as formulated in the PM is even more philosophical than that of the *Guide:* "It is stated in this dogma but not in the *Guide* that the intellects of the prophets were united with the Active Intellect."

44. Though I do not necessarily agree with all of Strauss' conclusions that view the prophet's primary role in his political leadership, I do accept it as one of the roles he assumes vis-à-vis the people. See *Philosophy and Law,* esp. part IV.

45. See also chapter 8 of Maimonides' introduction to his commentary ("Eight Chapters") on *Avot* in his PM. This is how Maimonides rationalized such biblical phenomena as the hardening of Pharoah's heart. See also Nahmanides' commentary on this troubling phenomenon (Exod 7:3), which would seem to undermine free will and responsibility; he follows in the same vein as Maimonides.

46. For an attempt at synthesizing the need for petitionary prayer and the contemplative ideal that focuses on a changeless and static divine will as "complementary dimensions of a distinctive form of ethical-intellectual worship" (another fine attempt at integrating the two enterprises of the *Guide* and the MT), see Benor, "Petition and Contemplation."

47. It would appear, on the basis of III:36, that the notion of repentance *(teshuvah)* itself is a necessary belief akin to anger. See H. Kasher, "Mitos Ha-El Ha-Ko'es," 100 n. 13. Once again, for a different conclusion based on what Maimonides said about the efficacy of *teshuvah* in attracting divine providence in MT *Laws of Fast Days* 1:2–3, see Twersky, "Halakha and Science," 151.

48. Maimonides understood Job to be evolving from one who is merely morally virtuous but lacking wisdom to one who acquires wisdom (GP III:22, 487). The theme of providence parallels this intellectual maturity in the narrative, that is, Job moves from being excluded from providence to coming within its purview, since providence is consequent upon intellect. See Kravitz, "Maimonides and Job," 155: "Of course! Lacking wisdom, Job lacked providence; virtues and uprightness could not protect him from accidents."

49. Though this "revelation" of 3:18 is a result of God's pity of 3:17, "as a man pities his own son," Maimonides is unequivocal that this does not imply any passion on the part of God but is only an attribute of action "similar to that which proceeds from a father in respect of His child" (GP I:54, 125). One must therefore bear in mind that Malachi is not portending some divinely orchestrated revelation; rather, this is a metaphor for a natural cognition.

50. Maimonides also cited in 7:2 the preceding verse in Psalms, "May God cut off *[yikaret]* all smooth lips, every tongue that speaks brazenly" (Ps 12:4). Considering Maimonides' definition of the punishment of "cutting off" *(karet)* as simply disappearing after death and being "destroyed like an animal" leaving no remnant of a soul, the choice of a verse with this consequence is most apropos. Since slander reflects a state of intellectual atrophy, the slanderer has not cultivated his human form, which is his intellect, which is his soul, which is the "thing that remains of man after death." See GP I:41, 91–92.

Chapter 3   Elisha ben Abuyah and the Hubris of the Heretic

1. 4:13 directly refers to the *pardes* of Elisha/Akiva fame. For the meaning of the term *pardes* within its talmudic context, see Scholem, *Jewish Gnosticism*, 16–17. For a medieval debate as to whether this entry into the *pardes* involves an actual ascension or is a metaphor for some form of contemplative ascent, see R. Solomon ben Isaac of Troyes (Rashi), who advocated the former, and a Tosafist who was a proponent of the latter, in their respective commentaries to the meaning of "entering the *pardes*" in b. *Hagigah* 14b. For the widespread understanding of the *pardes* as referring to esoteric doctrine regarding the nature of God, see Davidson, "The Study of Philosophy."

2. Maimonides quoted the characterization of Akiva's success but not that of Elisha's failure in GP I:32. Perhaps he did not wish to diminish the potency of the sobriquet Aher as the antithesis of Akiva's *shalom;* it becomes apparent at the conclusion of this chapter that these are two opposing states of being.

3. See his introduction to GP, xiii.

4. See, e.g., GP I:17, 26.

5. Liebes, *The Sin of Elisha*. For two recent treatments of Elisha/Aher that take issue with Liebes' methodology and conclusions, see Rubenstein, "Elisha ben Abuya," which has an appendix (211–25) devoted to a sustained critique of Liebes; and Goshen-Gottstein, *The Sinner and the Amnesiac,* 221–29. Rubenstein's criticisms are irrelevant to my preference for Liebes' reading. I am not dealing here with a talmudic passage on its own terms, but rather with how a major rabbinic figure, in this case Maimonides, received the rabbinic traditions and recast them. In fact, the very criticism directed at Liebes' study by Rubenstein may actually work in his favor for understanding the Maimonidean appropriation of Elisha. Being firmly rooted within the rabbinic tradition instead of a modern scholarly/literary/critical tradition, Maimonides would have been more prone to construct his own portrait on the basis of a "composite picture of Elisha that emerges from synthesizing and reconciling disparate texts" (Rubenstein, 223).

6. This outlook that all exists for the sake of man is labeled a "raving" *(hathiyan)*. Gellman ("Maimonides' Ravings," 312–15) has demonstrated that all instances of this term in Maimonides bear a technical connotation of a metaphysical category: the mistake of failing to "maintain a rigid metaphysical distinction between form and matter." This violation of Galen's principle, which considers matter as perfect as form, is precisely the error of Elisha that is at the heart of my argument.

7. Kugel, *The Idea of Biblical Poetry.*

8. It is striking how often Maimonides' positions and those of his later archnemesis converge on various issues. On this they are in complete accord with Spinoza, who also took a radical anti-teleological stance for some of the same reasons: "If God acts toward an end, He necessarily desires something He lacks." He even alludes to the same verse, Prov 16:4, as a criticism of anthropocentric theologies (Spinoza, *Opera,* vol. 3, *Ethica,* I, app. (6, II, 80, ll. 22–26). See also W. Z. Harvey, "A Portrait of Spinoza," 162–64.

9. Proverbs 25:27 was also cited by Maimonides in MT *Laws of Ethical Traits* 3:2 as a health warning against eating foods that are deleterious to our particular digestive temperament. Once again, this is an illustration of a self-inflicted harm. For the general purpose of the Torah's dietary restrictions, see GP III:35, 537: "to put an end . . . to taking the desire for food and drink as an end [in itself]."

10. *Lev Rabbah.* The motivating factor behind Maimonides' choice of contrasting Moses with the nobles may very well have been this *midrash,* which also plays Moses off of the nobles. There certainly was no dearth of midrashic offences attributed to Nadav and Avihu from which Maimonides could have chosen. See Shinan, "The Sins of Nadav and Avihu."

11. Though he was decidedly anti-teleological in matters pertaining to nature and the cosmos, he affirmed it within the sphere of human conduct: "There is, in the opinions of the Sages a cause for all the commandments; I mean to say

that any particular commandment or prohibition has a useful end" (GP III:26). For an example of his teleology of *mitzvot,* see Twersky, "On Law and Ethics in the *Mishneh Torah.*"

12. In all the extant versions of the Talmud, this verse is quoted in respect to Ben Zoma and not Elisha. It is too speculative to hypothesize an intentional switch here by Maimonides, as Stroumsa does. Although possible, the safer position is to not rule out the existence of a variant text possessed by Maimonides that indeed read as quoted by him. See Stroumsa, "Elisha ben Abuya and Muslim Heretics," 182–83.

13. See *Num Rabbah,* which correlates each segment of this verse to some pivotal event in David's life in which he was able to stave off grandiose behavior. Most relevant for my thesis is the correlation of the last phrase with his most unroyal conduct when returning the Ark to Jerusalem. What appears to some as undignified and "common" behavior is for Maimonides an illustration of the highest level of performing a *mitzvah* out of pure joy. See MT *Laws of Shofar, Sukkah, and Lulav* 8:16.

14. An officially sanctioned Aramaic translation and commentary originating in second-century Palestine.

15. See GP I:2 and II:30, 359, where "He is *Elohim*" = "He who governs."

16. In MT *Laws of the Foundations of the Torah* 3:3, Maimonides emphasized that the spheres are devoid of all physical properties including color, and therefore "what we see as blue *[tekhelet]* is really an optical illusion due to the atmospheric height." The color *tekhelet* is how the firmament *(rakia)* appears to the human eye, as qualified in MT *Laws of Fringes* 1:1, where one of the threads of the ritual fringes must bear this dye. That this relates to a color that only "appears" to the human eye when gazing at the firmament is reiterated in 2:1 of the same section in the MT. This qualification is rooted in the talmudic association of *tekhelet* with the "throne of glory" by way of a series of correspondences based on color similarity. The route the mind follows when looking at the *tekhelet* of the fringes is sea, firmament, throne of glory (b. *Sotah* 12a, b. *Menahot* 43b). The proof-text for the last association is "the work of the whiteness of a sapphire stone." Maimonides omits the intermediate step and draws a direct equivalence between the dye and what appears to be the color of the firmament. I suggest that the purpose of this *tekhelet* is to remind man that the domains of the firmament, the throne of glory, and the sapphire stone present themselves as optical illusions that are not to be mistaken for their true reality. The esoteric nature of this realm becomes evident in that it is an essential component of the Account of the Chariot. See GP III:4, where the color of the wheels of Ezekiel's chariot, "beryl," is also identified (though via the Aramaic *Targum*) with "the whiteness of a sapphire stone."

17. GP I:5. The *midrash* referred to can be found both in *Tanhuma Be-Ha'alotkha* and *Lev Rabbah,* end of chap. XX.

18. Maimonides may very well have been sensitive to the midrashic association of Moses with *tov.* Within the very *midrash* that is chosen to justify the

omission of "it was good" from the second day of creation, there is a reference to Moses' being called "good" *(tov) (Gen Rabbah* 4:5). R. Meir derives from the verse "And she saw that he was *tov*" (Exod 2:2) that Moses' name was in fact *tov (Exod Rabbah* 1:24). The midrashic personification of *tov* by Moses complements the Maimonidean Moses developed here.

19. That the reference is charged with the allusion is further corroborated by Maimonides' citation in his *mishnah* commentary of the talmudic opinion that identifies the transgression of sullying the honor of one's creator with committing a sin in secrecy (*b. Hagigah* 16a). The talmudic proof-text for this is one that connotes God's all-pervasive presence, to which private transgressions are an affront. The offender is likened to one who "shunts the feet of the Divine presence, for it says, *The heaven is my throne and the earth is my footstool* [Isa 66:1]." The heaven, which is God's throne, has already been identified with the *aravot*, which has been demonstrated to be the locale from which *tzedeq* and *mishpat* emanate. The reference then is further evidence of Elisha's apostasy on the issue of God's governance and evil.

20. See also his comments on Songs 4:11 in his introduction to PM, 35.

21. I agree with Davidson's incisive analysis of the import of this verse, which does not rank ethical virtue above intellectual virtue but rather mandates a kind of ethical conduct that automatically flows from the heights of intellectual accomplishment vis-à-vis knowledge of God. Jeremiah's exhortation is to model ethical conduct on God's attributes of action as follows: "Divine loving-kindness, righteousness, and judgment, are not characteristics in the being of God, but acts executed dispassionately. Analogously, human loving-kindness, righteousness, and judgment, growing out of knowledge of God, will not be characteristics in the soul of man, but acts again executed dispassionately." See Davidson, "The Middle Way," 71.

22. See Klein-Braslavy's discussion of the various hypotheses regarding the identity of the suprafirmament waters (*Maimonides' Interpretation of the Adam Stories*, 160–74).

23. For a survey of the debate among the medievals concerning the nature of the waters above the firmament (e.g., are they crystalline, ice, and so on?), see Grant, *Planets, Stars and Orbs*, 103–4; 332–34.

24. "Darkness" *(hoshekh)* in this verse means that which is empirically experienced as night, or the absence of light, as opposed to the elemental fire of Gen 1:2. For these equivocal meanings of *hoshekh*, see GP II:30, 351: "In view of the fact that the term darkness *[hoshekh]* as employed in the first place [Gen 1:2] which designates the element, differs in its meaning from the term darkness, as employed afterwards in the signification of obscurity, it begins to explain and differentiate, saying *And the hoshekh He called night.*"

25. For a striking example of the way in which Maimonides' rationalistic interpretations were transformed into mystical allegories, see Abraham Abulafia's version of Maimonides on this "water, water" episode, as discussed by Altmann,

"Maimonides' Attitude toward Jewish Mysticism," 208: "this does not mean a distinction between celestial and terrestrial matter—that is, a mere cosmological gradation—but the full breakthrough of the mystic conception of an ontological dualism." If Faur is correct in attributing sexual connotations to the expression "water, water" (see *Lev Rabbah* 23:3), then the signifier corresponds to its signified, or there is an indication of confusion between form and matter. Matter, in Maimonides, is very often depicted in feminine terms, as in GP I:6, 7, 14, and particularly III:8. There the relationship between matter and form is analogized to that between an unfaithful wife and her husband. Just as she "never ceases to seek for another man to substitute for her husband," so does matter, "whatever form is found in it, does but prepare it to receive another form" (GP III:8, 431). The "water, water" expression, then, captures the sexual infidelities of matter to form. See Faur, *Homo Mysticus,* 40.

26. Klein-Braslavy, *Maimonides' Interpretation of the Creation Account.*

27. The English translation is mine. See also Klein-Braslavy, ibid., who cites Crescas approvingly.

28. See also GP II:48, 410, where the point is made that prophetic language that attributes all material and moral events directly to God omits all the proximate natural series of causation between God and that phenomenon. A potent illustration of that prophetic trope is rain.

29. The chapter immediately preceding Maimonides' treatment of evil, GP III:9, dwells on matter as the inescapable handicap of the human condition, the perennial obstruction to a panoramic view of God. Numerous biblical citations are offered in which the imagery is of God ensconced in darkness *(hoshekh),* reaching its apogee with the Sinaitic theophany itself where God is enveloped in both darkness and rain. This image, of course, is restricted to the matter-biased perspective of man. However, the divine reality resides in "dazzling light, the overflow of which illumines all that is dark." The proof-text for the latter reality is "And the earth did shine with His glory *[kavod]*" (Ezek 43:2). *Kavod* is the counterbalance to man's *hoshekh.* When contemplating the darkness of matter, if man is not mindful of the light of *kavod,* then the equilibrium is shattered and he "does not have proper regard for the *kavod* of his Creator."

30. When addressing the omission of "it was good" from the second day of creation, Maimonides favored the midrashic solution that the creation of water was incomplete at that stage. This reason is qualified as "the best statement of its kind" but not necessarily the sole acceptable one. Particularly apt for R. Akiva's "peaceful" entry and return and cognizance of his own "water, water" warning is the midrashic opinion attributing the "good" omission to the conflict and tension introduced into the world that day, as evidenced by the "division" of the waters ("the sense is divisiveness"). But of course this is only a perceived "not good," and so Akiva, by placing each water in its proper context, resolves the conflict, sees the ultimate *tov,* and therefore returns in "peace" *(shalom).*

31. Chronologically, the editing process of the Palestinian Talmud predates the Babylonian Talmud. Friedman ("La-Aggadah Ha-Historit Ba-Talmud Bavli") has documented how the Babylonian Talmud literally reworked the Palestinian *aggadot* by revising and supplementing them in accordance with its own agenda. For this phenomenon with respect to the Elisha traditions, see Rubenstein, "Elisha ben Abuya," 200–203, 212–14.

Chapter 4 The King

1. It is universally acknowledged that Maimonides derived his formulation from Aristotle's *Nicomachean Ethics*; see, e.g., the English translation in Irwin, 1106a28–b7. For another formulation of the doctrine of the mean by Maimonides, see his introduction to his commentary on *m. Avot*, known as "Eight Chapters" (English translation in Raymond Weiss, *Ethical Writings*, 67–70). Weiss attributes Maimonides' choice of the term *deʿot* for ethical traits (rather than a more likely term such as *middot*) to that which distinguishes man from brute—his intellectual form. Maimonides thereby "intellectualizes the character traits by calling them *deʿot*. He also stresses the effect of moral conduct upon the mind by treating character traits as *deʿot*" (Raymond Weiss, "Language and Ethics," 430). Strauss translates *deʿot* as "ethics" ("Notes on Maimonides' Book of Knowledge," 270), while Schwarzschild prefers "morals" ("Moral Radicalism," 143). The laws of *deʿot* are an example of Maimonides' systemization of what is really a lacuna in biblical and rabbinic law. W. Z. Harvey makes the fascinating point that of all the chapters in the *Guide* that correspond to the commandments as codified in the *Mishneh Torah*, "chapter 38 dealing with laws concerning character traits is the only one that has no biblical quotation. This undoubtedly hints at the absence of a systematic ethic in the Written Law" ("Nuriel's Method," 33–36).

2. The other exception to the rule of the mean is anger, which requires a separate treatment; this study is restricted to the issue of humility. For that purpose, it suffices to accept the conclusion of Statman, citing Vital and Murphy, that hubris and anger both arise out of the same human impulses (Statman, "On Some Solutions," 361). See also D. Frank, "Anger As a Vice," who argues that Maimonides decidedly broke with Aristotle on the ethics of anger, judging the Aristotelian vice of inirascibility to be a virtue. Maimonides' "transvaluation of values," asserts Frank, is a result of an un-Aristotelian conception of the self that is measured by the divine standard of God's "ways."

3. In MT *Laws of Ethical Traits* 5:5, *anav* is the technical term that represents the median on the scale that measures pride and humility. The extreme of self-effacement is captured by the phrase *shafel-ruah*. The former is the ethical stance of the *hakham* while the latter is that of the *hasid* (ibid., 1:5) or of the *tzaddik* (ibid., 2:3). Schwarzschild claims that the distinction between the mean and

the extreme "is Maimonides' entrenched terminological distinction between the Aristotelian *homo philosophicus* and *homo religiosus*" ("Moral Radicalism," 142). Safran argues similarly that the *hakham* is identical to the Aristotelian paragon of virtue and the *hasid* is Maimonides' own unique "Jewish" category that "moves beyond as it turns theocentric" ("Maimonides and Aristotle," 151). Rawidowicz equates the two with "morality" and "Torah" (*Studies in Jewish Thought*, 464). Davidson traces shifting ethical positions between the distinctly Aristotelian one in Maimonides' earlier works of the Mishnah commentary and the *Mishneh Torah* endorsing the middle way and the more extreme ascetic position endorsed by the *Guide* that might have been influenced by Moslem pietistic works and more appropriately classified as Neoplatonic. See his "The Middle Way." Whatever shift may have occurred does not affect the argument of this chapter since it specifically deals with an extreme ethical position on humility that cuts across the earlier and later works. As Davidson himself notes, Maimonides' different positions "reflect a change of heart over a period of time—a change that was adumbrated in the Mishneh Torah itself" (61).

4. For a summary of these contradictions, see Kreisel, *Maimonides' Political Thought*, 161. Fox ("The Doctrine of the Mean") has argued incisively that Maimonides did not simply adopt wholesale the Aristotelian doctrine of the mean; rather, Maimonides' Aristotelianism was modified in accordance with his unswerving allegiance to Jewish law and tradition. Further on the issue of extreme humility, see Raymond Weiss, *Maimonides' Ethics*, 102–15; and D. Frank, "Humility As a Virtue."

5. For a vivid illustration of the extent to which this extreme of "lowly of spirit" should be taken, see the story (apparently of Sufi origins) recounted by Maimonides in PM *Avot* 4:4.

6. This is not a fixed dichotomy; note the insight of Benor, as elaborated by Kaplan ("An Introduction to Maimonides' Eight Chapters"), that what is meant by "mean" in the doctrine of the mean is not an arithmetic fixed mean, but rather a "relative shifting" one.

7. On the question of whether Maimonides subscribed to the Platonic/Farabian philosopher-king, see e.g. Berman, "The Political Interpretation," 60; GP "Translator's Introduction," lxxxvi; Melamed, *Philosopher King*, 211 n. 67. In both Maimonides' halakhic and philosophical writings, the king is clearly distinguished from the prophet. Indeed, the adoption of the "three crowns" model of Judaism in MT *Laws of Studying Torah* 3:1 disengages the "crown of Torah" (wisdom, philosophy) from the "crown of monarchy," with the former being clearly superior to the latter. The fact that it is only Moses who combines all the facets of the Platonic/Farabian ideal king who is also philosopher, legislator, and prophet is, in my opinion, the exception that proves the rule for Maimonides.

8. See also PM *Shevuot* 2:2: "Moses was a king and was counted among the kings in addition to his prophetic capacity and it is said of him 'And there was a king in Jeshurun [Deut 33:5].'" Moses is identified as a king in various rabbinic

sources; see, e.g., *b. Zevahim* 102a; *y. Sanhedrin* 1:3; *Lev Rabbah* 31:4 (also based on Deut 33:5); *Exod Rabbah* 48:4. Among the commentators, Nahmanides also relates the "king" of Deut 33:5, among other referents, to Moses, "for he was a king over us and all our tribes together." It is the ability to command a national tribal constituency, conveyed by the second colon of the verse, that is paramount in qualifying Moses as king for both Nahmanides and Abraham ibn Ezra.

9. This law is based on *b. Shevuot* 15a–b. Moses, acting in consonance with his brother Aaron and the seventy elders, was the precedent establishing the requisite participants in this decision: the king (Moses), the prophet (Moses), the *urim ve-tummim* (Aaron), and the Sanhedrin (seventy elders). For the list of all matters that require the deliberation and consent of the Sanhedrin of seventy-one, see MT *Laws of the Sanhedrin* 5:1.

10. Maimonides then distinguished the holiness of the remainder of the Land of Israel, which is, in a sense, man made. It arises as a result of a political process of national colonization *(kibbush rabbim)*, and consequently is lost with any reversal of that process. The boldness and novelty of these assertions are reflected in the aggressive arguments of the PM commentators Rabad of Posquieres and Joseph Karo ("Kesef Mishneh").

11. For a clear demonstration that holiness for Maimonides is not a hypostatic reality and does not bear any ontological qualities within the context of the Hebrew language, see Kellner, "Maimonides on the Normality of Hebrew"; Twersky, *Introduction to the Code of Maimonides,* 324, who refers to Maimonides' "consistent opposition to hypostasized entities endowed with intrinsic sanctity"; and Twersky, "Sanctifying the Name," 172–73, where he makes the point that holiness *(qeddushah)* is solely a function of the ennoblement of man via *mitzvot*.

12. See Kreisel, *Maimonides' Political Thought,* 151–56, and esp. 155, for a discussion of holiness.

13. From a popular theological perspective, since the Temple and Jerusalem uniquely draw their holiness from the *shekhinah,* an autonomous act by the king would have the appearance of usurping a divine prerogative. Confusion would arise over what is human conquest *(kibbush),* and therefore reflective of man, and what signifies God *(shekhinah).*

14. There are other restrictions on the king's power that are based on a similar rationale, most notably with respect to his ability to wage an elective war that is not halakhically mandated *(milhemet reshut).* This type of war, which includes "expanding the borders" of Israel, is waged for political or economic reasons, and requires the consent of the Sanhedrin. See MT *Laws of Kings* 5:1–2; and Kimmelman "The Laws of Warfare," 233–38.

15. In *b. Megillah* 31a this verse is cited as a proof-text for the observation that "wherever one finds the awesome power of God, there he will also find His humility." This verse is also cited in the *Guide* in support of the assertion that only those who have achieved a mastery of their passions can truly aspire to metaphysical knowledge.

16. See, e.g., GP I:59.

17. Davidson, "The Middle Way," 31–72.

18. Twersky cites this law as a prime illustration of the teleology of *mitzvot* that is characteristic throughout the *Mishneh Torah* and "shows that ritual acts, in the realm of theology or metaphysics, are also areas of ethics" ("On Law and Ethics in the *Mishneh Torah*," 46). Kaplan's analysis of the same *halakhah* shows that the "the theological motif is cited in order *to perform a halakhic function*" ("Hilkhot Megillah 2:17 Revisited," 18).

19. Halakhically, the convert is "like a new-born child" (*b. Yevamot* 22a, 48b, 62a, 97b; *b. Bekhorot* 47a). Maimonides adopted this classification for both the convert and the manumitted slave (MT *Laws of Forbidden Intercourse* 14:11). The logical extremes to which this is taken in halakhic terms can be seen in MT *Laws of Evidence* 13:2, where even twin converts are no longer considered brothers under the laws of evidence.

20. One need only look to ancient Egypt and its belief in divine kingship for a historical manifestation of this theological distortion. The king was viewed, not merely as divinely chosen or as a deity's representative, but as an actual product of divine procreation. His intimacy with the gods rendered him the focal point of the people's wants and needs. "The king was regarded as the actual author of the fertility of the fields and of the cattle. He was also instrumental in causing the flooding of the Nile upon which . . . the very existence of Egypt depended. . . . Without the king chaos would prevail in nature and human society" (Dvornik, *Early Christian and Byzantine Political Philosophy*, 13). See also Frankfort, *Kingship and the Gods*, 9–12.

21. For an earlier rabbinic source establishing a similar scale of charity, see *b. Shabbat* 63a, which lists almsgiving, lending, and offering a business partnership in ascending order of preference. Cronbach, comparing other medieval models of levels of charity, notes that the unitary sentiment informing all eight levels of charity (and recognized by most of the commentators) is "that of disguising the benevolence in order to shield the recipient against humiliation" ("The Gradations of Benevolence," 181).

22. Even though Maimonides drew on Neoplatonic sources to describe God's relationship to the world, I would not, as D. Schwartz does, go so far as to characterize his position on divine immanence as "rather ambiguous" ("Divine Immanence," 269). Maimonides' insistence on divine transcendence is relentless enough throughout the *Guide* to tip the balance well in favor of absolute transcendence. Negative theology expresses this in one sense, since the more one removes God from the world the closer one arrives at His reality. See GP I:59–60.

23. Davidson, "The Middle Way," 71.

24. My argument here supports Twersky's theory as to why Maimonides inserted the spiritual-ethical teaching regarding "gladdening the hearts" of the unfortunates specifically into the laws governing the holiday of Purim. Since it is a holiday that lacks intrinsic sanctity *(qeddushat ha-yom)*, he felt the "compelling

need to put its prescribed rejoicing in perspective . . . certainly a day of merrymaking without sanctification must be infused with a measure of spirituality and kindness" ("On Law and Ethics in the *Mishneh Torah,*" 145). My point here is that the rare expression *domeh le-shekhinah* is itself associated with sanctity and would offer a most appropriate inclusion in the laws of Purim to compensate for its lack of sanctity.

25. See also the discussion of holiness in Kreisel, *Maimonides' Political Thought,* 151–56. Compare the parallel passage in GP III:51, 623–24, which describes Moses as achieving a state "in which he talks with people and is occupied with his bodily necessities while his intellect is wholly turned toward Him so that in his heart he is always in His presence."

26. The necessity of emulating a state of *shefal-ruah* in order to pave the way toward this level of intellectual bliss is reinforced in another type who represents a total dedication to God that is also qualified as "holy"—the Levite. At the very end of MT *Laws of the Sabbatical Year and Jubilee,* the tribe of Levi is used as a paradigm for all who wish to dedicate themselves to God by eschewing all material wants. God metaphorically becomes the Levite's allotment, filling the vacuum left by the fact that Levi had no share in the land apportioned among the other tribes. The Levites are "separated from the ways of the world" (13:12). Further, the laws regarding the various tithes due to the Levites are codified in the *Mishneh* in the same section as those regarding charity; the *Guide* rationalizes their being grouped together since the Torah often does the same (listing together Levites, strangers, widows, and orphans), "for it always considers the Levite as one of the poor in view of the fact that he has no property" (GP III:39, 551). The Levite model is not restricted to Jews but is accessible to all who adopt this lifestyle; Kellner, *Maimonides on Judaism,* 73–74, uses this point in arguing for Maimonides' universalism.

27. See also the fifth principle of Maimonides' thirteen principles of faith, in which angels, stars, and spheres, described as lacking the ability to exercise governance or choice, must conform to the divine will (PM *Sanhedrin* 10:1). However, in GP II:7, they are in fact credited with some form of free choice. For a resolution of this apparent contradiction, see Kreisel, *Maimonides' Political Thought,* 49–50.

28. The vast majority of them relate to the Davidic line whose claim to the throne, although conditional on commitment to divine Law, is granted in perpetuity. See 1 Kgs 2:4, 8:20, 8:25, 9:5; 10:9; 2 Kgs 10:30, 16:12; 2 Chron 6:10, 6:16.

29. Kellner concludes that what is intended by this expression is "Judaism" (*Maimonides on Judaism,* 35–36). M. Lorberbaum concludes that the interchangeability of this term with *din* (law) suggests that for Judaism "the human relationship with God is mediated by, and institutionalized through, a law, the Torah" (*Politics and the Limits of Law,* 72–75).

30. Redemption *(ge'ulah)* is most often associated with freedom from servitude; see, e.g., MT *Laws of Leavened and Unleavened Bread* chaps. 7–9; *Laws of Slaves,* chap. 2. The other virtuous activity that attracts redemption is repentance

(teshuvah) (MT *Laws of Repentance* 7:5). It is of interest to note that ideal penance is also associated with extreme humility, "For the way of penitents is to be low and humble to the extreme" (ibid., 7:8).

31. In GP II:36, 373, the languor and sadness of exile that prevent philosophical and prophetic development are captured in the expatriate status of the king: "Her king and princes are among the nations, the Law is no more; her prophets find no vision from the Lord" (Lam 2:9). The despondency of exile is likened to being a "slave in bondage to the ignorant who commit great sins and in whom the privation of true reason is united to the perfection of the lusts of beasts." Therefore, the king's restoration to his throne in Israel marks the transition from a society that is intellectually vacuous and driven by physical passions to one that is the exact reverse.

32. Royal arrogance and supremacy rupture the king–court alliance. It is for this reason that when royal arrogance is manifest, the court is prohibited from exercising its ultimate jurisdiction over the king; challenging a tyrannical monarch would likely be self-defeating, as the judicial branch would be perilously exposing itself to the king's wrath. This attitude is also reflected in the law that a king of Israel (as opposed to the Davidic line) cannot be a subject of court proceedings: "their hearts are arrogant and religion *[dat]* would suffer tragedy and loss as a result" (MT *Laws of Kings* 3:7; *Laws of the Sanhedrin* 2:5). See also PM *Sanhedrin* 2:3. For the historical conflict that the Talmud credits as the impetus for this law, see *b. Sanhedrin* 19b.

33. In GP II:40, 382, Moses is clearly distinguished as the sole bearer of *nomos,* which followed from his intellectual perfection. The sovereign is someone who has "the faculty to compel people to accomplish, observe, and actualize that which has been established" by him and "who adopts the *nomos* in question."

34. See *Sifre Deut,* 156; *b. Sanhedrin* 20b; *t. Sanhedrin* 4:5. The harshly negative reaction of Samuel, and of God, to a request explicitly mandated by the Torah was a source of endless consternation for rabbinic exegetes throughout the ages. For but one example of a medieval disagreement with Maimonides' resolution, see Menahem ben Shlomoh Me'iri's novellae on *b. Horayot* 11a. Nahmanides adopts a similar argument to Maimonides in his comments to Gen 49:10 and Deut 17:14. He views the Deuteronomic command as both prescriptive and descriptive; the phrase "like all the nations around me" is not integral to the command to appoint a king, but rather predicts how the request was actually formulated.

35. Maimonides was disdainful of religious leaders in his own time who had become corrupted by power due to the politicization of their positions; in his letter to his student Joseph he stated: "when religion is joined to [political] authority, piety disappears" (Raymond Weiss, *Ethical Writings of Maimonides,* 120).

36. In MT *Laws of Phylacteries, Mezuzah and Scrolls of Torah* 7:2, this extra Torah is described as being "for himself, for the sake of the king, over and above that *sefer* which he already possessed as a commoner." Section 7:1 establishes the obligation common to all Jews to write a Torah scroll.

37. Maimonides combined alcoholic temperance with the mandate of concern for the public welfare, though these two notions are wholly unrelated in the rabbinic sources. The rule of temperance in the rabbinic sources is a universal one and not particularly related to any of the laws governing the king. D. Raffel, *Ha-Rambam Ke-Mehanekh*, 62–64, cites this as an example of a recurrent technique whereby Maimonides associated a certain personality with a particular ethical trait in order to highlight its importance. The rabbinic source promoting general alcoholic temperance cites the same biblical proof-text as Maimonides did for the king (Eccl 31:4). One interpretation of this verse, a highly inventive expansion of the word *lemo'el*, takes it as an admonishment by Bathsheba to Solomon to avoid the company of kings who drink excessively and then say "Why do we need God?" (*b. Sanhedrin* 70b). The idea that Maimonides possibly seized on is that intoxication encourages a self-centeredness to the exclusion of God.

38. See also GP III:48, 601, which considers the Nazirite on the same level as a High Priest as to holiness, because of his avoidance of wine. Levinger, "Abstinence from Alcohol," addresses the contradiction between this position on the Nazirite and that of the MT in *Laws of Ethical Traits* 3:1, which condemns the Nazirite as a premiere example of extreme conduct that violates the golden mean; the discrepancy is explained by the different audiences targeted by the *Guide* and the *Mishneh*.

39. The monarch's subservience to the Torah and its ideals is concretized, for example, in the law granting priority to the performance of a *mitzvah* over the performance of a royal decree when the two are in conflict: "When you are confronted with the words of the master and the words of the slave, the words of the master take precedence, and therefore one need not add that if the royal decree is intended to vitiate a *mitzvah* it is not heeded" (MT *Laws of Kings* 3:9). See also MT *Laws of Rebels* 6:12; *b. Sanhedrin* 29a, 49a.

40. This was a master copy of the Torah kept in the Temple courtyard (*m. Mo'ed Qatan* 3:4; *b. Bava Batra* 14b). According to Rashi it was the master text, transcribed by Moses himself, for all exilic scrolls.

41. Maimonides adopted these conditions for copying the royal Torah from *y. Sanhedrin* 2:6. The Babylonian parallel in *Sanhedrin* 21b omits them.

42. The septennial broadcast of excerpts from the Torah by the king constitutes a public display of the king's allegiance and subservience to God and Torah, "since the king is the emissary for publicizing the words of God" (MT *Laws of the Hagigah Sacrifice* 3:6).

43. A rabbinic source mentioning the three *ketarim* (crowns) is *m. Avot* 4:13. Stuart Cohen, "The Concept of the Three Ketarim," demonstrates that the tradition of the tripartite division of crowns (kingship, priesthood, Torah) encapsulates a rabbinic political theory that militates against the concentration of power in a single individual or body in favor of a diffusion of power among different agencies. The royal Torah is a supreme symbol of this political philosophy because it serves as a constant reminder of a higher authority—the source of the legislation

from which the king's authority derives—and of the fact that the king is no more privy to that higher authority than any of his subjects.

44. The democratization resulting from the study of Torah also ensues because of its ultimate telos—the attainment of human perfection. As H. Kasher has shown (*"Talmud Torah"*), Maimonides' definition of Torah as developed in his *Laws of Studying Torah* incorporates all the necessary prerequisites for that goal, through his unique definition of that section of Torah called Talmud. The latter includes the study of physics and metaphysics. If, then, *talmud torah* is the means by which man cultivates his essential humanity, it must, at least theoretically, be accessible to all. The king's engagement with it then highlights the human form that is common to all men regardless of social status, and is the sole definition of man qua man.

45. In contrast, the *nasi* and the parent may forgo the respect due them: MT *Laws of Studying Torah* 6:4; and *Laws of Rebels* 6:9.

46. In the Islamic tradition, an inviolately transcendent view of the caliph's person endowed his private space with a sacredness that stands in sharp contrast to the concept of the monarch reflected in Maimonides' legal distinction between public and private royal space. "The inviolability of the caliph's private quarters also reflects the sanctification of space . . . [the caliph's] aura rendered it doubly inviolable, almost sacred" (Al-Azmeh, *Muslim Kingship,* 142). In the Christian realm during the Carolingian period, the royal palace was similarly perceived as "a sacred space likened by poets to Solomon's Temple and seen as prefiguring the heavenly Jerusalem" (Nelson, "Kingship and Empire," 219). For Maimonides, the existence of the Temple would help deter the king's office from becoming sanctified in this way, as the Temple was the fixed locus of sacred space.

47. The use of the term "heart" here can accommodate all the metaphorical meanings canvassed by the *Guide* in I:39 devoted to this term: thoughts, opinions, will, and intellect. It is an internalized state of mind (thought, opinion, intellect) that guides the king's dictates (will). This is also captured in the *Guide's* treatment of God's soliloquies that are signified by the phrase "said unto His heart." This is rendered philosophically as "accomplished an act according to His will" (GP I:29, 62); the act is in complete consonance with the will—that is, it is an automatic consequence of His being.

48. This internal/external balance that must be maintained by the king is another example, in the very person of the king, of the tension between an earthly monarchy and a divine monarchy. Blidstein has identified this tension as "the dominant motif of rabbinic opposition to the political institution, whatever the specific historical stimuli may have been" ("The Monarchic Imperative," 17).

49. See also SM Positive Commandment 8.

50. Twersky has shown that *tzahut* (precision and elegance) is the hallmark of the *Mishneh Torah*; in particular, "scriptural references or aggadic allusions which are sure to be resonant . . . are used to entice and teach as well as to add

tonality and intonation" (*Introduction to the Code of Maimonides*, 346–49). Kreisel also notes "a surprising similarity in the writing technique he employs in dealing with philosophical topics" in both his halakhic and philosophical works (*Maimonides' Political Thought*, 264).

51. See Nahmanides on Exod 16:8 ,who compares the "what" *(mah)* of "what are we" to the "what is man that Thou art mindful of him" of Ps 8:5, and "what is man that Thou takest knowledge of him" of Ps 144:3. These are the very verses quoted by the *Guide* in its discussion of divine providence; I suggest they are imported by Maimonides in order to cast some doubt on any apparent endorsement of human individuals' being the subjects of divine providence. Once anthropocentrism is replaced by theocentrism, these verses call into question a simplistic notion of dependence on God and demand further refinement of what divine providence actually entails.

52. For a discussion of this perfection and its analogy in the thought of ibn Bajja, see Altmann, "Maimonides' Four Perfections," 67–68.

53. The battle against anthropocentrism was carried over by Maimonides even to include man's relationship with other species and his environment. For instance, the law against slaughtering an animal and its young on the same day, or that requiring the chasing of the mother bird away before taking its eggs, are sensitive to the emotional pain of the animals (GP III:48). One of the central tenets of the *Guide* is that man cannot determine the ultimate telos of any aspect of creation and therefore can never conclude that something exists for the sake of something else (GP III:25). Adopting this perspective obviates hubris. Silman, commenting on Maimonides and ibn Kaspi, argues that there is in general a tension between "cosmocentric" and "anthropocentric" views in the rabbinic tradition ("Ma'amad Ha-Adam," 346–47).

54. See GP I:1, where the following equation is constructed: image of God *(tzelem elohim)* = human form = intellectual apprehension = *imitatio dei*.

55. In terms of combating anthropocentrism, we may note that the biblical episode that follows the nursemaid image is replete with hints of God's unlimited capacity to provide basic necessities for the people, as opposed to the limited capacity of man. Moses cannot fathom the possibility of supplying the nation with the massive amounts of food it would require (Num 11:21). Moses therefore confuses the ultimate source of this supply. God responds "Is God's power limited?" (v. 23). It is also noteworthy that the spirit with which the seventy elders are endowed was not, strictly speaking, prophetic, but rather falls under Maimonides' second degree of "prophecy": inspirational wisdom "concerning governmental or divine matters" (GP II:45, 398). Since this group was the precursor of the Sanhedrin, this mechanism is also a reminder that adjudicatory pronouncements are not ex cathedra and are therefore fallible. Altmann argues that this is an essential distinction between the Sanhedrin of Judaism and the church of Christianity: "The Sanhedrin is not a 'sacral authority' like the church. . . . It is rather . . . halakhic *agency,* receiving its sanction only through the single fact of being appointed

by the Torah, but not through an actual pneumatic relation to the word of God" ("What Is Jewish Theology?" 46).

56. The memory of Israel's enslavement in Egypt is to be preserved: Deut 5:15, 16:12, 24:18, 22. This memory is particularly useful for the inculcation of humility. See, e.g., GP III:39, 552, which connects the first fruits and Egypt, and III:43, 572, where one is to connect Sukkot and Egypt "so that he should achieve humility and submission."

57. Blidstein quotes other examples where the phrases "according to the opinion of the majority of Israel" and "according to the high court" are used interchangeably ("Individual and Community in the Middle Ages," 247 n. 620). Rabbi J. B. Soloveitchik is credited as the source of this insight (*Qovetz Hiddushe Torah*, vol.II, 51–52).

58. The mutual enslavement of king and people is reflected in the royal power to impose taxation. The obligation to comply with the king's taxation arises from the verse "and you will be slaves to him" (1 Sam 8:17); however, that power is subject to the strict limitations dictated by the rule of law. See MT *Laws of Kings* 4:1; *Laws of Robbery and Loss* 5:12–14.

59. This idea is found biblically in Lev 25:39–40; see also *Sifra, Behar* 7:2; *b. Yevamot* 46a; and *b. Bava Metzia* 73b. The slave reference is also a continuation of the "brother" reference. *Sifra* picks up on the words of Lev 25:39, "And should your brother become impoverished," as indicating that, though he is your slave, he remains your brother and is deserving of brotherly treatment.

60. It is interesting that Joseph Karo ("Kesef Mishneh"), in his explication of MT *Laws of Robbery and Loss* 5:16, links this slave law with the status of slavery resulting from the nonpayment of royal taxes. Maimonides posited that one who pays the tax to the king on behalf of another who is impecunious is entitled to the latter's labor, "but cannot work him like a slave." Karo comments that his predicament is analogous to the "lowly" state described in *Laws of Slaves* 1:7, and thus total serfdom is prohibited; the king's laws cannot result in enslavement. It would seem from the outcome of Rehavam's rejection of the elders' advice that it was precisely a draconian policy of oppressive taxation that led to the disastrous split in the kingdom.

61. For a survey of the term "shepherd" as "one of the oldest appellations for kings in the ancient Near East," see Brettler, *God Is King*, 36–37.

62. The verse is the basis of a midrashic nexus between David's shepherding and Moses as the archetypical pastoral leader in Exod 3:1. Moses' humility is so extreme that it moves him to place an exhausted kid on his shoulders. See *Exod Rabbah* 2:3.

63. It is clear that the possessive suffix refers to God by virtue of verse 62 of Ps 78, as well as such verses as Deut 32:9.

64. In Ps 78 God is first portrayed as a shepherd (v. 52), rendering the concluding shepherding metaphor a model of *imitatio dei*. Keel comments, "According to Ps 78:52–54, Yahweh, like a shepherd, leads his people out of Egypt into

the land of Canaan. At the conclusion of the migration, Yahweh's office of shepherd is transferred, as it were, to David (70–72), a man fetched from the livestock pens.... Ps 78:70–72 makes a point of connecting David's shepherdship in Bethlehem with his shepherdship over Israel and God's shepherdship over His people" (*The Symbolism of the Biblical World,* 230). For other biblical representations of God as shepherd, see Gen 48:15, 49:24; Jer 31:7–9; Ezek 34; Ps 23, 80:2.

65. Brettler, *God Is King,* 37, shows that the metaphorical application of "shepherd" to God as king works to "reverse certain of the typical entailments of the shepherd sub-metaphor"; for example, the shepherd's crook, a symbol of royalty in Mesopotamian art, is an instrument of comfort rather than oppression in Ps 80:4.

66. The figure of the mortal king is ultimately, for Maimonides, the model for behavior vis-à-vis God. Since the king commands great reverence, "he who chooses to achieve human perfection and to be in true reality a *man of God* must give heed and know that the great king who always accompanies him and cleaves to him is greater than any human individual, even if the latter be David and Solomon" (GP III:52, 629). The king is useful insofar as he directs one's mind toward the Supreme King.

67. Given the importance of "lowly class" for understanding extreme humility, as I have argued, it is likely not mere coincidence that Maimonides illustrated the rabbinic use of the term *middot* for God's attributes with an example from *m. Avot* 5:12–13: "There are four characteristics [*middot*] among those who give charity."

68. Rosenberg notes a distinction between the *Mishneh*'s discussion of the *de'ot,* which is "directed to people in general," and that of the *Guide,* which "encompasses the quality of judgment as well, in the context of the need to guide leaders" ("You Shall Walk in His Ways," 8 n. 21). Though I would agree, my analysis leads ultimately to the collapsing of this distinction.

69. Even the expression of an emotion such as hate can be an act of *imitatio dei;* see Stern's explanation, with respect to the nation of Amalek, of the mechanics of hate, which the king in particular must inspire in his subjects in preparation for battle ("Maimonides on Amalek," 394–99).

70. Kaplan, in his analysis of this state, argues convincingly that Moses' "authorship" of the Law constitutes an act of *imitatio dei* par excellence, in that Mosaic Law "is a perfect imitation in political terms of the ideal cosmic law cognized by Moses. Through this act of legislation Moses governs the people, his political governance of the community imitating God's divine cosmic governance of man" ("'I Sleep, But My Heart Waketh,'" 139–40).

71. "Since the Creator is referred to by those terms which constitute the middle way in which we are obligated to walk, this path is called the "way of God *[derekh YHVH].*" The verse from which the command of *imitatio dei* is derived is "And you shall walk in His ways" (Deut 28:9), which Maimonides equates with the "median" *(benonim)* characteristics (MT *Laws of Ethical Traits* 1:5). Therefore, the "way of God" refers to those "ways" of Deut 28:9.

72. Rosenzweig incisively comments that it is precisely a moment of humiliation that brings to David, "who just then is for the first and only time in his life addressed as 'Messiah' (2 Sam 19:22), the realization that he is finally and in truth 'king over Israel' (19:23)" (*Ninety-Two Poems and Hymns,* 167).

73. For a comprehensive analysis of Maimonides' conception of the Messianic period and its normative significance, see Ravitzky, "'To the Utmost Human Capacity.'"

74. For similar descriptions of the utopian messianic polity, see GP II:29, 341; III:11, 441; PM *Eduyot* 8:12; and introduction to "Pereq Heleq" in Halkin, "Sanhedrin; Treatise on Resurrection," 222–23. Kraemer asserts that "Maimonides perceived a correlation between normalcy, tranquility, political freedom and relief from the burdens of Exile on the one hand and intellectual splendor on the other" ("On Maimonides' Messianic Posture," 139).

75. I do not mean here that the office of the king will become vacant during the messianic period, but only that the ideal king is one who presides over a kingdom in which there are no political concerns, only religious/philosophical ones. Weiler similarly argues that the messianic kingdom is not a "sovereign" one but a "holy" one. The state of universal political calm is considered by him to be nothing short of miraculous and he thus concludes, "The Messianic age, although politically conceived, serves no political ideal" (*Jewish Theocracy,* 161).

76. According to Nahmanides (commentary to Deut 17:20), the general stricture against haughtiness is derived from the specific biblical warning addressed to the king not to allow his "heart to be elevated . . . for Scripture prohibited even the king from indulging in conceit and haughtiness of heart, surely other people who are not of such commendable excellence are forbidden."

77. Levinas, *Beyond the Verse,* 181. On this statement of Levinas, I quote a most perceptive comment by an anonymous reader of this chapter: "The 'double life' which Levinas mentions here isn't simply the double life of war and Torah, but also the double life of the practical and the theoretical aspects of human perfection, in which the individual (by virtue of extirpating psychological characteristics) can simultaneously contemplate God and govern." See also Kreisel, *Maimonides' Political Thought.*

Chapter 5 The Sage/Philosopher

1. The letter forms an integral part of all standard editions of the *Guide* and can be found separately both in Judeo-Arabic and Hebrew translations in Iggerot, 246–53, and in Baneth's edition of *Iggerot Ha-Rambam,* 6–9. Baneth identified this Joseph as Joseph b. Judah ibn Shimon and not, as was long held, ibn Aknin, author of a commentary on the Song of Songs. My analysis follows Pines' English translation in GP, titled the "Epistle Dedicatory."

2. Heschel, "Did Maimonides Believe," discusses this letter and the relationship between Maimonides and Joseph. Heschel concludes that it was Maimonides' intention to "endow him [Joseph] with his own spirit and bring him under the wings of prophecy" (168).

3. For halakhic restrictions on both the explicit and public teaching of the "Account of the Creation" and "Account of the Chariot" see *m. Hagigah* 2:1 and Maimonides' commentary to it in PM. See also his comments in GP Intro., 6; I:17, 42; I:32; I:33, 72; II:29, 347; and Introduction to part III, 415, on the necessity for "flash pedagogy." See also MT *Laws of the Foundations of the Torah* 2:12; 4:10–13.

4. The perplexity is a stark choice of either "renounc[ing] the foundation of the Law" or "turning his back" on his intellect, bringing "loss to himself and harm to his religion."

5. The attainment of knowledge, according to Maimonides, is followed by an overwhelming and irresistible compulsion to share that knowledge. See, e.g., GP II:29, 347: "inasmuch as the divine commandment necessarily obliges everyone who has obtained a certain perfection to let it overflow toward others . . . every man endowed with knowledge . . . must indubitably say something." In II:37, 373–74, this phenomenon is a consequence of the measure of divine overflow, which "overflows from rendering him perfect toward rendering others perfect." An unbroken chain of transmission would thereby seem to be naturally guaranteed.

6. This is how Scott, *Proverbs, Ecclesiastes*, 256, understands *tiqqen*.

7. Gordis' rendering is "fashioning many proverbs" (*Koheleth*, 190); and at 340, "composing original contributions to this literature."

8. It would seem that the obscurity of the subject matter and the limitations of the human mind necessitate the use of the parable both for the multitude and the perfect, who understand it according to their capacity. See GP Intro., 9, which endorses the midrashic rationale for biblical parables, since "it is impossible to tell mortals of the power of the Account of the Beginning. For this reason Scripture tells you obscurely."

9. Here I wholly endorse Strauss' formulation in his introduction to GP that "[t]he *Guide* is then devoted above all to biblical exegesis (xiv)."

10. All the classical medieval commentators (Efodi, Shem Tov, Abravanel) point out that during Maimonides' face-to-face relationship with Joseph, the thought of writing down his teaching never even occurred to him. For Maimonides, at least, a text is a last resort, when live encounter is no longer possible. Faur, in a fascinating analysis of this introductory letter, states that the nature of esoteric teachings actually requires the physical absence of the student to be properly transmitted, so that a proper horizontal transference of knowledge can be effected: "Therefore, the absence of the student was not only a stimulus, but rather a condition sine qua non, for producing the *Guide*" ("The Character of Apophatic Knowledge," 71).

11. Nuriel's study ("The Use of the Term *Garib*") of the Arabic term, which can mean either "strange" or "wondrous," demonstrates that Maimonides consistently employed the term throughout the *Guide* to convey both senses.

12. See Ricoeur, "Biblical Hermeneutics," 29–145, 78.

13. Pines notes in the *Guide* (n. 59) that "religious community" means "the Jewish community."

14. Here Maimonides prefigured the Zohar, which cast itself ostensibly as ancient rabbinic tradition while winking its radical innovativeness at its mystically proficient audience. The paradoxical zoharic idiom "new old things" *(millin haditin atiqim)* can be equally applied to the *Guide*. See Matt, "*Matnita Dilan*."

15. No better evidence of this tension between the burden of community involvement, professional responsibility, and the yearning for solitude can be produced than the letter Maimonides wrote to ibn Tibbon outlining his daily routine. On a fine attempt to resolve the paradox of how Maimonides philosophically advocated an ideal life of contemplative solitude and yet lived a life thoroughly dedicated to the community, see S. Harvey, "Maimonides in the Sultan's Palace." Harvey offers the practical solution that Maimonides' work schedule and duties at the sultan's palace afforded him the opportunity to pursue the kind of solitude he preached.

16. Maimonides seems to be advocating a life of extreme asceticism that is at odds with the negative attitudes he expressed elsewhere in his writings toward asceticism (e.g., chapter 4 of his "Eight Chapters"). On these apparently contradictory positions, see Kreisel's discussion in *Maimonides' Political Thought*, 175–82.

17. See, e.g., ibn Bajja's reference in his *Governance of the Solitary* to perfected individuals as "strangers" in their own countries while their minds are at home elsewhere, "for although they are in their homelands and among their companions and neighbors, the Sufis say that these are strangers in their opinions, having traveled in their minds to other stations that are like homelands to them" (trans. by Berman, 128).

18. GP Intro., 16.

19. I adopt the logic of the Jewish Publication Society's translation, which has "the Lord" as the object of the remnant's calling ("Anyone who invokes the Lord will be among the survivors"), although its meaning is acknowledged as "uncertain." This is consistent with the way I believe Maimonides would have understood it, as evidenced by my analysis. The major medieval commentators such as Rashi, Radak, and ibn Ezra take "the Lord" to be the subject of the sentence, who respectively "invites," "decrees," and "honors" the remnants. Isaac Abravanel is one medieval commentator who anticipated the JPS by suggesting, as an alternative reading, the *Lord* as object.

20. See Baneth, *Iggerot Ha-Rambam*, 51.

21. See MT *Laws of Idolatry*, chap. 1.

22. Abraham's calling "in the name of the Lord, God of the World" is a reference to Gen 21:33, whose significance to Maimonides cannot be overstated; it is

employed as the epigraph for not only the GP but virtually all his writings, as noted by Lieberman in his *Hilkhot Yerushalmi,* 5 n. 7. See also Kafih's comments in his Hebrew translation of the *Guide* (*Moreh Ha-Nevukhim,* vol. 1, 1 n. 1) that this exhibits Maimonides' own perception of the *Guide* as a continuation of the "call" begun by Abraham.

23. See the portraits drawn of Abraham and Moses as the premier iconoclasts of their age in the first chapter of MT *Laws of Idolatry.*

24. Seeskin, in *Searching for a Distant God,* provides a probing account of the implications of this theology based on a fundamental dichotomy between "God and everything else."

25. In some ways, Maimonides' students are asked to adopt the stance of what J. B. Soloveitchik, in *Lonely Man of Faith,* classifies as "Adam" in his typological study of the different human beings represented by the two contradictory creation accounts of Adam in Gen 1 and 2.

26. Maimonides' references to Joel 3:5 in his other writings import a sense of a constricted social sphere and/or solitude. It is cited in the introduction to MT, at the end of tracing the history of the Oral Law's chain of transmission, to convey the aggravated state of Israel's exile and dispersion after Rav Ashi's generation, when rabbinic academies no longer attracted large numbers and rabbinic scholarship remained the province of "the remnant who call the Lord." In his *Epistle to Yemen,* exile, subjugation, and religious persecution are rationalized as means of ferreting out the stalwart Jews ("the remnant") who are entitled to lay claim to their ancestral heritage (Jacob; Sinai) because of their unflinching faith.

27. For the primordial existence of YHVH, see *Pirqe de-Rabbi Eliezer* 3 as quoted in I:61 of GP.

28. The talmudic source for these categories of *torah* is b. *Qiddushin* 30a. For Maimonides' innovative remodeling of this tripartite division of Torah, study see H. Kasher, "*Talmud Torah* as a Means of Apprehending God."

29. For a discussion of these laws, see Twersky, *Introduction to the Code of Maimonides,* 489–500. He characterizes these laws as together an "axial statement . . . capable of working a silent revolution in Jewish intellectual history" (489). Twersky adopts Hyamson's translation (*Mishneh Torah,* 58a) of the phrase *rohav libbo* as "breadth of mind," with which I am basically in agreement. For a biblical example of this term as indicating a broad expanse of intellect, see 1 Kgs 5:9, which describes Solomon's supreme wisdom. However, I do not think Hyamson's "maturity of intellect" captures the sense of *yiššuv da'at.* In MT *Laws of the Foundations of the Torah* 4:13, this is a quality that is attained through the study of the Oral Law (discussions of Abaye and Rava) that is universally accessible to "all, young and old, men and women, those who possess intellectual breadth and those whose intellects are limited." This quality, then, cannot possibly denote intellectual capacity. Appropriately, but inconsistently, Hyamson renders the phrase in this latter passage as "composure to the mind."

30. Proverbs 21:4 pairs broadmindedness *(rehav lev)* with "haughty eyes" as characteristic of the wicked. Gersonides, I believe, offers a thoroughly Maimonidean interpretation of this verse. According to him, the term "haughty eyes" signifies a blindness to the limits of human intelligence caused by intellectual capability *(rehav lev)*, which deceives the scholar into pursuing subjects that he cannot fathom.

31. On Maimonides' construct of Elisha/Aher's supreme intellectual arrogance, see chapter 3.

32. My use of the term "sage" in this chapter refers loosely to various classes of perfected individuals including philosophers and prophets who, while they may not be identical, share in some form of intellectual perfection. See, e.g., Kreisel, "The Sage and the Prophet," 158, who concludes that the paramount characteristic of the prophet is "the ultimate perfection of the intellect."

33. The very placement of the laws governing the teaching of Torah in the first book of the MT, *Book of Knowledge (Sefer Ha-Madda)*, reflects this. *Laws of the Foundations of the Torah* identifies the subject matter of physics and metaphysics, the ultimate disciplines of all academic study. This area of study is primarily self-perfecting and inward. The danger of self-centeredness is offset by *Laws of Ethical Traits* that follows, concentrating on the ethics of relating to others, a reminder that man is a social animal. Once the sage who has grasped the foundations of the Torah is cognizant of his living among others, he will become aware of his duty to impart his knowledge to others; thus the laws governing the study and teaching of Torah follow on the heels of the laws of foundations and of ethical traits. B. Cohen, "The Classification of the Law," 533, attributes this order of classification to the influence of Islam, which frequently includes the study of theology and science under the rubric of *'Ilm* (knowledge), the equivalent of *madda*. His historical thesis does not preclude my own rationale.

34. See also Maimonides' formulation of this *mitzvah* as Positive Commandment 11 in SM, 65.

35. On this feature, see Feintuch, *Sefer Ha-Mitzvot*, 152, for a discussion of Positive Commandment 11; he attributes the combination to Maimonides' eleventh principle for enumerating commandments, which is to combine *halakhot* that share in the same telos. Of interest here is Kafih's observation that both SM and MT posit teaching prior to learning.

36. The only circumstance for Maimonides that calls for a completely hermetic life is when society is thoroughly corrupt and coerces its citizens to participate in its corruption. Only then is the sage obligated to abandon society altogether for a life of solitude in caves or deserts (MT *Laws of Ethical Traits* 6:1).

37. Maimonides based this on the fact that among the four characteristics "pure and upright, who feared God, and turned away from evil," wisdom is missing. What is translated by Pines (GP III:22, 487) as "extraordinary" is the same term translated as "strange" in the introductory epistle to Joseph. See Nuriel,

"The Use of the Term *Garib.*" These are the types of biblical texts that particularly exercised Maimonides and his student during their study sessions.

38. The biblical proof-text for this is Gen 8:21, and a midrashic source is *Gen Rabbah* 34:10. For a comprehensive treatment of *Satan* in the *Guide,* see Nuriel, "The Concept of Satan"; he identifies three different Satans, all expressing different traits of matter.

39. Every mention of the "evil inclination" within a halakhic context in the MT is associated with the sexual urge. See *Laws of Marital Status* 24:9; *Laws of Forbidden Intercourse* 1:9; *Laws of Kings* 8:4; related to this last law, see GP III:41, 567. Since man is born with this tendency it needs to be reined in from birth. *Possibly* the most important rationale for circumcision is that "it weakens the faculty of sexual excitement . . . for if at birth this member has been made to bleed and has had its covering taken away from it, it must indubitably be weakened" (GP III:49, 609). I stress *possibly* since Maimonides offered another rationale that may be paramount: it is a mark of a covenant that "imposes the obligation to believe in the unity of God" (ibid., 610). On this, see Stern, "Maimonides on the Covenant of Circumcision," and his later reformulation on the same issue in *Problems and Parables of Law.*

40. Those who possess knowledge based solely on tradition, even if it is correct knowledge, occupy the lower end of the hierarchy in terms of the palace parable in GP III:51, 619; they wander around the palace precinct but never gain entry. Abraham is the founder of Judaism, so to speak, precisely because he broke with tradition, family, upbringing, and schooling—everything established religion considers sacrosanct—as a result of his reasoned passion for the truth. This is perhaps Abraham's greatest legacy. See MT *Laws of Idolatry,* chap. 1. Maimonides played with midrashic portrayals of Abraham to construct an ancient, New-Eastern Socrates willing to sacrifice everything for the truth. See also Turner, "The Portrayal of Abraham," who concludes that Maimonides followed in the path of the biblical and midrashic idealizations of Abraham "when he is portrayed as the archetype of all philosophers and the teacher of Aristotle."

41. Maimonides did consider knowledge conveyed by traditional authority to be a pragmatic method of spreading at least a semblance of true knowledge among the general populace, since the lengthy preliminary studies needed for true knowledge would be prohibitive and "lead to all people dying without having known whether there is a deity for the world, or whether there is not" (GP I:34, 75). Knowledge gained in this way is better than nothing, but is far inferior to grasping an "essence as it truly is" (GP I:33, 71). For a discussion of the usefulness of "tradition" and its Islamic counterpart *(taqlid),* see MN-S, vol.1, 76 n. 7.

42. Regarding the talmudic debate between R. Yohanan and Resh Laqish concerning the meaning of this verse (*b. Sanhedrin* 111a), Maimonides followed the latter, who takes the verse literally as referring to the miniscule number of exiles who will return to Zion. For R. Yohanan the verse is more compassionate, in that redemption comes to the many as a result of the merit of the few.

43. The rabbinic tradition attributed this Egyptian taboo to the fact that the Egyptians considered the animals of herdsmen to be their gods. See, e.g., Rashi's comment on this verse as well as on Exod 8:22. From a modern scholarly perspective this is highly questionable. See, e.g., Alter's comment on Gen 46:34 (*Genesis,* 278).

44. Maimonides' talmudic support for this is *b. Berakhot* 33b. Here, as is the norm, Maimonides relied on rabbinic sources, but, as always, with his own unique twist. For example, there is a talmudic position (*b. Megillah* 18a) that declares that "any one who praises God excessively will be uprooted from the world." Rashi, the nonphilosophical traditionalist, comments that since one is bound to miss some praise worthy of God, it is better to conform strictly to the rabbinic parameters of prayer than to omit possibilities through prayers of one's own. Rashi's position is that one can never exhaust all linguistic possibilities with respect to extolling God. Maimonides, on the other hand, considered all language applicable to God as inherently false and therefore defamatory. In addition, Rashi considers Ps 65:2 to be affirming the virtue of silence in general, not just with respect to God.

45. Kafih, in his edition of the *Guide (Moreh Ha-Nevukhim)*, I:59, n. 31, points to a parallel adage in Ghazali's works and a similar expression of this idea in Maimonides' introduction in PM to *Avot,* chap. 8 ("Eight Chapters"). According to Munk, another version of this can be found in Bahya ibn Pakudah's *Duties of the Heart,* chapter 10 of the section entitled "Gate of Unity."

46. On the essential paradox of this negative conception of God, particularly with respect to the light imagery, see Faur, "The Character of Apophatic Knowledge," 68–69. According to Faur there is in fact a double paradox: (1) understanding God lies precisely in understanding that He cannot be understood; and (2) such knowledge in turn cannot be communicated.

47. It is instructive here to contrast a kabbalistic approach that can live with positive God-talk and does not require a total disengagement into unmitigated silence. It does so by balancing the paradoxical tension between apophatic *en sof* and kataphatic *sefirot.* For a lucid presentation of this theosophic, approach see Wolfson, "Negative Theology and Positive Assertion." The contrast to Maimonides' rigorous apophasis is particularly vivid in the kabbalist's prayer posture, which Wolfson sums up as "this paradox that opens the Infinite in the heart of the mystic in the moment of visual contemplation through prayer or Torah study. That opening, in turn, floods the mystic's heart with knowledge of the Godhead" (xxii).

48. Even the first two commandments apparently heard by the entire assembly were not heard in the same way Moses heard them (GP II:33, 365). Maimonides seems to have ruled out any experience of collective revelation since prophecy is a factor of individual human perfection. For different mediaeval approaches to the enigma of the Sinaitic theophany, see Regev, "Collective Revelation and Mount Sinai."

49. For an excellent philosophical attempt to demonstrate that Maimonides' conception of prayer straddles the two opposing spiritual objectives of "the noeticity of contemplation and the ordinariness of dialogic of supplication," see Benor, *Worship of the Heart*, 7.

50. Maimonides' historical account of the rabbinic standardization of prayer presented in his MT traces its evolution from an individualistic to a communal spirituality. See *Laws of Prayer* 1:2–5 and Benor's analysis, *Worship of the Heart*, 110 and 218 n. 102: "Scriptural open-ended prayer, which is expressive of the spiritual ability of the individual, disappears, and a formalized rabbinic prayer takes its place. In rabbinic prayer, then, individuals participate in a worship that is essentially public." In my account the sage must suppress this public dimension. Every designated prayer time signals a struggle by the sage to resist falling prey to its public display of anthropomorphic notions of God even while participating in it.

51. Stern, "Maimonides on Language and the Science of Language," 202, sees this passage as drawing a distinction not between speech utterance and the total absence of any speech, "but between two types of language or representational systems corresponding to the distinction between external and internal speech . . . 'silence' does not refer to the vacuous state of mind but to representations of the mind." The medieval commentator Shem Tov also describes this silence in his comment on this passage as an "internal speech" *(dibbur penimi)*.

52. Blumenthal, "Maimonides: Prayer, Worship and Mysticism," 95, cogently argues that this plane of thought is a postcognitive devotion to God that is "completely post-intellectual, post ratiocinative." See also Blumenthal, "Maimonides' Intellectualist Mysticism," where he argues that Maimonides considered one of the aspects of Moses' superiority to be mystical and experiential in addition to intellectual.

53. Lerner, "Maimonides' Governance of the Solitary," 44–46, points out that the *Guide* never characterizes the solitary's involvement with others as a duty; rather, "a profound human understanding leads the perfect one to re-enter the world of practice." This translates in the Maimonidean corpus as a combination of the *Guide*'s concern for the few and the MT's concern for the community, which for Lerner "are alike instances of a most singular human *hesed*, one that might rightly be called pure worship of the noblest kind."

54. This is Aristotle's formulation of the object of divine contemplation in *Metaphysics*, bk. 12, chap. 9. That Maimonides subscribed to this notion of divine thought is no more clearly formulated than, of all places, in his legal code, the *Mishneh Torah*, in which he states that God knows all of creation "since he knows only himself." See *Laws of the Foundations of the Torah* 2:10.

55. Shiffman, *Moreh Ha-Moreh*, 325, on III:51 of the *Guide*. The English translation is taken from Jospe, "Rejecting Moral Virtue as the Ultimate End," 194. Jospe shows how Falaquera took Maimonides' position on intellectual perfection as the summum bonum to a logical extreme of asceticism and solitude. However,

even if Maimonides did not advocate the same form of asceticism, this assessment of the sage's predicament can be legitimately applied to his ideal sage.

56. See GP II:4, 259: "All spheres are living bodies, endowed with a soul and an intellect, having a mental representation and an apprehension of the deity and also a mental representation of their own first principles." See also MT *Laws of the Foundations of the Torah* 3:9, where the emphasis is on their praise of God. Maimonides ascribes his scheme of spheres and intellects to Aristotle, though its proponents are the Arabic Aristotelians and in particular Avicenna. See Davidson, *Alfarabi, Avicenna and Averroes on Intellect,* 197–99.

57. On this, see the discussion of Klein-Braslavy, *King Solomon and Philosophical Esotericism,* 168–69 and esp. n. 24.

58. See GP II:11, 275, where this relationship between God and the lower intellects strikingly parallels that between philosophers, prophets, and their disciples described in II:37: "For the overflow coming from Him for the bringing into being of separate intellects overflows likewise from these intellects so that one of them brings another into being."

59. The talmudic identification between children and students in *b. Sanhedrin* 19b is deduced from another biblical source.

60. See GP I:2, in which Adam's becoming an *elohim* as a result of his sin is interpreted in the sense of "rulers governing cities."

61. Kafih suggests that the specific "texts" he is referring to here within a Jewish context are those on which the Rabad of Posquieres relied in his gloss to MT *Laws of Repentance* 3:6. There Rabad cites biblical and rabbinic texts that justify, indeed promote, anthropomorphic conceptions of God. See Kafih, *Moreh Ha-Nevukhim,* n. 20 to I:31 and n. 38 to I:36.

62. Maimonides' explicitly endorsed rabbinic source is *Sifre Deut, Eqev*. It also appears in *b. Ketubbot* 111b. For a slightly different formulation of this commandment that poses the sage strictly as an ethical role model rather than both ethical and intellectual in SM, see MT *Laws of Ethical Traits* 6:2.

63. See Maimonides' letter to R. Phineas ben Meshullam, where he attributed his omission of sources to the kind of treatise he wished to compose—a code *(hibbur)* rather than a commentary *(perush)*. He also indicated his intentions (never realized) to write a companion volume that would supply the sources for his MT. The letter is quoted and discussed in Twersky, *Introduction to the Code of Maimonides,* 30–37. See his remark on 60 that the MT's "awesome erudition is masked not only by the decision to omit footnotes and source references, as required by the codificatory form, but also by the general thrust and tenor which determined that the constructive elements be greater than the critical ones." What I am doing here can be described as an attempt to determine the "constructive element" in a decision to cite a rabbinic source, normally considered as inimical to the goals of a legal code.

64. The clearest formulation of this is offered in MT *Laws of Repentance* 10:2, as the definition of true love for God. Paragraph 5 of that same chapter ac-

knowledges the political usefulness of teaching the public through anticipation of reward and fear of punishment.

65. This notion is maintained throughout Maimonides' lexicography in the *Guide*. For one vivid example, see I:19, 45, on the terms "approaching," "coming near," and "touching," which substitutes knowledge for space as a means of gaining proximity to God, "for nearness to Him, may He be exalted, consists in apprehending Him; and remoteness from Him is the lot of him who does not know Him."

66. See also Tosafot on this passage, who adopt Rashi's position. For a list of alternative interpretations of this rule, see Meiri's novellas on *b. Megillah* 25b, which cites five different views: (i) Rashi's; (ii) Maimonides'; (iii) the reader cannot be accompanied by the cantor; (iv) no other verses can be joined to these; (v) their recital is reserved for outstanding individuals (reading the term *yahid* as "unique" rather than one or alone).

67. Levinger, *Maimonides' Techniques of Codification*, 95–96. Levinger raises the possibility that Maimonides' formulation allows the reader to choose the option of Joshuan authorship, though he did not want to be explicit about this for fear of opening a Pandora's box with respect to Mosaic authorship in general; see 96 n. 24. Levinger cites this law as one example of how Maimonides combines innovation with loyalty to his rabbinic sources.

68. For a "rational" understanding of the midrashic tradition that Moses buried himself (see, e.g., Rashi on Deut 34:6), see Abraham ibn Ezra on ibid. For a Maimonidean perspective on this *midrash*, which extends the mind/body divide I have presented here to its most logical extreme, see Seforno's rationalization of Deut 34:6, which has Moses' separated intellect inter his now intellectually vacated body.

69. There is even a halakhic rule regarding the maximum permissible length of mourning, derived from the account of the mourning period subsequent to Moses' death. See MT *Laws of Mourning* 13:10.

70. Michael Fishbane describes this ecstatic death by the divine "kiss" as a "poetical way" of talking about the consummation of spiritual *eros* as the death of the earthly self," in his comprehensive study of spiritual death in Judaism (*The Kiss of God*, 26).

71. David Kimhi's understanding of this verse follows suit.

72. *Enneads,* VI.9. Armstrong translates it as "escape in solitude to the solitary," which captures better the sense of Maimonides' Moses in his face-to-face state.

73. The application of this verse to Adam is based on *Gen Rabbah* 21:4. See also W. Z. Harvey, "The Rambam on Job 14:20."

74. See Berman, "Maimonides on the Fall of Man," 8, where he characterizes Adam's fall as one that moves him from being a philosopher and a "solitary thinker" to "becoming a ruler of cities being informed by the imagination only." Pertinent to my argument here is Berman's comment in n. 22 that "Adam and

Moses were identical, the difference being that Adam, before the fall, represents the ideal for man, not living in society, while Moses represents the ideal for man living in society." What I believe the concluding verses of Deuteronomy represented for Maimonides is that Moses lived with pre-fall Adam in his mind and lived with his people only in his body.

75. See Nahmanides' critique of this position in his commentary to Deut 34:11. For him it is not the numbers but the caliber and staying power of the miracles themselves that have no equal.

76. My purpose in this chapter is not to enter into the much-debated issue as to whether Maimonides considered intellectual or political activity to be the summum bonum. Whichever side of the debate one supports, however, I believe that teaching is an integral component of human perfection. For but a sampling of two aspects of the debate, see Pines, "The Limitations of Human Knowledge" (political), and the sustained critique of this position by Davidson, "Maimonides on Metaphysical Knowledge."

77. What precisely Maimonides' position was with respect to miracles is not easy to determine. For some, Maimonides' statements that seem to endorse a traditional divine interventionist view of miracles are for popular consumption while his naturalistic view is the esoteric one intended for a philosophic audience. See, e.g., Reines, "Maimonides' Concept of Miracles." Others have argued that various positions can live together in a dialectic of religion and philosophy; see, e.g., Nehorai, "Maimonides on Miracles."

78. For this phrase and whom it contemplates, see *b. Shabbat* 11a, which includes Shimon bar Yohai and his comrades in this class. For what distinguishes this "profession" from others, see *b. Qiddushin* 82a–b. For a discussion of the halakhic parameters of this designation and whether it implies the study of Torah to the exclusion of any other gainful employment, see Septimus, "'Kings, Angels or Beggars,'" 322 n. 46.

79. Septimus, ibid., cites Nahmanides, who considered the designation "Torah is his profession" to apply to the one who makes "the study of Torah his primary occupation and his secular profession incidental."

80. Here Maimonides qualified the professional Torah scholar not as one "not engaged in any occupation whatsoever" (MT *Laws of Prayer* 6:8), but rather as one "who constantly engages in Torah study and whose Torah is his profession."

81. For a survey of the mishnaic and talmudic sources and description of this festivity, see Tabory, *Jewish Festivals,* 194–98. See also Rubenstein's discussion in *The History of Sukkot,* 131–52.

82. This phrase has been variously interpreted to refer to either exceptional moral qualities or miracle workers. Considering that the phrase appears in relation to Hanina ben Dosa, a known miracle worker, in *m. Sotah* 9:15, it is likely that its mishnaic sense is miracle workers. However, Maimonides would more than likely have appropriated it as a reference to some moral/intellectual qualities. See also Safrai, "Pious and Men of Deeds."

83. Twersky, *Introduction to the Code of Maimonides*, 176–87, lists this law as one of eight examples of what he calls "exegetical-expository facets of the *Mishneh Torah*."

84. According to Rubenstein, *The History of Sukkot*, 135, the classical rabbinic sources "rabbinize" the celebration by placing the rabbinic sages at the forefront and relegating the priests to idle bystanders. Maimonides continued this process of shaping the celebration in his own image and "intellectualizing" it. See also Blidstein, "The Concept of Joy," 158–60; he raises the possibility that Maimonides restricted this festivity to the elite since it was the kind of joy that was preparatory to prophecy and, therefore, out of reach of the common man.

85. Philo, despite subscribing to a rigidly apothatic God, attributed perfect joy *(chara)*—in the sense of an elevated, unchanging, rational joy—to God. The rationalization of joy was not unprecedented.

86. For a good discussion of what he calls "the thick texture of joy in Jewish theology," ranging from Maimonides' formulation here to Rabbi Nahman of Bratzlav in the eighteenth century, see Fishbane, "The Inwardness of Joy."

87. One of the major medieval kabbalists, Bahya ben Asher, took this to its logical extreme and interpreted the particle *akh* in the biblical command "to be *exceptionally [akh]* joyous" in its halakhic exclusionary sense to mean that the only legitimate forum for expressing joy is in the service of God. I do not believe that Maimonides would have been offended by this exegetical move. See this position as quoted by Fishbane, "The Inwardness of Joy," 75. For a similar view of joy in a halakhic context, see the *Responsa of Radbaz (R. David abi ibn Zimra)*, pt. 1, n. 434. He asserts that physicality is not the measure of "joy'" for halakhic purposes; he therefore rules that when circumcising a child of a forced convert a blessing that is restricted to joyous events is still required, despite the obvious pain of circumcision, since "joy is only of the heart."

88. Nahmanides applies the same logic in his comment on Deut 17:20, which obligates the king to keep a Torah (*mishneh torah* to be precise) with him at all times "to prevent his heart from *becoming lofty over his brothers.*" He derives the general rule against haughtiness from this particular one by way of an a fortiori argument, "for Scripture prohibited even the king from indulging in conceit and haughtiness of heart, surely [it would prohibit] other people who are not of such commendable excellence."

89. See a list of the various gymnastic and juggling feats performed by great rabbinic scholars in *b. Sukkah* 53a. By quoting Deut 28:47, in mandating joy as an essential ingredient of all religious devotion, Maimonides also imported a standard of civility that must govern all such festive occasions. The same verse is cited as demanding moderation in celebrating the joy of the festivals that runs the danger of turning into frivolous excess. This verse imposes restraints on the limits of joy, which must not deteriorate into "frivolity, lightheadedness, or inebriation" (MT *Laws of Holiday Repose* 6:20). Not only do the scholars exemplify

boundless joy, they also set the standard for its legitimate expression guided by restraint.

90. See the instruments listed in 2 Sam 6:5 and of course David's own gyrations in verse 16.

91. Muffs, *Love and Joy,* 126–28 and n. 33 on 135–36, has shown that in certain biblical contexts, understood correctly by the later Rabbis, the term *simhah* (joy) is "an expression of inner uncoerced willingness." This is precisely the type of joy experienced by the sage who has intellectually matured to the point that his performance of commandments flows naturally and not as a result of command and religious obligation.

92. The two halakhic formulations that are the subject of the excurses further develop Kreisel's well-developed thesis that for Maimonides the perfection of the individual and the perfection of society are not competing but are rather complementary goals. He demonstrates that when viewed in this way the numerous contradictions in the Maimonidean corpus can be reconciled in a coherent and unified ethical theory that is multifaceted (*Maimonides' Political Thought,* chap. 5).

93. The rabbinic sources for this are *b. Shabbat* 30b; *b. Pesahim* 117a. Maimonides also discussed sadness and worry as obstacles to prophecy, due to their weakening impact on the faculty most critical to prophecy's engagement—the imaginative. It is important to note that according to Maimonides, the cessation of prophecy was not due to some divine edict but was rather a natural consequence of Jewish statelessness. Exile is not conducive to happiness. See GP II:36, 373, and PM "Eight Chapters," chap. 7.

94. Maimonides specifically defined this phrase in the *Guide* when discussing the meaning of the term "child" *(ben).* Since giving birth can be a metaphor for the relationship between a teacher and student, "prophet's disciples were called the *sons of prophets*" (I:7, 32).

95. Though the classical Rabbis filled the religious vacuum left by the destruction of the Temple with Torah study, Maimonides, given his historical anthropological account of the rationale for the sacrificial cult, viewed this historical cause and effect in reverse sequence. Intellectual activity was always the ideal, and the sacrificial cult was introduced as a corrective to deterioration in right thinking. For an analysis of the rabbinic strategy to replace sacrifice with Torah study, see Anderson, "The Expression of Joy." He characterizes the rabbinic association of joy with Torah study as "such a fixed entity in the rabbinic imagination that it assumes ritual significance" (247).

96. Kaufman, *Toledot Ha-Emunah Ha-Yisraelit,* vol. 4, 324, dates this assembly to the year 444 BCE; he sees it as the culmination of years of grappling and searching for new expressions of Jewish worship and practice subsequent to the cataclysmic upheavals of the destruction of the first Temple, the ensuing Babylonian exile, and the eventual return and rebuilding under Persian hegemony.

97. See Lev 23:24–25; Num 29:1.

98. This probably refers to selections from the Pentateuch. According to Myers it would have been extracts from the "latest recension of the Pentateuch." See his commentary, *Ezra, Nehemiah*, 153.

99. These key terms inundate the chapter. See vv. 2–3, 7–9, 12–13.

100. The verse can be read as referring not to three different groups, but to one group whose members possess a certain intellectual maturity. Gersonides in his commentary to this verse reads it this way.

101. One of the metaphorical senses of the term "hear" *(shamoa)* is knowledge and "apprehension," in GP I:45, 96.

102. See also Rashi's comment that the Levites were engaged in translation.

103. On this as a primary source for Maimonides' universalism, see Kellner, *Maimonides on Judaism*, 74–75.

104. See Kaufman, *Toledot Ha-Emunah Ha-Yisraelit*, vol. XX, 326, who makes the similar observation that this chapter is entirely devoid of ritual except for the Torah recital. He comments, "There is no mention of any blast *(teruah)* appropriate for this day (Lev. 23:24). There is no mention of the pertinent sacrifice (Num 28:1–6). There is absolutely no reference to the temple or the priests, and even the Levites do not appear in the narrative in their official cultic capacity, they only appear as *those who cause to understand (mevinim).*"

105. See MT *Laws of Prayer* 12:10 for the custom, initiated during the time of Ezra, to have a simultaneous translation accompany every Torah recital "so that they *understand* the subject matter *[she-yavinu inyan ha-devarim]*," that is, have a substantive comprehension.

106. For the biblical use of this term as some aspect of wisdom, see Gen 48:14; 1 Sam 18:30 (David), 25:3 (Abigail). For its combination with wisdom and teaching, see Ps 52:10, 119:99; Dan 1:17, 12:10; Prov 12:8. For "understanding" *(binah)* and *sekhel* as possible synonyms, see 1 Chron 22:12; 2 Chron 2:11.

107. In *b. Megillah* 3a, which sees the educational process of this verse as involving translation, punctuation, and intonation (also a form of sentence structure)—that is, all the elements essential to a proper understanding of what is being read.

108. See, e.g., Rashi, Gersonides, and ibn Ezra, who all take this as going beyond simple translation to in-depth analysis.

109. This is the crux of his entire rationalization of commandments in the third part of the *Guide*. See esp. III:32, 527–29: "God does not change at all the nature of human individuals by means of miracles" (529).

110. This term is one of the intellectual features possessed by the separate intellects. See MT *Laws of the Foundations of the Torah* 3:9.

111. Fogelman, "The Sukkah in the Temple," traces the custom of synagogues constructing *sukkot* booths to this account, which is the earliest evidence of *sukkot* built for priests and Levites within the Temple precinct. Although the development of this custom may be relevant to our discussion, since the synagogue

is really a democratized temple, there is no reason to believe that the *sukkot* constructed within the Temple precinct in Neh 8 were for the use of the priests and Levites.

112. R. Meir Leibush ben Yehiel Michael (Malbim) (d. 1879) offers a novel explanation of the feature that distinguished this *Sukkot* holiday from all those preceding it that is pertinent to my reading. Jerusalem had always been considered an international city belonging to Israel as a whole and not the exclusive property of any one particular tribe. Consequently it was halakhically deemed to be "public property." Since Jewish law forbids the construction of festival booths on public property, the description here of the building of booths all over the roofs, courtyards, and streets of Jerusalem was in contravention of *halakhah*. For this *Sukkot*, Ezra and his court issued an extraordinary dispensation permitting the setting up of booths in Jerusalem. From a philosophical perspective this corroborates the religious model that I have claimed is endorsed by Neh 8. The presence of the booth on public property is a symbolic expression of the democratization of religion. It is not the exclusive preserve of any family, tribe, or class.

113. There is some confusion in the manuscripts of the Tosefta regarding the quotation of this verse. Some cite the word for scroll here *(ha-sefer)* as "the scribe" *(ha-sofer)*. See Lieberman's discussion in his *Tosefta Ki-Feshutah*, vol. XX, 682.

114. Since the people could not have actually seen the contents unless the scroll was in an upright position, it was assumed to have been so and is the source for the custom among Jews of Arab lands to recite the Torah from an upright scroll. See Tractate Soferim 14:14.

115. See, e.g., Gersonides' comment on verse 6 (Levi), which considers Ezra to have pronounced the Torah blessing prior to its reading. Even contemporary biblical scholars acknowledge the similarity between Ezra's ceremony and subsequent synagogue practice. See, e.g., the comments of Coggins on these verses, *Ezra and Nehemiah*, 108.

116. The Talmud concludes that this was an emergency measure *(hora'at sha'ah)* and is not to be taken as setting a precedent. According to Maimonides, the "articulated name" *(shem ha-meforash)* is YHVH. See MT *Laws of the Foundations of the Torah* 6:2.

117. Its talmudic source is *b. Sotah* 39a. Joseph Karo, in his commentary on the MT, "Kesef Mishneh," explains his preference for the position that endorsed verse 3 rather than verse 5 ("as he opened it all the people stood up") as due to the fact that the latter might only prove a very restricted moment of silence or respect at the time the Torah scroll is opened, while verse 3 better indicates the interval of reading. I would add that verse 3 is a far stronger metaphor for concentrating on the text than verse 5. The latter has people standing, or silenced, while the former has "their ears" glued to the scroll. See also *b. Berakhot* 8a, where Rav Sheshet is described as turning his back on the Torah reading to engage in his own scholarship, declaring, "let them be involved with theirs and we

with ours." The *Guide* advocates concentrated attention when listening to the Torah as another stage in an arduous training process that eventually leads to a single-minded focus on God (III:51, 622–23).

Chapter 6 God, the Supreme Outsider:

1. Heidegger, *Being and Time*, 155.
2. Strauss expresses amazement at the complete absence in I:8 of any mention of the postbiblical usage of the term *maqom* in reference to God. However, a source relevant to this rabbinic usage does in fact appear in I:70. The amazement should not be caused by its absence but by the fact that the proof-text Maimonides selected from the *midrash* is Deut 33:27 rather than the one that actually uses the term *maqom*, Exod 33:21; this is also the proof-text cited by one of the sages in that very same source. Strauss' inference from this absence is that it proves the *Guide* "is primarily concerned with the theology of the bible in contradistinction to post-biblical Jewish theology" (GP, "How to Begin to Study the Guide," xxxi). Maimonides explicitly singled out biblical theology, in opposition to rabbinic interpretation, as his concern in the section dealing with the rationale for the commandments. On the issue of the apparent biblical endorsement of *lex talionis* (eye for an eye) as opposed to the rabbinic replacement of *lex talionis* with monetary compensation, Maimonides instructed his readers to disregard the latter for the moment: "For at present my purpose is to give reasons for the [biblical] texts and not for the pronouncements of the legal science" (GP III:41, 558). For secondary literature dealing with the problematics of this statement, see MN-S, 578 n. 4.
3. GP I:54, 123: "He [God] drew his attention to a subject of speculation through which he can apprehend to the furthest extent that is possible for man."
4. Maimonides' radical displacement of God as a theological model for Judaism is in stark contrast to a kabbalistic model such as that subscribed to by Nahmanides; the latter's comment on Exod 33:21, "Behold there is a place by me," is "On this mountain where my *shekhinah* is located." See also Nahmanides' comments on Exod 3:2, with respect to the identities of God and the angel of God who appear in the burning bush, where he distinguishes between manifestations of angels and the *shekhinah*.
5. It is precisely because of its radical outlook that a commentator like Isaac Abravanel felt the need to offer a lengthy excursus on GP I:8 dealing with place, which challenges those who have interpreted Maimonides' metaphorical sense of place as exclusive to the point where even the binding of Isaac plays itself out in the mind and not in actual space. Before mounting a spirited defense that attempts to preserve the Aggadah's literal and figurative dimensions, he laments, "I have no idea whose womb spawned this confused belief that it is Maimonides' opinion that the entire Aggadah transpired in a prophetic vision." See p. 25b of MN.

6. What Pines has translated as "separation" ibn Tibbon translates in Hebrew (MN) as *hitboddedut* (isolating oneself), as does Schwartz in his modern Hebrew translation (MN-S); Kafih translates it as *hityahedut*. Kafih nicely captures the sense I wish to convey in his note, where he states "Its sense is that Moses isolated himself outside of the world of other people, living among whom impedes perfection."

7. Here again it is instructive to contrast Nahmanides' conception of Moses. Whereas Maimonides' Moses points to existence on a wholly abstract plane, Nahmanides conjures up an existence graded by levels of divinity and populated by divine beings such as angels. Nahmanides comments on Exod 23:20–21 that during Moses' career no angel accompanied or protected Israel; rather, "Moses filled his place." As an illustration of this, he provides the image of Moses raising and lowering his arms in the battle against Amalek (Exod 17:11). Though angelic beings are absent, Moses stands in their stead and therefore preserves a worldview that has levels of divinity operative inside the world. It is interesting to note that here the rabbinic position in *m. Rosh Hashanah* 3:8 on Moses' role against Amalek is much closer to Maimonides than to Nahmanides. The *Mishnah* finds Moses' magical role problematic and therefore considers his actions as merely reflective of the people's contemplative focus on God.

8. See GP III:32 and generally the section on the rationale for the commandments subsequent to this introductory chapter.

9. In what follows I am in agreement with Menachem Kellner's position in chapter 6 of his recent book *Maimonides' Confrontation with Mysticism*, 179–215, where he argues for Maimonides' non-ontological understanding of the term *shekhina*. The readings I offer here are supportive but very different than his presentation.

10. For example, the verse directly preceding Gen 14:13, the proof-text for the literal sense of "dwell," describes Lot as *yoshev* (residing) in Sodom.

11. It is important to note that it is the Arabic term *sakina* that is translated in this chapter as "Indwelling"; the Hebrew *shekhinah* does not appear. Once again Strauss infers from this that in this section Maimonides is concerned with biblical theology and omits any mention of *shekhinah* to draw "our attention to the difference between the biblical and the post-biblical teaching" (GP, xxxi–xxxii n. 2).

12. See GP III:22, 487: "The most marvelous and extraordinary thing about this story is the fact that knowledge is not attributed in it to Job. He is not said to be *wise* or *comprehending* or an *intelligent* man. Only moral virtue and righteousness in action are ascribed to him."

13. Maimonides derides this view as a "raving" *(hathiyan)*. For a study that understands "raving" as a technical term describing a particular philosophical error, see Gellman, "Maimonides' Ravings." Gellman demonstrates that the term is used consistently to refer to "the fallacy of confusing the attributes of matter with the attributes of form" (315).

14. Knowing where to "stop" is of course precisely what typifies Moses when he covers his eyes at the burning bush. His intellectual disciple is R. Akiva, who can "stay [his] progress because of a dubious point" (GP I:32, 68), while his antithesis is Elisha ben Abuyah, who has breached his limitations and whose intellectual progression cannot be "made to stop at its proper limit" (ibid., 69). For the meaning of "stop," see MN-S 73 n.3.

15. See my full-length study *Maimonides and the Hermeneutics of Concealment*.

16. For a full-length treatment of this point, see Seeskin, *Searching for a Distant God.*

17. Abravanel points out (MN) that the primary purpose of chapter I:30 is to "remove any doubts" about the meaning of God as a *consuming fire.*

18. For the difficulties with this position and possible resolutions, see note 33 in chapter 2 on the leper.

19. For the precise meaning of this term in Arabic, *taqlid*, see MN-S 76 n. 7. Belief in truth on the strength of authority is an inferior type of knowledge sufficient for those who cannot intellectually fend for themselves but unacceptable for those who can. See also Yafeh, "Some Notes on the Term *Taqlid*," who notes that in Ghazzali's writings as well, *taqlid* "has a distinctly negative derogatory connotation, and comes as the opposite to the faith which is founded on examination or study or on personal religious experience" (250). See also R. Frank, "Knowledge and *Taqlid.*"

20. See, e.g., the comments of Onkelos, Rashi, Nahmanides, and Seforno to this verse. See also *Sifre Deut pisqa* 353:16, which interprets the verse as "who performed the will of He who revealed Himself to Moses at the bush." The metaphor is particularly striking since the burning bush was located at "Horev, the mountain of God" (Exod 3:1), and *Sinai* assonates with *sneh* (bush).

21. See the discussion of eating in chapter 3 on the heretic.

22. Maimonides endorsed the rabbinic tradition (*Lev Rabbah* 20) that their punishment was stayed until they reached Taverah (GP I:5, 30).

23. According to Bacher, *Bibelexegese*, 71 n. 2, this is a backhanded swipe at Muhammad.

24. Once the prophetic period ends, the pedagogical model initiated by Moses and continued by the prophets extends to the sage. The sage, then, carries on the legacy of the dwelling teaching I have outlined here. In this light we can better appreciate Maimonides' midrashic flourish in MT *Laws of Studying Torah* 5:1, to buttress his halakhic formulation of the proper fear and respect the sage commands. Disrespect for the sage/teacher is tantamount to disrespect for the *shekhinah*, an equivalence drawn four times in the same *halakhah*, three of which analogize arrogant challenges against the sage to challenges against the *shekhinah*.

25. Also Num 9:16: "It was always so; the cloud covered it, appearing as fire by night."

26. This passage is consistent with Exod 25:8, which reads "and let them make me a Sanctuary that I may live among *them*." This formulation opens a door

for the later Maimonidean battle against anthropomorphism. See, e.g., Sarna's comment on Exod 25:8 (*Exodus,* 158) that "the sanctuary is not meant to be understood literally as God's abode, as are other such institutions in the pagan world. Rather, it functions to make perceptible and tangible the conception of God's immanence . . . to which the people may orient their hearts and minds."

27. Both Efodi and Abravanel (MN) establish this pairing of the three verses with the two alternative metaphors.

28. This revelation, followed by a declaration of the thirteen attributes, constitutes, according to Maimonides, the response to Moses' plea "Show me Thy ways" (Exod 33:13). This response is the pinnacle of human cognition, which "has not been apprehended by anyone before him nor will it be apprehended by anyone after him." Moses' apprehension of God's ways is of attributes of action. See GP I:54, 123–24.

29. Maimonides' attitude toward the Aramaic *Targum Onkelos* can at best be described as ambivalent and at worst (my own inclination) as derisive. For a good survey of his relationship to Onkelos throughout his philosophical and halakhic works, see Posen, "Targum Onkelos."

30. For a list of all those places in the GP in which alternative readings are offered, see MN-S vol.1, 43 n. 11.

31. See, e.g., GP I:59.

32. For a close reading of Maimonides' endorsement of this *midrash,* see my article "The Use of Midrash." See also Stern's series of studies, *Problems and Parables of Law*; he sees a tripartite structure of parables consisting of vulgar, external, and internal meanings corresponding to meaningless, exoteric, and esoteric (72–73). For a more recent study, see Y. Lorberbaum, "'The Men of Knowledge,'" 107–9, who sees this structure as intrinsically indispensable for the communication of esoteric knowledge.

33. Efodi comments that this "connective" strategy, on any issue in need of clarification, requires one "to connect the chapters and bear those relevant to the particular issue in mind, and then, upon accumulating all those chapters the matter will become perfectly clear to you, for the style of the author is to write sporadically *(a little here and a little here)* in order to conceal the matter" (MN, 9).

34. See note 13 in chapter 4, on the king.

35. For the centrality of the *shekhinah* as a divine hypostasis in kabbalistic thought, see the chapter "*Shekhina*: The Feminine Element in Divinity" in Scholem, *On the Mystical Shape of the Godhead,* 140–96.

36. This is a very large topic and one that became the subject of heated controversy over Maimonides. See, e.g., Nahmanides' blistering attack against the rationalists—those who see no intrinsic value other than to cater to the natural tendencies of the human psyche—in his comments to Lev 16:8 (Chavel, vol. 3, 222): "I cannot explain more for I would have to close the mouths of those who claim to be wise in the study of nature, following after that Greek [Aristotle] who denied everything except that which could be perceived by him and he and his

wicked disciples were so proud as to suspect that whatever he could not conceive of through his reasoning is not true." For an esoteric approach that considers structure and form instrumental to understanding Maimonides' *ta'ame ha-mitzvot* in general, and that sees their anthropocentric and theocentric dimensions as complementary, see Y. Ben-Sasson, "A Study of the Doctrine of *Ta'ame Ha-Mitzvot*." On sacrifices, see W. Z. Harvey, "Les sacrifices." For another study with which I am particularly sympathetic, see Henshke, "On the Question of Unity," who argues for a fundamental unity on this issue between the MT and GP, works usually seen to be at striking odds on the reasons for sacrifices. In chapter 2, dealing with the leper, I argue similarly for what Twersky has called a "symbiotic relationship" between the two works. For "nonlegal" statements in the MT on the rationality of *huqqim* (nonrational laws), see the conclusions in MT *Laws of Unlawful Use of Sacred Property* and *Laws of Exchange of Sacred Property*.

37. Here one needs to confront the vexing problem of the glaring inconsistency between this position regarding the sacrificial cult quite clearly articulated in the GP and that of the MT, which envisions the rebuilding of the Temple and the reestablishment of the cult (MT *Laws of Kings* 11:1). It would seem that these two positions are mutually exclusive. If the sacrificial cult is essentially a pagan mode of worship instituted to address Israel's historical weltanschauung in the ancient Near East, why would it be restored in a future historical period when that worldview no longer exits? For an intriguing solution to this problem that rests on Maimonides' particular sense of historical progress, see Seeskin, "Maimonides' Sense of History." According to Seeskin, Maimonides' sense of history "is open to the possibility of temporal change as long as it is political rather than conceptual." See esp. 133–36.

38. This strategy is based on the remedy adopted in MT *Laws of Ethical Traits* 2:3 of resorting to the extreme in order to bring a bad ethical characteristic back in line with the "golden mean."

39. See Nehorai, "Maimonides' System of the Commandments," who draws a conceptual and structural parallel between the *Guide*'s discussions of providence and *ta'ame ha-mitzvot*. His argument provides further support for my thesis of the integral link between the reason for sacrifices and correct knowledge of the mechanics of divine providence.

40. See GP II:36 for prophecy and III:17, 18 for reward and punishment as a function of intellectual perfection.

41. GP, xxxi–xxxii n. 2.

42. Here I take issue with Strauss' assertion that "*shekhina* and providence are certainly not identical."

43. The meaning of the Arabic *sakina* is ambiguous. Its origins are Quranic, where it appears six times. For a concise canvassing of its various possibilities, see Lobel, "A Dwelling Place for the Shekhina," 120 n. 47.

44. The three references that relate to Onkelos and "created light" or "created thing" are GP I:21, 50–51; I:27, 57; and I:28, 60. The fourth reference,

to just "created light" without a mention of Onkelos, is I:76, 229. The fifth reference is I:23, 53.

45. For an interesting study of another manipulative use of Onkelos by Maimonides to actually mouth his own radical views, see Roslyn Weiss' analysis of chapter I:48 ("See No Evil").

46. Here I disagree with Scholem's placement of Maimonides along the same intellectual continuum occupied by Halevi and Sa'adya, who "unanimously agree that the *Shekhina,* which is for them identical with the biblical concept of God, is a freely willed creation of God's" (Scholem, *On the Mystical Shape of the Godhead*). Urbach concurs in this assessment; as well, he lumps together Sa'adya, Maimonides, and Halevi as of one mind on the *shekhinah* as some created divine instrument (*The Sages,* 31–32). Maimonides' explicit contrast of his own view ("as we had interpreted in the first place," GP I:21, 51) to that of Onkelos, which does in fact adopt *shekhinah* as "a freely willed creation of God's," demonstrates that he himself emphatically rejects that view.

47. Although Maimonides never made mention of Halevi, Pines concludes that some passages in the GP are a "counterblast" to Halevi's *Kuzari,* "a book that Maimonides probably knew" (GP, "The Philosophic Sources of the *Guide*," cxxxiii). In his last appendix to his article "Shi'ite Terms," 248–51, Pines asserts much more confidently that it is a "practical certainty that Maimonides was familiar with the Kuzari; an important apologetic and theological work written by a celebrated member of the Jewish community of Spain would hardly have escaped his notice." He reiterates this position in a lengthy footnote to his article "On the Term Ruhaniyyut," 532–33 n. 77, stating "without any doubt he was well familiar [with the *Kuzari*]." Particularly intriguing is the close similarity Pines notes between Maimonides' granting of a positive role to Islam and Christianity in the historical evolution toward the Messianic period in MT *Laws of Kings* 11 and the position taken in the *Kuzari* 4:23. My argument here does not depend on this "certainty" of Maimonides' having actually read the *Kuzari,* and remains valid even if one accepts the position of Kreisel, who disagrees with Pines from a historical perspective and cites the absence of any references to the *Kuzari* as suggestive of the opposite conclusion ("Judah Halevi's Influence on Maimonides," 104–5). Yet even according to Kreisel, "certain aspects of Maimonides' thought might be better understood and appreciated if viewed in light of the *Kuzari*"; further, Halevi's influence "may have made a subtle contribution to Maimonides' position on a number of questions." The issue of *shekhinah* is one such question where Maimonides' view can be brought into a much sharper focus in light of Halevi's.

48. For a sampling of attempts to define this word, see Pines, "Shi'ite Terms," 172–78; Efros, "Some Aspects of Yehudah Halevi's Mysticism"; and Goldziher, "Mélanges Judeo-Arabes." Kogan, in his chapter on Halevi, 720–21, sums it up: "there is an elect core of humanity [Israel], who constitute an essentially separate order endowed with prophetic and even miraculous powers (*Kuzari,* 1:31–43;

2:14, 24). This group belongs to the *amr ilahi,* Halevi's multivalent term for diverse aspects of divine immanence."

49. Lobel, "A Dwelling Place for the Shekhina," 117.

50. Ibid., 120. Here the emphasis is on *Jewish* history as opposed to history of humankind. Recently, Hartman *(Israelis and the Jewish Tradition)* posed two distinct models of Judaism as antipodal options for the future of Judaism as a living tradition, exemplified by Halevi and Maimonides. The primary distinction between the two is the issue of universalism versus chosenness. For Halevi, Israel's uniqueness is ontologically grounded and its relationship to God "is the exclusive property of Israel" (28), while Maimonides categorically favors a universalist approach. On this issue, see also Kellner's thorough study *(Maimonides on Judaism and the Jewish People).*

51. It is noteworthy that Sa'adya is never mentioned by name when notions of "created things" are introduced in the *Guide.* According to Kreisel, this is a conscious ploy that "accords the notions even greater weight from a traditional standpoint" *(Prophecy,* 214). I believe that Maimonides' association of these phenomena with Onkelos is actually intended to undermine their legitimacy rather than to strengthen it. Since he wanted to relieve his ultimate audience, the learned ones, of this theology, ascribing it to the popular translation/commentary of Onkelos would be a far more effective indicator of its illegitimacy.

52. Scholem, *On the Mystical Shape of the Godhead,* 171.

Chapter 7   Deconstructing God's Indwelling

1. See also *Iggeret Teman* in Iggerot vol. 1, 126. This verse is also cited in support of the Torah's being impervious to change and addition. See PM, Introduction to *Zera'im* (vol. 1, 6).

2. Though hearsay testimony is not generally admissible in the North American judicial system, the rules of evidence do in fact allow such testimony as proof that statement *A* was said by person *B* or conveyed by *B* to *C,* but not as proof of the contents of statement *A.* That is the kind of testimony that the MT has described here.

3. For the distinction between the external *(zahir)* and internal *(batin),* see GP I:12, where the external = "wisdom that is useful in many respects," while the internal = "concerned with the truth as it is."

4. Ivry, "Ismaili Theology," 294.

5. Here I agree in part with Ivry's incisive assessment that "Maimonides' apparent acceptance of this voice as a disembodied being would thus not strike his readers as odd, particularly those who were not philosophically attuned to his style and true teaching, and not ready yet to absorb them" (ibid., 295). I both shore up Ivry's argument, by demonstrating how Maimonides actually signaled to his astute readers to part company with the unsophisticated, and extend it

even further. Maimonides was waging a subtle battle against prevailing theologies grounded in divine hypostases to which even the philosophically adept subscribed. My analysis has Maimonides advising them that they must reject those theologies under the popular guise of tolerating them. See also Ivry, "Neoplatonic Currents," 135–37.

6. Cited incorrectly by Pines, Kafih, Schwartz, and Munk as Exod 20:16.

7. David Kimhi follows suit with his comment on Isa 26:21 that God's going out of His place is to be read "metaphorically" *(al derekh mashal)* and, more explicitly, with his comment on Mic 1:3 that it is "a metaphor for the decrees that issue forth from Him." See also ibn Ezra's explication of Isa 26:21 as "the decrees which issue forth from God." For a more traditional view that the divine movement indicates a change in His adjudicatory mode from the "attribute of mercy [*rahamim*] to that of justice [*din*]," see Rashi's comments on both verses.

8. Both Pines and Kafih cite only Isa 26:21 as the source of "the Lord goeth out of His place," while Schwartz correctly cites Mic 1:3, where the identical phrase reappears as well.

9. See GP II:29, 343–45.

10. Shem Tov, in his comments on I:23, elaborates that all natural events are attributed to God only in the sense of a remote cause; God's decree or will initiated all existence and therefore anything that transpires thereafter can ultimately be traced back to God's will. See MN, 39b–40a.

11. See his PM *Avot* 5:6, which takes this list to be indicative only of miracles created during "twilight," whereas all other miracles were conditioned during the primal week of creation but at other junctures of the process. The sole difference between the natural and the miraculous is their frequency of appearance, the former occurring steadily while the latter only very rarely.

12. Onkelos neutralizes various instances of anthropomorphisms by replacing the offending phrase with "the word of the Lord." See, e.g., GP I:21, 49 on Gen 31:49. Passages indicating unmediated personal divine involvement are resolved by inserting a missing medium that Onkelos fills in; "sometimes he takes the omitted word to be *glory*, and sometimes he takes it to be *Indwelling*, and sometimes he takes it to be *word*" (GP I:21, 50).

13. See, e.g., *Targum Onkelos'* insertion of the missing *shekhinah* in Exod 33:3, 34:6; Num 23:21; Deut 3:24, 4:39, and 32:40, all listed by Urbach, *The Sages*, 32–33, as illustrations of Onkelos' programmatic removal of anthropomorphisms.

14. Although Urbach, ibid., 51, may be correct from an academic perspective when he asserts that "the notion of the *shekhina* as a separate creation does not have any source in the rabbinic tradition nor in later midrash like *Pirqe deRabbi Eliezer*," Maimonides himself may not have shared that conclusion. Even if he did, rabbinic usage of the term would certainly have been cause for consternation over its anthropomorphic qualities. My argument is that by his time the dangers posed by the anthropomorphic characteristics of *shekhinah* were exacerbated by its transformation into some divine creation on earth espoused by ear-

lier thinkers such as Sa'adya and Halevi. See, e.g., Sa'adya's rationalization of anthropomorphic prophetic revelations such as those seen by Daniel (7:9), Ezekiel (1:26), and Mikhayehu (1 Kgs 22:19) in his *Book of Beliefs and Opinions* (Rosenblatt, 121): they are "produced for the first time by the creator out of fire.... It is a form nobler even than that of the angels, magnificent in character, resplendent with light which is called *the glory of the Lord.* It is this form, too, that one of the prophets described *I beheld till thrones were placed and one that was ancient of days did sit* (Dan 7:9) and that the sages characterized as *shekhinah.*" For Maimonides, however, all these visions would have taken place within the mind's eye of the prophet; for example, he stated that 1 Kgs 22:19 "refers to intellectual apprehension and in no way to the eye's seeing" (GP I:4, 28).

15. See, e.g., *Sifre Num, Mas'e, pisqa* 3; and *Mekhilta de-Rabbi Ishmael, Bo, 14; b. Megillah* 29a; *y. Ta'anit* 3:1; *Num Rabbah* 7:10. Nahmanides' forceful critique of Maimonides' presentation of Onkelos' methodology, in his commentary to Gen 46:1, concludes by remarking that Onkelos' literal translation of God's promise to Jacob, "I will go down with you to Egypt" (Gen 46:4), contemplates this very midrashic motif of divine accompaniment by way of *shekhinah* in exile.

16. Davidson, "The Active Intellect in the *Cuzari,*" 389.

17. Ibid., 392.

18. Ibid., 392–95.

19. One of his boldest formulations of this proposition is his explanation of what we mean when we attribute anything to God. The correctness of this attribution lies in the sense that "every action that occurs in Being is referred to God, as we shall make clear, even if it is worked by one of the proximate efficient causes; *God, considered as efficient cause, is then the remotest one*" (GP I:69, 168; emphasis mine). Fox mounts a valiant attempt to salvage some traditional notion of a more involved God. He identifies three separate accounts of divine causality in the *Guide*—quasi-physical, metaphysical, and religious—all of which, as is Fox's wont, live together in a "dialectical tension," each one compensating for the limitations of the other but in a permanent and irresolvable tension. Fox has constructed a philosophically and existentially rich Maimonidean edifice that is most attractive to a modern philosophical sensibility. See his chapter "Maimonides' Account of Divine Causality" (*Interpreting Maimonides*, 229–50).

20. Another prophetic idiom to which this would apply is any attribution of worldly events to "angels." Maimonides, in GP II:6, virtually neutralizes the term to signify any point of natural causation encompassing all "individual natural and psychic forces," including sexual erections! On angels as natural forces, see Goodman, "Maimonidean Naturalism," esp. 160–67.

21. See *Kuzari* 5:23, where he distinguishes between the visible *shekhinah* and the invisible *shekhinah* that replaced it as a result of exile; and see ibid., 1:109; 2:58, 62; 3:41; and Davidson's discussion of the "visible shekhina," "The Active Intellect in the *Cuzari,*" 388–89. See also Kellner's discussion of Halevi's position in his *Maimonides's Confrontation*, 186–89.

22. GP 54 n. 6.

23. Schwartz (MN-S) follows Pines' lead in his translation with *davar*. Alharizi (MN) also translates as *davar* (100). Ibn Tibbon (MN) is slightly more nuanced with his rendering of *ha-inyan* (the matter). Friedländer, worried, I assume, that this might be misconceived, rendered it quite unliterally as "something ideal" (*Guide*, 87 n. 1). Munk's French translation of "la parole (divine)" (*Le guide*, 60) is more in accord with Kafih (*Moreh Ha-Nevukhim*, 39), although it is interesting that he felt the need to gloss "parole" with the adjective "divine," revealing a possible subconscious acceptance of *amr ilahi*.

24. See David Kimhi's comment on Isa 2:3 (which is typical) that the instructor here contemplates the messianic king.

25. This is most certainly the identification Maimonides or any Jewish coreligionist would have made.

26. It is of note that the halakhic implications of Isa 2:3, "for out of Zion shall the law go out," while exclusivist in their technical formulation, betrays a universal principle. Although the verse conditions the fixing of the calendar as the sole prerogative of experts residing within the geographical limits of Israel, this task is ultimately dependent on intellectual capacity. Should the superior sage reside outside of Israel then that prerogative transfers to him. The operative principle is wisdom. See SM, Positive Commandment 153, and MT *Laws of Sanctification of the Month* 1:8.

27. See MT *Laws of Idolatry* 1:3; GP II:39, 379; III:24, 502; and III:51, 624.

28. Here I am in total agreement with the thesis Kellner develops in chapter 5 of his book *Maimonides on Judaism and the Jewish People* that "the difference between Jew and Gentile will disappear by the time the messianic era reaches fruition" (33).

29. Ravitzky, "'To the Utmost Human Capacity,'" 232–34, views the circle of history as opening with the archetypal man, Adam, and closing with the messianic return to man's original stature. My argument remains the same, for here too the historical circle is rooted in and ends in a universalist vision of mankind. I chose Abraham as the originating point to return to since, for all intents and purposes, the present historical evolution toward intellectual utopia began with Abraham's rediscovery and promotion of the Adamic model.

30. See, e.g., Sa'adya, *Book of Beliefs and Opinions* (Rosenblatt, 121), who identifies the created glory with the rabbinic concept of *shekhinah;* and Altmann's discussion, *Studies in Religious Philosophy and Mysticism*, 152–54.

31. Perhaps it is for this reason that the laws governing the conduct of relations between student and teacher are virtually teeming with more references to the *shekhinah* than any other section of the MT. See *Laws of Studying Torah* 5:1, where Maimonides fully endorsed analogies drawn by the Talmud (*b. Sanhedrin* 110a) between offending a teacher and offending the *shekhinah* (four times).

32. Here I am indebted to Kreisel's assessment of this passage as a "a subtle and important critique" and "rejection of Halevi's doctrine. The *amr ilahi* does

not represent a special degree but is identified with the principle responsible for the forces of nature in general" ("Judah Halevi's Influence on Maimonides," 118–20). My contribution is to support this position by showing how the *Guide* conducts a sustained subtextual critique of the Halevian theology throughout the work, especially in its biblical exegesis. By his doing so, Maimonides rooted out the possibility of reading that doctrine into the tradition at its very source—namely, the Bible.

33. See Reines, "Maimonides' Concepts of Providence and Theodicy," 203–5. See also Klein-Braslavy, *Maimonides' Interpretation of the Adam Stories*, 214, who, based on a string of associations, draws the following equation: Samael = Satan = Evil inclination = imaginative faculty = angel. Satan, representing the imaginative faculty, would of course be the perfect foil to soul, representing the rational faculty. Based on the Maimonidean principle that providence is consequent upon intellect, if Satan dominates then man is exposed to the elements, and if soul dominates he is protected.

34. See, e.g., *Midrash Tehillim* 94:4 and the commentaries of David Kimhi and Seforno to the verse.

35. Psalms 144:5 and 8:5 are cited together in GP III:17, 472.

36. Rembaum, "Interpretation of Scripture in Judah Halevi's *Kozari*," 153, also points out an ongoing polemic in the *Guide* with Halevi largely due to this very point of contention that a "carefully transmitted body of revealed wisdom is . . . more valid than the results of humanly generated syllogistic logic."

37. *Kuzari*, 4:3, 200.

38. Ibid. For two different readings of Halevi's position with respect to the "reality" of these entities and with what human faculty they are perceived, particularly what is called the "inner eye," see Kreisel, "Judah Halevi's Influence on Maimonides," 126–32, and W. Z. Harvey, "Judah Halevi's Synesthetic Theory of Prophecy." The former sees him as vacillating between the philosophers and the sensualists while the latter attributes his hybrid position to a unique notion of the prophetic imagination.

39. Kafih, in his translation of the *Guide (Moreh Ha-Nevukhim)*, notes his own preference for honor being conferred on the place, "be it mountain, tabernacle or temple," and his disagreement with Shier's note to the Al-Harizi translation (*Guide*, 253–54) that relegates the honor to God.

40. The talmudic debate preceding this assertion would tend to support the Maimonidean perspective that the direction of the Temple was a ritual strategy to defeat pagan ideology. Various rabbis subscribe to the school that the *shekhinah* is not confined to one space but "is in all places." The following story (*b. Bava Batra* 25a) relates to one of them: "Rav Sheshet also held that the *shekhinah* is in all places for he would say to his attendant 'Face me in any direction except the east.' And this was not because the *shekhinah* is not there but because the *Minim* teach turning that way." Rashi identifies *Minim* as "the students of idolatry who promulgate prayer toward the east."

41. Maimonides' rationalist understanding of this posture is in stark contrast to that of a nonrationalist like Rashi, who comments on its talmudic source in *b. Yevamot* 105a that "eyes toward earth *[eretz]*" contemplates the direction of Israel *(eretz yisrael)*.

42. Kafih, ibn Tibbon, and Schwartz all translate the opposition as between *amittiyim* (true reality) and *dimyoniyim* (imagination).

43. *Book of Beliefs and Opinions* (Rosenblatt, 337–38). Consistently, Sa'adya interprets Isaiah's prophecies of chapters 65 and 66 regarding the creation of new heavens, new earth, and a new Jerusalem as referring to a new spatial accommodation for this special light in the world to come. Just as consistently, Maimonides challenged this interpretation by considering the very same prophecies as metaphors for the new intellectual and political climate that will prevail in the Messianic age (GP II:29, 341–42).

44. See his magisterial *Through a Speculum That Shines*, 167.

45. No better exploration of the humility engendered by the Maimonidean "quest" can be found than that in Seeskin, *Searching for a Distant God*.

46. The rabbinic locus classicus for this is *b. Qiddushin* 31a. See also MT *Laws of Ethical Traits* 5:6.

47. Maimonides refers to *m. Avot*, where there are two formulations advocating the avoidance of unnecessary speech (1:15, 17).

48. Ricoeur, "The Power of Speech, Science and Poetry," 66.

49. See the chapter titled "Metaphor and Symbol" in Ricoeur, *Interpretation Theory*.

Chapter 8   Sabbath

1. See *b. Sanhedrin* 58b, where a non-Jew who observes the Sabbath is considered guilty of a capital offense. Resh Laqish considers what seems to be a divine assurance in Gen 8:22 that the natural order will never cease to operate, night and day, as a prohibition. He transforms the plain sense of the verse "Day and night shall not cease" into "Thou shalt not rest day or night," imposing a continuous obligation on non-Jews to work. Various midrashic sources attribute the Sabbath's exclusivity to the unique relationship between the Sabbath and Israel. See, e.g., *Exod Rabbah* 25:6, 16; *Deut Rabbah* 1:18; *Mekhilta de-Rabbi Ishmael, parshah Ki Tissa*. Maimonides, though, considered the gravity of the offense to be in the "creation of a new religion." See also MT *Laws of Kings* 10:9. Justified indignation at this sanction against the non-Jew is somewhat alleviated by the fact that Maimonides restricted its administration to the "heavenly court." The non-Jew must be informed of this theoretical sanction to convey to him the seriousness of his offense. For contemporary halakhic discussions of Maimonides' view, see Feinstein, *Iggerot Moshe*, vol. 2, no. 7, 8–9; and Weinberg, *Seride Esh*,

vol. 2, no. 92, 229–33. For overviews of the issue of Gentile Sabbath observance, see A. Weiss, "Shevitat AKU"M"; and Adler, "The Sabbath Observing Gentile."

2. For the biblical connection, see Exod 20:11.

3. See also GP III:32, 531; III:41, 562; III:43, 570.

4. This is Maimonides' most mature assessment of the value of this belief; it was added to his formulation of the fourth principle of faith after the completion of the *Guide.* See Iggerot, 142; and Kellner, *Dogma in Medieval Jewish Thought,* 240–41. In GP II:13, 282, Maimonides evaluated creation as "undoubtedly a basis of the law of Moses our Master, peace be on him. And it is second to the basis that is the belief in the unity of God." Creation is also an integral component of his formulation at the very beginning of the MT: "The basic principle of all basic principles and the pillar of all sciences is to know that there is a First Being *who brought every existing thing into being.*" Creation is so critical to Judaism that a thinker like Isaac Abravanel, who was opposed to any creedal formulations, admitted in his *Principles of Faith* that "[w]ere I to choose principles to posit for the divine Torah I would only lay down one, the creation of the world" (Kellner, *Abravanel,* chap. 22, 192; see also Kellner's discussion on 33–36). True to his evaluation, Abravanel devoted an entire treatise to the problem of creation titled *Mifalot Elohim (The Deeds of God).*

5. On the Arabic term "tradition" *(taqlid),* see MN-S, 76 n. 7. Knowledge received by way of "tradition" is merely a preliminary stage toward true knowledge gained by self-teaching: "The opinions in question should first be known as being received through tradition; then they should be demonstrated" (GP III:54, 634). Job's initial misconceptions about God are due to the fact that "he had no true knowledge and knew the deity only because of his acceptance of authority, just as the multitude adhering to a law know it" (GP III:23, 492). See also Maimonides' *Letter on Astrology* (Mahdi), where he distinguished between three different methods of acquiring knowledge—reason, sense perception, and authoritative teaching (from prophets or the righteous)—with the warning that "every reasonable man ought to distinguish in his mind and thought all the things he accepts as trustworthy." For the interpretive debate as to whether Maimonides' conception of belief *(emunah)* can be reduced to rational knowledge or to some suprarational knowledge, see Rosenberg, "The Concept of *Emunah.*" For an analysis of the Arabic equivalent of "belief/knowledge" *(itiqad)* in understanding Maimonides' conception, see Rawidowicz, *Studies in Jewish Thought,* 317–23.

6. These are their respective roles as described in MT *Laws of Idolatry* chap. 1 and GP III:29.

7. See H. Kasher's analysis of this parable, "The Parable of the King's Palace"; and on this group, see ibid., 8.

8. In the *Guide,* his argument is that creation attests to the possibility of miracles, while in his *Pirqe Mosheh (Fusul Musa)* this reasoning works in reverse, that is, miracles are proof for creation. See Kafih's *Iggerot,* app. 2, 160.

9. Belief in miracles, however, was never included as a principle to begin with. Langermann, "Maimonides and Miracles," has recently argued that its conspicuous absence as a principle, together with certain texts from his early work, the *Commentary to the Mishnah,* are evidence of an early disregard for miracles consistent with his youthful deterministic bent. However, positions advanced in later works, such as this one in the *Guide,* support an ongoing reevaluation of that early position that was more accepting of miracles.

10. Shem Tov daringly responds to the hypothetical situation in which eternity could be rationally demonstrated, whereas a modern scholar such as Fox (*Interpreting Maimonides,* 43) only skirts this as "interesting to consider."

11. See *b. Betzah* 16a, where it is said of Shammai that the choices he made during the week were governed by their implications for the Sabbath.

12. Aquinas took issue with Maimonides' radical disposing of divine names, arguing for a hierarchy of meaningful predications that can apply to God. For a good analysis of this disagreement, see Jordan, "The Names of God." However, Jordan's conclusions regarding Aquinas seem equally apt for Maimonides. For instance, it is precisely "the failure of the divine names to make the signified present [that] is their success as a pedagogical device" (182); or in Derridean and Heideggerian terms, the names of God "were names which crossed themselves out. They were in short names which silenced themselves" (ibid.).

13. There is no dearth of scholarly literature on the subject of attributes of action. For an article that specifically zeroes in on these kinds of attributes, see Buijs, "Attributes of Action in Maimonides," and the literature cited therein. For present purposes, it is important to note his definition: "In keeping with their logical function, attributes of action identify an agent. They neither describe the agent nor explain the act" (100).

14. For attributes of action in the *Guide,* see I:54.

15. My suggestion as to the structure of the *Guide* here is consistent with the schematic developed by Strauss in his introduction to the GP (xi), which sees I:61–67 as one subunit, but for very different reasons. For Strauss, chapters 65–67 are necessitated by the fact that this unique name "is communicated to men by God and not coined or created by human beings" (xlix); therefore, "since God does not speak, Maimonides must therefore open the whole question of God's speaking, writing, and ceasing to speak or act." My proposal intersects with Strauss' on the point of the name "YHVH" as the crux that links the chapters. However, prophetic communication is only broached tangentially, and the bulk of the discussion in 65–67 by far concerns creation. I disagree with Rawidowicz's rationale for this succession of chapters ("The Structure of the *Moreh Nevukhim,*" 65–66), which sees the divine names as the completion of the discussion of attributes, with chapters 65–67 following on the basis of a string of associations. The bridge between chapters 64 and 65, according to him, is that the former concludes with a verse that uses the term "say": "And in His Temple all say glory" (Ps 29:9). First, that verse concerns human speech and not divine.

Second, were it not for this association, according to Rawidowitz, chapter 65's rightful place would be in the later discussion of prophecy. My proposal suggests a strong inherent thematic link that makes this just the right place to insert chapters 65–67.

16. Burrell, *Knowing the Unknowable God,* 62, succinctly captures this notion with the following formulation: "Underscoring God's hiddenness, the 'names of God' become icons or images, with the most sacred name—the one given from God to us—quite securely mysterious since we understand it not at all" [because, in his words, we know "so little of Hebrew"!].

17. It is difficult to reconcile this misconception with Maimonides' identification of Job's position with that of Aristotle (GP III:23, 494). How can Aristotle's opinion, which was previously encapsulated by the belief "The Lord hath forsaken the earth" (Ezek 9:9), be consistent with what is described here as Job's belief in immediate divine causality? On this question, see H. Kasher, "Job's Image and Opinion," and esp. 83. Suffice it to mention for my purposes that I am in agreement with her thesis that this is part of a strategy of dissemblance aimed at actually covering up what is a congruence between the final mature Job and Aristotle.

18. For a good analysis of how Maimonides "couches his emanative naturalism in terms of a critical appropriation of the biblical and rabbinic idea of angels," see Goodman, "Maimonidean Naturalism." The following characterization of angels is instructive: "[Angels are] the generative forms that organize and enliven the natural world, differentiating it from mere chaos. They are perceived from their effects, apprehended when we understand the structures of natural things and the characters and causes of natural processes" (167).

19. For Maimonides' summary of this school of thought, see GP III:17, 466–67. This is another example of W. Z. Harvey's characterization of Maimonides' critique of the Kalam as a religious critique as well as a philosophical one ("Why Maimonides Was Not a Mutakallim"). Just as Maimonides refused to accept their specious arguments "proving" creation, so he refused their arguments on providence as well, even though they seemed to be advocating more "religious" positions. Since only truth and falsehood provoke God's favor and anger, respectively, the "tendentiousness and sophistry of the *Kalam* are obnoxious to Maimonides' religious sensibility" (112).

20. See also GP II:12, 280, which equates the imagination with the evil impulse, and III:22, 489, where an identity is formulated between Satan, the evil inclination, and the angel of death. Therefore, Satan = imagination. I am indebted here to Kravitz's analysis, "Maimonides and Job." See also Levinger, "Maimonides' Exegesis of Job," who agrees with this equation (85).

21. Regardless of what Maimonides' actual position is on creation, his notion of the Sabbath, angels and what they reflect regarding the postcreation order may indicate a convergence with Aristotle on the question of divine providence. My argument here provides further evidence in support of H. Kasher's thesis ("Job's Image and Opinion").

22. Similarly, Sa'adya Gaon in his *Book of Beliefs and Opinions* links Gen 2:2 with Exod 20:11 as conveying "not relaxation from any kind of motion or exertion. It constituted merely the discontinuance of the production of what was to be created" (Rosenblatt, II:12, 128).

23. Similarly, Gersonides considers this detail a literary ploy to accentuate Naval's mean-spiritedness. However, for Gersonides the repose occurs prior to the messengers addressing Naval, indicating that they did not abruptly accost Naval with David's request but patiently waited for the right moment. Rashi and Radak favor a meaning of resting from exhaustion, both explicitly rejecting the sense of "cessation from speech" offered by *Targum Jonathan*. Alter's modern English translation concurs with the Maimonidean interpretation, rendering *va-yanuhu* as "and they paused" (*The David Story*, 154). According to Alter, David's message demonstrates deference and humility and is met with sarcasm and contempt by Naval.

24. Maimonides made it absolutely clear that this does not imply any kind of divine immanence in the world by pointing out that the analogy of divine form is imprecise. See D. Schwartz, "Divine Immanence in Medieval Jewish Philosophy," 266–69.

25. As D. Schwartz, ibid., points out, "God thus remains far removed, isolated from the world."

26. Fox (*Interpreting Maimonides*, chap. 9) has argued that this account of divine causality based on natural science is only one of three different accounts, the others being based on divine science and revelation ("religious account"). Each one on its own "suffers serious limitations"; but, Fox argues, none is meant to be dismissed by Maimonides. Rather, they coexist in a dialectical tension, the lesson being that "the price one pays for choosing to be both a philosopher and a Jew is that one sometimes must affirm the theses of both in the fullness of their tense opposition" (249).

27. Quoted from Ginsburg, *The Sabbath in the Classical Kabbalah*, 94; see esp. the section titled "Sabbath as Perfected Time," 93–101.

28. Eliade, *The Sacred and the Profane*, 68.

29. Maimonides was compelled to retain the term "angels" since it is such a prominent aspect of rabbinic teaching. In the *Guide*, however, he virtually stripped it of any rabbinic connotations and reconstructed it as a metaphor for the natural causal order. In his MT, he applied a parallel treatment by designating all prophetic descriptions of angels as metaphor (*Laws of the Foundations of the Torah* 2:4). For an interesting analysis of how Maimonides integrated the traditional teachings on angels with his philosophic outlook in the second chapter of *Laws of the Foundations of the Torah*, see Blumenthal, "Maimonides on Angel Names." There Maimonides conducted a subtler balancing act between audiences of various levels of philosophical sophistication.

30. See, e.g., GP I:54, where the pinnacle of Moses' quest for knowledge of God consists in observing all created things and apprehending "their nature and the way they are mutually connected," by which God is ultimately known.

31. For similar attitudes to contemporary incompetence in the nuances of biblical Hebrew, see Halevi, *Kuzari*, II:68; ibn Tibbon's comments on the need for a lexicon of words used in his translation *mipene qotzer leshonenu* in his *Explanation of Strange Words (Perush Ha-Millim Ha-Zarot)* appended to MN, 2b; and generally Halkin, "The Medieval Jewish Attitude toward Hebrew," esp. 238–39. Maimonides also attributed the institution of standardized prayers to the increasing bastardization of Hebrew over the course of various exiles, to the point where "everybody's speech was a mixture of many tongues. No one was able, when he spoke, to express his thoughts in any one language, otherwise than incoherently" (MT *Laws of Prayer* 1:4). See also PM *Bikkurim* 3:7.

32. That this was a radical view on the nature of the messianic era can be seen from the tortuous reasoning resorted to by traditional commentators on the MT in order to come to terms with it. See the critical gloss of Rabad, along with compromise interpretations of Radbaz (Maimonides' naturalism applied to the rest of the world but not the land of Israel), and Elijah of Vilna (Gra), who distinguishes between the periods of the messiah ben Joseph, where nature prevails, and the messiah ben David, which supersedes nature and is the *le'atid lavo* (end of days). See also Abravanel's *Yeshu'ot Meshiho,* 3:7, 56b, where he takes Maimonides to task for misrepresenting a solitary opinion (Samuel) as one that is universally accepted. See also "Lehem Mishneh" on MT *Laws of Repentance* 8:8, who resorts to attributing to Maimonides a quasi-adoption of Samuel's position rather than a full-fledged endorsement in order to resolve various halakhic inconsistencies in the MT.

33. The extent of Maimonides' naturalistic messianism is open to debate. Scholem has argued for its most extreme form, which considers the messianic period a realization of purely human restorative endeavors (*The Messianic Idea in Judaism,* 24–35). Funkenstein, *Perceptions of Jewish History,* 134–55, offers a more nuanced understanding of it as a "realistic utopianism," which preserves its miraculous quality since, though realized through this-worldly processes, "it also excels every previous historical period by leaps" (155). As a result, he concludes, it would be wrong both to deny its political character and to simply relegate it to "the realm of ordinary political processes" (154). Recently Berger ("Some Ironic Consequences") has gone even further and argued that, while rationalistic, Maimonides' messianism does not promote human activism, but, on the contrary, counsels a patient quietism.

34. The literature on this aspect of Maimonides' thought is vast. For a comprehensive bibliography, see Dienstag, "Reasons for the Commandments."

35. See generally his preface to the *ta'ame ha-mitzvot* in III:26–33, where this notion of first and second intentions is fully developed.

36. The sources are *b. Shabbat* 87b and *b. Sanhedrin* 57b, although they add others such as the seven Noahide Laws and honoring one's parents. Rashi cites a tradition that adds the law of the red heifer to the list. See also M. Kasher's survey of variant traditions concerning what was legislated at Marah (*Torah Shelemah,* vol. 14, 168–69 n. 267).

37. Stern, "The Idea of a *Hoq*," trenchantly calls attention to the change in use of first and second intentions from value assessment to chronology—that is, the first legislation occurred at Marah and the second at Sinai. Maimonides also made it clear, by conflating "first" and "primary," that the legislation at Marah is also theoretically superior, since "in the first legislation there was nothing at all concerning burnt offerings and sacrifices, for, as we have mentioned, these belong to the second intention" (GP III:32, 531).

38. This may pose another solution to the quandary of how *mitzvot* can survive their historically conditioned contexts and continue to be effective means of religious pursuit. This is dealt with by Stern, "The Idea of a *Hoq*." As long as any *mitzvah* is performed in the shadow of Marah, it can accomplish its goal regardless of its particular form.

39. See, e.g., Rashi, Joseph Kara, Abraham ibn Ezra, David Kimhi, and Metzudot David on this verse.

40. See, e.g., ibn Shmuel's sense of Maimonides' reading as "I will remain fixed and resolute until I witness the downfall of my enemies" (*Sefer Moreh Ha-Nevukhim,* pt. 1, vol. 2, 355). Munk *(Le guide)* translates *anuah* as "ferme (ou tranquille)," which is consistent with my rendering as "firm, fixed, stable, constant" *(ferme)* or "still, undisturbed" *(tranquille).*

41. This is the locus classicus of Maimonides' theory of providence. His account has been widely discussed in the scholarly literature. For but one sober analysis of the "overflow" and providence, see Ivry, "Providence, Divine Omniscience, and Possibility"; he states that it is man who appraises "God's actions from the point of view of reward and punishment, we who personalize the actions of the divine overflow"; in reality, it "is essentially impersonal and functions of necessity, but for the element of will which Maimonides, as is customary in medieval philosophy, regards as essential to the divine being" (152).

42. For this assertion as contradicting other statements in the *Guide,* see Disendruck, "Samuel and Moses ibn Tibbon on Maimonides' Theory of Providence."

43. Nuriel, "Providence and Governance," offers a philological solution to the well-known contradictions on this issue by distinguishing between divine "providence," which can be attained by intellectual perfection, and "governance," which acknowledges a certain amount of chance inherent in the natural working order. It is only with respect to the former that Nuriel claims there can be total immunity since it adheres to a disembodied intellect. See also W. Z. Harvey's subsequent analysis, "Nuriel's Method."

44. For an extended discussion of the precise meaning of *asah* in the Maimonidean lexicon of the creation account, see Klein-Braslavy, *Maimonides' Interpretation of the Creation Account,* 96–99.

45. For the precise meaning of this phrase and others related to the prevailing state of affairs prior to creation, see Ivry's incisive philological analysis "Maimonides on Creation," asserting that the "no thing" or "non existence" that preceded the material world is not absolute nothingness, or what has been con-

sidered as *ex nihilo,* but rather some *thing* that is wholly outside the framework of human cognition and experience. As he states, this precreation nothingness "is not anchored either in the material foundation known as prime matter or in the purely non-material, like God. This absolute non existence has a certain reality, though it is beyond our comprehension" (121–22).

46. For a contrasting medieval view of the functional meaning of *asah* and its role in the creation process, see Nahmanides' comment on Gen 1:7: "The word *asiyyah* always means adjusting something to its required proportion" (Chavel, vol. 1, 34). Samuelson, "Creation in Medieval Philosophical, Rabbinic Commentaries," 250, translates this sentence as "To set something in order according to its proportion."

47. A possible midrashic source for Maimonides' reading of *va-yinnafash* as the completion and perfection of God's will can be found in *Midrash Ha-Gadol, Exodus,* 31:17 (Margulies, 673): "He ceased from the sayings of the creation account and all his will was perfected."

48. For a decisive argument that Maimonides emptied such notions as "holiness" and ritual "purity" or "impurity" of any sense reflecting metaphysical realities in favor of one reflecting social realities (or, as he aptly frames it, Maimonides as a Durkheimian as opposed to Otto-ian on these issues), see Kellner, "Maimonides on the Nature of Ritual Purity and Impurity." As he asserts at xxiii, "The laws of ritual purity and impurity refer to matters that exist in the mind only; they are halakhic institutions, with no objective referent in the super-social universe."

49. It is important to note that Maimonides' negative theology does not necessarily rule out the possibility of any God-talk whatsoever. Religious language about God remains a viable option if the critical distinction between "an epistemic [thesis] concerning the unknowability of God [and] a semantic one concerning the intelligibility of language about God" is maintained, as Buijs has argued ("The Negative Theology," 724). For a well-argued thesis that picks up on this distinction, arguing that Maimonides' negative theology is in fact a solution to how one can legitimately talk about an unknowable God, see Benor, "Meaning and Reference." His thesis, which has Maimonides promoting the "symbolic function of God-talk" so that "intellectual lovers of God are therefore not beyond the realm of human-bound religious language" (343), would, I believe, equally apply to religious "acts" such as the halakhic observance of Sabbath. Both speech and act constitute a symbolic path toward a pure conception of God.

50. The cherubim and their evident violation of the strict prohibition against the crafting of graven images, particularly within the holiest of spaces known to Judaism, troubled the Rabbis as well. See, e.g., *Mekhilta de-Rabbi Ishmael Ba-Hodesh* 10 (Lauterbach, vol. 2, 282–83), which struggles with the glaring contradiction between the stricture of Exod 20:20 and the cherubim, restricting the latter to a rare exception to the general rule. It concludes its discussion in an attempt to avert the inherent danger posed by images in the Temple: "Lest you

say: since the Torah has given permission to make the cherubim in the Temple, I am also going to make them in the synagogues and in the schoolhouses, Scripture says *Ye shall not make unto you [gods of silver or gold]*." For a suggestion as to how Maimonides may have halakhically reconciled the two, see Klein, "The Significance of the *Keruvim*."

51. For a midrashic parallel of this formulation, see *Midrash Ha-Gadol, Exodus*, 25:18, which reads in part: "Why do I need these *cherubim*? In order to know that *cherubim* exist on high . . . and one should be sufficient. They might come to err and they will say it is a deity." See also M. Kasher's note to this *midrash*, which already draws the parallel between it and Maimonides' statement on the cherubim (*Torah Shelemah*, vol. 20, 35 n. 129). It is more likely than not that the *Midrash Ha-Gadol* actually postdated Maimonides and was itself influenced by him. One theory actually ascribes authorship of the *Midrash Ha-Gadol* to Maimonides' own son, Abraham. See Fisch's introduction to his edition of the *Midrash Ha-Gadol, Numbers*, 16 ff.

52. MT *Laws of the Foundations of the Torah* 2:7; GP II:4, 258: "For the intellects are the angels, which are near to Him, by means of whom the spheres are moved"; GP II:10, 273: "For all created things are divided into three parts: the separate intellects which are the angels." See Blumberg, "The Separate Intelligences."

53. GP II:6, 264–65, where cherub is distinguished from angel in a *midrash* that is taken to be descriptive of the prophetic process in which angel = imaginative faculty and cherub = intellect.

54. GP III:3, 422–23, where they are identified with the *hayot* (living creatures) seen by Ezekiel in his vision of the chariot. See Blumenthal, "Maimonides on Angel Names," 365, who notes its use as a homonym. Altmann, *Encyclopedia Judaica*, already pointed this out: Maimonides "considered the word 'angel' a homonymous term denoting not only the separate intelligences but all natural and psychic forces, both generic and individual." H. Kasher, "Is There an Early Stratum," considers the different meanings of "angel" as evidence for sifting out different strata in Maimonides' writings, reflecting earlier and more mature positions; see esp. 109–16.

55. Maimonides' theory of divine accommodation to rationalize many of the *mitzvot* was his most controversial and "had touched a nerve that sent tremors throughout the Jewish world. His theory met incessant caustic criticism; the battle was joined to repel his interpretation" (Benin, "'Cunning of God,'" 189). Maimonides' most prominent opponent on this issue, Nahmanides, had this to say about this offensive theory in his biblical commentary to Lev 1:9: "Heaven forbid that these rituals should have no other purpose and intention save the elimination of idolatrous opinions from the minds of fools."

56. Kugel, *The God of Old*, 194, points out that the pervasiveness of angels assigned to control every possible natural and human phenomenon in the closing centuries of the biblical period was a way of bringing a remote God down

to earth: "God's remoteness seems to have compromised His standing as the only divine power in the world: in practice divinity was once again shared." See also Silver's assessment of the proliferation of angels: "The more the theological spirit of the age raised God to the heaven of heavens, the more the folk peopled the lower spheres with angels, spirits, and emanations of the world-soul" (*History of Judaism,* 202).

57. A parallel obsession with angels developed in the Christian tradition and angelology became part of the scholastic curriculum; in response to Greek philosophy, as with Maimonides, it took a decidedly different approach. As Keck, *Angels and Angelology in the Middle Ages,* 71, observes: "The flowering of medieval angelology in the thirteenth century was the result of formalized, logical reflections on certain natural and metaphysical aspects of angels raised by Aristotelian categories and problems."

58. *Eccl Rabbah* on Eccl 10:20, of which Maimonides quoted only two out of six links in a communicative chain that works its way from the body all the way up to God.

59. As Rosenberg points out ("On Biblical Exegesis in the *Guide,*" 110), this reflects the general structure of prophecy "which in the prophetic perception something immanent in man (imaginative faculty) appears as if it exists external to him (angel)."

60. For the implications of this distinction, see Bland, "Moses and the Law."

61. According to Blumenthal, "Maimonides on Angel Names," 365 n. 14, the two cherubim from between which God communicates with Moses represent the Agent Intelligence and Moses' intellect. Faur, *Homo Mysticus,* 19, draws a striking equation between the cherubim and intellectual perfection, which strengthens my point here, as follows: "The *Chariot* represents God's Divine Providence steering the Cosmos, like a rider steering his mount (Dt.33:26). The *Kerubim* are the holy beings pulling the Chariot. They seem like full-grown humans with children's faces and are identified with 'the natural individual forces' in humans effecting human rationality. Probably *kerub* is a metathesis of *rakhub* (mount). Upon perfection, the individual and community undergo a metamorphosis, becoming God's mount, a medium carrying on His will." The *keruv* thus ultimately represents "natural forces" in man, who is the ultimate purveyor of divine providence in the world. Providence translates itself through human efforts, through natural means.

62. The translation of Kafih's Hebrew is mine. For the phrase "and he was standing between the two cherubim," Maimonides switched from Judeo-Arabic to Hebrew in the original.

63. Scholem, *On the Kabbalah and Its Symbolism,* 139.

64. Idel, "Sabbath," 82, where this characterization was made in reference to Moses Cordovero.

65. See Green, "Sabbath as Temple," and esp. 300, for Bahya ben Asher's interpretation of Lev 19:30.

66. See *b. Berakhot* 57b and *m. Tamid* 7:4, among others listed by Wolfson, "Coronation of the Sabbath Bride," 307 n. 19.

67. See, e.g., GP I:40 and MT *Laws of Repentance* 8:2–3. For a recent study of Avicenna's influence on this subject, see Eran, "Al-Ghazali and Maimonides," and the works cited therein on the issue of Maimonides' position on immortality.

68. PM Introduction to *Pereq Heleq,* as translated by Abelson, "Maimonides on the Jewish Creed." Judah Halevi also attributes the world-to-come-like nature of the Sabbath to the fact that the creation of man caps all of natural creation that is contingent on time and comes closest to the angels who transcend both nature and time (*Kuzari* 5:10). Though both Maimonides and Halevi share the angels analogy, for Halevi it is based on a conception of the Sabbath as transcending nature and not as representative of it.

69. Wolfson, "Coronation of the Sabbath Bride," 308 and 313, where he describes what would have been, according to my thesis, anathema to Maimonides: "But it is the Sabbath that truly anticipates the eschatological overcoming of time and the *transposition of the natural order*" (emphasis mine). Maimonides, in MT *Laws of the Sabbath* 30:2, cited the talmudic model for greeting the Sabbath, where the early sages would prepare each other with the words "Come let us go to greet Sabbath the king." Our versions of *b. Shabbat* 119a and *b. Bava Qama* 32a–b have these scholars addressing the Sabbath as "queen" (and some as the "bride" and "queen") (see also *Gen Rabbah* 10:9). Though the discrepancy may very likely boil down to the simple matter of textual variants and which document Maimonides worked from (see *Book of Seasons,* vol. 4, Mossad Harav Kook edition, 256 n. 6; and MT, vol. 3, 629 n. 3), it may be worth considering the possibility of an intentional variance to distance the Sabbath from any feminine connotations and counter what may already have become a strong tendency to associate the Sabbath with *shekhinah* and ontic reifications of the feminine aspects of the Godhead. See Ginsburg, *The Sabbath in the Classical Kabbalah,* 101–3. For a thorough discussion of those who followed Maimonides' lead in resisting the feminization of the Sabbath in the Talmud as "queen" by replacing it with "king," see Kimmelman, *The Mystical Meaning,* 1–8. As Kimmelman demonstrates, that resistance was slowly eroded and eventually overcome by kabbalistic tendencies, beginning with the turning of the tide by the *Zohar* and culminating in the Sabbath's total feminization as "bride" and "queen" in sixteenth-century Safed.

70. Burrell, in his *Freedom and Creation in Three Traditions,* has criticized the Islamic *kalam*'s position on human autonomy as amounting to a "zero-sum game in which one protagonist's gain is the other's loss," a position that ignores a metaphysics that can account for "how the originating activity of the creator continues to make the creature to be an agent in its own right" (94). My argument here does not amount to the same zero-sum game where human freedom and God are irreconcilable polarities. Precisely as Sabbath marks a beginning for human freedom it also recalls a God that makes way for that beginning. Every human act

needs to be cognizant of both. God's "disengagement" is itself a kind of engagement that informs every act with its ultimate origins. Sabbath as an *end* to divine activity is necessary for preserving an unadulterated intellectual grasp of divine nature and unity. At the same time, Sabbath also looks back at God as creator and the world as a product of His untrammeled will.

71. There is a serious disagreement as to the precise translation of the final sentence of chapter II:31. Pines translates it as "Accordingly the Sabbath is, as it were, *of universal benefit,* both with reference to a true speculative opinion and to the well-being of the state of the body." The principal term of contention is "universal benefit," which ibn Tibbon (MN) translates as "and it is as if it were a benefit *which includes [kolel]* a true speculative . . . ." The other major translations adopt ibn Tibbon's rendering rather than that of Pines:

Schwartz (MN-S): "which includes" *(ha-kolel).*
Friedländer picks up loosely on the ibn Tibbon sense: "The Sabbath is therefore a *double blessing.*"
Alharizi (Scheyer): identical to ibn Tibbon *(kolel).* In this version the chapter is I:32.
Munk: "C'est en quelque sorte un bienfait qui sert *a la fois.*"

I have consulted with other Judeo-Arabic scholars who conclude that both are plausible readings. Since there are basically two viable readings of the chapter's conclusion, I adopt Pines' for internal literary and structural reasons. First, it is consistent with the assertion made at the beginning of the chapter that Sabbath observance promotes widespread knowledge (Pines: "in order that the principle of the creation of the world in time be established and universally known in the world"; ibn Tibbon followed by Schwartz: *va-yitparsem ba-metziut*) of creation in time. Second, the phrase "as it were" (ibn Tibbon: *ke'ilu;* Schwartz: *me'en*) seems to qualify the previous sentence that identifies the *benefit* as a particular one unique to Jewish history: "God bestowed upon us by giving us rest *from under the burden of the Egyptians.*" The reference to the biblical verses Exod 6:6, 7 identifies the "us" as Jews. The "as it were," then, universalizes a benefit that is originally particularistic. What I believe Maimonides to have asserted is that Israel's historical experience of good fortune turns into good fortune for the world in that it transcends its own parochialism as an exemplar of two universal teachings, one practical and the other theoretical.

The eminent Judeo-Arabic scholar Haggai Ben-Shammai, in a communication with me, cautions that the Arabic original is unclear and that Pines' translation may be misleading. It is his belief, however, that what Pines intended by "universal" is also "comprehensive" with respect to the specific things that the Rambam mentions subsequently. In light of Ben-Shammai's expertise, my reading remains tentative.

72. Medieval commentators such as Abravanel and Shem Tov already address this problem of the introduction of Sabbath at this juncture rather than in the third part at the subject *ta'ame ha-mitzvot.*

73. The debate arises out of seemingly contradictory positions taken by Maimonides. On the one hand, MT (*Laws of Repentance,* chap. 5) and PM ("Eight Chapters," chap. 8) vigorously endorse human autonomy, while GP II:48 paints a wholly deterministic picture of humanity. Altmann, "The Religion of the Thinkers," and Pines, "Studies in Abul Barakat al-Baghdadi's Poetics and Metaphysics," are eminent advocates of an esoteric determinist position, while others have attempted a reconciliation between the two. See, e.g., Gellman, "Freedom and Determinism," and Sokol, "Maimonides on Freedom." Burrell has forcefully argued for a third alternative to the strict dichotomy of libertarian versus determinist that accounts for human freedom in terms of response to God as creator and revealer rather than initiative. Though his primary expositors of this third alternative are Augustine and Aquinas (see *Freedom and Creation,* esp. 83–94), his claim is that Maimonides' conception of human freedom would be more closely aligned with them than with post-Enlightenment thinking on the issue. Though Burrell's important and thoughtful alternative itself deserves pursuing, suffice it for the purposes of this chapter to respond that it might be more attuned to Augustine and Aquinas than Maimonides. What I believe is a critical difference that would affect their positions on freedom is one which Burrell himself identifies in his more recent *Faith and Freedom,* on creation. Whereas Maimonides simply presumed that an everlasting creation emerges at an initial moment of time, Aquinas "refuses to foreclose the conceptual possibility of a free creator creating everlastingly. In short, it need not be part of the meaning of 'free creator' that there exists an initial moment of time" (152–53). A responsive model of freedom works better with a "free creator creating everlastingly." Of course even on this issue there is debate as to Maimonides' position and whether the world's everlastingness is due to God's keeping it that way or to its inherent indestructibility. On this debate, see the typically lucid discussion of Seeskin, *Maimonides on the Origin of the World,* 157–68, and Feldman, "The End of the Universe in Medieval Jewish Philosophy," who endorses the former position, as opposed to R. Weiss, "Maimonides on the End of the World," who argues for the latter.

74. The same *midrash* continues with a derivation from *va-yannihehu,* stating that God "granted him the commandment of Sabbath," based on the linguistic analogy between the terms *va-yannihehu* of Gen 2:15 and *va-yanach* of Exod 20:11. The creation of man and of the Sabbath intersect by virtue of the use of the identical term in the originating moment of "established" order. The choice of this *midrash* by Maimonides could not have been merely fortuitous.

75. See Lieberman, *Hilkhot Yerushalmi,* 5 n. 7, who calls attention to Maimonides' pervasive use of this phrase to introduce virtually every one of his writings.

76. For a later rationalist's subtle and "diplomatic" formulation of what the phrase "possessor of heaven and earth" in Gen 14:19 connotes, see Seforno's commentary on this verse in which he defines the phrase as follows: "The heaven and earth are His possession to do with them as He wills, for they have no natural cause as some of the scholars thought. Rather, He is the willing agent for them and

acts upon them as He wills." Note that his emphasis is on the origins of the world; that is, it is a result of an unfettered act of divine will. This formulation does not rule out the view that nature takes over from where divine will leaves off.

77. No chapter can be strictly differentiated from any other thematically, but each must be read in light of every other. This is why, as Strauss has stressed, the *Guide* is divided into parts and chapters "without supplying the Parts and the chapters with headings indicating the subject matter of the Parts or of the chapters" (GP, "How to Study the Guide," xv). Their porous nature prohibits narrow classification by subject matter. Just as the *Guide* must be subjected to this kind of reading intratextually, Maimonides' entire literary output must often be read intertextually for a "totality" of meaning. For one example, see Levinger, "Abstinence from Alcohol," esp. his remarks on 304–5.

78. See *b. Yoma* 85b; *b. Sanhedrin* 74a; *b. Avodah Zarah* 27b, 54a. This rule is so paramount that if one violates it and chooses observance over life (outside of those three rare circumstances that demand self-sacrifice) he is considered to have committed the most grievous of sins. See MT *Laws of the Foundation of the Torah* 5:1. The normative implications of Lev 18:5, "and shall live by them," clearly apply to life in the present world, although it also harbors an aggadic dimension that sees it as referring to the future world where there is *real* living. See MT *Laws of Unlawful Use of Sacred Property* 8:8; *Sifra Ahare Mot* 8:10.

79. Translation from S. Gandz and H. Klein, 11. Twersky, *Introduction to the Code of Maimonides*, 344, identifies this as a classic anti-Karaite polemic and raises the possibility that describing the laws of the Torah as "not vengeance" is a polemic against the Christian view of Jewish law (432 n.190).

80. For a lengthy analysis of this law, see Blidstein, *Authority and Dissent*, 109–27, and esp. 122–25. Blidstein points out that this formulation is purely rhetorical, intended to persuade, rather than halakhic like its parallel in the *Laws of the Sabbath* just quoted.

81. See, e.g., *b. Shabbat* 118a.

82. See also *Bate Midrashot* 47:62; *Deut Rabbah* 3:1, 20.

Works Cited

Abelson, J. 1907. "Maimonides on the Jewish Creed." *Jewish Quarterly Review* 19: 38–39.
Abravanel, Isaac. 1967. *Yeshu'ot Meshiho*. Ketavim al Mahashevet Yisrael 1. Jerusalem. Reprint of 1861 Konigsberg edition.
———. 1967. *Mifalot Elohim*. Ketavim al Mahashevet Yisrael 5. Jerusalem. Reprint of 1863 Lemberg ed.
Adler, E. 2002. "The Sabbath Observing Gentile: Halakhic, Hashkafic and Liturgical Perspectives." *Tradition* 36(3): 14–45.
Agus, Jacob. 1946. *Banner of Jerusalem*. New York: Bloch.
———, trans. 1946. *Abraham Isaac Kook. Olat Re'iyah*. In *Banner of Jerusalem*, 217–20. New York: Bloch.
Al-Azmeh, A. 1997. *Muslim Kingship*. London: Tauris.
Alter, Robert. 1996. *Genesis*. New York: Norton.
———. 1999. *The David Story*. New York: Norton.
Altmann, Alexander. 1969. *Studies in Religious Philosophy and Mysticism*. Ithaca: Cornell University Press.
———. 1972. *Encyclopedia Judaica*, vol. 2, 975. S.v. "Angels and Angelology in Jewish Philosophy."
———. 1974. "The Religion of the Thinkers: Free Will and Predestination in Saadia, Bahya and Maimonides." In *Religion in a Religious Age*, 25–51. Edited by S. D. Goitein. Cambridge, Mass.: Association for Jewish Studies.
———. 1981. "Maimonides' Four Perfections." *IOS* 2 (1972):15–24. Reprinted in *Essays in Jewish Intellectual History*, 65–76. Hanover: Brandeis University Press.

———. 1981. "Maimonides' Attitude toward Jewish Mysticism." In *Studies in Jewish Thought: An Anthology of German Jewish Scholarship*, 200–219. Edited by A. Jospe. Detroit: Wayne State University Press.

———. 1991. "What Is Jewish Theology?" In *The Meaning of Jewish Existence: Theological Essays, 1930-1939*, 46–56. Hanover: Brandeis University Press.

Anderson, G. 1990. "The Expression of Joy as a Halakhic Problem in Rabbinic Sources." *Jewish Quarterly Review* 80(3–4): 221–52.

Armstrong, A. H., trans. 1984. *Plotinus Enneads*. Loeb Classical Library. Cambridge, Mass.: Harvard University Press.

Bacher, W. 1896. *Die Bibelexegese Moses Maimuni's*. Budapest.

Baneth, D. 1935. "On the Philosophical Terminology of the Rambam." *Tarbitz* 6: 254–84.

———. 1946. *Iggerot Ha-Rambam*. Jerusalem: Meqitze Nirdamim.

Barnes, J., trans. 1995. *The Complete Works of Aristotle*. 2 vols. Princeton: Princeton University Press.

Benin, S. 1984. "'Cunning of God' and Divine Accommodation." *Journal of the History of Ideas* 45: 179–91.

Benor, Ehud. 1994. "Petition and Contemplation in Maimonides' Conception of Prayer." *Religion* 24: 59–66.

———. 1995. *Worship of the Heart: A Study in Maimonides' Philosophy of Religion*. Albany: SUNY Press.

———. 1995. "Meaning and Reference in Maimonides' Negative Theology." *Harvard Theological Review* 88(3): 339–60.

Ben-Sasson, Haim Hillel. 1969–74. "The Uniqueness of Israel According to Twelfth Century Thinkers." *Peraqim* (Schocken Institute Yearbook) 2, 145–218.

Ben-Sasson, Y. 1959. "A Study of the Doctrine of *Ta'ame Ha-Mitzvot* in Maimonides' *Guide* [Hebrew]." *Tarbitz* 29: 268–81.

Berger, D. 1991. "Some Ironic Consequences of Maimonides' Rationalistic Messianism [Hebrew]." *Maimonidean Studies* 2: 1–8.

Berman, L. 1961. "The Political Interpretation of the Maxim: The Purpose of Philosophy is the Imitation of God." *Studia Islamica* 15: 53–61.

———. 1963. "Avempace: The Governance of the Solitary." In *Medieval Political Philosophy: A Sourcebook*, 122–33. Edited by R. Lerner and M. Mahdi. New York: Free Press.

———. 1980. "Maimonides on the Fall of Man." *AJS Review* 5: 1–15.

Bland, Kalman. 1982. "Moses and the Law According to Maimonides." In *Mystics, Philosophers and Politicians*, 49–66. Edited by J. Reinharz and J. Swetschinski. Durham: Duke University Press.

Blau, J., ed. and trans. 1958. *Teshuvot Ha-Rambam*. Jerusalem: Mekitze Nirdamim.

Blenkinsopp, J., trans. 2002. *Isaiah 40-55*. Anchor Bible Series 19A. New York: Doubleday.

Blidstein, Gerald. 1980. "The Concept of Joy in Maimonides [Hebrew]." *Eshel Be'er-Sheva* 2: 145–63.

———. 1981. "Individual and Community in the Middle Ages: Halakhic Theory." In *Kinship and Consent: The Jewish Political Tradition and its Contemporary Uses*, 215–56. Edited by D. J. Elazar. Ramat Gan: University Press of America.

———. 1982–83. "The Monarchic Imperative in Rabbinic Perspective." *AJS Review* 8–9: 15–39.

———. 1994. *Prayer in Maimonidean Halakhah* [Hebrew]. Jerusalem: Mossad Bialik.

———. 1996. "Parents and Children in Maimonides' Philosophy and Halakha." *Da'at* 37: 27–36.

———. 2002. *Authority and Dissent in Maimonidean Law* [Hebrew]. Tel Aviv: Ha-Kibbutz Ha-Meuhad.

Blumberg, H. 1971. "The Separate Intelligences in Maimonides' Philosophy [Hebrew]." *Tarbitz* 40: 216–25.

Blumenthal, D. R. 1977. "Maimonides' Intellectualist Mysticism and the Superiority of the Prophecy of Moses." *Studies in Medieval Culture* 10: 51–67.

———. 1986. "Maimonides on Angel Names." In *Hellenica et Judaica*, 357–69. Edited by A. Caquot et al. Leuven: Éditions Peeters.

———. 1987. "Maimonides: Prayer, Worship and Mysticism." In *Prière, mystique et Judaisme*, 89–106. Edited by R. Goetschel. Paris: Presses Universitaires de France.

Brettler, M. 1989. *God Is King: Understanding an Israelite Metaphor*. Sheffield: JSOT Press.

Broadie, A. 1989. "Maimonides on Divine Knowledge." In *Of Scholars, Savants and Their Texts: Studies in Philosophy and Religious Thought: Essays in Honor of Arthur Hyman*, 47–67. Edited by R. Link-Salinger. New York: Lang.

Buber, Martin. 1973. *Meetings*. LaSalle, Ill.: Open Court.

Buijs, J. 1988. "The Negative Theology of Maimonides and Aquinas." *Review of Metaphysics* 41: 723–38.

———. 1989. "Attributes of Action in Maimonides." *Vivarium* 27(2): 85–102.

Burrell, David. 1986. *Knowing the Unknowable God: Ibn-Sina, Maimonides, Aquinas*. Notre Dame: University of Notre Dame Press.

———. 1993. *Freedom and Creation in Three Traditions*. Notre Dame: University of Notre Dame Press.

———. 2004. *Faith and Freedom: An Interfaith Perspective*. Malden, Mass.: Blackwell.

Chavel, Charles, trans. 1971–76. *Nahmanides's Commentary on the Torah*. 5 vols. New York: Shilo.

Coggins, R. J. 1976. *Ezra and Nehemiah*. Cambridge: Cambridge University Press.

Cohen, Boaz. 1935. "The Classification of the Law in the Mishneh Torah." *JQR* 25: 519–40.

Cohen, Shaye. 1999. *The Beginnings of Jewishness: Boundaries, Varieties, Uncertainties*. Berkeley: University of California Press.

———. 2005. *Why Aren't Jewish Women Circumcised?: Gender and Covenant in Judaism*. Berkeley: University of California Press.

Cohen, Stuart. 1984. "The Concept of the Three Ketarim: Its Place in Jewish Political Thought and Its Implications for a Study of Jewish Constitutional History." *AJS Review* 9: 27–54.
Cronbach, Abraham. 1941. "The Gradations of Benevolence." *HUCA* 16: 163–86.
Danby, H., trans. 1954. *The Code of Maimonides*, vol. 10, *The Book of Cleanness*. Yale Judaica Series. New Haven: Yale University Press.
Davidson, Herbert. 1972. "The Active Intellect in the *Cuzari* and Hallevi's Theory of Causality." *Revue des études juives* 131: 381–95.
———. 1974. "The Study of Philosophy as a Religious Obligation." In *Religion in a Religious Age*, 53–68. Edited by S. D. Goitein. Cambridge, Mass.: Association for Jewish Studies.
———. 1987. "The Middle Way in Maimonides' Ethics." *PAAJR* 54: 31–72.
———. 1992. *Alfarabi, Avicenna and Averroes on Intellect*. Oxford: Oxford University Press.
———. 1992–93. "Maimonides on Metaphysical Knowledge." *Maimonidean Studies* 3: 49–103.
———. 2001. "The Authenticity of Works Attributed to Maimonides." In *Me'ah Shearim: Studies in Medieval Jewish Spiritual Life in Memory of I. Twersky*. Edited by G. Blidstein et al. Jerusalem: Magnes Press.
Diamond, James. 1996. "The Use of Midrash in Maimonides' *Guide of the Perplexed.*" *AJS Review* 21: 39–60.
———. 2002. *Maimonides and the Hermeneutics of Concealment: Deciphering Scripture and Midrash in* The Guide of the Perplexed. Albany: SUNY Press.
Dienstag, J. I. 1998. "Reasons for the Commandments in Maimonidean Thought [Hebrew and English]." *Da'at* 41: 101–15.
Disendruck, Z. 1936. "Samuel and Moses ibn Tibbon on Maimonides' Theory of Providence." *Hebrew Union College Annual* 11: 341–56.
Dvornik, Francis. 1966. *Early Christian and Byzantine Political Philosophy*. Washington: Dumbarton Oaks Center for Byzantine Studies.
Efros, I. 1941. "Some Aspects of Yehudah Halevi's Mysticism." *PAAJR* 11: 7–9.
Eliade, Mircea. 1957. *The Sacred and the Profane*. New York: Harcourt, Brace.
Eran, A. 2001. "Al-Ghazali and Maimonides on the World to Come and Spiritual Pleasures." *Jewish Studies Quarterly* 8: 137–66.
Fackenheim, Emil. 1961. *Metaphysics and Historicity*. Milwaukee: Marquette University Press.
Faur, Jose. 1997. "The Character of Apophatic Knowledge in Maimonides' Guide." In *Theodicy*, 65–74. Edited by D. Cohn-Sherbok. Lewiston: Edwin Mellen Press.
———. 1998. *Homo Mysticus: A Guide to Maimonides'* Guide for the Perplexed. Syracuse: Syracuse University Press.
Feinstein, M. 1973. *Iggerot Moshe*. 8 vols. New York: Balshon Printing.
Feintuch, A. 2000. *Sefer Ha-Mitzvot Le-Ha-Rambam im Perush Piqude Yesharim*. Jerusalem: Ma'aliyot Press.

Feldman, Seymour. 1986. "The End of the Universe in Medieval Jewish Philosophy." *AJS Review* 11: 53–77.
Finkelstein, Louis, ed. 1989. *Sifre to Deuteronomy*, vol. 1. New York: Jewish Theological Seminary of America.
Fisch, S., trans. 1940. *Midrash Ha-Gadol, Numbers*. Manchester: Manchester University Press.
Fishbane, Michael. 1994. *The Kiss of God: Spiritual and Mystical Death in Judaism*. Seattle: University of Washington Press.
———. 1995. "The Inwardness of Joy in Jewish Spirituality." In *In Pursuit of Happiness*, 71–88. Edited by L. Rouner. Notre Dame: University of Notre Dame Press.
Fogelman, R. M. 1950. "The Sukkah in the Temple [Hebrew]." *Sinai* 26: 89–95.
Fox, Marvin. 1990. "The Doctrine of the Mean in Aristotle and Maimonides: A Comparative Study." In *Studies in Jewish Religious and Intellectual History*, 93–120. Edited by Siegfried Stein and R. Loewe. Tuscaloosa: University of Alabama Press. Reprinted in *Interpreting Maimonides*, 93–123. Chicago: University of Chicago Press.
———. 1990. *Interpreting Maimonides*. Chicago: University of Chicago Press.
———. 1996. "Prayer in the Thought of Maimonides." In *Prayer in Judaism*, 119–41. Edited by G. Cohn and H. Fisch. Northvale: Jason Aaronson.
Frank, Daniel H. 1989. "Humility As a Virtue: A Maimonidean Critique of Aristotle's Ethics." In *Moses Maimonides and His Time*, 89–99. Edited by Eric Ormsby. Washington, D.C.: Catholic University of America Press.
———. 1990. "Anger As a Vice—A Maimonidean Critique of Aristotle's Ethics." *History of Philosophy Quarterly* 7: 269–81.
Frank, R. M. 1989. "Knowledge and *Taqlid*." *JAOS* 109: 37–62.
Frankel, Shabse, ed. 1975–2001. *Mishneh Torah*, 12 vols. Bene, Brak: Hotsa'at Shabse Frankel Ltd.
Frankfort, H. 1948. *Kingship and the Gods*. Chicago: University of Chicago Press.
Friedländer, Michael, trans. 1956. *The Guide for the Perplexed*. 2d ed. New York: Dover Publications.
Friedman, Shamma. 1993. "La-Aggadah Ha-Historit Ba-Talmud Bavli." In *Saul Lieberman Memorial Volume*, 119–63. New York: Jewish Theological Seminary.
Frydman-Kohl, Baruch. 1992. "Covenant, Conversion and Chosenness: Maimonides and Halevi on 'Who Is a Jew?'" *Judaism* 41(1): 64–79.
Funkenstein, A. 1993. *Perceptions of Jewish History*. Berkeley: University of California Press.
Gandz, S., and H. Klein. 1961. *The Code of Maimonides*, vol. 14, *The Book of Seasons*. Yale Judaica Series. New Haven: Yale University Press.
Gellman, Jerome. 1989. "Freedom and Determinism in Maimonides' Philosophy." In *Moses Maimonides and His Time*, 139–50. Edited by E. Ormsby. Washington: Catholic University Press of America.
———. 1991. "Maimonides' Ravings." *Review of Metaphysics* 45: 309–28.

Ginsburg, E. 1989. *The Sabbath in the Classical Kabbalah.* Albany: SUNY Press.

Goitein, S. D. 1980. "Moses Maimonides, Man of Action: A Revision of the Master's Biography in Light of the Genizah Documents." In *Homage à Georges Vajda: Études d'histoire et de pensée juives.* Louvain: Peeters.

———. 1999. *A Mediterranean Society. An Abridgment in One Volume.* Berkeley: University of California Press.

Goldziher, Ignaz. 1905. "Mélanges Judeo-Arabes: Le 'Amr Ilahi *(hainyan haelohi) chez Juda Halevi.*" *Revue des études juives* 50: 32–41.

Goodman, Lenn. 1992. "Maimonidean Naturalism." In *Neoplatonism and Jewish Thought,* 157–94. Albany: SUNY Press.

Gordis, R. 1951. *Koheleth—The Man and His World.* New York: Jewish Theological Seminary.

Goshen-Gottstein, Alon. 2000. *The Sinner and the Amnesiac: The Rabbinic Invention of Elisha ben Abuya and Eleazer ben Arach.* Stanford: Stanford University Press.

Grant, Edward. 1996. *Planets, Stars and Orbs: The Medieval Cosmos 1200-1687.* Cambridge: Cambridge University Press.

Green, A. 1980. "Sabbath as Temple: Some Thoughts on Space and Time in Judaism." In *Go and Study: Essays in Honor of Alfred Jospe,* 287–305. Edited by R. Jospe and S. Fishman. Washington, D.C.: B'nai Brith Hillel Foundation.

Gruenwald, Ithamar. 1991. "Maimonides' Quest Beyond Philosophy and Prophecy." In *Perspectives on Maimonides,* 141–57. Edited by J. Kraemer. Oxford: Littman Library.

Guttman, Julius. 1964. *Philosophies of Judaism. The History of Jewish Philosophy from Biblical Times to Franz Rosenzweig.* Translated by D. Silverman. New York: Holt, Rinehart, and Winston.

Halamish, M. 1983. "Some Aspects of the Attitudes of the Kabbalists toward Gentiles." In *Filosofyah Yisre'elit,* 49–71. Edited by A. Kasher and M. Halamish. Tel Aviv: Papirus.

Halevi, Judah. 1996. *The Kuzari.* Translated by Joseph Kafih. Kiryat Ono: Makhon Mishnat Ha-Rambam.

Halkin, A. S. 1963. "The Medieval Jewish Attitude toward Hebrew." In *Biblical and Other Studies,* 233–48. Edited by A. Altmann. Cambridge: Harvard University Press.

———, trans. 1985. "Sanhedrin; Treatise on Resurrection." In *Crisis and Leadership: Epistles of Maimonides,* 222–23. Philadelphia: Jewish Publication Society.

Ha-Meiri, Shelomoh. 1978. *Hiddushe Ha-Meiri al Sanhedrin, Makkot, Shevuot, Avodah Zarah, Horayot, Eduyot.* Zihron Yaakov: Ha-Makhon Le-Hotsa'at Sefer.

Harris, Jay. 1995. *How Do We Know This: Midrash and the Fragmentation of Modern Judaism.* Albany: SUNY Press.

Hartman, David. 2000. *Israelis and the Jewish Tradition: An Ancient People Debating Its Future.* New Haven: Yale University Press.

Harvey, Steven. 1991. "Maimonides in the Sultan's Palace." In *Perspectives on Maimonides,* 47–75. Edited by J. Kraemer. Oxford: Littman Library.

Harvey, Warren Zev. 1981. "A Portrait of Spinoza as a Maimonidean." *Journal of the History of Philosophy* 19: 151–72.

———. 1988. "Crescas versus Maimonides on Knowledge and Pleasure." In *A Straight Path: Studies in Medieval Philosophy and Culture: Essays in Honor of Arthur Hyman*, 113–23. Edited by R. Hackett et al. Washington, D.C.: Catholic University of America Press.

———. 1991. "Why Maimonides Was Not a Mutakallim." In *Perspectives on Maimonides*, 105–14. Edited by J. Kraemer. Oxford: Littman Library.

———. 1994. "Nuriel's Method for Deciphering the Secrets of the *Guide* [Hebrew]." *Da'at* 32–33: 69–70.

———. 1994. "Political Philosophy and Halakha in Maimonides." In *Jewish Intellectual History in the Middle Ages*, Binah 3, 47–64. Edited by Joseph Dan. Westport, Conn.: Praeger. Translated from *Iyyun* 29 (1980), 198–212.

———. 1995. "Les sacrifices, la prière, et l'étude chez Maimonide." *Revue des études juives* 154: 97–103.

———. 1996. "Judah Halevi's Synesthetic Theory of Prophecy and a Note on the Zohar [Hebrew]." *Jerusalem Studies in Jewish Thought* 12: 141–55.

———. 1997. "The Rambam on Job 14:20 and the Garden of Eden Story [Hebrew]." In *Sefer Yovel Le-Yitzhak Barzilai*, 143–48. Edited by S. Nash. Tel Aviv: Ha-Kibuts Ha-Meuhad.

Heidegger, Martin. 1962. *Being and Time*. New York: Harper and Row.

Henshke, D. 1996. "On the Question of Unity in Maimonides' Thought [Hebrew]." *Da'at* 37: 37–51.

Heschel, A. J. 1945. "Did Maimonides Believe That He Was Worthy of Prophecy? [Hebrew]" In *Louis Ginzberg Jubilee Volume*, 164–66. New York: American Academy for Jewish Research.

———. 1954. "Prayer and the Community." In *Man's Quest for God*, 44–46. New York: Charles Scribner.

Hyamson, M. 1971. *Mishneh Torah*. Jerusalem: Feldheim.

ibn Shmuel, Y., ed. 2000. *Sefer Moreh Ha-Nevukhim Le-Rabbenu Mosheh ben Maimon*. With *Perush Ha-Millim Ha-Zarot* by Shmuel ibn Tibbon. Jerusalem: Mossad Ha-Rav Kook.

ibn Tibbon, Shmuel. 1960. Hebrew trans. *Moreh Nevukhim*. With Commentaries by Efodi, Shem Tov, Crescas, Abravanel. Repr. from 1904, Jerusalem.

Idel, M. 2004. "Sabbath: On Concepts of Time in Jewish Mysticism." In *Sabbath: Idea, History, Reality*, 57–93. Edited by G. Blidstein. Beer Sheva: Ben Gurion University of the Negev Press.

Irwin, T., trans. 1985. *Aristotle. Nicomachean Ethics*. Indianapolis: Hackett.

Ivry, Alfred L. 1985. "Providence, Divine Omniscience, and Possibility: The Case of Maimonides." In *Divine Omniscience and Omnipotence in Medieval Philosophy*, 143–59. Edited by T. Rudavsky. Boston: Reidel.

———. 1990. "Maimonides on Creation [Hebrew]." *Mehqere Yerushalayim Be-Mahshevet Yisrael* 9: 115–37.

———. 1991. "Neoplatonic Currents in Maimonides' Thought." In *Perspectives on Maimonides*, 114–40. Edited by J. Kraemer. Oxford: Littman Library.

———. 1995. "Ismaili Theology and Maimonides' Philosophy." In *The Jews of Medieval Islam: Community, Society and Identity*, 271–99. Edited by D. Frank. Leiden: E. J. Brill.

Jordan, Mark. 1983. "The Names of God and the Being of Names." In *The Existence and Nature of God*, 161–87. Edited by A. J. Freddoso. Notre Dame: University of Notre Dame Press.

Jospe, R. 1986. "Rejecting Moral Virtue as the Ultimate End." In *Studies in Islamic and Judaic Traditions*, 185–204. Edited by W. Brinner and S. Ricks. Atlanta: Scholars Press. Hebrew version: "Negating Moral Virtue as the Ultimate End." *Jerusalem Studies in Jewish Thought* 5 (1986): 93–112.

Kafih, Joseph, ed. and trans. 1965. *Mishnah im Perush Rabbenu Mosheh ben Maimon*. 6 vols. Jerusalem: Mossad Ha-Rav Kook.

———. 1971. *Sefer Ha-Mitzvot*. Jerusalem: Mossad Ha-Rav Kook.

———. 1972. *Moreh Ha-Nevukhim*. 3 vols. Jerusalem: Mossad Ha-Rav Kook.

———. 1972. *Iggerot Le-Rabbenu Mosheh ben Maimon*. Jerusalem: Mossad Ha-Rav Kook.

———. 1984. *Sefer Mishneh Torah*. 22 vols. Jerusalem.

———. 1997. *Maimonides' Treatise on Logic* [Hebrew]. Kiryat Ono: Makhon Mishnat Ha-Rambam.

Kaplan, Lawrence. 1985. "Maimonides on the Singularity of the Jewish People." *Da'at* 15: v–xxvii.

———. 1990. "'I Sleep, but My Heart Waketh': Maimonides' Conception of Human Perfection." In *The Thought of Moses Maimonides: Philosophical and Legal Studies*, 130–66. Edited by I. Robinson et al. Lewiston: Edwin Mellen Press.

———. 1991. "Hilkhot Megillah 2:17 Revisited: A Halakhic Analysis." *Tradition* 26(1): 4–21.

———. 2002. "An Introduction to Maimonides' Eight Chapters." *Edah Journal* 2(2): 10–13.

Karo, Joseph. 2001. *Kesef Mishneh*, in *Mishneh Torah*. Jerusalem.

Kasher, Hannah. 1985. "Job's Image and Opinion in *The Guide of the Perplexed* [Hebrew]." *Da'at* 15: 81–87.

———. 1986. "*Talmud Torah* as a Means of Apprehending God in Maimonides' Teachings [Hebrew]." *Mehqere Yerushalayim Be-Mahashevet Yisrael* 5: 71–81.

———. 1989. "The Parable of the King's Palace in *The Guide of the Perplexed* as Instruction for the Student [Hebrew]." *AJS Review* 14(2): 1–19.

———. 1992–93. "Is There an Early Stratum in *The Guide of the Perplexed*?" *Maimonidean Studies* 3: 105–29.

———. 1995. "Mitos Ha-El Ha-Ko'es Ba-Moreh Nevukhim." *Eshel Be'er Sheva* 4: 95–111.

———. 1996. "Preferential Concern for Kin in Maimonides' Thought [Hebrew]." *Iyyun* 45: 115–24.

———. 1998. "Biblical Miracles and the Universality of Natural Laws: Maimonides' Three Methods of Harmonization." *Journal of Jewish Thought and Philosophy* 8: 25–52.

Kasher, Menachem. 1953–1970. 8 vols. *Torah Shelemah.* New York: American Biblical Encyclopedia Society.

Kaufman, Y. 1969. *Toledot Ha-Emunah Ha-Yisraelit.* 4 vols. Jerusalem: Mosad Bialik.

Keck, D. 1998. *Angels and Angelology in the Middle Ages.* New York: Oxford University Press.

Keel, O. 1978. *The Symbolism of the Biblical World.* Translated by T. Hallett. New York: Seabury Press.

Kellner, Menachem. 1986. *Dogma in Medieval Jewish Thought: From Maimonides to Abravanel.* Oxford: Littman Library.

———. 1990. *Maimonides on Human Perfection.* Brown Judaic Series 202. Atlanta: Scholars Press.

———. 1991. *Maimonides on Judaism and the Jewish People.* Albany: SUNY Press.

———. 1993. "Chosenness, Not Chauvinism: Maimonides on the Chosen People." In *A People Apart: Chosenness and Ritual in Jewish Philosophical Thought,* 61–62. Edited by D. Frank. Albany: SUNY Press.

———. 1999. "Could Maimonides Get Into Rambam's Heaven?" *Journal of Jewish Thought and Philosophy* 8(2): 231–42.

———. 2001. "Maimonides on the Normality of Hebrew." In *Judaism and Modernity: The Religious Philosophy of David Hartman,* 435–71. Edited by J. Malino. Jerusalem: Shalom Hartman Institute.

———. 2001. "Was Maimonides Truly Universalist?" *Terumah* 11: 3–15.

———. 2003. "Maimonides on the Nature of Ritual Purity and Impurity." *Da'at* 50–52: i–xxx.

———. 2006. *Maimonides' Confrontation with Mysticism.* Portland: Littman Library.

———, trans. 1982. *Abravanel. Principles of Faith* [*Rosh Amanah*]. Rutherford: Fairleigh Dickenson.

Kimmelman, R. 1992. "The Laws of Warfare and its Parameters [Hebrew]." In *Sanctity of Life and Martyrdom,* 233–53. Edited by I. Gafni and A. Ravitzky. Jerusalem: Shazar Center.

———. 2003. *The Mystical Meaning of* Lekhah Dodi *and* Kabbalat Shabbat [Hebrew]. Jerusalem: Magnes Press.

Klein, A. 2003. "The Significance of the *Keruvim* in Maimonides' Teaching [Hebrew]." *Megadim* 37: 33–46.

Klein-Braslavy, Sara. 1986. *Maimonides' Interpretation of the Adam Stories in Genesis* [Hebrew]. Jerusalem: Reuven Maas.

———. 1987. *Maimonides' Interpretation of the Creation Account* [Hebrew]." Revised ed. Jerusalem: Reuven Maas.

———. 1996. *King Solomon and Philosophical Esotericism in the Thought of Maimonides* [Hebrew]. Jerusalem: Magnes Press.

Kogan, B. 1996. "Judah Halevi." In *A History of Islamic Philosophy,* vol. 1, 718–24. Edited by S. Nasr and O. Leaman. New York: Routledge.

Kraemer, Joel. 1984. "On Maimonides' Messianic Posture." In *Studies in Medieval Jewish History and Literature,* vol. 2, 109–42. Edited by I. Twersky. Cambridge, Mass.: Harvard University Press.

Kravitz, L. S. 1967. "Maimonides and Job: An Inquiry as to the Method of the Moreh." *Hebrew Union College Annual* 58: 149–58.

Kreisel, Howard. 1986. "The Sage and the Prophet in the Thought of the Rambam and His School." *Eshel Be'er-Sheva* 3: 149–69.

———. 1991. "Judah Halevi's Influence on Maimonides." *Maimonidean Studies* 2: 95–121.

———. 1996. "Love and Fear of God in Maimonides' Thought [Hebrew]." *Da'at* 37: 127–51.

———. 1999. *Maimonides' Political Thought: Studies in Ethics, Law and the Human Ideal.* Albany: SUNY Press.

———. 2001. *Prophecy: The History of an Idea in Medieval Jewish Philosophy.* Dordrecht: Kluwer Academic.

Kugel, James. 1981. *The Idea of Biblical Poetry.* New Haven: Yale University Press.

———. 2003. *The God of Old: Inside the Lost World of the Bible.* New York: Free Press.

Langermann, Y. Tzvi. 2004. "Maimonides and Miracles: The Growth of a (Dis)belief." *Jewish History* 18(2–3): 147–72.

Laqueur, Walter. 1996. *Fascism.* New York: Oxford University Press.

Lasker, Daniel. 1990. "Proselyte Judaism, Christianity, and Islam in the Thought of Judah Halevi." *Jewish Quarterly Review* 81: 75–91.

Lauterbach, J. Z., trans. 1933. *Mekhilta de Rabbi Ishmael.* 3 vols. Philadelphia: Jewish Publication Society.

Lebowitz, Y. 1989. "Divine Providence in Maimonides [Hebrew]." In *Mehkarim Be-Hagut Yehudit,* 79–86. Edited by S. Willensky and M. Idel. Jerusalem: Magnes Press.

Lerner, Ralph. 1991. "Maimonides' Governance of the Solitary." In *Perspectives on Maimonides,* 33–46. Edited by J. Kraemer. Oxford: Littman Library.

Levi, Y., ed. 1992–99. *Persushe Ha-Torah Le-Rabbenu Gershom ben Levi.* 5 vols. Jerusalem: Mossad Ha-Rav Kook.

Levinas, E. 1994. *Beyond the Verse: Talmudic Readings and Lectures.* Translated by G. Mole. Bloomington: Indiana University Press.

Levinger, Jacob. 1965. *Maimonides' Techniques of Codification: A Study in the Method of the Mishneh Torah* [Hebrew]. Jerusalem: Magnes Press.

———. 1967. "Abstinence from Alcohol in Maimonides' *Guide of the Perplexed* [Hebrew]." *Bar Ilan* 4–5 (decennial vol.): 299–305.

———. 1988. "Maimonides' Exegesis of Job." In *Creative Biblical Exegesis,* 81–88. Edited by B. Uffenheimer and H. G. Reventlow. Sheffield: Sheffield Academic Press.

Lieberman, Saul. 1955-88. *Tosefta Ki-Feshutah.* 10 parts. New York: Jewish Theological Seminary.

———. 1947. *Hilkhot Yerushalmi.* New York: Jewish Theological Seminary of America.

Liebes, Yehuda. 1990. *The Sin of Elisha: The Four Who Entered* Pardes *and the Nature of Talmudic Mysticism* [Hebrew]. Jerusalem: Academon.

Lobel, Diana. 1999-2000. "A Dwelling Place for the Shekhina." *Jewish Quarterly Rreview* 90: 103-25.

Lockshin, Martin, trans. 2001. *Rashbam's Commentary on Leviticus and Numbers.* Brown Judaic Studies 330. Providence.

Lorberbaum, Menachem. 1993. "Maimonides' Letter to Ovadyah: An Analysis." *Svara* 3(2): 59-66.

———. 2001. *Politics and the Limits of Law: Secularizing the Political in Medieval Jewish Thought.* Stanford: Stanford University Press.

Lorberbaum, Y. 2001-2002. "'The Men of Knowledge and the Sages Are Drawn, as It Were, Toward This Purpose by the Divine Will': On Maimonides' Conception of Parables [Hebrew]." *Tarbitz* 71: 86-132.

Mahdi, M. 1963. "Maimonides *Letter on Astrology.*" In *Medieval Political Philosophy,* 227-36. Edited by R. Lerner and M. Mahdi. New York: Free Press.

Mani, Aaron. 1956. *Sefer Moreh Ha-Nevukhim.* Jerusalem: Weinfeld.

Margulies, M., ed. 1966. Midrash *Ha-Gadol, Exodus.* Jerusalem: Mossad Ha-Rav Kook.

Matt, Daniel. 1989. "*Matnita Dilan*: A Technique of Innovation in the Zohar [Hebrew]." *Jerusalem Studies in Jewish Thought* 8 (The Age of the *Zohar*): 123-45.

McGovern, W. 1941. *From Luther to Hitler: The History of Fascist-Nazi Political Philosophy.* Cambridge, Mass.: Riverside Press.

Melamed, Abraham. 2003. *Philosopher King in Medieval and Renaissance Jewish Thought.* Albany: SUNY Press.

Milgrom, Jacob. 1991. *Leviticus 1-16.* Anchor Bible Series 3. Garden City: Doubleday.

Muffs, Y. 1992. *Love and Joy: Law, Language and Religion in Ancient Israel.* New York: Jewish Theological Seminary.

Munk, Saloman, trans. 1979. *Le guide des égarés.* Revised ed. by Charles Mopsik. Paris: Verdier.

Myers, J. 1965. *Ezra, Nehemiah: Introduction, Translation, and Notes.* Anchor Bible Series 14. Garden City: Doubleday.

Nehorai, Michael. 1984. "Maimonides' System of the Commandments [Hebrew]." *Da'at* 13: 29-42.

———. 1990. "Maimonides on Miracles [Hebrew]." *Jerusalem Studies in Jewish Thought* 9(2): 1-18.

———. 1993. "Review of M. Kellner, *Maimonides on Judaism* [Hebrew]." *Da'at* 30: 127-29.

Nelson, Janet. 1988. "Kingship and Empire." In *The Cambridge History of Medieval Political Thought*, 211–25. Edited by J. H. Burns. Cambridge: Cambridge University Press.

Nuriel, A. 1986. "The Concept of Satan in *The Guide of the Perplexed* [Hebrew]." *Jerusalem Studies in Jewish Thought* 5: 83–91.

———. 1990. "The Use of the Term *Garib* in *The Guide of the Perplexed*: A Remark on the Esoteric Method in the *Guide*." *Sefunot* 5: 137–43.

———. 2000. "Providence and Governance in *Moreh Ha-Nevukhim* [Hebrew]." *Tarbitz* 49: 346–55. Reprinted in *Concealed and Revealed in Medieval Jewish Philosophy*, 83–92. Jerusalem: Magnes Press.

Pines, Shlomo. 1960. "Studies in Abul Barakat al-Baghdadi's Poetics and Metaphysics." *Scripta Hierosolymitana* 6: 195–98.

———. 1979. "The Limitations of Human Knowledge According to al-Farabi, ibn Baja, and Maimonides." In *Studies in Medieval Jewish History and Literature*, 82–109. Edited by I. Twersky. Cambridge: Harvard University Press.

———. 1980. "Shi'ite Terms and Conceptions in Judah Halevi's *Kuzari*." *Jerusalem Studies in Arabic and Islam* 2: 165–261.

———. 1986. "The Philosophical Purport of Maimonides' Halachic Works and the Purport of *The Guide of the Perplexed*." In *Maimonides and Philosophy*, papers presented at the Sixth Jerusalem Philosophical Encounter, May 1985, 1–14. Edited by S. Pines and Y. Yovel. Dordrecht: Nijhoff.

———. 1988. "On the Term Ruhaniyyut and Its Origin and on Judah Halevi's Doctrine [Hebrew]." *Tarbitz* 57: 511–40.

———, trans. 1963. *The Guide of the Perplexed*. 2 vols. Introductory essay by Leo Strauss. Chicago: University of Chicago Press.

Pinhas of Koretz. 2000. *Midrash Pinhas*. Edited by S. Valtsis. Ashdod: Yashlim.

Porton, Gary. 1994. *The Stranger within Your Gates: Converts and Conversion in Rabbinic Literature*. Chicago: University of Chicago Press.

Posen, R. 2001. "Targum Onkelos in Maimonides' Writings [Hebrew]." In *Sefer Zikkaron leRav Yosef ben David Kafih*, 236–56. Edited by Z. Amar and H. Seri. Ramat Gan: Bar Ilan University.

Raffel, C. M. 1987. "Providence as Consequent upon the Intellect: Maimonides' Theory of Providence." *AJS Review* 12: 25–71.

Raffel, Dov. 1998. *Ha-Rambam Ke-Mehanekh*. Jerusalem: Yediot Ahronot.

Ravitzky, A. 1991. "'To the Utmost Human Capacity': Maimonides on the Days of the Messiah." In *Perspectives on Maimonides*, 221–56. Edited by J. Kraemer. Oxford: Littman Library.

Rawidowicz, S. 1935. "The Structure of the *Moreh Nevukhim* [Hebrew]." In *Sefer Ha-Rambam shel Ha-Tarbitz*, 41–89. Jerusalem: Hebrew University Press.

———. 1969. *Studies in Jewish Thought* [Hebrew]. Jerusalem: Rueven Maas.

———. 1974. *Studies in Jewish Thought*. Philadelphia: Jewish Publication Society.

Regev, S. 1990. "Collective Revelation and Mount Sinai: Maimonides and His Commentators [Hebrew]." *Jerusalem Studies in Jewish Thought* 9(2): 251–65.

Reines, A. 1972. "Maimonides' Concepts of Providence and Theodicy." *Hebrew Union College Annual* 43: 169–206.
———. 1975. "Maimonides' Concept of Miracles." *Hebrew Union College Annual* 45: 243–85.
———. 1986. "Maimonides True Belief Concerning God." In *Maimonides and Philosophy*, 24–35. Edited by S. Pines and Y. Yovel. Dordrecht: Nijhoff.
Rembaum, J. 1991. "Interpretation of Scripture in Judah Halevi's *Kozari*: A Study in Theological Exegesis." In *Threescore and Ten: Essays in Honor of Rabbi Seymour J. Cohen*, 151–64. Edited by A. Karp et al. Hoboken: Ktav.
Ricoeur, Paul. 1975. "Biblical Hermeneutics." *Semeia* 4: 29–145.
———. 1985. "The Power of Speech, Science and Poetry." *Philosophy Today* 29: 59–70.
———. 1991. "The Model of the Text: Meaningful Action Considered as a Text." In *From Text to Action: Essays in Hermeneutics II*, 144–67. Translated by K. Blamey and J. Thompson. London: Athlone Press.
———. 1996. *Interpretation Theory: Discourse and the Surplus of Meaning*. Fort Worth: Texas Christian University Press.
Rosenberg, S. 1981. "On Biblical Exegesis in the *Guide* [Hebrew]." *Jerusalem Studies in Jewish Thought* 1: 85–157.
———. 1984. "The Concept of *Emunah* in Post-Maimonidean Jewish Philosophy." In *Studies in Medieval Jewish History and Literature*, vol. 2, 273–307. Edited by I. Twersky. Cambridge, Mass.: Harvard University Press.
———. 2001. "You Shall Walk in His Ways." *Edah Journal* 2(2): 2–17. Translated by J. Linsider from *Filosofyah Yisraelit*. Edited by M. Halamish and A. Kasher. Tel Aviv: Papyrus, 1982–83.
Rosenblatt, S., trans. 1948. *Sa'adya Gaon. Book of Beliefs and Opinions*. New Haven: Yale University Press.
Rosenzweig, Franz. 2000. *Ninety-Two Poems and Hymns of Yehuda Halevi*. Translated by T. Kovach et al. Albany: SUNY Press.
Rubenstein, Jeffrey. 1995. *The History of Sukkot in the Second Temple and Rabbinic Periods*. Atlanta: Scholars Press.
———. 1998. "Elisha ben Abuya: Torah and the Sinful Sage." *Journal of Jewish Thought and Philosophy* 7: 129–225.
Safrai, S. 1985. "Pious and Men of Deeds [Hebrew]." *Tzion* 50: 133–54.
Safran, Bezalel. 1990. "Maimonides and Aristotle on Ethical Theory." In *Alei Shefer: Studies in the Literature of Jewish Thought*, 133–61. Edited by M. Halamish. Ramat Gan: Bar Ilan University Press.
Samuelson, N. 1989. "Creation in Medieval Philosophical, Rabbinic Commentaries." In *From Ancient Israel to Modern Judaism: Essays in Honor of Marvin Fox*, vol. 2, 231–59. Edited by J. Neusner et al. Atlanta: Scholars Press.
Sarna, Nahum. 1991. *Exodus. The JPS Torah Commentary*. Philadelphia: Jewish Publication Society.

Scheyer, Simon, ed. 1952. *Judah ben Solomon Harizi. Moreh Ha-Nevukhim*. Tel Aviv: Mahbarot Le-Sifrut.
Scholem, Gershom. 1965. *Jewish Gnosticism, Merkabah Mysticism, and Talmudic Tradition*. New York: Jewish Theological Seminary.
———. 1970. *On the Kabbalah and Its Symbolism*. New York: Schocken Books.
———. 1971. *The Messianic Idea in Judaism*. New York: Schocken Books.
———. 1991. *On the Mystical Shape of the Godhead*. New York: Schocken Books.
Schwartz, Dov. 1994. "Divine Immanence in Medieval Jewish Philosophy." *Journal of Jewish Thought and Philosophy* 3: 249–78.
Schwartz, Michael, trans. 2002. *Moreh Nevukhim*. Edited by David Tzeri. Tel Aviv: University of Tel Aviv.
Schwarzschild, Steven. 1990. "Moral Radicalism and 'Middlingness' in the Ethics of Maimonides." *Studies in Medieval Culture* 11 (1978): 65–94. Reprinted in *The Pursuit of the Ideal*, 37–160. Edited by M. Kellner. Albany: SUNY Press.
Scott, R. B. Y. 1965. *Proverbs, Ecclesiastes: Introduction, Translation, and Notes*. Anchor Bible Series 18. Garden City: Doubleday.
Seeskin, Kenneth. 2000. *Searching for a Distant God: The Legacy of Maimonides*. New York: Oxford University Press.
———. 2004. "Maimonides' Sense of History." *Jewish History* 18: 129–45.
———. 2005. *Maimonides on the Origin of the World*. New York: Cambridge University Press.
Seforno, Obadiah ben Jacob. 1980. *Beur Al Ha Torah*. Jerusalem: Mossad Ha-Rav Kook.
Septimus, B. 1984. "'Kings, Angels or Beggars': Tax Law and Spirituality in a Hispano–Jewish Responsum." In *Studies in Medieval Jewish History and Literature*, vol. 2, 309–32. Edited by I. Twersky. Cambridge, Mass.: Harvard University Press.
Shailat, I., ed. 1987. *Iggerot Ha-Rambam*. 2 vols. Jerusalem: Ma'aliyot Press.
Shiffman, Yair, ed. 2001. *Moreh Ha-Moreh*. Jerusalem: World Union of Jewish Studies.
Shinan, Avigdor. 1979. "The Sins of Nadav and Avihu in Rabbinic Literature [Hebrew]." *Tarbitz* 48(3/4): 201–14.
Silman, Y. 2001. "Ma'amad Ha-Adam Be-Yekum Be-Aspaklaryah shel Ha-Sifrut Ha-Rabbanit." *Bar-Ilan Annual* 28–29: 335–51.
Silver, D. J. 1974. *History of Judaism*. New York: BasicBooks.
Slotki, J. trans. 1939. *Numbers Rabbah*. London: Soncino Press.
Sokol, M. 1998. "Maimonides on Freedom the Will and Moral Responsibility." *Harvard Theological Review* 91(1): 25–39.
Soloveitchik, Haym. 1980. "Maimonides' Iggeret Ha-Shemad: Law and Rhetoric." In *Rabbi Joseph Lookstein Memorial Volume*, 281–319. Edited by L. Landman. New York: Ktav.
———. 1994. "Rupture and Reconstruction: The Transformation of Contemporary Orthodoxy." *Tradition* 28(4): 64–130.

———. 1995. "On Some Solutions to the Paradox of Humility in Jewish Sources [Hebrew]." *Iyyun* 44, 355–70.
Soloveitchik, J. B. 1992. *Lonely Man of Faith*. Garden City: Doubleday.
Sontag, Susan. 1978. *Illness as Metaphor*. New York: Farrar, Straus, and Giroux.
Spinoza, Baruch. 1925. *Spinoza Opera, im Auftrag der Heidelberger Akademie der Wissenschaft*. 5 vols. Edited by C. Gebhardt. Heidelberg: Winter.
Statman, Daniel. 1995. "On Some Solutions to the Paradox of Humility in Jewish Sources." *Iyyun* 44: 355–70.
Stern, Josef. 1986. "The Idea of a *Hoq* in Maimonides' Explanation of the Law." In *Maimonides and Philosophy*, 92–130. Edited by S. Pines and Y. Yovel. Dordrecht: Nijhoff.
———. 1989. "Al Setirah KiBe-Yakhol ben *Moreh Nevukhim Le-Mishneh Torah*" ["On an Alleged Contradiction between Maimonides' *Guide of the Perplexed* and *Mishneh Torah*]." *Shenaton Ha-Mishpat Ha-Ivri* xiv–v: 283–98. Reprinted in 1998 in English in *Problems and Parables of Law*, chap. 3. Albany: SUNY Press.
———. 1993. "Maimonides on the Covenant of Circumcision." In *The Midrashic Imagination: Jewish Exegesis, Thought and History*, 131–54. Edited by M. Fishbane. Albany: SUNY Press.
———. 1998. *Problems and Parables of Law: Maimonides and Nahmanides on Reasons for the Commandments*. Albany: SUNY Press.
———. 2000. "Maimonides on Language and the Science of Language." In *Maimonides and the Sciences*, 211, 173–226. Boston Studies in the Philosophy of Science. Edited by R. Cohen and H. Levine. Dordrecht: Kluwer Academic.
———. 2001. "Maimonides on Amalek, Self-Corrective Mechanisms and the War against Idolatry." In *Judaism and Modernity: The Religious Philosophy of David Hartman*, 371–410. Edited by J. Malino. Jerusalem: Shalom Hartman Institute.
Strauss, Leo. 1967. "Notes on Maimonides' Book of Knowledge." In *Studies in Mysticism and Religion presented to G. Scholem*, 269–83. Jerusalem: Magnes.
———. 1987. *Philosophy and Law*. Translated by F. Baumann. Philadelphia: Jewish Publication Society.
Stroumsa, Sara. 1992–93. "Elisha ben Abuya and Muslim Heretics in Maimonides' Writings." *Maimonidean Studies* 3: 173–93.
Tabory, J. 1995. *Jewish Festivals in the Time of the Mishnah and the Talmud*. Jerusalem: Magnes.
Tate, J. 1929. "Plato and Allegorical Interpretation." *Classical Quarterly* 23: 142–54.
Turner, M. 1996. "The Portrayal of Abraham the Patriarch in *The Guide of the Perplexed* [Hebrew]." *Da'at* 37: 181–92.
Twersky, I. 1967. "Some Non-Halakhic Aspects of the *Mishneh Torah*." In *Jewish Medieval and Renaissance Studies*, 95–118. Edited by A. Altmann. Cambridge: Harvard University Press.
———. 1980. *Introduction to the Code of Maimonides*. New Haven: Yale University Press.

———. 1988–89. "Halakha and Science: Perspectives on the Epistemology of Maimonides [Hebrew]." *Shenaton Ha-Mishpat Ha-Ivri* xiv–xv: 121–51.

———. 1989. "On Law and Ethics in the *Mishneh Torah*: A Case Study of Hilkhot Megillah II:17." *Tradition* 24(2): 138–49.

———. 1992. "Sanctifying the Name and Sanctity of Life: Perspectives on 'Holiness' in the Thought of the Rambam [Hebrew]." In *Sanctity of Life and Martyrdom*, 167–90. Edited by I. Gafni and A. Ravitzky. Jerusalem: Shazar Center.

———, ed. 1972. *A Maimonides Reader*. New York: Behrman House.

Urbach, E. 1971. *The Sages: Their Concepts and Beliefs* [Hebrew]. Jerusalem: Magnes Press.

Wasserstein, D. 1993. "A Fatwa on Conversion in Islamic Spain." In *Studies in Muslim-Jewish Relations*, vol. 1, 177–88. Edited by R. Nettler. Switzerland: Harwood Academic.

Weiler, Gershon. 1988. *Jewish Theocracy*. Leiden: Brill.

Weinberg, R. Y. Y. 1962. *Seride Esh*. 4 vols. Jerusalem: Mossad Ha-Rav Kook.

Weiss, A. 1963. "Shevitat AKU"M." *Bar Ilan Annual* 1: 143–48.

Weiss, Raymond. 1971. "Language and Ethics: Reflections on Maimonides' Ethics." *Journal of the History of Philosophy* 9: 425–33.

———. 1975. *Ethical Writings of Maimonides*. New York: Dover Press.

———. 1991. *Maimonides' Ethics: The Encounter of Philosophic and Religious Morality*. Chicago: University of Chicago Press.

Weiss, Roslyn. 1992–93. "Maimonides on the End of the World." *Maimonidean Studies* 3: 195–218.

———. 2000. "See No Evil: Maimonides on Onqelos's Translation of the Biblical Expression 'And the Lord Saw.'" *Maimonidean Studies* 4: 135–62.

Wijnhoven, Jochanan. 1995. "The Zohar and the Proselyte." In *Readings on Conversion to Judaism*, 47–65. Edited by L. J. Epstein. Northvale, N.J.: Jason Aaronson.

Wolfson, Elliot. 1994. "Negative Theology and Positive Assertion in the Early Kabbalah." *Da'at* 32–33: v–xxii.

———. 1994. *Through a Speculum That Shines: Vision and Imagination in Medieval Jewish Mysticism*. Princeton: Princeton University Press.

———. 1997. "Coronation of the Sabbath Bride: Kabbalistic Myth and the Ritual of Androgynisation." *JJTP* 6(2): 301–43.

———. 2004. "Beneath the Wings of the Great Eagle: Maimonides and Thirteenth-Century Kabbalah." In *Moses Maimonides (1138–1204): His Religious, Scientific, and Philosophical* Wirkungsgeschichte *in Different Cultural Contexts*, 209–37. Edited by George Hasselhoff and Otfried Fraisse. Wurzburg: Ergon Verlag.

———. 2006. *Venturing Beyond: Law and Morality in Kabbalistic Mysticism*. Oxford: Oxford University Press.

Yafeh, H. Lazarus. 1971. "Some Notes on the Term *Taqlid* in the Writings of al-Ghazzali. *Israel Oriental Studies* 1: 249–56.

Citations Index

HEBREW BIBLE

Genesis
1:1, 72
1:2, 247n24
1:4, 73
1:7, 73, 293n46
1:8, 73
1:18, 75
1:26, 119
1:28, 59
1:31, 58, 60, 68
2:2, 194, 195, 196, 201, 290n22
2:15, 222, 298n74
2:18, 5
3:7, 5, 135
3:21, 5
4:9, 5
4:15, 239n11
5:3, 121
8:21, 265n38
8:22, 286n1
13:17, 13, 19
14:12, 276n10
14:13, 276n10
14:19, 298n76
14:22, 223
14:23, 224
17:5, 29
18:19, 13, 16, 17, 18
21:33, 223, 262n22
31:49, 282n12
36:31, 237n61
39:2, 132
46:1, 283n15
46:4, 283n15
46:33–34, 116
46:34, 266n43
47:3, 116
48:14, 273n106
48:15, 259n64
49:10, 254n34
49:24, 259n64

Exodus
2:2, 246n18
2:22, 119
3:1, 258n62, 277n20

3:2, 149, 275n3
3:6, 61, 143
4:14, 242n33
6:6, 297n71
6:7, 297n71
7:3, 243n45
8:22, 266n43
12:48–49, 232n19
15:25, 206
16:7, 96
16:8, 95, 96, 97, 257n51
16:18, 97
17:11, 276n7
18:3, 119
19:9, 160, 161, 163
19:22, 144
19:24, 117
20:1, 162
20:2, 8
20:11, 192, 194, 199, 201, 210, 219, 222, 287n2, 290n22, 298n74
20:16, 282n6
20:19, 162
22:20, 236n51
23:20–21, 276n7
24:2, 176, 177
24:10, 65
24:15–18, 147
24:16, 147, 148, 149, 155, 181, 184
24:17, 148, 184
25:8, 277n26
25:22, 216, 217
28:42, 211
29:43–44, 153
29:45, 151, 153, 154
29:46, 151, 153
31:17, 209
31:18, 168
32:16, 168
33:3, 281n13
33:13, 45, 68, 102, 103, 278n28
33:18, 102, 175
33:19, 45, 68
33:21, 114, 143, 144, 175, 176, 275nn2–3
34:6, 151, 156, 281n13
34:29, 113
35:35, 179
40:34, 180, 181, 182, 184
40:35, 180
40:38, 150

Leviticus
10:2, 67
13–14, 34
13:2, 238n3
13:46, 240n14
13:47, 238n2
14:34, 238n2
16:8, 278n36
18:5, 225, 299n78
19:30, 211, 214, 218, 295n65
22:32, 15, 128
23:24, 273n104
23:24–25, 272n97
25:39–40, 258n59
26:27–28, 50

Numbers
9:16, 277n25
11:1, 67, 68
11:12, 97
11:16, 98
11:21, 257n55
11:23, 257n55
12:3, 35, 81, 95
12:6, 40
12:8, 40
12:9, 41, 42, 43, 241n28, 242n33
12:10, 39, 172
14:27, 129
15:15, 14, 23, 24, 25
16–17, 84
16:3, 84
23:21, 281n13
28:1–6, 273n104
29:1, 272n97

Deuteronomy
3:24, 281n13
4:11, 163
4:24, 122, 148
4:39, 281n13
5:15, 30, 210, 219, 219–20, 237n59, 258n56
5:28, 113, 114
6:4, 214
6:7, 113, 120, 121
10:18, 9
10:19, 27
10:20, 122, 123
10:21
11:1, 27
11:22, 122, 123
13:5, 174
16:7, 155
16:12, 30, 237n59, 258n56
17:14, 254n34
17:15, 91, 237n61
17:19, 91
17:20, 260n76
24:8–9, 39
24:9, 35
24:18, 258n56
24:22, 258n56
26:5–10, 28–29
28:9, 18, 94, 123, 174, 259n71
28:47, 130, 271n89
31:17–18, 42, 75, 77, 170
31:18, 42
32:9, 258n63
32:40, 281n13
32:41, 8
33:1, 155
33:4, 23
33:5, 250n8
33:16, 149, 155
33:26, 64, 65, 295n61
33:27, 142, 275n2
34:5–12, 125
34:6, 269n68
34:7, 126
34:10, 126
34:10–12, 127

Joshua
1:8, 92, 93

1 Samuel
8, 91
8:7, 91
8:17, 258n58
18:30, 273n106
25:3, 273n106
25:9, 199
25:10, 200
25:14, 200

2 Samuel
6, 132
6:5, 272n90
6:16, 131, 132, 133, 272n90
6:22, 131, 132
19:22, 260n72
19:23
21:10, 207

1 Kings
2:4, 253n28
7:14, 179
8:20, 253n28
8:25, 253n28
9:5, 253n28
10:9, 253n28
12:7, 100
22:19, 283n14

2 Kings
10:30, 253n28
16:12, 253n28
17:9, 36, 43, 46, 51
24:20, 243n42

Isaiah

2:2-3
2:3, 173, 284n24, 284n26
2:5, 174, 175
5:20, 72, 73, 74, 75
6:3, 180, 181, 182, 188
11:6, 8
26:21, 166, 167, 172, 281nn7-8
40:11, 101
44:5, 14, 30, 31
45:7, 72, 73, 76
55:1, 57
55:2, 57
56:3, 13, 19, 20
56:7, 19, 20
57:15, 85, 86
58:14, 226
65:17, 8
66:1, 247n19

Jeremiah

3:14, 4, 116
3:15, 116
7:22-23, 154, 213
9:22-23, 71
12:2, 118
17:7, 88
27-28, 243n42
31:7-9, 259n64

Ezekiel

1:26, 283n14
3:12, 175
9:9, 289n17
34, 259n64
43:1, 164
43:2, 164, 248n29
44:1, 164
44:2, 160, 164, 165

Hosea

5:15, 166, 169, 170

Joel

3:5, 111, 262n26

Micah

1:3, 166, 167, 281nn7-8

Habakkuk

3:16, 207, 208

Zechariah

5:10, 207

Malachi

3:13, 52
3:15, 51
3:17, 36, 244n49
3:18, 52, 244n49

Psalms

4:5, 118, 119
8:5, 179, 257n51, 285n35
12:4, 244n50
12:5, 52
19:2-4, 120
23, 259n64
29:9, 184, 288n15
31:18, 47
31:19, 35, 47, 49
33:6, 167, 168, 169, 172
36:10, 187
52:10, 273n106
65:2, 116, 266n44
68:5, 64
73:9, 36, 51
73:11-13, 51
78:52, 258n64
78:62, 258n63
78:70-72, 259n64
78:70-71, 101
78:71, 101
80:2, 259n64
80:4, 259n65
89:15, 64

91:7, 208
94:2, 84, 85
109:22, 94
119:99, 273n106
131:1, 63, 64
144:3, 179, 257n51
144:5, 178, 179, 285n35
145:9, 78

Proverbs
5:17, 71
12:8, 273n106
16:4, 60, 245n8
21:4, 264n30
24:13, 57, 58
24:14, 57
25:6, 131
25:16, 62, 63
25:17, 62, 63
25:27, 57, 58, 60, 63, 245n9

Job
2:5, 178
2:6, 178
3:4, 146
3:5, 146, 147
14:20, 126
22:21, 76
32:1, 196, 199

Song of Songs
4:11, 70, 71, 247n20
4:12, 70
4:12–13, 5
4:13, 71

Ruth
2:12, 16, 231n11
3:13, 78

Lamentations
2:9, 254n31

Ecclesiastes
2:5, 228n8
4:17, 62, 145
5:1, 46, 47, 189
5:2, 35, 46, 49
7:8, 78
7:16, 63
9:14–15, 115
12:9, 109
12:10, 109
31:4, 255n37

Esther
9:27, 20

Daniel
1:17, 273n106
7: 9, 283n14
12:10, 273n106

Nehemiah
2:8, 228n8
8, 135, 274n112
8:1 138
8:2, 136, 138
8:2–3, 273n99
8:3, 139, 274n100
8:4, 138
8:5, 139, 274n100
8:5–6, 138–39
8:7, 136
8:7–9, 273n99
8:8, 137
8:9, 137
8:10, 137
8:11, 138
8:12–13, 273n99
8:13, 138
8:14, 138
8:16, 138
8:17, 138
8:18, 138

1 Chronicles
22:12, 273n106
28:2, 99

2 Chronicles
2:11, 273n106
6:10, 253n28
6:16, 253n28
36:13, 48
36:16, 35, 47–48, 48, 49
36:17–21, 48

RABBINIC WORKS

Mishnah

Avot
1:15, 286n47
1:17, 242n38
5: 6, 167
5:12–13, 259n67

Bikkurim
1:4, 29
3:4, 237n58

Hagigah
2:1, 2, 261n3
2:3, 69

Mo'ed Qatan
3:4, 255n40

Nega'im
3:1, 238n6

Rosh Hashanah
3:8, 276n7

Sanhedrin
7:6, 211

Sotah
9:15, 270n82

Sukkah
5:4, 129

Tamid
7:4, 296n66

Tosefta

Sanhedrin
4:5, 254n34

Sukkah
4:2, 129

Halakhic Midrash

Mekhilta de-Rabbi Ishmael
Ba-Hodesh 10, 293n50
Bo 14, 283n15
Ki Tissa, 286n1
Mishpatim 18, 229n19, 237n60

Sifra
Ahare Mot 8:10, 299n78
Be-Har 7:2, 258n59
Qedoshim 7:8, 211

Sifre numbers
Num 12:1, 240n16
Mas'e, 3, 283n15

Sifre Zuta
Num 12:1, 240n16

Sifre Deuteronomy
Eqev, 268n62
33, 231n8
34, 113, 121
41, 14
156, 254n34
353:16, 277n20

Palestinian Talmud

Bikkurim
1:4, 29

Sanhedrin
1:3, 251n8
2:6, 255n41

Ta'anit
3:1, 283n15

Babylonian Talmud

Arakhin
16a, 240n16

Avodah Zarah
27b, 299n78
54a 229n10
54b, 167

Bava Batra
14b, 255n40
15a, 125
25a, 285n40
81a, 232n17, 237n56

Bava Metzia
73b, 258n59

Bava Qama
32a–b, 296n69

Bekhorot
47a, 252n19

Berakhot
3b, 105
7a, 68
8a, 15, 274n117
17a, 186
26b, 14
33b, 266n44
57b, 202, 296n66

Betzah
16a, 288n11

Hagigah
7a, 62
13a, 64, 228n3
14b, 56, 228n7, 244n1
16a, 247n19

Horayot
8a, 161
11a, 254n34

Keritot
9a, 23

Ketubbot
111a, 239n10
111b, 268n62

Makkot
24a, 161

Megillah
3a, 273n107
18a, 266n44
23b, 15
29a, 283n15
31a, 251n15

Menahot
30b, 125
43b, 246n16

Nedarim
32b, 115

Pesahim
117a, 272n93

Qiddushin
30a, 263n28
31a, 286n46
44b, 239n10
70b, 234n31
73a, 31
82a–b, 270n78

Sanhedrin
16b, 98
19b, 254n32, 268n59
20b, 254n34
21b, 255n41
29a, 255n39
32b, 222
39b, 230n1
49a, 255n39
57b, 291n36
58b, 286n1
70b, 255n37
74a, 299n78
99a–b, 49
110a, 284n31
111a, 265n42

Shabbat
11a, 270n78
30b, 272n93
63a, 252n21
87b, 291n36

105b, 42
118a 299n81
119a, 296n69
119b, 48

Shevuot
15a–b, 251n9

Sotah
12a, 246n16
39a, 274n117

Sukkah
53a, 271n89

Taanit
2a, 14

Yevamot
22a, 252n19
46a, 258n59
47b, 231n11
48b, 252n19
62a, 252n19
91b, 236n47
97b, 252n19
105a, 286n41

Yoma
69b, 139
85b, 299n78

Zevahim
102a, 251n8

Extra-Canonical Tractates

Gerim
4:3, 237n60

Soferim
14:14, 274n114

Aggadic Midrash

Bate Midrashot
47:62, 299n82

Deuteronomy Rabbah
1:18, 286n1
3:1, 299n82
3:20, 299n82

Ecclesiastes Rabbah
Ecclesiastes 10:20, 295n58

Exodus Rabbah
1:24, 247n18
2:3, 258n62
25:12, 226
25:16, 286n1
48:4, 251n28

Genesis Rabbah
4:5, 247n18
5:5, 229n11
10:9, 296n69
10:12, 201
16:5, 222
21:4, 269n73
22:15, 239n11
34:10, 265n38
68:9, 142

Leviticus Rabbah
16:1, 240n16
20, 277n22
23:3, 248n25
31:4, 251n8

Midrash Ha-Gadol
Exodus 25:18, 294n51
Exodus 31:17, 293n47
Numbers, 12:1, 240n16

Midrash Tehillim
94:4, 285n34

Numbers Rabbah
4:20, 230n23
7:10, 283n15

Pesiqta Rabbati
22:3, 161

Pirqe de-Rabbi Eliezer
3, 67, 195, 202, 263n27

Song of Songs Rabbah
1:2, 161
1:8, 153

Tanhuma
5:10, 240n16

MAIMONIDES' WORKS

GP

I, Introduction, 2, 3, 9, 77, 95, 108, 110, 121, 134, 135, 153, 154, 157, 165, 181, 224, 242n34, 245n3, 261n3, 261n8, 262n18
I:1, 4, 68, 119, 123, 174, 257n54
I:2, 5, 114, 127, 135, 137, 246n15, 268n60
I:4, 175, 283n14
I:5, 61, 62, 66, 67, 68, 112, 144, 152, 246n17, 277n22
I:6, 248n25
I:7, 16, 121, 272n94
I:8, 142, 143, 166, 175, 176, 177, 275n2, 275n5
I:9, 99, 100
I:11, 145
I:13, 113
I:15, 48, 114
I:16, 114, 176, 231n8
I:17, 261n3, 245n4
I:18, 176, 177
I:19, 179, 181, 182, 184
I:20, 84
I:21, 152, 156, 157, 279n44, 280n46, 281n12, 281n12
I:22, 160, 165, 166
I:23, 166, 167, 168, 169, 170, 172, 173, 174, 280n44, 281n10
I:24, 18, 41, 123, 170, 172, 173, 174, 242n34
I:25, 88, 145, 157, 173, 184
I:26, 6, 254n4
I:27, 279n44
I:28, 65, 66, 67, 279n44
I:29, 118, 256n47
I:30, 57, 68, 122–3, 124, 148, 149
I:30–36, 56
I:31, 121
I:32, 56, 58, 62, 113, 244n2, 261n3, 277n14, 297n71
I:33, 192, 265n41
I:34, 4, 111, 116, 228n3, 265n41

I:36, 43, 44, 123, 148, 149
I:37, 75, 239n8, 242n34
I:38, 77
I:39, 118, 256n47
I:40, 239n8, 296n67
I:41, 57, 178, 208–9, 209, 239n8, 244n50
I:43, 231n11
I:44, 239n8
I:45, 68, 273n101
I:46, 217
I:48, 280n45
I:50, 118, 192
I:51, 217, 242n37
I:51–52, 232n13
I:54, 43, 45, 68, 86, 88, 94, 102, 103, 175, 232n16, 242n36, 244n49, 275n3, 277n28, 290n30
I:56, 46
I:59, 21, 44, 51, 116, 117, 148, 189, 252n116, 277n31
I:59–60, 252n22
I:60, 111, 212, 213
I:61, 112, 183, 195, 263n27
I:61–63, 183
I:61–64, 195
I:61–67, 288n15
I:64, 69, 181, 181–82, 183, 184
I:65, 117, 183, 184, 195,
I:66, 167, 168
I:67, 194, 194–95, 203
I:68, 68
I:69, 201, 283n19
I:70, 64, 65, 67, 142, 275n2
I:76, 280n44
II:2, 177
II:4, 235n39, 268n56, 294n52
II:5, 26, 74, 75, 119
II:6, 89, 197, 198, 202, 203, 215–16, 283n20, 294n53
II:7, 89
II:10, 178, 294n52
II:11, 268n58
II:12, 163, 164, 207–8, 289n20

II:13, 223, 287n4
II:16, 192, 193
II:23, 192
II:25, 193, 204
II:26, 65, 67
II:29, 127, 167, 204–5, 229n10, 229n15, 234n29, 239n10, 260n74, 261n3n5, 281n9, 286n41
II:30, 70, 72, 73, 74, 76, 77, 209, 219, 221, 222, 223, 246n15, 247n24
II:31, 191, 210, 219, 220, 221, 222, 297n71
II:32, 117, 150, 219
II:33, 25, 117, 118, 162, 165, 266n48
II:34, 150
II:35, 39, 40, 44, 127
II:36, 48, 216, 254n31, 272n93, 279n40
II:37, 120, 243n42, 261n5, 268n58
II:39, 18, 234n33, 284n27
II:40, 243n42, 254n33
II:41, 48
II:42, 48
II:45, 131, 132, 216, 257n55
II:48, 171, 248n28, 299n73
III, Introduction, 261n3
III:2, 126
III:3, 294n54
III:4, 246n16
III:7, 69
III:8, 61, 248n25
III:9, 163, 165, 166, 248n29
III:10, 58, 66, 68, 76
III:11, 60, 229n15, 260n74
III:12, 47, 52, 59, 61, 62, 78, 87, 96–7, 97, 146
III:13, 24, 58, 59, 60, 87
III:16, 47
III:17, 41, 63, 70, 147, 208, 279n40, 285n35, 289n19
III:17–23, 241n29
III:18, 41
III:19, 51, 146
III:22, 38, 114, 178, 196, 244n48, 264n37, 276n12, 289n20
III:23, 38, 52, 115, 147, 196, 198, 287n5, 289n17
III:24, 18, 96, 284n27
III:25, 257n53
III:26, 24, 59, 246n11, 291n35
III:26–33, 291n35
III:27, 90
III:28, 42
III:29, 24, 111, 205, 287n6
III:30, 72
III:31, 24, 192
III:32, 99, 154, 185, 205, 206, 212, 213, 215, 235n42, 273n109, 276n8, 287n3, 292n37
III:33, 91, 92, 161
III:34, 25, 204
III:35, 61, 245n9, 244n47
III:36, 49–50, 244n47
III:37, 239n10
III:39, 30, 101, 116, 155, 231n7, 253n26, 258n56
III:41, 265n39, 275n2, 287n3
III:43, 18, 220, 221, 258n56, 287n3
III:45, 4, 83, 84, 136, 137, 185, 211, 212, 214, 232n20, 240n18
III:46, 232n20
III:47, 34–36, 53, 62, 82, 210
III:48, 255n38, 257n53
III:49, 265n39
III:50, 237n61
III:51, 14, 18, 42, 44, 45, 47, 75, 76, 103, 111, 114, 119, 125, 126, 170, 171, 177, 187, 193, 208, 253n25, 265n40, 267n55, 275n117, 284n27
III:52, 46, 210, 235n44, 259n66
III:54, 71, 72, 97, 287n5

Iggerot
Letter to Ovadyah, 12–14
233, 15, 16
234, 15, 17, 19, 20, 22
235, 22, 25, 29
240, 28

Letter to Joseph bar Yehudah (Rosh Yeshivah) 300–301, 3

MT

Book of Knowledge, 264n33
Foundations of the Torah
1:1–2, 201
1:3–6, 17
1:7, 215
1:9, 8
1:11, 42
2, 290n29
2:1, 235n43
2:2, 26, 239n9
2:4, 290n29
2:7, 48, 294n52
2:10, 267n54
2:12, 261n3
3:3, 246n16
3:9, 26, 268n56, 273n110
4:10–13, 261n3
4:13, 5, 55, 113, 244n1, 263n29
5:1, 299n78
6:2, 274n116
7:4, 133
7:6, 40, 89, 120, 240n18
8:1, 160, 239n10
8:2, 239n10
9:5, 235n10
10:1, 37
Ethical Traits
1:1, 91
1:3, 80
1:5, 88, 249n3
1:5–7, 16, 18
1:6, 94, 174
1:7, 104, 174
2:2, 91
2:3, 10, 42, 52, 80, 230n21, 240n15, 249n3, 279n38
2:4, 243n38

3:1, 63, 255n38
3:2, 245n9
5:5, 249n3
5:6, 286n46
6:1, 264n36
6:2, 268n62
6:4, 27, 229n19, 235n44
7:2, 244n50
7:3, 52, 53
7:10, 27, 86
Studying Torah
1:2, 113, 120, 231n8
1:8, 93
1:11, 112
1:12, 112
3:1, 93, 250n7
3:9, 93
5:1, 277n24, 284n31
6:4, 256n45
6:11, 48
Idolatry
1, 262n21, 263n23, 265n40, 287n6
1:3, 15, 17, 20, 104, 234n33, 284n27
2:1, 240n12
3:3, 136
11:16, 239n10
Repentance
3:6, 268n61
5, 299n73
6:3, 49
7:5, 254n30
7:8, 254n30
8:2–3, 296n67
8:2–4, 187
8:8, 291n32
9:2, 104, 220n12
10:2, 27, 268n64
10:5, 268n64

Book of Love, 235n43
Reading the Shema
1:4, 104

Prayer
1:2, 14
1:2–4, 235n40n41
1:2–5, 267n50
1:2–6 128
1:4, 21, 291n31
2:5, 14
4:16, 186
5:3, 186
5:4, 186
6:8, 128, 270n80
8:1, 15
8:4, 124
8:5, 129
8:6, 15, 128
8:11, 15
12:1, 128
12:3, 124
12:9, 128, 139
12:10, 273n105
12:18, 228n4
13:6, 124

Phylacteries, Mezuzah and Torah Scrolls
7:1, 254n36
7:2, 91, 254n36

Fringes
1:1, 246n16
2:1, 246n16

Book of the Seasons, 296n69
Sabbath
2:3, 225
30:2, 296n69
30:15, 226

Holiday Repose
6:17, 20
6:20, 271n89
6:24, 228n3

Leavened and Unleavened Bread
7–9, 253n30
7:4, 89–90

Shofar, Sukkah, and Lulav
8:13, 129
8:14, 130
8:15, 130–31
8:16, 246n13

Sanctification of the Month
1:8, 284n26
5:2, 239n9
9:8, 239n9

Fasts
1:2–3, 244n47
4:4, 20

Megillah and Hanukkah
2:17, 86

Book of Women
Marital Status
24:9, 265n39

Book of Agriculture
Gifts to the Poor
8:17–18, 237n61
10:1, 89
10:2, 21
10:5, 86
10:7, 87
10:19, 88

Second Tithe
11:17, 237n61

First Fruits
1:3, 29
4:3, 232n17

Sabbatical Year and Jubilee
13:12, 253n26
13:12–13, 136
13:13, 232n22

Book of Holiness
Forbidden Intercourse
1:9, 265n39
12:17, 237n61

13:1–4, 23
13:4, 231n11
14:2, 231n10, 235n37
14:11, 252n19
15:7, 31
21:9, 240n12

Book of Temple Service

The Temple
6:11, 81
6:16, 82
7:1, 211
7:7, 211

Temple Vessels
3:8, 137
8:12, 4
10:4, 4

Yom Kippur Service
2:6–7, 139

Unlawful Use of Sacred Property
8:8, 299n78

Book of Sacrifices

Hagigah Sacrifice
3:1, 89
3:6, 255n42

Sacrifices for Unintentional Sin
15:6, 105

Exchange of Sacred Property

Book of Cleanliness

Leprosy Defilement
9:2, 238n6
16:10, 34, 37, 38, 39, 53

Food Defilement
16:12, 89

Book of Damages

Robbery and Loss
5:12–14, 258n58
5:16, 258n60

The Murderer and Preservation of Life
6:3, 239n9
6:12, 37
13:14, 21

Book of Acquisition

Sale
19:5, 239n9

Slaves
1:7, 86, 100, 258n60
2, 253n30
8:11, 86

Book of Judges

The Sanhedrin
1:3, 98
2:5, 254n32
4:8, 239n9
4:10, 239n9
5:1, 251n9
25:2, 98, 99

Evidence
13:2, 252n19
16:4, 239n9

Rebels
2:4, 225
5:11, 27
6:3, 239n9
6:7, 27
6:9, 256n45
6:12, 255n39

Mourning
13:1, 240n12
13:10, 269n69

Kings and their Wars
1:1–2, 83
1:2, 91
1:3, 90
1:4, 237n61
2:5, 93, 94
2:6, 94

3:1, 91, 92
3:5, 91
3:6, 91
3:7, 254n32
3:9, 255n39
4:1, 258n58
4:10, 89
5:1–2, 251n14
8:4, 265n39
8:5, 231n11
8:10, 23
10:9, 286n1
11:1, 279n 37
12:1, 7, 8, 89, 205
12:4, 104
12:5, 20, 104

PM

Book of Zera'im, 281n1

Avot
Introduction
(Eight Chapters), 120, 249n1
4, 242n32, 262n16
7, 240n18, 272n93
8, 233n29, 243n45, 266n45, 299n73
1:17, 242n38
4:4, 240n17, 250n5
5:5, 229n11, 239n10
5:6, 233n29, 281n11

Bikkurim
1:4, 236n53
3:7, 291n31

Eduyot
8:12, 260n74

Gittin
5:8, 228n 4

Hagigah
2:1, 261n3
2:3, 69

Horayot
1:6, 99

Nega'im
12:5, 37

Sanhedrin
1:5, 82
2:3, 254n32
10, Introduction, 109, 120, 243n43
10:1, 253n27

Shevuot
2:2, 250n8

SM
Positive Commandments
6, 122, 123
8, 85, 174, 256n49
11, 211, 264n34–35
153, 284n26
207, 235n44

Names Index

Abelson, J., 296n68
Abravanel, Isaac, 241n28, 242n33, 261n10, 262n19, 275n5, 277n17, 278n27, 291n32, 297n72
Abulafia, Abraham, 247n25
Adler, E., 287n1
Al-Azmeh, A., 256n46
Alter, Robert, 266n43, 290n23
Altmann, Alexander, 247n25, 257n52, 257n55, 284n30, 294n54, 298n73
Anderson, G., 272n95
Aquinas, Thomas, 288n12, 298n73
Augustine, 298n73
Avicenna, 268n56, 296n67

Bacher, W., 277n23
Bahya ben Asher, 271n87, 295n65
Baneth, D., 260n1, 262n20
Benin, S., 294n55
Benor, Ehud, 233n26, 243n46, 250n6, 267n49, 267n50, 293n49
Ben-Sasson, Haim Hillel, 234n32, 235n35
Ben-Sasson, Y., 279n36

Ben-Shammai, Haggai, 297n71
Berger, D., 291n33
Berman, L., 250n7, 269n74
Bland, Kalman, 234n34, 240n19, 295n60
Blenkinsopp, J., 237n60
Blidstein, Gerald, 233n27, 236n49, 256n48, 258n57, 271n84, 299n80
Blumberg, H., 294n52
Blumenthal, D. R., 267n52, 290n29, 294n4, 295n61
Brettler, M., 258n61, 259n65
Broadie, A., 243n40
Buber, Martin, 230n4
Buijs, J., 293n49
Burrell, David, 289n16, 296n70, 298n73

Coggins, R. J., 274n115
Cohen, Boaz, 264n33
Cohen, Shaye, 229nn16–17, 232n12, 236n56
Cohen, Stuart, 255n43
Crescas, Asher, 74, 241n28, 248n27
Cronbach, Abraham, 252n21

Danby, Herbert, 238n4
Davidson, Herbert, 17, 171, 232n14,
    239n8, 244n1, 247n21, 250n3,
    252n17, 252n23, 268n56, 270n76,
    283nn16–18, 283n21
Derrida, Jacques, 288n12
Diamond, James, 234n33, 278n32
Dienstag, J. I., 291n34
Disendruck, Z., 242n37, 292n42
Dvornik, Francis, 252n20

Efodi, 4, 241n28, 242n33, 261n10,
    278n27, 278n33
Efros, I., 280n48
Eliade, Mircea, 202, 290n28
Elijah, Vilna Gaon, 291n32
Eran, A., 296n67

Fackenheim, Emil, 227n2
Faur, Jose, 232n19, 248n25, 261n10,
    266n46, 295n61
Feinstein, M., 286n1
Feintuch, A., 264n35
Feldman, Seymour, 298n73
Fisch, S., 294n51
Fishbane, Michael, 269n70,
    271nn86–87
Fogelman, R. M., 273n111
Fox, Marvin, 231n5, 233n26, 250n4,
    283n19, 290n26,
Frank, Daniel, 241n30, 249n2, 250n4
Frank, R. M., 277n19
Frankfort, H., 230n24, 252n20
Friedländer, Michael, 162, 284n23,
    297n71
Friedman, Shamma, 249n31
Frydman-Kohl, Baruch, 234n31
Funkenstein, A., 291n33

Gellman, Jerome, 245n6, 276n13, 298n73
Gersonides (R. Levi b. Gershon), 137,
    238n2, 273n108, 274n115, 290n23

Ginsburg, E., 290n27, 296n69
Goitein, S. D., 228n6, 230n3
Goldziher, Ignaz, 280n48
Goodman, Lenn, 283n20, 289n18
Gordis, R., 261n7
Goshen-Gottstein, Alon, 245n5
Grant, Edward, 247n23
Green, A., 295n65
Gruenwald, Ithamar, 241n23
Guttman, Julius, 240n19

Halamish, M., 231n11
Halkin, A. S., 260n74, 291n31
HaMe'iri (Menahem ben Shlomo),
    254n34, 269n66
Harris, Jay, 228n9
Hartman, David, 281n50
Harvey, Steven, 228n6, 262n15
Harvey, Warren Zev, 242n35, 245n8,
    249n1, 269n73, 279n36, 285n38,
    289n19, 292n43
Heidegger, Martin, 142, 275n1,
    288n12
Henshke, D., 279n36
Heschel, A. J., 231n6, 261n2
Hyamson, M., 263n29

ibn Bajja, 257n52, 262n17
ibn Ezra, Abraham, 251n8, 262n19,
    269n68, 273n108, 282n7, 292n39
ibn Shmuel, Y., 292n40
ibn Tibbon, Samuel, 239n8, 242n37,
    262n15, 276n6, 284n23, 286n42,
    297n71
Idel, M., 295n64
R. Issac of Dampierre, 237n56
Ivry, Alfred, 162, 241n29, 281n4, 281n5,
    292n41, 292n45

Jordan, Mark, 288n12
Jospe, R., 267n55
Judah, Tibi, 230n1

Kafih, Joseph, 162, 172, 236n53, 238n6, 262n22, 264n35, 266n45, 268n61, 276n6, 282n6, 282n8, 284n23, 285n39, 286n42, 287n6, 295n62

Kaplan, Lawrence, 232n15, 242n36, 250n6, 252n18, 259n70

Karo, Joseph ("Kesef Mishneh"), 236n48, 236n56, 251n10, 258n60, 274n117, 292n39

Kasher, Hannah, 234n29, 237n61, 241n31, 242n33, 244n47, 256n44, 263n28, 289n17, 289n21, 291n36, 294n54

Kasher, Menachem, 229n14, 287n7, 294n51

Kaufman, Y., 272n96, 273n104

Keck, D., 295n57

Keel, O., 258n64

Kellner, Menachem, 40, 230n2, 232n18, 233n25, 235n38, 241n22, 251n11, 253n26, 253n29, 272n103, 276n9, 283n21, 284n28, 287n2, 293n48

Kierkegaard, Søren, 232n16

Kimmelman, R., 296n69

Klein, A., 294n50

Klein-Braslavy, Sara, 74, 247n22, 248nn26–27, 268 57, 285n33, 292n44

Kogan, B., 280n48

Kook, R. Abraham Isaac, 230n4

Kraemer, Joel, 260n74

Kravitz, L. S., 244n48, 289n20

Kreisel, Howard, 235n43, 250n4, 251n2, 253n25, 253n27, 257n50, 260n77, 262n16, 264n32, 272n92, 284n32, 285n38

Kugel, James, 228n5, 245n7, 294n56

Langermann, Y. Tzvi, 234n29, 288n9

Laqueur, Walter, 229n20

Lasker, Daniel, 234n31

Lebowitz, Y., 241n29

Lerner, Ralph, 267n53

Levinas, Emmanuel, 105, 260n77

Levinger, Jacob, 125, 255n38, 269n67, 289n20, 299n77

Lieberman, Saul, 263n22, 274n113, 298n77

Liebes, Yehuda, 59, 245n5

Lobel, Diana, 157, 279n43, 281n49–50

Lorberbaum, Menachem, 29, 236n54, 237n61, 253n29

Lorberbaum, Y., 278n32

Malbim (R. Meir Leibush ben Yehiel Michael), 274n112

Matt, Daniel, 262n14

McGovern, W., 230n22

Melamed, Abraham 250n7

Metzudat David. *See* Radbaz

Milgrom, Jacob, 238n1

Muffs, Y., 272n91

Munk, Saloman, 266n45, 282n6, 284n23, 292n40, 297n71

Nahmanides (R. Moses b. Nahman), 34, 229n14, 236n51, 238n2, 243n45, 251n8, 254n34, 257n51, 260n76, 270n75, 270n79, 271n88, 275n4, 276n7, 277n20, 278n36, 283n15, 293n46, 294n55

Nehorai, Michael, 232n18, 270n77, 279n39

Nelson, Janet, 256n46

Nuriel, A., 241n29, 262n11, 264n37, 265n38, 292n43

Pines, Shlomo, 69, 172, 243n43, 250n7, 260n1, 262n13, 264n37, 270n76, 276n6, 280nn47–48, 282n6, 282n8, 284n23, 297n71, 298n73

Pinhas of Koretz, 230n4

Names Index

Porton, Gary, 229n18
Posen, R., 278n29

Rabad (R. Abraham ben David of Posquieres), 236n55, 251n10, 268n61, 291n32
Rabbenu Tam, 232n17, 237n56
Radak (R. David Kimhi), 235n35, 243n39, 262n19, 269n71, 282n7, 284n24, 290n23, 292n39
Radbaz (R. David ibn abi Zimra), 291n32, 292n39
Raffel, C. M., 241n29, 242n37, 255n37
Rashbam (R. Samuel b. Meir), 34
Rashi (R. Solomon b. Isaac), 34, 125, 237n60, 240n14, 241n20, 243n39, 244n1, 255n40, 262n19, 266n43, 266n44, 269n66, 269n68, 273n102, 273n108, 277n20, 282n7, 285n40, 290n23, 291n36, 292n39
Ravitzky, A., 229n13, 260n73, 284n29, 286n41
Rawidowicz, S., 250n3, 287n5, 288n15
Regev, S., 266n48
Reines, A., 233n26, 239n10, 241n29, 270n77, 285n33
Rembaum, J., 285n36
Ricoeur, Paul, 41, 189, 241n26, 261n12, 286nn48–49
Rosenberg, S., 259n68, 287n5, 295n59
Rosenzweig, Franz, 260n72
Rubenstein, Jeffrey, 245n5, 249n31, 270n81, 271n84

Safrai, S., 270n82
Safran, Bezalel, 250n3
Samuelson, N., 293n46
Sarna, Nahum, 278n26
Scheyer, Simon, 297n71
Scholem, Gershom, 157, 218, 244n1, 278n35, 280n46, 281n52, 291n33, 295n63

Schwartz, Dov, 252n22, 290n24, 290n25
Schwartz, Michal, 276n6, 282n6, 282n8, 284n23, 286n42, 297n71
Schwarzschild, Steven, 249n1, 249n3
Scott, R. B. Y., 261n6
Seeskin, Kenneth, 234n29, 262n24, 279n37, 286n45, 298n73
Seforno, 269n68, 277n20, 298n76
Septimus, B., 270nn78–79
Shailat, I., 230n2, 233n28
Shem Tov ibn Falaquera, 119, 194, 241n28, 242n33, 261n10, 267n51, 282n10, 288n10, 297n72
Shiffman, Yair, 267n55
Shinan, Avigdor, 245n10
Silman, Y., 257n53
Silver, D. J., 295n56
Sokol, M., 298n73
Soloveitchik, Haym, 237n62
Soloveitchik, J. B., 258n57, 263n25
Sontag, Susan, 240n13
Spinoza, Baruch, 245n8
Statman, Daniel, 249n2
Stern, Josef, 238n5, 259n69, 265n39, 267n51, 278n32, 292n37, 292n38
Strauss, Leo, 56, 156, 243n41, 243n44, 249n1, 275n2, 279n42, 288n15, 299n77
Stroumsa, Sara, 246n12

Tabory, J., 270n81
Tate, J., 229n9
Tosafot, 232n17, 244n1, 269n66
Turner, M., 265n40
Twersky, I., 36, 230n2, 232n15, 236n52, 238n5, 238n7, 240n12, 244n47, 246n11, 251n11, 252n18, 252n24, 256n50, 263n29, 268n63, 271n83, 279n36, 299n79

Urbach, E., 282nn13–14

Wasserstein, D., 230n3
Weiler, Gershon, 260n75
Weinberg, R. Y. Y., 286n1
Weiss, A., 287n1
Weiss, Raymond, 249n1, 250n4, 254n35, 298n73

Weiss, Roslyn, 243n38, 280n45
Wijnhoven, Jochanan, 231n11
Wolfson, Elliot, 188, 219, 227n1, 233n22, 266n47, 296n66, 296n69

Yafeh, H. Lazarus, 277n19

Subject Index

Abraham
    and *aqedah* as parable, 18–19, 275n5
    as "lover" of God, 27
    as teacher of ethical golden mean, 16
Account of the Chariot, 4, 70, 112, 228n3
Account of Creation, 4, 70, 112
Active Intellect, 198
Adam
    post-sin role, 5, 121
    pre-sin role, 270n74
R. Akiva
    as antithesis to Elisha ben Abuyah, 55–56, 61
    journey to *pardes,* 55–56
    relation to peace, 75–76
    warning about "water," 72–73, 74, 75, 248n30
amr ilahi
    as used by Halevi, 157, 171, 172, 173, 234n31
    as used by Maimonides, 171, 172, 178, 179

angels
    Active Intellect as, 198
    in Christian tradition, 295n57
    imaginative faculty as, 198, 215–16
    in Kalamic tradition, 197
    as points of natural causation, 197, 198, 202
    prophets as, 215, 216

cherubim. *See also* angels
    defined, 294n53
    as intellect, 214, 216, 217
    and Mosaic prophecy, 216
    rabbinic view, 293n50
circumcision, 231n12, 235n35, 265n39
cloud, as metaphor, 147, 148, 150
convert
    as authentic Jew, 11, 12, 19–20
    as beneficiary of miracles, 22
    as beneficiary of Sinaitic law, 23
    and *bikkurim* doxology, 28–29, 39
    conversion as replication of Sinai, 22–23, 25

convert *(cont.)*
   as "descendant" of Abraham, 15, 16, 17, 18
   duty to parents, 27–28
   and ethnocentric liturgy, 11–12
   and Israelite historical conscience, 14, 19
   in Kabbalistic view, 231n11, 233n22
   as legal "orphan," 9, 28
   as "lover" of God, 27
   as member of congregation, 30
   as prayer leader, 14
   purity of faith, 9
   reason as motivation, 25, 26

David
   as antithesis to Elisha ben Abuyah, 63–64
   as exemplar of "joy," 131–33, 246n13
   governance of, as ideal, 10, 105
   as "shepherd," 258n62
   and Temple-building, 99
de'ot as ethical traits, 249n1. *See also imitatio dei*

eating
   excess
      —as misperception of evil, 61, 63
      —as putting-off of form, 68
      —as repudiation of God's omniscience 62
   as metaphor for knowledge, 56, 57
   moderation as corollary of ethical golden mean, 63
ethical golden mean. *See also* eating
   anger as exception, 249n2
   humility as exception, 80
   as *imitatio dei*, 16
   and Nazirite, 255n38
evil, 58, 59, 60, 61, 65, 66, 68, 70, 72, 114

"eye," as metaphor, 126
Ezra, intellectual role of, 138–39

"face," hiding of as metaphor, 75
fire
   connected with "eating," 67, 124, 148, 149
   connected with God, 122–23, 148, 149, 150
form. *See also* matter
   "putting-off," 57, 108, 124
   as wisdom, 121

garden *(pardes)* as metaphor for esoteric knowledge, 5, 56, 71, 112, 244n1
God. *See also* fire; providence; Sabbath; *shekhinah*
   "anger," 42, 43, 44, 49–50, 123, 241n31, 242nn33–34
   "approaching"/"coming near," 176–79
   aravot/throne of glory, 64, 65, 66
   attributes of action, 71, 195, 196, 247n21
   "coming," 160–66
   "creating," 70, 72
   "dwelling," 145, 146, 147, 149, 151, 152, 154, 155
   El olam, 223, 224
   as exemplar of writing, 3, 168
   fear of, 211
   "filling," 179–81
   glory *(kavod),* 164, 175, 176, 181, 182, 183, 184, 187
   "going," 41, 42, 170–75
   "going out"/returning, 166–70
   human contact with
      —outside human physical and cognitive experience, 147, 148
      —through intellect, 174, 176, 177, 179, 181
   "jealous," 148

knowledge of, as Jewish identity, 20
"making" *(asoh)*, 70
names of
— other than Tetragrammaton: in Aquinas' view, 288n12; as attributes of action, 195
— Tetragrammaton: as essence, 183; in Halevi's view, 182–83
"passing," 151–52
placelessness, 142, 151, 180, 213
"possessing" *(qoneh)*, 70, 222, 223, 224
"raising," 85
"resting," 194, 195, 196, 198, 201
— *nefesh,* 194, 208, 209, 210
— *nihah,* 199, 200, 202, 206, 207, 209, 222
— *shavat,* 194, 199, 209
"saying/speaking," 117, 171. See also *amr ilahi*
shepherding, 258n64, 259n65
"touching," 178, 179
as ultimate form, 201
"voice," as intellectual apprehension, 161
volition of, and creation, 169, 195. See also Sabbath
good *(tov),* 57, 58, 59, 60, 68, 72, 73, 76, 77, 78, 114

heart, as metaphor, 118, 256n47
heresy
of Elisha ben Abuyah, 55
as intellectual failure,
— anthropocentrism, 59–60
— attributing deficiency to God, 66
— failure to distinguish form and matter, 245n6
— failure to distinguish heaven and earth, 67
— failure to form a coherent theodicy, 59, 68, 77, 78
— failure to situate evil within good, 75
— intellectual arrogance, 69, 77
— lack of *kavod,* 60, 69, 70
— linking sin and punishment, 63, 74, 146
— obsession with material, 61, 62
— reviling scholars, 49
of Israelite nobles, 61, 65, 66, 67, 149
of Nadav and Avihu, 61, 67
honey, as metaphor, 57, 58, 62, 70

idolatry, 124, 148
imitatio dei, 16–17, 18, 85–86, 102, 123, 142, 259n69. See also ethical golden mean; king
de'ot as ethics based on *imitatio dei,* 103
freeing of slave as, 225
solitude of slave as, 119
Isaac, as teacher, 20, 104

Jacob
ladder as intellectual ascent, 48, 243n41
as teacher, 20, 104
Job. See also Sabbath
achieving correct knowledge, 147, 244n48
as reflecting Aristotelian theology, 289n17
as reflecting Kalamic theology, 197, 199
joy
Philo's definition, 271n85
relation to intellect, 133–34, 137–38

king. See also David; Moses
anthropocentrism as danger to, 9–10, 29, 81, 87, 88
and elective war, 251n14

king (*cont.*)
  essential traits
    —absence of classism, 93
    —attachment to Torah, 91, 92, 254n36, 255n39, 255nn42–43
    —charity, 89, 90
    —dependence, 88
    —humility/*shefal-ruah*, 10, 64, 83, 86, 99
    —intellect-driven, 104
    —power over holy precincts curtailed, 82–88
    —power shared with judiciary and prophets, 90, 98, 99, 254n32
    —practical/theoretical balance, 90, 256n48
    —temperance, 92, 255n37
    —theocentrism, 267n54
  as exemplar of God-human divide, 10
  imitatio dei
    —construction of Temple, 85
    —dispassionate governance, 86, 88, 95
    —gladdening the needy, 86, 88
    —grace and mercy, 94
    —shepherding, 102
  in messianic era, 89–90
  Moses as model of restraint, 81–85
  in Platonic/Farabian view, 250n7
  and sacred space, 256n46

leper
  false conceptions
    —arrogance, 52
    —corporealizing God, 43–44, 46, 51
    —denial of fundamental principle (*kofer ba-iqqar*), 43, 44, 48, 50, 51
    —denying God's omniscience, 36, 51, 52
    —denying human-God divide, 44
    —discrediting prophets, 35, 47–49, 51, 52
    —discrediting righteous, 35, 47, 51

  fear as antidote, 52
  "leprosy"
    —as miracle/"sign and wonder," 34, 37, 38, 239n11, 240n12
    —as moral disorder, 34
    —as physical malady, 34, 238n1
    —as punishment for slander, 34, 35, 36, 38
    —as theological category, 238n6
  rehabilitation parallel to Job's, 38
  repentance (*teshuvah*), 49, 50
Levites
  as example of humility, 253n26
  as teachers, 104, 136–37
lex talionis, 275n2
light
  in Halevi's view, 182, 188
  as metaphor for intellect, 117, 163, 187, 188
  in Sa'adya Gaon's view, 187, 188
  as sensory perception, 152–53

Maimonides, techniques and views
  adaptation to different intellects, 2, 3, 8, 261n8
  anti-teleological views, 245n8, 245n11
  asceticism, 267n55
  autonomy versus determinism, 298n73
  biblical language
    —as metaphor, 2, 3, 8, 9, 17
    —as parable, 2, 3, 9, 109, 134, 135, 153, 189
    —treatment of miracles, 6–7, 22, 127, 167–68, 204, 233n29, 270n77, 273n109
  body as parable, 40
  creation and eternity, 7, 8, 193, 194
  divide between heaven and earth, 228n5
  Guide of the Perplexed, 110
  Hebrew grammar, 203, 204

influences on
— Avicenna, 268n56, 296n67
— Aristotle, 193, 250n3, 267n54, 268n56
— Halevi, 280n47
— Neoplatonists, 250n3, 251n22
intertextual and intratextual strategies, 30, 175
and Kalam, 289n19
nature as analogue to Torah, 6, 7
negative theology, 212, 293n49
rabbinic literature
— commitment to rabbinic tradition, 1, 135
— lack of sources in MT, 29, 236n55, 268n63
— use of Palestinian Talmud, 29, 30
relationship between philosophical and juridical works, 30, 36, 243n46, 279n36
role of exodus, 154–55
role of outsider, summarized, 6, 9
role of prayer, 14
role of priests, 228 n4
role of reward and punishment, 63, 268n64
role of sacrifice, 63, 154–55, 279n39
role of tradition, 265n41
and *Targum Onkelos*, 152, 156
theory of divine accommodation, 294n55
thirteen principles of faith, 40, 51, 243n43, 253n27
as universalist, 128, 281n50
view of anthropocentrism, 257n53
view of holiness, 251n11
manna, as metaphor, 96–97
Marah, as normative ideal, 206
matter. *See also* form
relation to form, 248n25
R. Meir, and rehabilitation of Elisha ben Abuyah, 78

messianic era
dependent on charity, 89
MT structure as parallel of journey to messianic era, 7–8
role of hermeneutics, 8
rules of nature operative in, 7, 229n12
Miriam, leprosy of, as existential error, 35, 41
Moses
as archetypical sage, 113
death of, 122, 123, 124–29
as first king of Israel, 81, 83, 85, 250n8
God-centered intellectual focus, 44, 45
having highest cognition of God, 44, 45
humility of, 61, 65, 68, 81, 95–96, 240n17
imitatio dei of, 242n36
intellect/material dichotomy, 89, 113, 114, 125, 126, 144, 177, 253n25
intellectual self-restraint, 144
as lawgiver, 234nn33–34
as pastoral leader, 258n62
sin of, 242n32
ultimate in human form, 68
uniqueness as prophet, 39, 40, 44, 126, 216, 217, 240n18, 241n24
uniqueness of miracles, 127, 239n10
Mt. Horev, as metaphor, 144

Onkelos, method of, 168, 282n12

peace *(shalom)*, 76–77
place, as metaphor, 166
prayer
halakhic observance as "God-talk," 116
kabbalistic view, 266n47
standardization of, 21, 267n50
wordless, as ideal, 26, 116, 117, 119

prophets. *See also* Moses
  as "angels of God," 48
  connected with Active Intellect, 48, 243n42
  degrees of prophecy, 240n18
  qualifications of, 150
  role of, after Moses, 150
providence
  as consequent on intellect, 41, 45, 46, 48, 50, 147
  Moses as supreme beneficiary of, 45
  relation to *shekhinah*, 155, 156
  withdrawal of, as human responsibility, 42

Rehavam, as antithesis of ideal king, 100, 258n60
Ruth, as archetypical convert, 16, 231n11

Sabbath
  faith-based versus reason-based, 193
  as feminine, 218
  Halevi's view, 218
  human life takes precedence, 225
  Kabbalistic views, 219
  mystical views, 202
  observance by non-Jews, 286n1
  as portent of messianic era, 205
  rabbinic views, 218, 225
  rationales for
  —in Deuteronomy, 219
  —in Exodus, 192, 219
  as recalling creation, 192
  —demarcation between chaos and order, 202, 203
  —demarcation between divine will and human action, 209, 210, 219, 220
  —demarcation between divine will and laws of nature, 198, 203, 219, 220
  —exodus as parallel, 220, 221, 222
  —Job's journey as parallel, 196, 197–99
  —Naval as rejection of, 199–200
  —temporal analogue to Temple, 213
sage. *See also* student; Sukkot
  defined, 264n32
  duty of individual to obey, 277n24
  duty of individual to seek out, 122
  in Islamic tradition, 111
  and joy, 108, 130–31, 133, 134, 137–38
  Maimonides as exemplar, 107–9, 110–11
  obligation to teach, 120, 121, 264n33
  and prayer, 116–19
  priests as metaphor for, 4
  private space halakhically preserved, 128, 129
  relation to student, 231n9
  solitude/society dichotomy, 4, 5, 111, 112, 113, 115, 119
Satan
  as evil inclination, 285n33
  as imagination, 198, 285n33, 289n20
  as vulnerability of matter, 178
shefal-ruah, defined, 80, 249n3
shekhinah
  absence of term in *shakhon* chapter of GP, 156
  in afterlife, 186n7
  Halevi's view, 156, 234n31, 280n46
  and holy precincts, 251n13
  not localized, 154, 173
  Onkelos' view, 157
  as related to providence, 169, 170
  rabbinic view, 170
  Sa'adya Gaon's view, 280n46

Sinai experience
  law of, as lesser than Marah law, 206
  multiple levels of, 117, 118, 160, 161, 162, 184, 266n48
  prayer assembly as reenactment, 117
song, as medium of teaching, 136–37
spheres, 74–75, 120, 178, 235n39, 246n16, 286n56
student. *See also* sage
  evolving to teacher, 109
  R. Jospeh ben Judah as example, 108, 109
  as link in chain of transmission, 111
  qualifications to read Maimonides, 263n25
  qualifications to study under Abraham, 17, 18
  quest of, 123
  stages of learning, 108
Sukkot
  as exercise in self-demeanment, 127–34
  intellectualization of, 134–39

Temple. *See also* king; Sabbath
  as emphasizing minimal divine presence, 145, 180, 184, 212, 213
  enduring holiness of, 82
  as focal point for intellect, 4, 185, 186
  as God's throne/residence, 99, 100
  rationale for cult regulations, 62, 82, 210, 211
  rationale for location, 185–86, 211, 212
Torah study. *See also* king
  contingent on humility, 93
  as democratizating, 93, 113, 137, 138, 256n44
  "Torah speaks in the language of man," 5–6, 228n9
  tripartite classification, 112

water
  R. Akiva's warning, 72–73, 74, 75, 248n30
  connected with "eating," 57

James A. Diamond

is the Joseph and Wolf Lebovic Chair of Jewish Studies at the University of Waterloo. He is the author of *Maimonides and the Hermeneutics of Concealment: Deciphering Scripture and Midrash in* The Guide of the Perplexed.

www.ingramcontent.com/pod-product-compliance
Lightning Source LLC
Chambersburg PA
CBHW071758300426
44116CB00009B/1120